"Many in the scholarly and political field prai̇...
ness to think big, raise controversial questio̊...
ethical prophet."

THE NEW ᴠᴏʀᴋ ᴛᴛᴛᴛᴇ

"Rifkin warns that in the coming years new, more sophisticated software technologies are going to bring civilization ever closer to a near worker-less world. His book is timely and . . . is arousing enormous interest."

FINANCIAL TIMES

"The End of Work is rich in detail, absorbing in its real-life relevance, and large in scope. An indispensable introduction to a problem that we [and our children] will be living with for the rest of our lives."

ROBERT L. HEILBRONER, economist

"Jeremy Rifkin addresses boldly and expertly a most important problem facing contemporary society, a problem most economists are reluctant to discuss. This is a very readable and important book."

WASSILY LEONTIEF, Nobel laureate
and professor of economics,
New York University

"Rifkin does an extremely comprehensive and insightful analysis of our current economic situation. While not everyone will agree with his recommendations, nevertheless, this book is extremely provocative about how we design a society that better meets the needs of all its citizens."

GLEN L. URBAN, Dean,
MIT Sloan School of Management

The End of Work

OTHER BOOKS BY JEREMY RIFKIN

Common Sense II

Own Your Own Job

Who Should Play God (with Ted Howard)

The Emerging Order

The North Will Rise Again (with Randy Barber)

Entropy (with Ted Howard)

Algeny

Declaration of a Heretic

Time Wars

Biosphere Politics

Beyond Beef

Voting Green (with Carol Grunewald)

The Biotech Century

The Age of Access

The Hydrogen Economy

■ ■ ■

THE END OF WORK

The Decline of the Global Labor Force
and the Dawn of the Post-Market Era

JEREMY RIFKIN

Jeremy P. Tarcher/Penguin
a member of
Penguin Group (USA) Inc.
New York

*In memory of my father, Milton Rifkin, who understood, better than anyone
I know, the workings of the marketplace*

*For my mother, Vivette Rifkin, who personifies the volunteer spirit in
American society*

For Ernestine Royster and her family and their dream of a better tomorrow

Most Tarcher/Penguin books are available at special quantity discounts for bulk
purchases for sales promotions, premiums, fund-raising, and educational needs.
Special books or book excerpts also can be created to fit specific needs.

For details, write Penguin Group (USA) Inc. Special Markets
375 Hudson Street, New York, NY 10014

Jeremy P. Tarcher/Penguin
a member of Penguin Group (USA) Inc.
375 Hudson Street
New York, NY 10014
www.penguin.com

First trade paperback edition 1996

The Library of Congress Cataloging-in-Publication Data

Rifkin, Jeremy.
    The end of work: the decline of the global labor force
and the dawn of the post-market era / Jeremy Rifkin.
        p.   cm.
    Originally published: New York: G.P. Putnam's Sons, c1995.
    Includes bibliographical references and index.
    ISBN 1-58542-313-0
    1. Technological unemployment.   2. Labor productivity.   3. Work—
    Forecasting.   I. Title.
    HD6331.R533   2004   2003068708
    331.13'7042-dc22

Design by Lee Fukui

Printed in the United States of America
10 9 8 7 6 5 4 3

This book is printed on acid-free paper. ∞

Contents

Acknowledgments

I WOULD LIKE to give special thanks to Jeff Kellogg, who assisted me in the research for *The End of Work*. Mr. Kellogg's in-depth research as well as his many editorial suggestions and comments have been invaluable in the preparation of the manuscript. I'd also like to thank Andy Kimbrell for his help in editing the final manuscript and for serving as a sounding board for many of the ideas that have gone into the book. I would also like to thank several other people for their contribution to the research and preparation of *The End of Work*: Anna Awimbo, Clara Mack, Carolyn Bennett, and Jennifer Beck. Finally, I'd like to thank the late Ping Ferry for his encouragement and support while I was researching and writing the book.

2004 Introduction

IN THE NINE YEARS that have elapsed since I published *The End of Work*, the global economy went on a wild ride, careening to new heights, then plummeting just as fast, leaving in its wake a worldwide recession. But, even at the peak of the economic cycle, structural unemployment remained dangerously high in countries around the world, despite gains in both global productivity and gross domestic product. In 1995, 800 million people were unemployed or underemployed. By 2001, more than a billion people fell into one of these two categories.[1]

Today, millions of workers across America find themselves underemployed or without jobs and with little hope of obtaining full-time employment. This sobering reality is all the more painful when we recall that just a few short years ago, business leaders and elected officials were making exuberant claims that the United States had solved its unemployment problems. "Official" unemployment dropped from 6.6 percent in January of 1994 to 4 percent in January of 2000, leading some economists to boast that unemployment was a thing of the past.[2] Their predictions turned out to be ill founded. By the spring of 2003, official U.S. unemployment had climbed back to 6 percent and become the most worrisome problem facing the country.[3] Nor is the U.S. alone.

The world's most highly developed nations continue to be plagued by chronic high unemployment. Germany's unemployment at the end of 2003 was 10.4 percent, and 60 percent of the unemployed had been without a job for more than a year.[4] France's and Italy's unemployment in 2003 hovered around 9 percent, while Spain's was nearly

12 percent.[5] Overall, unemployment in the European Union was 7.9 percent, and in the expanded Euro-zone it was more than 8.7 percent.[6]

The other side of the world is doing no better. Japan's unemployment reached 3.68 million people at the beginning of 2003 with an overall unemployment rate of 5.5 percent, the largest percentage of unemployed workers since record keeping began in the 1950s. Indonesia's unemployment rate was 9.1 percent and India's was 8.8 percent. In the Caribbean and Latin America, the average unemployment rate was 10 percent.[7]

What has become clear throughout this period is that the structural problems behind rising unemployment that were first discussed in *The End of Work* have only deepened in the interim years, making the future of employment the critical issue of our age. Interestingly enough, the analysis and trends taken up in the body of the book hold greater resonance now than when the book was first published.

I have taken the opportunity in this new introduction to bring the reader up to date on the future of work, with emphasis on lessons that can be learned from the tumultuous economic events of the past several years. I have also expanded on some of the many suggestions for addressing the jobs crisis that appear in the first edition with a range of new ideas for rethinking the nature of work. My hope is that these proposals might help us navigate our way into a new world where each person's avocation and contribution to the lot of humanity and the well-being of the Earth will likely be of a far different sort than anything previously imagined.

Every nation is in the throes of a great debate about the future of work. Saddled with high unemployment, high taxes, burdensome welfare systems, and convoluted regulatory regimes, which some say only perpetuate economic stagnation, critics in government, industry, and civil society are locked in a fierce ideological struggle about whether the rules governing employment, commerce, and trade need to be reformed, and if so, how. While politicians and business and labor leaders squabble over the issues of creating a flexible labor policy, lowering taxes, and rewriting the rules governing welfare and pension allotments, the real cause of global unemployment is going unaddressed in the public policy debate.

If the key to creating new jobs was only a matter of making the above-mentioned reforms, then the United States of America should be experiencing robust employment. After all, we have made virtually all of the reforms that other countries are now attempting to implement.

Yet American workers—and for that matter workers in virtually every other national economy in the world—are experiencing hard times.

Until recently, when official U.S. unemployment figures began to rise, the rest of the world looked to America for inspiration and guidance. What the other countries didn't know is that real unemployment in the U.S., even during the boom years of the second half of the 1990s, when the government was reporting a 4 percent unemployment rate, was really much higher. A University of Chicago study found that if the hidden unemployment were added in, real unemployment was closer to the unemployment levels, at the time, in the European Union.[8] That is because even though some Americans did find jobs after the 1989–92 recession, millions of other discouraged workers simply gave up and dropped out of the workforce and therefore were no longer counted in the official statistics.[9] Many others were incarcerated. In 1980, the prison population stood at 503,000 inmates. By the year 2000, nearly two million people were in prison.[10] Currently, 1.8 percent of the adult male workforce is in prison.[11] Moreover, many of the workers who did find employment in the bull market between 1995 and 2000 were temporary and part-time, without benefits, and for the most part underemployed. Many of them sank back into the ranks of the unemployed by the end of 2003.

THE RISE AND FALL OF THE "AMERICAN MIRACLE"

Much of the so-called American economic miracle of the late 1990s, including the temporary bubble in employment, turns out, in hindsight, to have been illusory. It wasn't so much America's superior management skills, entrepreneurial abilities, and productivity gains that fed the commercial expansion but, rather, the unprecedented extension of consumer credit, which allowed Americans to go on an extended spending spree. The American miracle was, to a great extent, bought on credit. Indeed, it is impossible to understand the temporary reduction in U.S. unemployment in the late 1990s without examining the close relationship that developed between job creation and the amassing of record consumer debt.

Consumer credit has been growing for nearly a decade. The burst in consumer spending put people back to work for a few years to make all the goods and provide all the services being purchased on credit. The result was that America's family savings rate, which was about 8 percent in the early 1990s, sank to around 2 percent by the year 2001.[12]

An analogous situation occurred in the mid- to late 1920s. Like to-day, the 1920s was a period of disruptive technological change. Electricity replaced steam power across every major industry, greatly increasing the productive capacity of the country. Productivity gains, however, were not matched by a significant increase in worker compensation. Instead, wages remained relatively flat, while many marginal workers were let go in the wake of cheaper, more efficient technology substitutions. By the late 1920s, American industry was running at only 75 percent of capacity in most key sectors of the economy. The fruits of the new productivity gains were not being distributed broadly enough among workers to sustain increased consumption and empty the inventories. Concerned over ineffective consumer demand, the banking community provided consumer loans and the retail trade extended cheap credit in the form of installment buying to encourage workers to buy more and keep the economy growing. By late 1929, consumer debt was so high that it could no longer be sustained. Even the bull market was being stoked by record purchases of stocks on margin (i.e., the amount paid by the customer when using a broker's credit to buy or sell a security). Finally, the entire house of cards collapsed.

The same phenomenon is occurring today. The productivity gains brought on by the information and telecommunication revolutions are finally being felt. The problem is that virtually every industry is facing global underutilization of capacity and insufficient consumer demand. American manufacturers reported that they were using less than 73 percent of their capacity in October 2003.[13] Once again, in the United States, consumer credit has become the palliative of sorts, a way to keep the economic engines throttled up, at least for a time.

Consumer credit is growing by a staggering 9 percent annual rate, and personal bankruptcies are increasing. In 1994, 780,000 Americans filed for bankruptcy. By 2002, the number of bankruptcies had soared to 1,576,133.[14] Until recently, some economists argued that the near zero percent savings rate was not really as bad as the figures might suggest, because millions of Americans experienced record gains in the stock market, making their equity portfolios a substitute for traditional bank savings. Of course, the recent downturn in the stock market has muted such claims. Moreover, it should be noted that nearly 90 percent of the gains of the stock market went to the top 10 percent of households, while more than half of all Americans did not benefit at all from the bull market, as they owned no stock.[15]

The U.K. is the only other G-8 country to follow the U.S. lead by dramatically increasing consumer credit to boost its economy. And, in the short run, its policy has met with success. U.K. unemployment is among the lowest in the world and the economy is growing. The problem is that, like the U.S., the U.K. economic miracle has less to do with keen business savvy and streamlined government oversight and more to do with runaway credit and mounting debt. Household debt is now at a record high of $1.4 trillion. The average British subject is now spending 120 percent to 130 percent of his or her annual income, using the same credit instruments that Americans have become so fond of, including credit cards, refinancing of home mortgages, loans, and overdrafts.[16] British consumers now enjoy the dubious distinction of increasing their personal debt even more than Americans.

If the continental countries of the European Union had lowered their family savings rate from around 14.6 percent in the early 1990s to 2 percent in the year 2001, as the United States did, they could have significantly reduced their unemployment rate.[17] Millions of people spending money—on credit—would assuredly have brought millions of additional European workers back to work to make the goods and perform the services being purchased on credit. But following the U.S. lead would only have resulted in a short-term fix while creating the conditions for an even more profound long-term period of economic instability when the extension of credit reached its limits, pushing consumers into default and the economy into a downward spiral, as occurred in the late 1920s and early 1930s.

Now, in the aftermath of the stock-market-bubble burst, Americans have slowed their spending, and the temporary decline in unemployment has given way to a steady climb back to the unemployment levels experienced nearly a decade ago. The U.S. economy is experiencing its worst hiring slump in more than twenty years.[18]

The Permanent Jobless Recovery

The U.S. is two years into its recovery from the last recession, without significant job growth. The so-called jobless recovery has economists and political leaders worried. This is the first time since before World War II that employment has failed to show any signs of real growth despite a long period of increased growth in gross domestic product.[19] Nearly three million jobs were lost between March 2001 and September 2003.[20] Only twice in the past half century has the U.S. lost as many jobs—between 1956 and 1958 and from 1980 to 1983.[21] Most of the jobs—2.5 million—were lost in the manufacturing sector.[22] The retail sector also eliminated a large number of jobs in the period stretching from March 2001 to May 2003.[23] One hundred and twenty-one thousand jobs disappeared in the service industries in just the six-month period between October 2002 and April 2003.[24] Between June of 2000 and June of 2003, a startling 18 percent of American workers reported being laid off.[25] "What's unique about the economy today," says Lawrence Mishel, president of The Economic Policy Institute in Washington, D.C., "is that even though the recession . . . ended apparently in November 2001, here we are in August–September 2003, and we have far fewer jobs than when we started this whole process . . . that has never happened since the Great Depression."[26]

For years, government leaders and economists have urged workers to upgrade their educational skills so they could be prepared for the new, more sophisticated high-tech jobs of the "Age of Access." Ironically, better educated, more skilled workers are also feeling the brunt in this new jobless era. Nearly 44 percent of the long-term unemployed in 2002—workers unemployed for more than six months— were educated beyond high school. A staggering 22.7 percent of college graduates, 22.8 percent of laid-off executives and managerial and professional workers and 25.6 percent of unemployed mid-career workers were looking for employment for more than half a year. That compares to 18 percent of the rest of the unemployed workforce still looking for work after six months without a job.[27]

The current trends in unemployment bode ill for America's college graduates. Companies said that they planned on hiring 36 percent fewer college grads in 2002 than in 2001.[28] Recruitment of MBAs—the hottest job category in the last half of the 1990s—was down by 45 percent. Only 25 percent of college graduates in 2002 were expected to find employment.[29] Many moved back in with their parents.

Until recently, hourly wages were declining across virtually every income category, with the exception of CEOs. Even during the rapid economic recovery of the second half of 2003, the average hourly wage of nonsupervisory jobs in offices and factories went up only 3 cents, according to the Bureau of Labor Statistics—barely enough to keep even with inflation. This is the slowest wage growth America has experienced in more than 40 years.[30] Moreover, the jobs being lost pay around $17.00 per hour, while the new jobs being created pay only $14.50 per hour.[31] At the same time, corporate profits, as a percentage of national income, reached its highest level since the 1960s.[32]

Equally disturbing, the average workweek for rank and file employees—approximately 80 percent of the U.S. workforce—stood at thirty-four hours, matching the lowest level since the government began keeping records in 1964.[33] That means that many of those who are employed are, in reality, underemployed. In mid-2003, more than 4.8 million Americans wanted full-time work but were only able to find part-time employment—this represents a 50 percent increase in the level of underemployment from just the year before and the highest in a decade.[34]

Most economists are at a loss. The conventional benchmarks for measuring economic stimulus are all way up. Tax cuts, record low interest rates, home mortgage refinancing, a dramatic increase in military spending, rising corporate profits, and increased expenditures on new capital equipment have boosted GDP. But even with the U.S. economy growing at 3.3 percent in the second quarter and a blistering 7.2 percent in the third quarter of 2003, and with productivity averaging a robust 6.8 percent in the second quarter and 9.4 percent in the third quarter, the ranks of the unemployed continue to remain high.[35] Incredibly, in the three-month period between June and September of 2003, the U.S. lost an additional 146,000 jobs, despite the fact that the economy grew at its fastest rate since the first quarter of 1984.[36]

With a decline in real wages and diminishing jobs, what's continuing to keep the American economy afloat is consumer debt. While the bear market of 2000[37] significantly reduced the wealth of the 50 percent of the population who owned equities, many Americans were able to rebound—despite layoffs—by taking advantage of record low interest rates and refinancing home mortgages. The refinancing of home mortgages and the stimulus from the government tax cuts put an additional $300 billion into the economy annually.[38] The infusion of cash, however, is quickly being spent. And with credit card debt soaring and bankruptcies mounting, the question on everyone's mind on Wall Street is, Where does the money come from to maintain consumer spending? David Rosenberg, chief economist at Merrill Lynch, worries that "once the steroids from the home refinancing wave and the tax cuts wear off, the economy is likely to slow down."[39] Another tax cut is unlikely, say Washington insiders in the wake of mushrooming military expenditures in the Middle East and elsewhere, and the ballooning government deficit, now estimated to exceed $370 billion in 2004 alone.[40]

Still more ominous, for the millions of Americans saddled with record debts, even a temporary layoff can spell disaster. According to a Gallup survey conducted in 2003, four in ten Americans say they could survive without a job for only about a month before "experiencing significant financial hardship."[41]

By mid-summer 2003, nine million Americans, or 6.1 percent of the workforce, were looking for employment. But if you count discouraged workers—an additional 4.4 million Americans—who have given up searching for work and therefore are no longer counted as unemployed, the number of unemployed is closer to 13.2 million Americans. John A. Challenger, president of the outplacement company Challenger, Gray and Christmas, puts the real unemployment rate at 9 percent.[42] The reason so many workers are dropping out of the workforce is that it currently takes up to five months or more for a job seeker to find new employment, and generally the jobs pay less in wages and benefits than the worker's previous employment. The bottom line is that the United States is now experiencing the longest period without job growth since before World War II.[43]

The Productivity Conundrum

Despite a 2.8 percent growth in the economy in 2002, and a steep rise of 4.7 percent in labor productivity—the biggest increase since 1950—more than one million workers left the job market altogether in the last year.[44] They simply gave up looking for work and are, therefore, no longer counted as unemployed. Why did those jobs disappear? Some critics blame the increasing unemployment on cheap labor and cheaper imports from abroad, and rail against American companies for relocating production and services south of the border and overseas. While there is some truth to the claim, the deeper cause of the spreading unemployment in America and around the world lies with the dramatic boosts in productivity.

The old logic that technology gains and advances in productivity destroy old jobs but create as many new ones is no longer true. Productivity has always been looked to as the engine for job creation and prosperity. Economists have long argued that productivity allows firms to produce more goods at cheaper costs. Cheaper goods, in turn, stimulate demand. The increase in demand leads to more production and greater productivity, which, in turn, increases demand even more, in a never-ending cycle. So even if technological innovations throw some people out of work in the short term, the spike in demand for the cheaper products will assure additional hiring down the line to meet expanded production runs. And even if the technological advances result in sizable layoffs, eventually the ranks of the unemployed will swell, depressing wages to the point that it will be cheaper to re-hire the workers than to invest in new labor-saving technology.

The problem is that this bedrock foundation of capitalist economic theory appears no longer to be applicable. Productivity is rising quickly in the U.S., and with every increase, more workers are let go. According to a just-released report on productivity at the nation's one hundred largest companies, it now takes only nine workers to produce what ten workers did in March of 2001.[45] William V. Sullivan, a senior economist at Morgan Stanley, says "structural shifts in the labor market"—notably, advances in productivity growth and the introduction of new labor-saving technology—could "impede new hiring."[46] Richard D. Rippe, chief economist of Prudential Securities, agrees, saying, "We can produce more output without adding a lot of workers."[47]

Edmund Andrews, of *The New York Times*, summed up the unfolding labor crisis facing the United States, and every other country, noting that the reason payrolls are continuing to decline despite rapid economic growth "stems primarily from an extraordinary gain in productivity which has allowed companies to produce far more goods with far fewer people."[48]

In November of 2003, Alliance Capital Management published an eye-opening study on manufacturing jobs in the world's twenty largest economies, showing the correlation between increases in productivity and the dramatic disappearance of factory-related employment. According to the study, 31 million manufacturing jobs were eliminated between 1995 and 2002.[49] Manufacturing employment declined every year and in every region of the world. The employment decline occurred during a period when manufacturing productivity rose by 4.3 percent and global industrial production rose by more than 30 percent.[50] The incredible increase in productivity has allowed manufacturers to produce far more goods with far fewer workers. Manufacturing jobs, worldwide, fell by nearly 16 percent.[51] The U.S. lost more than 11 percent of its own manufacturing jobs.[52]

Most Americans and many Europeans complain that domestic manufacturing jobs are being lost to China's burgeoning economy. While China is producing and exporting a far greater percentage of manufactured goods, the study found that manufacturing jobs are also being eliminated en masse in China. Between 1995 and 2002, China lost more than fifteen million factory jobs, or 15 percent of its total manufacturing workforce.[53] Like every other region, Chinese manufacturers are increasing productivity and thus need far fewer workers to produce goods. If the current rate of decline continues—and it is more than likely that the rate of decline will accelerate—global manufacturing employment will dwindle from the current 163 million jobs to just a few million jobs by 2040, virtually ending the era of mass factory labor in the world.[54]

The best way to grasp the enormity of this change in factory labor is to look at a single industry. The steel industry in the United States is typical of the transition taking place. In the past twenty years, U.S. steel production rose from 75 million tons to 102 million tons.[55] In the same twenty-year period, from 1982 to 2002, the number of steelworkers in the U.S. declined from 289,000 to 74,000.[56] American steel manufacturers, like manufacturers all around the world, are producing more output with far fewer workers, thanks to dramatic increases in productivity. "Even if manufacturing holds on to its share of GDP," says University of Michigan economist Donald Grimes, "we are likely to continue to lose jobs because of productivity growth."[57] Grimes laments that there is little we can do about it. "It's like fighting a huge headwind."[58]

The white-collar and service industries are experiencing similar job losses as intelligent technologies increase productivity and replace more and more workers. Banking, insurance, and the wholesale and retail sectors are introducing smart technologies into every aspect of their business operations and fast eliminating support personnel in the process. The Internet banking company NetBank is illustrative of the high-tech trend. NetBank has $2.4 billion in deposits. A typical bank that size employs approximately 2000 people. NetBank runs its entire operation with just 180 workers.[59] Industry observers expect the decline in white-collar jobs to shadow the decline in manufacturing jobs over the course of the next four decades, as companies, whole industries, and the world economy become connected in a global neural network. Inexpensive sensors—small processors—are being attached to everything from grocery items to human organs, connecting the whole world in a seamless web of continuous conversation and information exchange. Paul Saffo, director of the Institute for the Future, in Menlo Park, California, observes that "in the 1980s business was about people talking to other people—now, it's about machines talking to machines."[60]

Conversations between machines is increasingly being accompanied by conversation between human beings and machines. Voice-recognition technology is already well developed and will continue to substitute for conversations between people. Consider Sprint. The phone company has been steadily replacing human operators with voice-recognition technology. In the year 2002, Sprint's productivity jumped 15 percent and revenue increased by 4.3 percent, while the company reduced its payroll by 11,500 workers.[61] New computer software is even perfecting the ability of machines to translate conversations from one language to another, in real time. Like the manufacturing sector, expect intelligent technologies to reduce white-collar and service industry workforces to a fraction of their present sizes as the digital communication revolution connects everything on the planet into intelligent conversational networks embedded in a global grid.

Herein lies the conundrum. If dramatic advances in productivity, in the form of cheaper, more efficient technology and better methods for organizing work can replace more and more human labor, resulting in more workers being let go from the workforce, where will the consumer demand come from to buy all the potential new products and services made available by the gains in productivity? As mentioned earlier, for a period of time, consumer credit, the stock-market bubble and home-mortgage refinancing allowed underemployed and unemployed workers to keep buying. Now that credit is maxed out, the stock market bubble has burst, and interest rates on home mortgages are rising, we are being forced to face up to an inherent contradiction at the heart of the capitalist system that has been present since the very beginning, but is only now becoming irreconcilable.

Market capitalism is built, in part, on the logic of reducing input costs, including the cost of labor, in order to increase profit margins. There is always a search to find cheaper, more efficient technologies to force down human wages or eliminate human labor altogether. Now, the new intelligent technologies can replace much of human labor—both physical and mental. While the introduction of new labor-saving and time-saving technology has greatly increased productivity, it has done so at the expense of more workers being marginalized into part-time employment or given their pink slips. A shrinking workforce, however, means diminished income, reduced consumer demand and an economy unable to grow. This is the new structural reality that government and business leaders and so many economists are reluctant to acknowledge.

Traditionally, resolving the dilemma rested with organized labor. Trade unions, and political parties representing their interests, have served as the counterweight to management, forcing companies to share the fruits of productivity gains broadly among the workers, in the form of increased wages, shorter working hours, and improved working conditions and benefits. But, in many countries, unions have been weakened by the forces of globalization and especially by the ability of management to move capital and plants elsewhere and play the game of "beggar thy neighbor."

The unions have long relied on the one weapon at their disposal to exact gains—the ability to withhold their labor through the strike. Strikes, however, become less effective when management can simply shift production to plants in other countries or outsource to anonymous subcontractors. Moreover, with increasing automation of factories and offices, management can often continue to run production and maintain services—at least for short periods—with skeleton crews. The result is that the productivity gains, rather than being shared with the workers in the form of increased wages and benefits, mainly accrue to the benefit of shareholders in the form of increased dividends as well as bloated salaries for senior management. Of course, in the end, the whole system suffers when the paychecks of working people shrink or disappear altogether.

Some economists put forth the argument that even though workers' wages and benefits are shrinking, increases in productivity are making goods and services cheaper and, therefore, allow working people to buy more with less income. If that were the case, working people would not be going deeper and deeper into debt to survive.

What's become obvious is that productivity gains, by themselves, don't automatically lift the boat of working people. Rekindling consumer demand requires sharing some of the productivity gains with employees. Since management will not voluntarily do this on its own, the only real answer to increasing consumer demand is to rejuvenate the trade union movement and extend its geographic reach to match the reach of finance capital. Trade unions, civil society organizations representing consumers and local communities, and political parties need to establish people-to-people networks (P2P) on a global playing field to counter the "beggar thy neighbor" policy with "worker and community solidarity." Arguably, a difficult challenge, but, in the final analysis, only by organizing a global labor and community response to the global flow of capital will it be possible to increase the share of disposable income everywhere and boost consumer spending.

Still, even though organizing a new counterforce to management is essential if some of the dramatic productivity gains brought on by the new technologies are going to be more equitably shared with workers, it is still not enough to address the deep problem of a growing loss of jobs all over the world. That is because it is the concept of employment, itself, that is changing.

THE END OF WORK

The global economy is in the midst of a radical change in the nature of work, with profound consequences for the future of society. In the Industrial Age, mass human labor worked side by side with machines to produce basic goods and services. In the Age of Access, intelligent machines, in the form of computer software, robotics, nanotechnology, and biotechnology, increasingly replaced human labor in the agriculture, manufacturing, and service sectors. Farms, factories, and many white-collar service industries are quickly becoming automated. More and more physical and mental labor, from menial repetitive tasks to highly conceptual professional work, will be done by cheaper and more efficient thinking machines in the twenty-first century. The cheapest workers in the world likely will be not as cheap as the technology coming online to replace them. By the middle decades of the twenty-first century, the commercial sphere will have the technological wherewithal and organizational capacity to provide goods and basic services for an expanding human population using a fraction of the workforce presently employed. Perhaps as little as 5 percent of the adult population will be needed to manage and operate the traditional industrial sphere by the year 2050. Near-workerless farms, factories, and offices will be the norm in every country.

Few of the CEOs I talk to believe that mass amounts of human labor will be needed to produce conventional goods and services fifty years from now. Virtually all believe that intelligent technology will be the workforce of the future.

Of course, the coming era will bring with it all sorts of new goods and services that, in turn, will require new occupational skills, especially in the more sophisticated knowledge arena. However, these new jobs, by their nature, are elite and restricted in numbers. We will never again see thousands of workers stream out of factory gates and service centers as we did in the twentieth century.

Even the more highly skilled professional jobs are increasingly vulnerable to technological displacement. Sophisticated diagnostic technology is replacing the more labor-intensive diagnostic testing previously done by physicians, nurses, and technicians. Computer-aided design has eliminated many draftsmen and engineers. New software programs have taken over much of the standard work previously done by accountants. While the best and the brightest professionals will still be needed, garden-variety professionals in most disciplines will likely be culled out of the workforce as intelligent technology proves to be a more adept, faster and cheaper alternative. The workforce of the future will be increasingly boutique.

The Industrial Age ended slave labor. The Age of Access will end mass wage labor. This is both the opportunity and challenge facing the world economy as we move into the new era of intelligent technology. Freeing up successive generations from toiling long hours at the workplace could usher in a second Renaissance for the human race or lead to great social division and upheaval. The question is, What do we do with the millions of young people who will be needed less or not at all, in an increasingly automated global economy?

Several options for addressing the future of employment lie before us. Each requires a leap of human imagination: i.e., the willingness to both rethink the very nature of work as well as explore alternative ways human beings might define their role and contribution to society in the coming century.

CREATING MILLIONS OF JOBS IN THE NEW HYDROGEN AGE

New "smart" technologies are moving the global economy away from mass labor and toward smaller professional workforces over the next half century. There is, however, one new area where many new jobs will open up—at least temporarily—in the manufacturing and high technology industries. We are on the cusp of a new energy regime that will alter our way of life as fundamentally as the introduction of coal and steam power in the nineteenth century and the shift to oil and the internal combustion engine in the twentieth century.

Qualitative leaps in employment always occur during periods in history when new energy regimes are being established and accompanying infrastructures are being laid out. The harnessing of coal and steam power and the laying down of a continental rail infrastructure between the end of the Civil War and the beginning of World War I in the United States and Europe created millions of jobs as did the harnessing of oil and the introduction of the internal combustion engine and the laying down of roads and the electrification of factories and communities in the first sixty years of the twentieth century. Once operational, these new energy regimes—the first and second industrial revolutions—spawned great leaps in productivity and made possible new kinds of goods, services, and markets, again resulting in the creation of still more jobs.

Hydrogen energy and fuel-cell technology is entering the commercial arena. Its widespread dissemination will likely have a greater impact on the global economy than any other single development in the foreseeable future. Reconfiguring the energy infrastructure as the global economy makes the historic shift out of the fossil-fuel age and into the hydrogen era will create millions of new jobs—enough jobs to absorb at least a portion of the new entrants into the workforce. And because the installation of renewable resource technologies and the establishment of a hydrogen infrastructure as well as the reconfiguration and decentralization of every nation's power grids are geographically tied, the employment generated will all be within each country. The jobs will buy some precious time, while other more far-reaching solutions to the future of work are phased in.

The dawn of new energy regimes is always a key indicator of the future success of countries and economies. Recall that England succeeded in dominating the global economy in the nineteenth century, in large measure because it was the first nation in the world to exploit its rich deposits of coal and establish steam technology—laying the base for the first industrial revolution. Similarly, the United States owes much of its success in the twentieth century to its large domestic oil reserves, which provided it with an abundant source of cheap energy to power automobiles and maintain an unrivaled military machine, giving the U.S. a commanding position in the unfolding of the second industrial revolution.

In October 2002, the European Union unveiled a bold long-term plan for making the transition out of the fossil-fuel age and into a fully integrated renewable-based hydrogen economy. I was serving, at the time, as a personal adviser to Romano Prodi, the President of the European Commission, the governing body of the European Union. In that capacity, I provided President Prodi with the initial strategic memorandum that led to the EU hydrogen energy initiative. President Prodi said that the transformation of Europe's energy regime would be the next great development in European integration after the introduction of the Euro, and likened the effort to the American Space program in the 1960s and 1970s, which spawned the subsequent high-tech economic revolution of the 1980s and 1990s.[62]

Hydrogen has the potential to end the world's reliance on imported oil and help diffuse the dangerous geopolitical game being played out between Muslim militants and Western nations. It will dramatically cut down on carbon dioxide emissions and mitigate the effects of global warming. And because hydrogen is so plentiful and exists everywhere on Earth, every human being could be "empowered," making it the first truly democratic energy regime in history.

Commercial fuel cells powered by hydrogen are just now being introduced into the market for home, office, and industrial use. The major automakers have spent more than $2 billion developing hydrogen-powered cars, buses, and trucks, and the first mass-produced vehicles are expected to be on the road in just a few years.

The hydrogen economy makes possible a broad redistribution of power, with far-reaching beneficial consequences for society. Today's centralized, top-down flow of energy, controlled by global oil companies and utilities, becomes obsolete. In the new era, every human being could become the producer as well as the consumer of his or her own energy—so-called distributed generation. In the new hydrogen fuel-cell era, even the automobile itself is a "power station on wheels" with a generating capacity of twenty kilowatts. Since the average car is parked most of the time, it can be plugged in, during non-use hours, to the home, the office, or the main interactive electricity network, providing premium electricity back to the grid. If just 25 percent of drivers used their vehicles as power plants to sell energy back to the grid, all of the power plants in the country could be eliminated.

When millions of end users connect their fuel cells into local, regional, and national hydrogen energy webs (HEWs), using the same design principles and smart technologies that made possible the World Wide Web, they can begin to share energy—peer-to-peer—creating a new decentralized form of energy use.[63]

Silicon valley is just beginning to understand the critical role that the software and communications revolutions will play in ushering in a new energy era. The great pivotal changes in world history have occurred when new energy regimes converge with new communication regimes. When that convergence happens, society is restructured in wholly new ways. For example, the coming together of coal-powered steam technology and the printing press gave birth to the first industrial revolution. It would have been impossible to organize the dramatic increase in the pace, speed, flow, density, and connectivity of economic activity made possible by the coal-fired steam engine using the older codex and oral forms of communication. In the late nineteenth and early twentieth centuries, the telegraph and telephone converged with the introduction of oil and the internal combustion engine, becoming the command and control mechanism for organizing the second industrial revolution.

A great communications revolution occurred in the 1990s. Personal computers, the Internet, the World Wide Web, and wireless communication technologies connected the central nervous system of more than a billion people on Earth at the speed of light. And, although the new software and communication revolutions have begun to increase productivity in every industry, their true potential is yet to be fully realized. That potential lies in their convergence with the new distributed hydrogen energy regime. The software and communication revolution is the command and control mechanism to reconfigure every power grid in the world so that power can be generated by the people and shared with each other just as information is on the World Wide Web. The coming together of decentralized communications technology and distributed hydrogen energy technology marks the next great turning point in the way people organize the energy of the planet.

The biggest beneficiaries of the new decentralized hydrogen energy regime will be the developing world. Today, more than one billion people on Earth live on less than one dollar a day and three billion people—half of the human race—live on less than two dollars a day.[64] The reason people are powerless is literal. They have no power. One-third of the human race has no access to electricity, and nearly two-thirds of the human race has never made a telephone call.[65]

Without electricity, it is impossible to produce goods and services and create jobs. In South Africa, according to a recent report, for every one hundred households electrified, ten to twenty new businesses were created.[66] Electricity frees human labor from day-to-day survival tasks. It provides power to run farm equipment, operate small factories and craft shops, and light homes, schools, and businesses.

While developed nations are making a historic shift from mass to elite workforces, there is still opportunity in the third world, at least in the short run of the next fifty years, to harness electricity to create businesses and expand employment for a portion of the population. Getting renewable technologies, fuel cells, and mini power grids installed in every village, town, and city in the third world is crucial to creating new job opportunities.

Laying down a new energy infrastructure in the poorest countries of the world will require a considerable infusion of investment capital.

Even though the costs of renewable technologies, hydrogen storage, and fuel cells will continue to go down as the technology matures and as economies of scale are realized in the developed countries, they will still be expensive to employ in the third world. Developing countries will need to begin leveraging their micro and macro credit, but even that won't be enough to operate a state-of-the-art hydrogen power grid.

There is, however, another source of investment capital that could be brought to bear to the task. South American economist Hernando De Soto makes the telling point that large amounts of potential capital already exists in the third world, but are not usable because the appropriate property rights regime is not in place to allow for their conversion into instruments of credit. De Soto says that just the real estate alone held by the poor in the third world exceeds $9 trillion. He argues that "[b]ecause the rights to these possessions are not adequately documented, these assets cannot readily be turned into capital, cannot be traded outside of narrow local circles where people know and trust each other, cannot be used as collateral for loans, and cannot be used as a share against investment."[67] What separates the haves from the have-nots, says De Soto, is the kind of formal property law that allows property to be turned into capital and be used as an investment tool.

The developing nations, then, are going to need to create a formal private property regime so that a portion of the property their citizens own can be made use of as credit instruments to underwrite the creation of a hydrogen energy infrastructure. The power grid, in turn, will open up new possibilities for businesses and employment.

THE THIRTY-FIVE-HOUR WORKWEEK
AND BEYOND

The shift to a new energy regime and the laying down of an accompanying power grid across the world will create many new jobs. Still, it will not be enough to accommodate the growing population of young people in search of employment. Traditionally, when new technologies have increased productivity, the result has been a reduction in the number of hours worked and an increase in wages and benefits. (Remember, the industrial revolution began with a seventy-hour workweek, subsistence wages, and a Draconian work environment.) Improvements in productivity mean that more goods and services can be produced with less human labor. Therefore, the question has always been, Do we reduce the workweek or the workforce to accommodate productivity advances? In other words, do we choose more leisure or longer unemployment lines? For more than one hundred years, society chose to continue to reduce the workweek and increase the pay and benefits with each successive improvement in productivity.

Every nation needs to create a formal mechanism that ties productivity gains with ever-shorter work hours. A shorter workweek means that more people can be kept on the employment rolls.

France was the first country in the world to adopt a thirty-five-hour workweek. The publication of *The End of Work* in France helped ignite a discussion on the shorter workweek. The proposals in the book were taken up, at the time, by Philippe Séguin, the president of the French National Assembly and a member of the ruling Rally for the Republic Party. Michel Rocard, the influential former democratic socialist prime minister, wrote a lengthy forward to the book and publicly championed the idea of the thirty-five-hour workweek. The nonpartisan support helped lead to the passage of the historic legislation.

In January of 2000, all French companies with more than twenty workers reduced their workweek to thirty-five hours, and in January of 2002, firms with fewer than twenty workers made the switchover to the shorter workweek. Under the new thirty-five-hour workweek law, employees will still be paid for thirty-nine hours of work. To ensure that French companies remain competitive, the government subsidizes the increase in employee remuneration per hour by lowering employers' social security contributions.[68] In addition, the government provides an incentive to companies to create new jobs by agreeing to subsidize the social payments (retirement, health care, workers compensation, and unemployment insurance) of any newly hired low-wage workers. The annual subsidies amount to at least $3.3 billion per year.[69] Much of the funds have come from so-called sin taxes on tobacco and alcohol.

The new thirty-five-hour workweek was credited with creating more than 285,000 new jobs and pushing the unemployment rate down to 8.7 percent in 2001, an eighteen-year low.[70] Although French employers were at first skeptical of the new reduced workweek, many became enthusiastic converts because the new legislation built in provisions to allow greater workforce flexibility, something companies had desperately sought for years, but which the unions had fought. The adoption of the shorter workweek has been accompanied by a greater willingness on the part of workers and unions to accept more flexible work schedules. For example, Samsonite workers have agreed to work a forty-two-hour workweek in the summer when demand for luggage is generally high, in return for a thirty-two-hour workweek in the winter when demand is slack. The giant French retailer Carrefour has made an agreement with its cashiers to adjust their work schedules to fit customers' peak shopping times in the stores.[71]

In 2002, the French government passed additional legislation raising maximum overtime from 130 to 180 hours to further accommodate employers' need for flexibility in matching production quotas to hours needed to complete the work.[72]

French workers, overall, have been enthusiastic about the new reduced workweek. Eighty percent of workers polled felt that their lives had improved with the reduced work schedule.[73] Some French workers complain that the shorter workweek has created additional stress by forcing them to do more work in less time. Most workers, however, say they feel more rested and are better able to be more productive during the hours they do work.

Many French workers now start their weekend on Thursday and return to work on Tuesday. Working mothers often take off work on Wednesday, when French children are not in school. More time off has also increased spending. Cafés, movie theaters, and retail stores report brisk business.[74]

American economists and business leaders derided the French thirty-five-hour workweek as retrogressive and predicted it would undermine the French economy. In fact, the new shorter workweek has increased French competitiveness. French productivity is now the highest of any major industrialized country in the world. In 2002, French workers produced $41.85 of output per hour or $3.02 per hour more than American workers—that's 7 percent greater productivity.[75] French managers attribute at least part of this success to the thirty-five-hour workweek. In a survey of corporate directors conducted in 2001, 60 percent of the respondents polled said that the new law helped improve productivity by introducing more flexible work arrangements and by creating a new dialogue with workers, which improved morale.[76]

Reducing the workweek to thirty-five hours, while maintaining remuneration for thirty-nine to forty hours of work, will require the kind of government assistance that France has provided. In an increasingly competitive global market, companies cannot remain competitive if their labor costs soar. Therefore, governments need to compensate companies by freeing them of payroll or other corporate taxes in direct proportion to the expenses incurred in shortening the workweek. Governments will lose revenue at the front end, but they will pick it up at the back end. More people working means fewer people on welfare, more paychecks, more consumption, increased personal savings and investment, and more employed people paying both personal income and sales taxes, all increasing the government's revenue base.

Countries across Europe are following France's lead. Belgium put into effect a thirty-eight-hour workweek in January 2003. European trade unions have also made the thirty-five-hour workweek a high priority. The European Trade Union Confederation, the European Metal Workers Federation, and the European Federation of Public Service Unions have all adopted resolutions calling for a thirty-five-hour workweek across Europe.[77]

Union efforts have already resulted in collective bargaining agreements that have reduced the workweek in a number of industries. The result is that even without government initiatives, the average workweek in the EU countries is now 38.2 hours. In Germany, the U.K., the Netherlands, Denmark, and Norway, the average workweek is closer to thirty-seven hours.[78] Governments around the world should set a goal of dropping the workweek to thirty-five hours by 2010 and aim for a thirty-hour workweek, or a six-hour day, by 2020. (The drop in the length of the workweek needs to be tied to a commensurate rise in productivity.)

The decrease in work hours should also be made flexible to accommodate the human resource needs of companies and the lifestyles of workers. Employers, if they had their way, would prefer a "just in time" workforce, employing people only when they are needed. This is the ultimate goal of a so-called flexible labor policy. From a pure market perspective, employing human resources only when needed makes sense. The problem is that from the point of view of society at large, such a policy would create social havoc. Workers are not just another factor in production. They have families to feed and futures to plan. While management gurus might laud the virtue of every worker becoming his or her own contractor or entrepreneur, in reality, economies would likely collapse if workers could not be sure of whether they will have work or a paycheck week-to-week.

A flexible hours policy needs also to take into consideration the security and needs of workers. Belgium has led the way in creating flexible labor policies. The government has introduced novel legislation called "time credits," which went into effect in January 2002. The law is designed to create a more flexible balance between one's work and home life, and updates an older law called "career breaks."[79]

Under the new "time credits" law, workers can take a maximum of one year off over their entire career or interrupt their work, or reduce it to a half-time job without severing their employment contract and without loss of social security rights. To receive a general career break, the employee has to give a three-month advance notice to the employer, but does not have to give any reason for the request. The time credit can be extended up to five years by an agreement with the company. Employees who have worked less than five years receive a monthly government allowance of €379. The allowances rise to €505 for workers who have been employed longer.[80] Workers can also request "thematic leaves" to take care of a family member, to provide medical assistance to a relative, or to take care of a child. Each of these specific career breaks comes with different allowances and allocated times. Each worker can also choose to reduce his or her working hours by 20 percent, which generally works out to be a four-day workweek. Older workers over the age of fifty can reduce their work hours by one-fifth to one-half over an unlimited period of time.[81]

Although American employers would be incredulous at the thought of providing career breaks and time credits and wonder how Belgium's companies could maintain their competitive edge with these kinds of flexible labor schedules, it's interesting to note that, like France, the Belgian workforce enjoys higher productivity in terms of output per hour than does the American workforce.[82]

In an era increasingly characterized by reduced requirements for human labor, being able to create a flexible labor policy that accommodates the needs of both employers and employees is going to be essential to maintaining a healthy and sustainable economy.

Avocations and Social Capital in the Third Sector

Finally, even with new job opportunities opening up with the transformation to a new energy regime, the reduction of the workweek and the adoption of a more flexible labor employment scheme, there is likely not going to be enough work to accommodate all of the new entrants coming into the workforce. What about government jobs? It's probably safe to assume that governments are not going to significantly enlarge their public payrolls but will, in fact, continue to pare down their historic role as employers of last resort. Of course, the fourth sector, which includes the informal and black markets and organized crime, is a prospective arena for employment. In many countries, this is now the fastest-growing employment sector. The informal economy generally provides only marginal subsistence. The criminal economy, on the other hand, is often a lucrative source of employment, but if allowed to grow and prosper, could further erode social relations in every country and lead to an increasingly dangerous and destabilized world.

There is, however, another sector where people's skills, talents and expertise can be energized—the third sector, or civil society. This sector includes all of the formal and informal not-for-profit activities that make up the cultural life of the society. It is the sector where people create both the bonds of community and social order.

Community pursuits include a range of activities, from social services to health care, education and research, the arts, sports and recreation, religion, and advocacy. In the first edition of *The End of Work*, I suggested the possibility of creating millions of new jobs in the third sector. In the nine years since, employment has mushroomed in the not-for-profit sector. A study conducted by the Johns Hopkins Comparative Nonprofit Sector Project covering twenty-two nations found that the nonprofit sector is a $1.1 trillion industry employing 19 million full-time equivalent paid workers. Nonprofit expenditures in these countries averaged 4.6 percent of the gross domestic product, and nonprofit employment constituted 5 percent of all non-agricultural employment, 10 percent of all service employment, and 27 percent of all public employment.[83]

Several European nations now boast employment levels in the nonprofit sector that exceed the United States. In the Netherlands, 12.6 percent of total paid employment is in the nonprofit sector. In Ireland, 11.5 percent of all workers are in the nonprofit sector, and in Belgium, 10.5 percent of workers are in this sector. In the U.K., 6.2 percent of the workforce are in the not-for-profit sector, and in France and Germany the figure is 4.9 percent. Italy currently has more than 220,000 nonprofit organizations, and its not-for-profit sector employs more than 630,000 full-time workers.[84]

The growth in employment in the nonprofit sector was stronger in Europe in the 1990s than in any other region of the world, expanding by an average of 24 percent in France, Germany, the Netherlands, and the U.K.[85] The expansion in nonprofit employment in these countries alone accounted for 40 percent of total employment growth, or 3.8 million jobs.[86]

It is interesting to note that in the ten European countries where revenue data was available, fees for services and products accounted for one-third to one-half of the income in the nonprofit sector between 1990 and 1995. Globally, of the twenty-two countries for which data is available, 49 percent of nonprofit revenue comes from fees for services and products. In the U.S., 57 percent of all nonprofit revenue comes from fees for services and products.[87] The share of funds coming from the philanthropic and public sector, however, has declined in many countries, thus dispelling the long-harbored myth that the nonprofit sector is virtually dependent on government or private charity to sustain itself.

Community service is very different from labor in the marketplace. One's contribution is freely given out of a sense of caring for others. While economic consequences often flow from the activity, they are secondary to the social exchange. The goal is not the accumulation of wealth but, rather, social cohesion.

Unlike market capitalism, which is based on Adam Smith's notion that the common good is advanced by each person pursuing his or her own individual self-interest, the civil society starts with the exact opposite premise—that by each person giving of himself or herself to others and optimizing the social good of the larger community, one's own well-being will be advanced.

In a globalized economy of impersonal market forces, the civil society has become an important social refuge. It is the place where people create a sense of intimacy and trust, shared purpose and collective identity. The third sector is the antidote to a world increasingly defined in strictly commercial terms.

Every country will need to explore new opportunities to educate and train young people for active participation—and paid compensation—in the third sector. Financing millions of people to engage in the creation of social capital in their communities will require the expenditure of government funds. Although, as mentioned, fees for services already account for between one-third and one-half of revenue in the third sector, much of the remaining funds will have to be made up largely through government expenditures. Private philanthropy currently makes up approximately 11.7 percent of the revenue of nonprofit organizations around the world.[88]

Serious consideration should be given to using "tax shifting" arrangements to bolster employment opportunities in the third sector. Such schemes have been used effectively for more than a decade— mostly in Europe—to create a more sustainable approach to economic development. The idea is to tax environmentally destructive practices and activities and earmark the revenues specifically to reducing taxes on corporate profits, labor, and personal income. In the European Union, 50 percent of the tax burden falls on labor, whereas less than 10 percent falls on the use of natural resources.[89] Thus, human labor is penalized and polluting activity is given free rein. Many of the industries that are among the biggest polluters are further rewarded with large subsidies for their negative activities. By shifting the burden from taxing labor to taxing the use of environmental resources and eliminating subsidies, governments hope to redress the inequities and create a more balanced, environmentally sensitive approach to economic activity as well as to stimulate employment.

Increased taxes on gasoline, home heating oil, electricity, automobile use, and the like fall disproportionately on working people and the poor in terms of higher energy and transportation costs. Governments that have adopted tax-shifting measures have made adjustments by granting greater tax cuts on personal income for lower-income groups as well as by extending other offsetting benefits, including housing benefits, increases in pensions, student grants, child allowances, and tax credits in the form of lump-sum payments. These compensating benefits, say the architects of tax shifting, "must be designed in such a way that these households will be motivated to make energy savings." In the Netherlands, a portion of the tax-shifting revenue is used to improve home energy efficiency.[90]

Environmental Fiscal Reform (EFR), as it is sometimes referred to, has been taken up by a number of countries, including Sweden, Denmark, the Netherlands, the U.K., Finland, Norway, Italy, and Germany. In Sweden, taxes raised on diesel fuel, heating oil, and electricity, amounting to 6 percent of the total tax revenue, were used to cut personal income taxes and fund continuous education. The pollution tax resulted in a 4 percent decline in CO_2 emissions in the ten-year period from 1990 to 2000.[91] In Denmark, in the 1990s, an increase in taxes on gasoline, electricity, water, waste, cars, CO_2, and SO_2 amounting to more than 6 percent of total tax revenue, went to reducing personal income taxes and social security contributions. Industrial production grew by 27 percent during the same decade while CO_2 emissions fell by 7 percent and SO_2 emissions by 24 percent. In the Netherlands, a CO_2 tax was used to reduce corporate profit taxes. Germany, which is among the most enthusiastic supporters of tax shifting, has phased in an increase in taxes on gasoline, heating oil, and electricity, and used the revenue to reduce payroll taxes. By reducing the social security contribution equally between employers and employees, the tax shifting gained the support of both management and the workforce. The cuts reduced labor costs for the employers and provided workers with additional income, which allowed them to pay their higher energy bills and still have additional income for other spending. The gasoline tax resulted in the decline in motor fuel use by 5 percent in 2001 over 1999 and a growth in carpooling by 25 percent.[92]

In Europe, most of the environmental tax shift has been directed toward reduction in payroll taxes to encourage job growth. The European Commission, the governing body of the European Union, has recommended an EU-wide tax on carbon emissions and energy use that could be shifted to cutting payroll taxes across the continent. Government economists estimate that a tax shift of this sort could generate 1.5 million new jobs. A World Bank study on the effects of EFR on employment found that in 73 percent of the cases studied, the influence on job creation was positive.[93]

At present, environmental tax shifting comprises only about 3 percent of tax revenues worldwide, but the potential is enormous.[94] A World Watch report on the subject notes that 90 percent of the $7.5 trillion in government revenues generated annually worldwide are from taxes on work and investment, including payrolls, personal income, corporate profits, capital gains, retail sales, trade, and built-in property, while less than 5 percent comes from taxes on environmental harm. A tax on fossil fuels alone could raise more than a trillion dollars annually. The revenue, in turn, could be used to cut existing taxes on wages and profits by 15 percent and stimulate new hires, leaving the overall tax burden unchanged.[95]

Ending environmentally harmful subsidies to polluting industries could free up an additional $500 billion per year globally, which could be used to significantly reduce taxes on labor, income, and corporate profits, which would stimulate both investment and job creation. According to surveys conducted in both the U.S. and Europe, 70 percent of the public favors such tax-shifting practices.[96]

Interestingly, the evidence shows that while increases in taxes on corporate pollution is not very well received by the companies, it forces them to eliminate resource inefficiencies and makes them more competitive in world markets. Studies show that many of the countries "that have the highest levels of environmental taxes also have industries that are the best in international competitiveness."[97]

Economists refer to tax shifting as the "double dividend."[98] The tax shift helps preserve vital resources and protects the environment while forcing employers to become more efficient and competitive. At the same time, the revenue generated helps reduce labor taxes, income taxes, and corporate profit taxes, putting more money into the economy and thus stimulating additional employment.

To ensure that firms in energy-intensive industries don't suffer adversely during the transition to becoming more energy-efficient and competitive players, tax rebates are offered, but only if the companies can show that they are in need of the assistance and committed to making the necessary changes to cut energy use and pollution. And again, it should be emphasized that in all the countries where EFRs have been implemented, a phase-in approach is used, with taxes increasing gradually each year, to allow companies the time to make the appropriate changes in their commercial practices to mitigate inefficient energy use, rein in wasteful use of resources, and curtail polluting practices.

Tax-shifting policies to promote sustainable development and employment are likely to become increasingly popular in countries around the world in the years ahead. Other tax-shifting ideas are also under active consideration by governments, including initiatives designed to discourage socially harmful behavior. Sin taxes on cigarette consumption, alcohol use, and gambling are already widespread and a growing source of revenue for governments. Recently, the British Medical Association (BMA) rolled out a controversial proposal to charge a 17.5 percent Value Added Tax (VAT) on high-fat foods. The tax, which would bring in millions of pounds in revenue to the government, is under serious discussion because of the growing concern over the dramatic rise in obesity in the U.K. and the increase in health costs associated with it. Nearly 20 percent of men and 25 percent of women in the U.K. are obese, and the numbers are expected to rise sharply in the years ahead. The rise in obesity, which has now become a worldwide concern, is a major cause of diabetes, heart disease, high blood pressure, and cancer-related illnesses. Many U.K. physicians say they "strongly support the concept of a tax on saturated fats" as a way of slowing the trend toward obesity.[99]

Tax shifting geared to both harmful environmental and social behavior could be earmarked to help finance third-sector organizations, bolstering civil society employment and promoting social capital development around the world. Cleaning up the environment, creating sustainable ways of conducting commerce, making companies more energy and resource efficient and competitive, discouraging social behavior that is harmful to personal health and one's quality of life, while stimulating the rebuilding of the third sector and creating millions of paid jobs that serve the social good of neighborhoods and communities is a win-win-win, for the environment, the economy, and the civil society.

In the coming century, human contribution is increasingly going to shift from the commercial arena to the civil society. Tax shifting is an important tool to helping make the transition a reality.

PARALLEL CURRENCY

In the twenty-two-country survey reporting on third-sector activity, conducted by Johns Hopkins University Center for Civil Society Studies, researchers found that, on average, 28 percent of the population in these countries contributed their time to nonprofit civil society organizations.[100]

The third sector is, in fact, a parallel economy. Its mission, however, is to create social capital, not market capital. Civil society proponents argue, with some justification, that without the social economy, the market economy could not exist. The social economy is the "core" sector, the place where people create formal and informal bonds, relationships, and institutions to care for one another. It's where human beings establish the social trust that allows them to reach out and engage in commercial relations. Social capital always precedes market capital in every society.

The problem is that as the human population has grown and social relations have become both more dense and dispersed, the kind of intimate personal relations that facilitated the creation of social capital have become more difficult to maintain. In smaller, more tight-knit communities, reciprocity between kin and neighbors is traditionally high. It is customary for individuals to contribute their expertise, skills, and knowledge to help one another and to build community relationships and institutions. As human communities have mushroomed into giant cities and spread out into sprawling suburbs, intimacy has given way to anonymity, and a sense of shared obligation and mutual aid has suffered.

While the social economy has waned, the market economy has waxed, in part because the mechanisms of exchange between people in the commercial realm are based on arm's-length, adversarial behavior. Money, which is an impersonal medium, allows people spread out across space and time to exchange their human time and labor without having to establish an intimate bond with one another.

What's sorely missing in the civil society is the kind of fungibility that would allow people to exchange their time, skills, and expertise in not-for-profit activity that builds the social capital in their communities. Social currency provides a solution. The technology is now available with debit and credit cards, Internet services, the World Wide Web, and mobile technology to establish a parallel currency in the civil society that can begin to make fungible the pent-up human capital that is available in every neighborhood and community.

The creation of social currency is the key to creating whole new ways for people to share their personal resources with one another. For the millions of people who find themselves underemployed or unemployed and without sufficient means to ensure their survival, social currency will increasingly fill the vacuum and eventually could become a powerful parallel means for providing a quality of life, outside the marketplace economy.

Social currency, in one form or another, dates back to the early years of the twentieth century. Its recent reincarnation, however, is attributable to Edgar Cahn, a law professor at the David C. Clarke School of Law of the University of the District of Columbia. He developed the idea of the "time bank" at the London School of Economics, and established the first operational bank in the late 1980s.[101]

The idea is a simple one based on the notion of helping a neighbor with the expectation that a neighbor—not necessarily the same one—will then help you somewhere down the line. Its inspiration is similar to the principle behind the notion of giving blood at the blood bank.

There are now more than 250 "time dollar" bank schemes operating in the United States involving thousands of people, and similar projects exist in the U.K., Japan, and a host of other countries under different names, like "fair shares" and "service credits." Here's how it works.

An individual gives an hour of his or her volunteer time and is rewarded with one time dollar. Unlike the market economy, where people's hourly time is compensated on a descending scale measured by their perceived expertise, social currency is equally weighted. Everyone, regardless of their expertise, from doctors to cab drivers, receives an hour credit for an hour of commitment, reflecting the idea that each person's contribution is equally valued in producing the social capital of the community.

The accrued time dollars can be used to secure goods and services from others in the time bank, including food, clothing, computers, legal services, health-care services, housing, transportation services, and even enrollment in school programs. Some critics have bemoaned the idea of being rewarded for giving one's time to not-for-profit civil society activities. Its advocates point out, however, that the idea of creating reciprocal obligations among equals is a far superior form of engagement than just volunteering one's services to others in need. The latter often creates an unequal relationship of dependency—the feeling that one is being given charity—because it doesn't allow the person in need a way to reciprocate. Time dollars reinforces the idea of "mutual aid": that is, bringing together many more people into cooperative relationships with one another.

Elderplan, a Brooklyn, N.Y., health maintenance organization (HMO), was one of the first organizations to use the time-dollar model. Elderplan, like other HMOs, was anxious to reduce the cost of emergency medical treatment and long hospital stays by providing quality care-giving, counseling, and other services at home. The company transformed its own passive recipients of medical services into active providers of health care with its time-dollar program.

Under the program, HMO members help chronically ill and homebound members by cooking meals for them, transporting them to doctors and therapy appointments, and picking up their prescriptions. Some have even been trained in counseling the bereaved. Most of the volunteers are seniors. From 1987 to 1998, they could cash in their time dollars for a 25 percent discount on their health-care insurance. Today, their time dollars can be used at the Time Dollar Credit Shop to purchase digital blood-pressure monitors, bathtub spas, and other health-related products.[102] With time dollars, the members of the HMO become part of a health community network. They help one another.

The Grace Hill settlement in St. Louis is still another example of the successful use of time banks. The organization runs eleven neighborhood centers and four health centers in the poorer areas of the city. Eight hundred and twenty families with pre-school children are involved in the organization's Head Start program and other Grace Hill activities. Some of the parents are trained in child care and other skills. They are rewarded with time dollars for their contributions, which can be used to make purchases in time-dollar stores stocked with donated goods and located around the city. Grace Hill also runs a neighborhood college where local residents can exchange time dollars for course instruction.[103]

Other time-dollar programs allow people to exchange their hours donated to the community for a range of services, including car repair, carpentry, plumbing, accounting, legal services, and dancing lessons. Even rent can be partially paid for with time dollars.[104]

It should be emphasized that time-dollar programs are not the same as barter. There is no bargaining. All contributions are valued equally. That is, each hour of work is comparable, regardless of the nature and kind of contribution. The U.S. government's Internal Revenue Service has ruled that time dollars, unlike barter, are not taxable.[105]

According to a 2001 survey by the Independent Sector, 44 percent of the adult American population, or eighty-four million people, contributed an average of 3.6 hours of their time each week to one or more of the 1.2 million nonprofit organizations in the U.S. Most Americans believe we have the most developed third sector, but the fact is that several Western European countries have an even larger nonprofit sector in proportion to their total employment.[106] The point is, the third sector is a growing force in countries around the world, but despite its size and importance in the life of every country, it has lacked, up to now, the one essential element that would allow it to connect and mobilize the vast human potential that exists into a formidable parallel social force comparable in clout to the market economy. Social currency, in the form of time dollars and other similar schemes, is the way to begin bringing together large numbers of people in the process of creating and exchanging social capital. For unemployed youth and retired seniors, and for the millions of people who are currently either underemployed or unemployed, social currency is a way to be able to utilize their full human potential to both serve the community and provide for their own families' needs.

All of the social-currency programs presently in operation around the world are small in scope and scale. They are, however, suggestive of the great human potential that could be unleashed were more bold programs put into effect. There should be serious discussion on how to expand these piecemeal efforts into a single national social currency in each country—using debit cards and other state-of-the-art banking technology—so that people can contribute their time and skills to the community, and use their time dollars for securing access to goods and services anywhere in the region where they reside. Extending the time-dollar concept to a region allows for a broader playing field for the exchange of personal contributions while still maintaining a degree of geographic locality. Special allowances could even be made to exchange time dollars nationally in cases where access to expertise, services, and goods is not readily available regionally. A parallel national social currency, running alongside the existing commercial currency, will help establish the third sector or civil society arena as a viable alternative for the utilization of human resources.

It is possible to imagine intelligent technology replacing much of human labor in the commercial sphere by the twenty-second century, allowing most human beings to be educated and trained for avocations in the cultural arena. After all, work should be what machines do. Work is only about producing utility values. People, on the other hand, should be freed to generate intrinsic values and to reinvigorate a sense of shared community. Liberating people from work so that they can make a deep contribution to the creation of social capital in the civil society represents a great potential leap forward for humanity in the coming century. What is required now is the will and determination to begin this next phase in the human journey.

—Jeremy Rifkin
January 2004

Foreword

Robert L. Heilbroner

Economists have always been uneasy about what machinery does for us and to us. On the one hand, machines are the very embodiment of the investment that drives a capitalist economy. On the other hand, most of the time when a machine moves in, a worker moves out—sometimes many workers. Economists have always granted that a machine may displace a few workers here and there, but in the end, they have maintained, productivity will be vastly augmented, and as a consequence, the national income.

But who gets the income? In 1819 the famous economist David Ricardo wrote that the amount of employment in an economy was of no consequence, as long as rent and profits, out of which flowed its new investment, were undiminished. "Indeed?" replied Simonde de Sismondi, a well-known Swiss critic of the times. "Wealth is everything, men are absolutely nothing? What? . . . In truth then, there is nothing more to wish for than that the king, remaining alone on the island, by constantly turning a crank, might produce, through automata, all the output of England."[1]

Jeremy Rifkin's mind-opening book is about a world in which corporations have taken the place of kings, turning cranks that set into motion the mechanical, electrical, and electronic automata that provide the goods and services of the nation. This is by no means a recent development. If we could look down over the man-machine history of the United States—or for that matter, any modern nation—we would see that for two hundred years there has been a great migration of workers leaving jobs that technology had taken away, looking for others that it was creating.

As the curtain rises on this drama, at the beginning of the 19th century, machines were not highly visible. North, south, east and west, farming was the quintessential occupation; largely manual, helped along with hoes and spades, horse-drawn plows, carts, and the like.

Then, around the middle of the century, things began to change. Cyrus McCormick invented the reaper; John Deere the steel plow; the tractor appeared. As a consequence, by the three-quarter mark of the century, the proportion of the national labor force in agriculture had decreased from around three quarters to half; by 1900 to a third, by 1940 to a fifth, today to about 3 percent.

What happened to those whose jobs were taken over by machines? They moved to other fields, in which technology was creating new places for work. In 1810 a mere 75,000 persons worked in the infant "manfactories" that made pig iron and lumber and the like; fifty years later, over 1,500,000; by 1910, over 8 million; by 1960, twice that. In terms of percentages, the industrial labor force grew by leaps and bounds until it offered work to some 35 percent of the total labor force.

The figures did not, however, climb indefinitely. Technology was not only opening up jobs in the new automobile plants, home appliance factories, and power plants, but also trimming them down as the assembly line followed the lathe, as drills and presses increased their speeds, and as remarkable new "calculators" began to simplify the work of foremen. Between 1960 and 1990, output of manufactured goods of all kinds continued to rise, but the number of jobs needed to create that flow of production fell by half.

We are almost finished with our drama. During all the time that labor was moving into, and then out of the factory, a third great sector was offering growing possibilities for employment. This was the expanding range of "service" employments—teachers and lawyers, nurses and doctors, maids and baby-sitters, government officials and traffic cops, file clerks, typists, custodians, salespeople. It is impossible to estimate with any degree of accuracy the number of "service" employees in the early 19th century, but by 1870 there were perhaps 3 million in the diverse branches of this sector, and by the 1990s nearly 90 million. Service employment thus saved this—and other modern economies—from absolutely devastating unemployment.[2]

As with manufacturing, technology in the service sector created with one hand and took away with the other. The sector grew on the back of the typewriter and the telephone, shrank under the impact of the Xerox machine and the mail order catalogue. But it was the computer, of course, that brings the drama to a close, threatening to allow the corporation to sit on its island, turning its crank while the automata go to work.

That is the historic transformation about which Jeremy Rifkin is writing. His book is rich in detail, absorbing in its real-life relevance, and large in scope, spelling out the global, as well as the national implications of the change in the reach and impact of technology in our time. If he is right—and his range and depth of research strongly suggest that he *is* right—we are pushing the relationship of machines and work beyond the uneasy accommodation of the last two hundred years into a new relationship about whose configuration we can say little except that it will have to be markedly different from that of the past.

Rifkin explores some of the obvious changes that will be forced upon us by this emerging relationship—changes that range from the dislocations and dysfunctions that will assuredly accompany a studied indifference to the problem, through reconfigurations in the patterns of work life as dramatic as those that separate today's work-years and work-days from those in Dickens's time, to possibilities for the creation of a new employment-offering sector that I will allow him to describe.

This is a book that ought to become the center of a long-lasting and deep-probing conversation for the nation. I would describe it as an indispensable introduction to a problem that we will be living with for the rest of our own and our children's lives.

Robert L. Heilbroner is the author of many books and articles in economics, most recently Visions of the Future.

Introduction

G LOBAL UNEMPLOYMENT has now reached its highest level since the great depression of the 1930s. More than 800 million human beings are now unemployed or underemployed in the world.[1] That figure is likely to rise sharply between now and the turn of the century as millions of new entrants into the workforce find themselves without jobs, many victims of a technology revolution that is fast replacing human beings with machines in virtually every sector and industry of the global economy. After years of wishful forecasts and false starts, the new computer and communications technologies are finally making their long-anticipated impact on the workplace and the economy, throwing the world community into the grip of a third great industrial revolution. Already, millions of workers have been permanently eliminated from the economic process, and whole job categories have shrunk, been restructured, or disappeared.

The Information Age has arrived. In the years ahead, new, more sophisticated software technologies are going to bring civilization ever closer to a near-workerless world. In the agricultural, manufacturing, and service sectors, machines are quickly replacing human labor and promise an economy of near automated production by the mid-decades of the twenty-first century. The wholesale substitution of machines for workers is going to force every nation to rethink the role of human beings in the social process. Redefining opportunities and responsibilities for millions of people in a society absent of mass formal employment is likely to be the single most pressing social issue of the coming century.

While the public continues to hear talk of better economic times ahead, working people everywhere remain perplexed over what appears to be a "jobless recovery." Every day, transnational corporations announce that they are becoming more globally competitive. We are told that profits are steadily rising. Yet, at the same time, companies are announcing massive layoffs. In the single month of January 1994, America's largest employers laid off more than 108,000 workers. Most of the cutbacks came in service industries, where corporate restructuring and the introduction of new laborsaving technologies are resulting in greater productivity, larger profits, and fewer jobs.[2]

Corporate downsizing and re-engineering continue to accelerate with no end in sight. On November 15, 1995, AT&T announced it was letting go more than 77,000 managers in an effort to cut labor costs and improve profit margins.[3] Other companies are pursuing an equally aggressive labor-cutting policy. According to a 1995 survey of 2,000 corporate executives from the world's leading industrial nations, 94 percent of the respondents reported that their companies had been through a reorganization in the past two years, resulting in a permanent reduction in their workforce. More than 66 percent of the business leaders predicted that the pace of downsizing and re-engineering would increase in the years ahead. The companies surveyed employ 18 million people, more than 6 percent of the work force in the six leading industrialized countries.[4]

We are entering a new phase in world history—one in which fewer and fewer workers will be needed to produce the goods and services for the global population. *The End of Work* examines the technological innovations and market-directed forces that are moving us to the edge of a near workerless world. We will explore the promises and perils of the Third Industrial Revolution and begin to address the complex problems that will accompany the transition into a post-market era.

In Section I, "The Two Faces of Technology," we will present an overview of the current technology revolution with an eye toward understanding its effect on employment and the global economy. To better assess both the impacts and potential outcomes of the Third Industrial Revolution, we will examine the two competing visions of technological progress that have spurred the drive to an automated society and ask how each is likely to influence the ultimate course society takes as it makes its way into the high-tech global village.

To provide some background on the current technology and employment debate, we will turn our attention in Section II, "The Third Industrial Revolution," to a look at how the early innovations in automation affected the livelihoods of African-American workers and trade unionists. Their experience could be a harbinger of what lies ahead for millions of service and white collar workers as well as a growing number of middle-class management and professional employees around the world. We will end the section with an analysis of the revolutionary changes being made in corporate organizational structures and management practices to accommodate the new high technologies of the twenty-first century.

In the past, when new technologies have replaced workers in a given sector, new sectors have always emerged to absorb the displaced laborers. Today, all three of the traditional sectors of the economy—agriculture, manufacturing, and service—are experiencing technological displacement, forcing millions onto the unemployment rolls. The only new sector emerging is the knowledge sector, made up of a small elite of entrepreneurs, scientists, technicians, computer programmers, professionals educators and consultants. While this sector is growing, it is not expected to absorb more than a fraction of the hundreds of millions who will be eliminated in the next several decades in the wake of revolutionary advances in the information and communication sciences. In Section III, "The Decline of the Global Labor Force," we will explore in depth the vast technological and organizational changes taking place in the agricultural, manufacturing, and service sectors that are greatly reducing the number of workers needed to produce the world's goods and service.

The restructuring of production practices and the permanent replacement of machines for human laborers has begun to take a tragic toll on the lives of millions of workers. In Section IV, "The Price of Progress," we will look closely at how the Third Industrial Revolution is affecting the global labor force. The information and communications technologies and global market forces are fast polarizing the world's population into two irreconcilable and potentially warring forces—a new cosmopolitan elite of "symbolic analysts" who control the technologies and the forces of production, and the growing numbers of permanently displaced workers who have little hope and even fewer prospects for meaningful employment in the new high-tech global economy. We will assess the impact of the new technology revolution on both industrialized and developing nations. We will pay particular attention to the disturbing relationship between increased technological unemployment and the rising incidence of crime and violence around the world. Just outside the new high-tech global village lie a growing number of destitute and desperate human beings, many of whom are turning to a life of crime and creating a vast new criminal subculture. The new outlaw culture is beginning to pose a very real and serious threat to the ability of central governments to maintain order and provide security for their citizens. We will look at this new phenomenon in detail and at how the United States and other countries are attempting to cope with its societal implications and consequences.

The Third Industrial Revolution is a powerful force for good and evil. The new information and telecommunication technologies have the potential to both liberate and destabilize civilization in the coming century. Whether the new technologies free us for a life of increasing leisure or result in massive unemployment and a potential global depression will depend in large part on how each nation addresses the question of productivity advances. In the final section, "The Dawn of the Post-Market Era," we will explore several practical steps for coping with productivity advances in an effort to mitigate the effects of mass technological displacement while reaping the rewards of the high-technology revolution.

For the whole of the modern era, people's worth has been measured by the market value of their labor. Now that the commodity value of human labor is becoming increasingly tangential and irrelevant in an ever more automated world, new ways of defining human worth and social relationships will need to be explored. We will conclude the book with the formulation of a new post-market paradigm and discuss the possible ways of making the transition from a market-oriented vision of the world to a new third-sector perspective.

PART I

THE TWO FACES
OF TECHNOLOGY

· 1 ·

The End of Work

FROM THE BEGINNING, civilization has been structured, in large part, around the concept of work. From the Paleolithic hunter/gatherer and Neolithic farmer to the medieval craftsman and assembly line worker of the current century, work has been an integral part of daily existence. Now, for the first time, human labor is being systematically eliminated from the production process. Within less than a century, "mass" work in the market sector is likely to be phased out in virtually all of the industrialized nations of the world. A new generation of sophisticated information and communication technologies is being hurried into a wide variety of work situations. Intelligent machines are replacing human beings in countless tasks, forcing millions of blue and white collar workers into unemployment lines, or worse still, breadlines.

Our corporate leaders and mainstream economists tell us that the rising unemployment figures represent short-term "adjustments" to powerful market-driven forces that are speeding the global economy into a Third Industrial Revolution. They hold out the promise of an exciting new world of high-tech automated production, booming global commerce, and unprecedented material abundance.

Millions of working people remain skeptical. Every week more employees learn they are being let go. In offices and factories around the world, people wait, in fear, hoping to be spared one more day. Like a deadly epidemic inexorably working its way through the marketplace, the strange, seemingly inexplicable new economic disease spreads, destroying lives and destabilizing whole communities in its wake. In the United States, corporations are eliminating more than 2 million jobs annually.[1] In Los Angeles, the First Interstate

Bankcorp, the nation's thirteenth-largest bank holding company, recently restructured its operations, eliminating 9,000 jobs, more than 25 percent of its workforce. In Columbus, Indiana, Arvin Industries streamlined its automotive components factory and gave out pink slips to nearly 10 percent of its employees. In Danbury, Connecticut, Union Carbide re-engineered its production, administration, and distribution systems to trim excess fat and save $575 million in costs by 1995. In the process, more than 13,900 workers, nearly 22 percent of its labor force, were cut from the company payroll. The company is expected to cut an additional 25 percent of its employees before it finishes "reinventing" itself in the next two years.[2]

Hundreds of other companies have also announced layoffs. GTE recently cut 17,000 employees. NYNEX Corp said it was eliminating 16,800 workers. Pacific Telesis has riffed more than 10,000. "Most of the cuts," reports *The Wall Street Journal*, "are facilitated, one way or another, by new software programs, better computer networks and more powerful hardware" that allow companies to do more work with fewer workers.[3]

While some new jobs are being created in the U.S. economy, they are in the low-paying sectors and generally temporary employment. In April of 1994, two thirds of the new jobs created in the country were at the bottom of the wage pyramid. Meanwhile, the outplacement firm of Challenger, Gray and Christmas reported that in the first quarter of 1994, layoffs from big corporations were running 13 percent over 1993, with industry analysts predicting even steeper cuts in payrolls in the coming months and years.[4]

The loss of well-paying jobs is not unique to the American economy. In Germany, Siemens, the electronics and engineering giant, has flattened its corporate management structure, cut costs by 20 to 30 percent in just three years, and eliminated more than 16,000 employees around the world. In Sweden, the $7.9 billion Stockholm-based food cooperative, ICA, re-engineered its operations, installing a state-of-the-art computer inventory system. The new laborsaving technology allowed the food company to shut down a third of its warehouses and distribution centers, cutting its overall costs in half. In the process, ICA was able to eliminate more than 5,000 employees, or 30 percent of its wholesale workforce, in just three years, while revenues grew by more than 15 percent. In Japan, the telecommunications company NTT announced its intentions to cut 10,000 employees in 1993, and said that, as part of its restructuring program, staff would eventually be cut by 30,000 —15 percent of its workforce.[5]

The ranks of the unemployed and underemployed are growing daily in North America, Europe, and Japan. Even developing nations are facing increasing technological unemployment as transnational companies build state-of-the-art high-tech production facilities all over the world, letting go millions of laborers who can no longer compete with the cost efficiency, quality control, and speed of delivery achieved by automated manufacturing. In more and more countries the news is filled with talk about lean production, re-engineering, total quality management, post-Fordism, decruiting, and downsizing. Everywhere men and women are worried about their future. The young are beginning to vent their frustration and rage in increasing antisocial behavior. Older workers, caught between a prosperous past and a bleak future, seem resigned, feeling increasingly trapped by social forces over which they have little or no control. Throughout the world there is a sense of momentous change taking place —change so vast in scale that we are barely able to fathom its ultimate impact. Life as we know it is being altered in fundamental ways.

SUBSTITUTING SOFTWARE FOR EMPLOYEES

While earlier industrial technologies replaced the physical power of human labor, substituting machines for body and brawn, the new computer-based technologies promise a replacement of the human mind itself, substituting thinking machines for human beings across the entire gamut of economic activity. The implications are profound and far-reaching. To begin with, more than 75 percent of the labor force in most industrial nations engage in work that is little more than simple repetitive tasks. Automated machinery, robots, and increasingly sophisticated computers can perform many if not most of these jobs. In the United States alone, that means that in the years ahead more than 90 million jobs in a labor force of 124 million are potentially vulnerable to replacement by machines. With current surveys showing that less than 5 percent of companies around the world have even begun to make the transition to the new machine culture, massive unemployment of a kind never before experienced seems all but inevitable in the coming decades.[6] Reflecting on the significance of the transition taking place, the distinguished Nobel laureate economist Wassily Leontief has warned that with the introduction of increasingly sophisticated computers, "the role of humans as the most important factor of production is bound to diminish in the same way that the role of horses in agricultural production was first diminished and then eliminated by the introduction of tractors."[7]

Caught in the throes of increasing global competition and rising costs of labor, multinational corporations seem determined to hasten the transition from human workers to machine surrogates. Their revolutionary ardor has been fanned, of late, by compelling bottom-line considerations. In Europe, where rising labor costs are blamed for a stagnating economy and a loss of competitiveness in world markets, companies are hurrying to replace their workforce with the new information and telecommunication technologies. In the United States, labor costs in the past eight years have more than tripled relative to the cost of capital equipment. (Although real wages have failed to keep up with inflation and in fact have been dropping, employment benefits, especially health-care costs, have been rising sharply.) Anxious to cut costs and improve profit margins, companies have been substituting machines for human labor at an accelerating rate. Typical is Lincoln Electric, a manufacturer of industrial motors in Cleveland, which announced plans to increase its capital expenditures in 1993 by 30 percent over its 1992 level. Lincoln's assistant to the CEO, Richard Sobow, reflects the thinking of many others in the business community when he says, "We tend to make a capital investment before hiring a new worker."[8]

Although corporations spent more than a trillion dollars in the 1980s on computers, robots, and other automated equipment, it has been only in the past few years that these massive expenditures have begun to pay off in terms of increased productivity, reduced labor costs, and greater profits. As long as management attempted to graft the new technologies onto traditional organizational structures and processes, the state-of-the-art computer and information tools were stymied, unable to perform effectively and to their full capacity. Recently, however, corporations have begun to restructure the workplace to make it compatible with the high-tech machine culture.

RE-ENGINEERING

"Re-engineering" is sweeping through the corporate community, making true believers out of even the most recalcitrant CEOs. Companies are quickly restructuring their organizations to make them computer friendly. In the process, they are eliminating layers of traditional management, compressing job categories, creating work teams, training employees in multilevel skills, shortening and simplifying production and distribution processes, and streamlining administration. The results have been impressive. In the United States, overall productivity jumped 2.8 percent in 1992, the largest rise in two decades.[9] The giant strides in productivity have meant wholesale reductions in the workforce. Michael Hammer, a former MIT professor and prime mover in the restructuring of the workplace, says that re-engineering typically results in the loss of more than 40 percent of the jobs in a company and can lead to as much as a 75 percent reduction in a given company's workforce. Middle management is particularly vulnerable to job loss from re-engineering. Hammer estimates that up to 80 percent of those engaged in middle-management tasks are susceptible to elimination.[10]

Across the entire U.S. economy, corporate re-engineering could eliminate between 1 million and 2.5 million jobs a year "for the foreseeable future," according to *The Wall Street Journal*.[11] By the time the first stage of re-engineering runs its course, some studies predict a loss of up to 25 million jobs in a private sector labor force that currently totals around 90 million workers. In Europe and Asia, where corporate restructuring and technology displacement is beginning to have an equally profound impact, industry analysts expect comparable job losses in the years ahead. Business consultants like John C. Skerritt worry about the economic and social consequences of re-engineering. "We can see many, many ways that jobs can be destroyed," says Skerritt, "but we can't see where they will be created." Others, like John Sculley, formerly of Apple Computer, believe that the "reorganization of work" could be as massive and destabilizing as the advent of the Industrial Revolution. "This may be the biggest social issue of the next 20 years," says Sculley.[12] Hans Olaf Henkel, the CEO of IBM Deutschland, warns, "There is a revolution underway."[13]

Nowhere is the effect of the computer revolution and re-engineering of the workplace more pronounced than in the manufacturing sector. One hundred and forty-seven years after Karl Marx urged the workers of the world to unite, Jacques Attali, a French minister and technology consultant to socialist president François Mitterrand, confidently proclaimed the end of the era of the working man and woman. "Machines are the new proletariat," proclaimed Attali. "The working class is being given its walking papers."[14]

The quickening pace of automation is fast moving the global

economy to the day of the workerless factory. Between 1981 and 1991, more than 1.8 million manufacturing jobs disappeared in the U.S.[15] In Germany, manufacturers have been shedding workers even faster, eliminating more than 500,000 jobs in a single twelve-month period between early 1992 and 1993.[16] The decline in manufacturing jobs is part of a long-term trend that has seen the increasing replacement of human beings by machines at the workplace. In the 1950s, 33 percent of all U.S. workers were employed in manufacturing. By the 1960s, the number of manufacturing jobs had dropped to 30 percent, and by the 1980s to 20 percent. Today, less than 17 percent of the workforce is engaged in blue collar work. Management consultant Peter Drucker estimates that employment in manufacturing is going to continue dropping to less than 12 percent of the U.S. workforce in the next decade.[17]

For most of the 1980s it was fashionable to blame the loss of manufacturing jobs in the United States on foreign competition and cheap labor markets abroad. Recently, however, economists have begun to revise their views in light of new in-depth studies of the U.S. manufacturing sector. Noted economists Paul R. Krugman of MIT and Robert L. Lawrence of Harvard University suggest, on the basis of extensive data, that "the concern, widely voiced during the 1950s and 1960s, that industrial workers would lose their jobs because of automation, is closer to the truth than the current preoccupation with a presumed loss of manufacturing jobs because of foreign competition."[18]

Although the number of blue collar workers continues to decline, manufacturing productivity is soaring. In the United States, annual productivity, which was growing at slightly over 1 percent per year in the early 1980s, has climbed to over 3 percent in the wake of the new advances in computer automation and the restructuring of the workplace. From 1979 to 1992, productivity increased by 35 percent in the manufacturing sector while the workforce shrank by 15 percent.[19]

William Winpisinger, past president of the International Association of Machinists, a union whose membership has shrunk nearly in half as a result of advances in automation, cites a study by the International Metalworkers Federation in Geneva forecasting that within thirty years, as little as 2 percent of the world's current labor force "will be needed to produce all the goods necessary for total demand."[20] Yoneji Masuda, a principal architect of the Japanese plan to become the first fully computerized information based society, says that "in the near future, complete automation of entire plants will come into

being, and during the next twenty to thirty years there will probably emerge . . . factories that require no manual labor at all."[21]

While the industrial worker is being phased out of the economic
process, many economists and elected officials continue to hold out
hope that the service sector and white collar work will be able to
absorb the millions of unemployed laborers in search of work. Their
hopes are likely to be dashed. Automation and re-engineering are
already replacing human labor across a wide swath of service related
fields. The new "thinking machines" are capable of performing many
of the mental tasks now performed by human beings, and at greater
speeds. Andersen Consulting Company, one of the world's largest
corporate restructuring firms, estimates that in just one service industry, commercial banking and thrift institutions, re-engineering will
mean a loss of 30 to 40 percent of the jobs over the next seven years.
That translates into nearly 700,000 jobs eliminated.[22]

Over the past ten years more than 3 million white collar jobs were
eliminated in the United States. Some of these losses, no doubt, were
casualties of increased international competition. But as David Churbuck and Jeffrey Young observed in *Forbes*, "Technology helped in a
big way to make them redundant." Even as the economy rebounded
in 1992 with a respectable 2.6 percent growth rate, more than 500,000
additional clerical and technical jobs simply disappeared.[23] Rapid
advances in computer technology, including parallel processing and
artificial intelligence, are likely to make large numbers of white collar
workers redundant by the early decades of the next century.

Many policy analysts acknowledge that large businesses are shedding record numbers of workers but argue that small companies are
taking up the slack by hiring on more people. David Birch, a research
associate at MIT, was among the first to suggest that new economic
growth in the high-tech era is being led by very small firms—
companies with under 100 employees. At one point Birch opined that
more than 88 percent of all the new job creation was taking place in
small businesses, many of whom were on the cutting edge of the new
technology revolution. His data were cited by conservative economists
during the Reagan-Bush era as proof positive that new technology
innovations were creating as many jobs as were being lost to technological displacement. More recent studies, however, have exploded
the myth that small businesses are powerful engines of job growth in
the high-tech era. Political economist Bennett Harrison, of the H. J.
Heinz III School of Public Policy and Management at Carnegie-
Mellon University, using statistics garnered from a wide variety of

sources, including the International Labor Organization of the United Nations and the U.S. Bureau of the Census, says that in the United States "the proportion of Americans working for small companies and for individual establishments . . . has barely changed at all since at least the early 1960s." The same holds true, according to Harrison, for both Japan and West Germany, the other two major economic superpowers.[24]

The fact is that while less than 1 percent of all U.S. companies employ 500 or more workers, these big firms still employed more than 41 percent of all the workers in the private sector at the end of the last decade. And it is these corporate giants that are re-engineering their operations and letting go a record number of employees.[25]

The current wave of job cuts takes on even greater political significance in light of the tendency among economists continually to revise upward the notion of what is an "acceptable" level of unemployment. As with so many other things in life, we often adjust our expectations for the future, on the basis of the shifting present circumstances we find ourselves in. In the case of jobs, economists have come to play a dangerous game of accommodation with steadily rising unemployment figures, sweeping under the rug the implications of an historical curve that is leading inexorably to a world with fewer and fewer workers.

A survey of the past half-century of economic activity discloses a disturbing trend. In the 1950s the average unemployment for the decade stood at 4.5 percent. In the 1960s unemployment rose to an average of 4.8 percent. In the 1970s it rose again to 6.2 percent, and in the 1980s it increased again, averaging 7.3 percent for the decade. In the first three years of the 1990s, unemployment has averaged 6.6 percent.[26]

As the percentage of unemployed workers edged ever higher over the postwar period, economists have changed their assumptions of what constitutes full employment. In the 1950s, 3 percent unemployment was widely regarded as full employment. By the 1960s, the Kennedy and Johnson administrations were touting 4 percent as a full employment goal. In the 1980s, many mainstream economists considered 5 or even 5.5 percent unemployment as near full employment.[27] Now, in the mid-1990s, a growing number of economists and business leaders are once again revising their ideas on what they regard as "natural levels" of unemployment. While they are reluctant to use the term "full employment," many Wall Street analysts argue that unemployment levels should not dip below 6 percent, lest the economy risk a new era of inflation.[28]

The steady upward climb in unemployment, in each decade, becomes even more troubling when we add the growing number of part-time workers who are in search of full-time employment and the number of discouraged workers who are no longer looking for a job. In 1993, more than 8.7 million people were unemployed, 6.1 million were working part-time but wanted full-time employment, and more than a million were so discouraged they stopped looking for a job altogether. In total, nearly 16 million American workers, or 13 percent of the labor force, were unemployed or underemployed in 1993.[29]

The point that needs to be emphasized is that, even allowing for short-term dips in the unemployment rate, the long-term trend is toward ever higher rates of unemployment. The introduction of more sophisticated technologies, with the accompanying gains in productivity, means that the global economy can produce more and more goods and services employing an ever smaller percentage of the available workforce.

A WORLD WITHOUT WORKERS

When the first wave of automation hit the industrial sector in the late 1950s and early 1960s, labor leaders, civil rights activists, and a chorus of social critics were quick to sound the alarm. Their concerns, however, were little shared by business leaders at the time who continued to believe that increases in productivity brought about by the new automated technology would only enhance economic growth and promote increased employment and purchasing power. Today, however, a small but growing number of business executives are beginning to worry about where the new high-technology revolution is leading us. Percy Barnevik is the chief executive officer of Asea Brown Boveri, a 29-billion-dollar-a-year Swiss-Swedish builder of electric generators and transportation systems, and one of the largest engineering firms in the world. Like other global companies, ABB has recently re-engineered its operations, cutting nearly 50,000 workers from the payroll, while increasing turnover 60 percent in the same time period. Barnevik asks, "Where will all these [unemployed] people go?" He predicts that the proportion of Europe's labor force employed in manufacturing and business services will decline from 35 percent today to 25 percent in ten years from now, with a further decline to 15 percent twenty years down the road. Barnevik is deeply pessimistic about Europe's future: "If anybody tells me, wait two or three years and there will be a hell of a demand for labor, I say, tell me where? What jobs? In what cities? Which companies? When I add it all together, I find a clear risk that the 10% unemployed or underemployed today could easily become 20 to 25%."[30]

Peter Drucker, whose many books and articles over the years have helped facilitate the new economic reality, says quite bluntly that "the disappearance of labor as a key factor of production" is going to emerge as the critical "unfinished business of capitalist society."[31]

For some, particularly the scientists, engineers, and employers, a world without work will signal the beginning of a new era in history in which human beings are liberated, at long last, from a life of back-breaking toil and mindless repetitive tasks. For others, the work-erless society conjures up the notion of a grim future of mass unemployment and global destitution, punctuated by increasing social unrest and upheaval. On one point virtually all of the contending parties agree. We are, indeed, entering into a new period in history— one in which machines increasingly replace human beings in the process of making and moving goods and providing services. This realization led the editors of *Newsweek* to ponder the unthinkable in a recent issue dedicated to technological unemployment. "What if there were really no more jobs?" asked *Newsweek*.[32] The idea of a society not based on work is so utterly alien to any notion we have about how to organize large numbers of people into a social whole, that we are faced with the prospect of having to rethink the very basis of the social contract.

Most workers feel completely unprepared to cope with the enor-mity of the transition taking place. The rash of current technological breakthroughs and economic restructuring initiatives seem to have descended on us with little warning. Suddenly, all over the world, men and women are asking if there is a role for them in the new future unfolding across the global economy. Workers with years of education, skills, and experience face the very real prospect of being made redundant by the new forces of automation and information. What just a few short years ago was a rather esoteric debate among intellectuals and a small number of social writers around the role of technology in society is now the topic of heated conversation among millions of working people. They wonder if they will be the next to be replaced by the new thinking machines. In a 1994 survey conducted by *The New York Times,* two out of every five American workers expressed worry that they might be laid off, required to work reduced hours, or be forced to take pay cuts during the next two years. Seventy-seven percent of the respondents said they personally knew of someone who had lost his or her job in the last few years, while 67 percent said that joblessness was having a substantial effect on their communities.[33]

In Europe, fear over rising unemployment is leading to widespread social unrest and the emergence of neo-fascist political movements. Frightened, angry voters have expressed their frustration at the ballot box, boosting the electoral fortunes of extreme-right-wing parties in Germany, Italy, and Russia. In Japan, rising concern over unemployment is forcing the major political parties to address the jobs issue for the first time in decades.

We are being swept up into a powerful new technology revolution that offers the promise of a great social transformation, unlike any in history. The new high-technology revolution could mean fewer hours of work and greater benefits for millions. For the first time in modern history, large numbers of human beings could be liberated from long hours of labor in the formal marketplace, to be free to pursue leisure-time activities. The same technological forces could, however, as easily lead to growing unemployment and a global depression. Whether a utopian or dystopian future awaits us depends, to a great measure, on how the productivity gains of the Information Age are distributed. A fair and equitable distribution of the productivity gains would require a shortening of the workweek around the world and a concerted effort by central governments to provide alternative employment in the third sector—the social economy—for those whose labor is no longer required in the marketplace. If, however, the dramatic productivity gains of the high-tech revolution are not shared, but rather used primarily to enhance corporate profit, to the exclusive benefit of stockholders, top corporate managers, and the emerging elite of high-tech knowledge workers, chances are that the growing gap between the haves and the have-nots will lead to social and political upheaval on a global scale.

All around us today, we see the introduction of breathtaking new technologies capable of extraordinary feats. We have been led to believe that the marvels of modern technology would be our salvation. Millions placed their hopes for a better tomorrow on the liberating potential of the computer revolution. Yet the economic fortunes of most working people continue to deteriorate amid the embarrassment of technological riches. In every industrial country, people are beginning to ask why the age-old dream of abundance and leisure, so anticipated by generations of hardworking human beings, seems further away now, at the dawn of the Information Age, than at any time in the past half century. The answer lies in understanding a little-known but important economic concept that has long dominated the thinking of both business and government leaders around the world.

· 2 ·

Trickle-down Technology and Market Realities

FOR MORE THAN A CENTURY, the conventional economic wisdom has been that new technologies boost productivity, lower the costs of production, and increase the supply of cheap goods, which, in turn, stimulates purchasing power, expands markets, and generates more jobs. This central proposition has provided the operating rationale for economic policy in every industrial nation in the world. Its logic is now leading to unprecedented levels of technological unemployment, a precipitous decline in consumer purchasing power, and the specter of a worldwide depression of incalculable magnitude and duration.

The notion that the dramatic benefits brought on by advances in technology and improvements in productivity eventually filter down to the mass of workers in the form of cheaper goods, greater purchasing power, and more jobs is essentially a theory of trickle-down technology. While technology enthusiasts, economists, and business leaders rarely use the term trickle-down to describe technology's impact on markets and employment, their economic assumptions are tantamount to an implicit acceptance of the idea.

The trickle-down-technology argument dates back to the writings of the early nineteenth-century French economist Jean Baptiste Say, who was among the first to argue that supply creates its own demand. According to Say, "A product is no sooner created than it, from that instant, affords a market for other products to the full extent of its own value. . . . The creation of one product immediately opens up a vent for other products."[1] Later in the century, Say's ideas on markets, known as Say's law, were taken up by neoclassical economists who argued that new laborsaving technologies increase productivity, allowing suppliers to produce more goods at a cheaper cost per unit. The increased supply of cheaper goods, according to the neoclassical argument, creates its own demand. In other words, falling prices resulting from productivity advances stimulate consumer demand for the goods being produced. Greater demand in turn stimulates additional production, fueling demand again, in a never-ending cycle of expanding production and consumption. The increased volume of goods being sold will assure that any initial loss of employment brought about by technological improvements will quickly be compensated by additional hiring to meet the expanded production levels. In addition, lower prices resulting from technological innovation and rising productivity will mean consumers have extra money left over to buy other products, further stimulating productivity and increased employment in other parts of the economy.

A corollary to the trickle-down argument states that even if workers are displaced by new technologies, the problem of unemployment will eventually resolve itself. The growing number of unemployed will eventually bid down wages. Cheaper wages will entice employers to hire additional workers rather than purchase more expensive capital equipment, thereby moderating the impact of technology on employment.[2]

The idea that technological innovation stimulates perpetual growth and employment has met with stiff opposition over the years. In his first volume of *Capital*, published in 1867, Karl Marx argued that producers continually attempt to reduce labor costs and gain greater control over the means of production by substituting capital equipment for workers wherever and whenever possible. The capitalists profit not only from greater productivity, reduced costs, and greater control over the workplace, but also secondarily by creating a vast reserve army of unemployed workers whose labor power is readily available for exploitation somewhere else in the economy.

Marx predicted that the increasing automation of production would eventually eliminate the worker altogether. The German philosopher looked ahead to what he euphemistically referred to as the "last ... metamorphosis of labor," when "an automatic system of machinery" finally replaced human beings in the economic process. Marx foresaw a steady progression of increasingly sophisticated machine substitutes for human labor and argued that each new technological breakthrough "transforms the worker's operations more and more into mechanical operations, so that at a certain point the mechanism can step into his place. Thus we can see directly how a particular form of labor is transferred from the worker to capital in the form of the machine and his own labor power devalued as a result of this transposition. Hence we have the struggle of the worker against machinery. What used to be the activity of the worker's labor becomes that of the machine."[3]

Marx believed that the ongoing effort by producers to continue to replace human labor with machines would prove self-defeating in the end. By directly eliminating human labor from the production process and by creating a reserve army of unemployed workers whose wages could be bid down lower and lower, the capitalists were inadvertently digging their own grave, as there would be fewer and fewer consumers with sufficient purchasing power to buy their products.

Many orthodox economists agreed, in part, with Marx's analysis. They were willing to admit that productivity gains and the substitution of machines for human beings created a reserve army of the unemployed. Unlike Marx, however, many conceived technology displacement as a necessary evil required to advance the overall prosperity of the economy. By "releasing" workers, the capitalists were providing a cheap labor pool that could be taken up by new industries which in turn would use the surplus labor to increase their own profits. The profits would then be reinvested in new laborsaving technology that would once again displace labor, reduce unit costs, and increase sales, creating a perpetual upward cycle of economic growth and prosperity. John Bates Clark, founder of the American Economic Association, observed that "a supply of unemployed labor is always at hand, and it is neither possible or normal that it should be altogether absent. The well-being of workers requires that progress should go on, and it cannot do so without causing temporary displacement of laborers."[4]

Another American economist, William Leiserson, echoed Clark's enthusiasm, suggesting that "the army of the unemployed is no more unemployed than are firemen who wait in fire-houses for the alarm to sound, or the reserve police force ready to meet the next call."[5]

THE ROARING TWENTIES

The question of whether modern machine technology creates job growth and prosperity or unemployment, recession, and even depression was put to the test in the 1920s. As today, a fundamental restructuring of work and a spate of new laborsaving technologies were altering the economic landscape. The Ford assembly line and the General Motors organizational revolution radically changed the way companies produce goods and services. The internal combustion engine and the automobile were quickening the pace of transportation. Electricity provided a cheap and abundant supply of energy to drive the production process. Productivity had been rising steadily since the turn of the century. In 1912, 4,664 worker-hours were required to build a car. By the mid-1920s one could be built in less than 813 worker-hours.[6] Similar productivity gains were realized in many other industries.

Between 1920 and 1927, productivity in American industry rose by 40 percent. In manufacturing, output per man-hour rose by an astounding 5.6 percent a year between 1919 and 1929. At the same time, more than 2.5 million jobs disappeared. In the manufacturing sector alone more than 825,000 blue collar workers were let go.[7]

In 1925 the Senate Committee on Education and Labor, chaired by Robert Wagner, held hearings on the increasing numbers of working people being displaced by new technologies and rising productivity. The committee found that most of the workers who lost their jobs because of "technology improvements" remained unemployed for an extended period, and when they did find work, it was generally at a lower wage level.[8]

As productivity soared in the 1920s and a growing number of workers were handed pink slips, sales dropped off dramatically. The press began to run stories about "buyers' strikes" and "limited markets." Faced with a glut of overproduction and not enough buyers, the business community began to marshal its public-relation resources to rally the consumer public. The National Association of Manufacturers called on the public to "end the buyers' strike." In New York, businessmen organized the Prosperity Bureau and urged consumers to "Buy Now" and "Put the Money Back to Work," reminding the public that "Your Purchases Keep America Employed." Local chambers of commerce took up the banner and spread the corporate message across the country.[9] The business community hoped that by convincing those still working to buy more and save less, they could empty their warehouses and shelves and keep the American economy going. Their crusade to turn American workers into "mass" consumers became known as the gospel of consumption.

THE GOSPEL OF MASS CONSUMPTION

The term "consumption" has both English and French roots. In its original form, to consume meant to destroy, to pillage, to subdue, to exhaust. It is a word steeped in violence and until the present century had only negative connotations. As late as the 1920s, the word was still being used to refer to the most deadly disease of the day—tuberculosis. Today the average American is consuming twice as much as he or she did at the end of World War II.[10] The metamorphosis of consumption from vice to virtue is one of the most important yet least examined phenomena of the twentieth century.

The mass-consumption phenomenon did not occur spontaneously, nor was it the inevitable by-product of an insatiable human nature. Quite the contrary. Economists at the turn of the century noted that most working people were content to earn just enough income to provide for their basic needs and a few luxuries, after which they preferred increased leisure time over additional work hours and extra income. According to economists of the day like Stanley Trevor and John Bates Clark, as people's income and affluence increase, a diminishing utility of returns sets in, making each increment in wealth less desirable. The fact that people preferred to trade additional hours of work for additional hours of leisure time became a critical concern and a bane to businessmen whose inventories of goods were quickly piling up on factory floors and in warehouses across the nation.

With an increasing number of workers being displaced by new laborsaving technologies and with production soaring, the business community desperately searched for new ways to reorient the psychology of existing wage earners, to draw them into what Edward Cowdrick, an industrial relations consultant of the time, called "the new economic gospel of consumption."[11]

Converting Americans from a psychology of thrift to one of spend-thrift proved a daunting task. The Protestant work ethic, which had so dominated the American frontier ethos, was deeply ingrained. Parsimony and savings were cornerstones of the American way of life, part of the early Yankee tradition that had served as a guidepost for generations of Americans as well as an anchor for newly arrived immigrants determined to make a better life for their children's generation. For most Americans, the virtue of self-sacrifice continued to hold sway over the lure of immediate gratification in the marketplace. The American business community set out to radically change the psychology that had built a nation—to turn American workers from investors in the future to spenders in the present.

Early on, business leaders realized that in order to make people "want" things they had never previously desired, they had to create "the dissatisfied consumer." Charles Kettering of General Motors was among the first to preach the new gospel of consumption. GM had already begun to introduce annual model changes in its automobiles and launched a vigorous advertising campaign designed to make consumers discontent with the car they already owned. "The key to economic prosperity," said Kettering, "is the organized creation of dissatisfaction." The economist John Kenneth Galbraith put it more succinctly years later, observing that the new mission of business was to "create the wants it seeks to satisfy."[12]

The long-standing emphasis on production, which had so preoccupied economists earlier in the century, was suddenly matched by a newfound interest in consumption. A new subfield of economics, "consumption economics," emerged in the 1920s as more and more economists turned their intellectual attention to the consumer. Marketing, which had previously played a peripheral role in business affairs, took on a new importance. The producer culture was being converted overnight to the consumer culture.[13]

The new interest in marketing reflected a growing awareness on the part of the business community of the central importance of the consumer in maintaining the economy. Historian Frederick Lewis Allen summed up the emerging consciousness: "Business had learned as never before the importance of the ultimate consumer. Unless he could be persuaded to buy and buy lavishly, the whole stream of six cylinder cars, super heterodynes, cigarettes, rouge compacts, and electric ice boxes would be dammed up at its outlets."[14]

It was not long before advertisers began to shift their sales pitches from utilitarian arguments and descriptive information to emotional appeals to status and social differentiation. The common man and woman were invited to emulate the rich, to take on the trappings of wealth and prosperity previously reserved for the business aristocracy and social elite. "Fashion" became the watchword of the day as companies and industries sought to identify their products with the vogue and the chic.

Consumption economists like Hazel Kyrk were quick to point out the commercial advantages of turning a nation of working people into status-conscious consumers. Growth, she declared, required a new level of consumer buying. "Luxuries for the well-off," she argued, had to be "turned into necessities for the poorer classes." Overproduction and technological unemployment could be mitigated, even eliminated, if only the working class could be re-educated toward the "dynamic consumption of luxuries."[15]

Transforming the American worker into a status-conscious consumer was a radical undertaking. Most Americans were still making most of their own goods at home. Advertisers used every available means and opportunity to denigrate "homemade" products and to promote the "store-bought" and "factory-made" items. The young were particularly targeted. Advertising messages were designed to make them feel ashamed of wearing or using homemade products. Increasingly, the battle lines were drawn around the issue of being "modern" or "old-fashioned." Fear of being left behind proved a powerful motivating force in stimulating purchasing power. Labor historian Harry Braverman captured the commercial spirit of the times, remarking that "the source of status is no longer the ability to make things but simply the ability to purchase them."[16]

New concepts of marketing and advertising, which had been slowly gaining ground for several decades, took off in the 1920s, reflecting the business community's growing determination to empty its warehouses and increase the pace of consumption to match the ever-accelerating productivity. Brand names, once an oddity, became a permanent feature of the American economy. After the Civil War the only brand-name product one was likely to see in the local general store was Baker's chocolate. Even as late as 1900, most general stores sold staples like sugar, vinegar, flour, nails, and pins unmarked and unlabeled from barrels and bins.

Manufacturers anxious to move their products and impatient with the slow pace of jobbers and wholesalers began to sell directly to the public under brand labels. Many of the products were novel and required changing the lifestyles and eating habits of consumers. Author Susan Strasser recounts the many marketing problems encountered by companies trying to sell products that never before existed and create needs that people had never before perceived: "People who never before bought corn flakes were taught to need them: those formerly content to buy oats scooped from the grocer's bin were informed about why they should prefer Quaker Oats in a box. At the same time, they learned how packaged breakfast cereals fit modern urban life-styles, suiting people seeking convenience."[17]

Many companies sought new ways to reorient their products to increase sales. Coca-Cola was originally marketed as a headache remedy. It was repositioned as a popular beverage. Asa Candler, who bought the patent on the process from an Atlanta pharmacist, reasoned that "the chronic sufferer from headaches may have but one a week. Many persons have only one a year. There was one dreadful malady, though, that everybody . . . suffered from daily . . . which during six or eight months of the year would be treated and relieved, only to develop again within less than a hour. That malady was thirst."[18]

In 1919 the American Sugar Refining Company introduced Domino Golden Syrup, a new product that could be produced throughout the year. Up until then, most Americans used molasses, which was produced in the fall season and used on pancakes during the "winter pancake season." Finding it difficult to convince consumers to eat pancakes all year 'round, Domino came up with an alternative use for its new syrup. It began to sell the product to soda fountains, where it was marketed as the Domino Syrup Nut Sundae and sold during the hot summer months.[19]

Companies also experimented with a number of direct marketing schemes to promote their products and increase sales. Premiums and other giveaways were commonplace by the mid-1920s. Many major manufacturers of household products also relied heavily on coupons and ran extensive advertising campaigns in local newspapers.

Nothing, however, proved more successful in reorienting the buying habits of American wage earners than the notion of consumer credit. Buying on installment was seductive, and for many became addictive. In less than a decade, a nation of hardworking, frugal Americans were made over into a hedonist culture in search of ever-new avenues of instant gratification. At the time of the great stock market crash, 60 percent of the radios, automobiles, and furniture sold in the United States were purchased on installment credit.[20]

Many factors converged in the 1920s to help create a psychology of mass consumption. Perhaps the most enduring of the changes that took place in that decade of transition was the emergence of the suburb. Here was a new kind of domicile, designed in part to emulate the leisurely country life of the rich and famous. Economist Walter Pitkin predicted that "the suburban home-owner would become the ideal consumer."[21]

In the 1920s more than 7 million middle-class families migrated to the suburbs.[22] Many viewed the transition from city to suburb as a rite of passage, a declaration of having arrived in American society. Suburban homeownership conferred a new kind of status—one reflected in the aristocratic-sounding names of the streets and subdivisions—Country Club Lane, Green Acre Estates. The suburban home became as much a display as a dwelling. "Keeping up with the Joneses" became a preoccupation, and for many a suburban homeowner, a near obsession. Advertisers zeroed in on the new suburban "aristocrats" determined to fill their castles with an endless array of new products and services.

By 1929 the mass psychology of consumerism had taken hold in America. The traditional American virtues of Yankee frugality and frontier self-sacrifice were fading. That year President Herbert Hoover's Committee on Recent Economic Changes published a revealing report on the profound change in human psychology that had taken place in less than a decade. The report ended with a glowing prediction of what lay ahead for America:

> The survey has proved conclusively what has long been held theoretically to be true, that wants are insatiable; that one want satisfied makes way for another. The conclusion is that economically we have a boundless field before us; that there are new wants which will make way endlessly for newer wants as fast as they are satisfied. . . . By advertising and other promotional devices . . . a measurable pull on production has been created . . . It would seem that we can go on with increasing activity . . . Our situation is fortunate, our momentum remarkable.[23]

Just a few short months later the stock market crashed, plunging the nation and the world into the darkest depression of the modern age.

The Hoover Committee, like many of the politicians and business leaders of the day, was so fixated on the idea that supply creates demand that it was unable to see the negative dynamic that was careening the economy into a major depression. In order to compensate for the rising technological unemployment brought about by the introduction of new laborsaving technologies, American corporations poured millions of dollars into advertising and marketing campaigns, hoping to convince the still-employed workforce to engage in an orgy of spending. Unfortunately, the income of wage earners was not rising fast enough to keep up with the increases in productivity and output. Most employers preferred to pocket the extra profit realized from productivity gains rather than pass the savings along to the workers in the form of higher wages. Henry Ford, to his credit, suggested that workers be paid enough to buy the products companies were producing. Otherwise, he asked, "who would buy my cars?"[24] His colleagues chose to ignore the advice.

The business community remained convinced that it could continue to reap windfall profits, depress wages, and still prime the consumer pump sufficiently to absorb the overproduction. The pump, however, was running dry. The new advertising and marketing schemes did stimulate a new psychology of mass consumption. However, lacking sufficient income to purchase all of the new products flooding the market, American workers continued to buy on credit. Some critics at the time warned that "goods are being put in hock faster than they can be produced."[25] The warnings went unheeded until it was too late.

The business community had failed to understand that its very success was at the root of the growing economic crisis. By displacing workers with laborsaving technologies, American companies increased productivity, but at the expense of creating larger numbers of unemployed and underemployed workers who lacked the purchasing power to buy their goods. Even during the depression years, productivity gains continued to result in labor displacement, greater unemployment, and a further depression of the economy. In a study of the manufacturing sector published in 1938, Frederick Mills found that while 51 percent of the decline in man-hours worked was directly related to a fall in production, a surprising 49 percent was tied to rising productivity and labor displacement.[26] The economic system seemed caught in a terrible and ironic contradiction from which there appeared no escape. Trapped by an ever-worsening depression, many companies continued to cut costs by substituting machines for workers, hoping to boost productivity—only to add fuel to the fire.

At the depth of the depression, the British economist John Maynard Keynes published *The General Theory of Employment, Interest and Money*, which was to fundamentally alter the way governments regulate economic policy. In a prescient passage, he warned his readers of a new and dangerous phenomenon whose impact in the years ahead was likely to be profound: "We are being afflicted with a new disease of which some readers may not yet have heard the name, but of which they will hear a great deal in the years to come—namely 'technological unemployment.' This means unemployment due to our discovery of means of economizing the use of labor outrunning the pace at which we can find new uses for labor."[27]

By the 1930s, many mainstream economists were suggesting that increased efficiency and rising productivity, brought on by laborsaving technology, was only exacerbating the economic plight of every industrial nation. Trade unionists, business leaders, economists, and government officials began looking for a way out of what many had come to see as the ultimate contradiction of capitalism. Organized labor began lobbying for a shorter workweek as an equitable solution to the crisis, arguing that working people had a right to share in the productivity gains brought on by the new laborsaving technologies. By employing more people at fewer hours, labor leaders hoped to reduce unemployment, stimulate purchasing power, and revive the economy. Union members across the country joined together under the "share the work" banner.

THE SHARE THE WORK MOVEMENT

In October of 1929 fewer than one million people were unemployed. By December 1931 more than 10 million Americans were without work. Six months later, in June of 1932, the number of unemployed had climbed to 13 million. Unemployment peaked at more than 15 million at the height of the depression, in March 1933.[28]

A growing number of economists blamed the depression on the technological revolution of the 1920s that had increased productivity and output faster than demand could be generated for goods and services. More than a half century earlier, Frederick Engels wrote, "The ever increasing perfectibility of modern machinery is . . . turned into a compulsory law that forces the individual industrial capitalist always to improve his machinery, always to increase its productive force . . . [but] the extension of the markets cannot keep pace with the extension of production. The collision becomes inevitable."[29]

Engels' views, once considered unduly pessimistic and even wrongheaded, were now being taken up by conventional economists and engineers. Dexter Kimball, the dean of the College of Engineering at Cornell University, like many others, came to see an inextricable relationship between new laborsaving, timesaving technologies, greater efficiency, and rising unemployment. "For the first time," Kimball observed, "a new and sharp question is raised concerning our manufacturing methods and equipment, and the fear is expressed that our industrial equipment is so efficient that permanent overproduction . . .

has occurred and that consequently technological unemployment has become a permanent factor."[30]

Labor leaders at the time turned to the notion of matching productivity gains with a reduction in hours worked as a way of putting people back to work, increasing purchasing power, and jump-starting an idle economy. Although throughout the 1920s labor had argued that productivity gains should be shared with the workers in the form of reduced work hours, the argument for the shorter week had concentrated more on the psychological and social benefits of leisure rather than the economic benefits. Historian Benjamin Hunnicutt notes that at the 1929 American Federation of Labor (AFL) convention, the Executive Council's final report on shorter hours "made no mention of unemployment or higher wages, presenting instead a lengthy praise of worker leisure, describing it as necessary for rounded development of the body, mind and spirit . . . the richness of life . . . social progress . . . and civilization itself."[31]

By 1932 organized labor had shifted the argument for reduced hours from quality of life concerns to economic justice. Labor leaders viewed technological unemployment as "a natural result of increased efficiency, economic surpluses, and limited markets."[32] They argued that if the nation were to avoid widespread and permanent unemployment it was necessary for the business community to share the productivity gains with its workers in the form of reduced working hours. Redistribution of hours was increasingly seen as a survival issue. If new technologies increased productivity and led to fewer workers and overproduction, the only appropriate antidote was to reduce the number of hours worked so that everyone would have a job and enough income and purchasing power to absorb the increases in production. Bertrand Russell, the great English mathematician and philosopher, stated labor's case. "There should not be eight hours per day for some and zero for others but four hours per day for all."[33]

On July 20, 1932, the AFL Executive Council, meeting in Atlantic City, drafted a statement calling on President Hoover to convene a conference of business and labor leaders for the purpose of implementing a thirty-hour workweek to "create work opportunities for millions of idle men and women."[34] Anxious to stimulate consumer purchasing power, and seeing no other viable solution on the horizon, many business leaders reluctantly joined the campaign for a shorter workweek. Major employers, including Kellogg's of Battle Creek, Sears, Roebuck, Standard Oil of New Jersey, and Hudson Motors voluntarily cut their workweeks to thirty hours to keep people employed.[35]

The Kellogg's decision was the most ambitious and innovative of the plans. W. K. Kellogg, the owner, reasoned that "if we put in four six-hour shifts . . . instead of three eight-hour shifts, this will give work and paychecks to the heads of three hundred more families in Battle Creek." To insure the adequate purchasing power of its employees, the company raised the minimum wage of its male workers to $4.00 per day, and increased hourly wages by 12.5 percent, which offset the loss of two hours of work each day.[36]

Kellogg's management argued that its workers ought to be able to benefit from increases in productivity by enjoying higher wages and shorter workweeks. The company produced reports showing that reduced work schedules improved enthusiasm and efficiency on the job. In 1935 the company published a detailed study showing that after "five years under the six hour day, burden [or overhead] unit cost was reduced by 25 per cent . . . labor unit costs reduced by 10 per cent . . . accidents reduced 41 percent . . . [and] 39 per cent more people [were] working at Kellogg's than in 1929."[37] The company was proud of its accomplishments and eager to share its insights with others in the business community: "This isn't just a theory with us. We have proved it with five years actual experience. We have found that, with the shorter working day, the efficiency and morale of our employees is [sic] so increased, the accident and insurance rates are so improved, and the unit cost of production is so lowered that we can afford to pay as much for six hours as we formerly paid for eight."[38]

The Kellogg philosophy extended well beyond notions of improved worker efficiency and reduced unemployment. President Lewis L. Brown spoke for the Kellogg family when he said that the goal of increased productivity should be not only profit, but also more leisure time for millions of American workers so they could renew their commitments to family and community and explore their own personal freedom. The company introduced a number of innovations at the plant and in the community to advance the leisure ethic, including the erection of a gymnasium and recreation hall, an outdoor athletic park, a recreation park, employee garden plots, day-care facilities, and a nature center to allow its employees to enjoy the beauty of the Michigan countryside.[39]

A survey of 1,718 business executives conducted by the Industrial Conference Board found that by 1932 more than half of American industry had reduced the number of hours worked, in order to save jobs and promote consumer spending.[40] H. I. Harriman, president of the National Chamber of Commerce, spoke out in favor of spreading the work more equitably among American workers, saying, "It is better for all of us to be at work some of the time than for some of us to be at work all of the time while others are not at work at all."[41]

On December 31, 1932, Senator Hugo L. Black of Alabama introduced a bill in the U.S. Senate calling for a thirty-hour workweek as the "only practical and possible method of dealing with employment." Black addressed the nation on radio, urging Americans to support the "30 Hour Work Week Bill." He predicted that its passage would lead to the immediate re-employment of more than 6.5 million jobless Americans and benefit industry by increasing the purchasing power of millions of newly hired wage earners.[42]

At congressional hearings held on the Black bill in January and February of 1933, William Green of the AFL testified that he was firmly convinced that "the shorter work day and the shorter work week must be applied generally and universally if we are to provide and create work opportunity for the millions of workmen who are idle and who are anxious to work."[43]

Much to the surprise of the country, the Senate passed the Black bill on April 6, 1933, by a vote of 53 to 30, mandating a thirty-hour week for all businesses engaged in interstate and foreign commerce. The Senate vote electrified the public and sent shudders through Wall Street. *Labor*, a union publication, ran the banner headline, GREAT VICTORY. Its editors, as incredulous as the rest of the country over what had transpired on the Senate floor, reflected on the importance of the event. They wrote, "Ten years ago, such a bill would have been smothered in committee. Last week a tremendous majority of Senators, progressives and conservatives alike, were in favor of it. This marks the most amazing change in public opinion in recent history."[44]

The Black bill went immediately to the House of Representatives, where William P. Connery, Jr., of Massachusetts, the chairman of the Labor Committee, predicted quick passage. The bill was voted out of committee with a recommendation that the House pass the legislation. The legislation seemed assured. Most Americans thought they were about to be the first labor force in the world to work a thirty-hour week. The excitement in the country was to be short-lived. President Roosevelt—joined by the nation's business leaders—moved immediately to kill the legislation. While the Administration acknowledged that a reduction in the number of hours worked would provide jobs in the short run and boost purchasing power, Roosevelt was concerned that it would have a negative long-term impact, slowing growth and hurting America's ability to effectively compete overseas. The business community, although in favor of voluntary short-term strategies to reduce the number of hours worked, was opposed to federal legislation that would institutionalize the thirty-hour week and make it a permanent feature of the American economy.

Roosevelt convinced the House Rules Committee to scuttle the Black-Connery bill in return for passage of the National Industrial Recovery Act (NIRA), which contained provisions allowing the government to set the length of the workweek for targeted industries. Both Congress and organized labor capitulated, in large part, because the NIRA legislation guaranteed labor the right to organize and bargain collectively with management, a demand the unions had long sought in federal legislation. In essence, the demand for shorter hours was sacrificed in return for the right of labor to have the full protection of federal law in their efforts to organize the American workplace.

Roosevelt later "voiced regret that he did not get behind the Black-Connery Thirty Hour Week Bill and push it through Congress."[45] In 1937 he delivered an address to a special session of Congress convened to deal with the worsening employment picture that year. He asked his colleagues a question that is as timely and significant today as it was when he spoke before Congress more than a half century ago. "What does the country ultimately gain if we encourage businessmen to enlarge the capacity of American industry to produce unless we see that the income of our working population actually expands to create markets to absorb that increased production."[46]

With the "gospel of consumption" crusade stalled by collapsing consumer credit, and the "share the work" movement stymied by congressional inaction, the country finally turned to the federal government to bail out the ailing economy. It came in the form of the New Deal and a new approach to solving the twin problems of widespread technological unemployment and ineffective consumer demand in America.

THE NEW DEAL

Just months after being elected to office, President Franklin Delano Roosevelt enacted the first in a series of legislative programs designed to put America back to work. The National Industrial Recovery Act

(NIRA) of 1933 committed the country to employing millions in an expanded public-works program. Unveiling the new program to the American people, Roosevelt made it clear that "our first purpose is to create employment as fast as we can." The New Deal Administration saw its role as an employer of last resort, a kind of backup mechanism that could effectively jump-start a weakened economy. Roosevelt emphasized government's new role, saying that "the aim of this whole effort is to restore our rich domestic market by raising its vast consuming capacity. . . . The pent-up demand of the people is very great and if we can release it on so broad a front, we need not fear a lagging recovery."[47]

The NIRA was followed by the Civil Works Administration in 1933 and 1934, which found jobs for more than 4 million unemployed workers.[48] In 1935 Roosevelt launched a still more ambitious job creation effort—the Works Progress Administration, or WPA. The aim of the WPA was to stimulate immediate consumer purchasing power by initiating what the Roosevelt administration called "light projects," programs that were labor-intensive, cost little to implement, and could be completed quickly. The idea was to use more manpower than materials and machinery and to get paychecks in the hands of as many laborers as possible, as quickly as possible. By emphasizing work for unskilled and semiskilled laborers, and purposely deemphasizing large capital expenditure, the White House hoped to put money directly in the hands of the group most likely to spend it immediately in order to help stimulate retail business.[49] Harry Hopkins, who headed up the WPA effort for Roosevelt, argued persuasively that the first priority of the government was "to get the national income up [so that] the underprivileged one third of the American people can become consumers, and thus participate in the economy." To Hopkins and others in the Roosevelt brain trust, it had become all too apparent that the principal cause of the depression lay in the fact that "consumer incomes did not increase fast enough to take the goods off the market."[50] The government's task was to provide jobs, income, and increased purchasing power to restart the economic engine.

In addition to the WPA, the Roosevelt administration launched the Tennessee Valley Authority (TVA) and built the Boulder and Grand Coulee dams as well as other electricity-generating plants to boost government work rolls and bring cheap electrical power to rural communities and businesses. The National Youth Administration was set up in 1935 to train and employ the nation's youth. The Federal

Theater Project and the Federal Writers' Project put many of the nation's artists back to work. The Federal Housing Administration (FHA) was established and the Homeowner's Loan Association set up to boost employment in the construction industry and assist financially stressed homeowners. Finally, the Agriculture Adjustment Act of 1933 and the Soil Conservation Act of 1936 were passed to help farmers survive the depression.

To aid older Americans and stimulate consumer spending, the Roosevelt administration passed the Social Security Act of 1935. Unemployment compensation was established to ease the burden of workers temporarily laid off. The Administration also passed the Fair Labor Standards Act to guarantee minimum wage standards and the National Labor Relations Act to help make it easier for unions to organize. It was believed that a strong union movement could more effectively bargain for improved wages and provide additional consumer purchasing power to grease the economy.

The New Deal Administration also sought to manipulate purchasing power by its tax policies. Some economists, like Marriner Eccles, fought hard for tax policies that would stimulate the economy by lowering the taxes on consumption—which represented nearly 60 percent of the federal tax revenues—and by raising the taxes on incomes, gifts, corporate profits, and estates. The idea was to take money from the wealthy, who are more likely to "oversave" it, and give more money to the middle, working class, and the poor, who were more likely to spend it, thus boosting sales and economic growth.[51]

The New Deal was at best only a partial success. In 1940 the nation's unemployment still hovered at nearly 15 percent. Although the rate was considerably lower than in 1933, when it had reached a high of 24.9 percent, the economy continued in a depression.[52] Still, FDR's many reform programs established a new role for the federal government—one that has remained firmly entrenched in public policy ever since. Thereafter, government was to play a key part in regulating the economic activity of the country by attempting to assure adequate levels of employment and income to keep the economy from faltering.

Despite the many new government programs pushed through during the 1930s in the United States and in other countries, the endemic weaknesses in the industrial system that had precipitated the worldwide economic crisis in the first place continued to plague the international economic community. It was only global war that saved the

American economy. Within a year after the United States entered World War II, government expenditures climbed from $16.9 billion to more than $51.9 billion. By 1943, federal outlays on the war totaled more than $81.1 billion. Unemployment was cut in half in 1942, and in half again in 1943.[53]

THE POSTWAR WORLD

The war economy continued after V-J day in the form of a vast military-industrial complex, a labyrinth of Pentagon-financed endeavors that came to dominate the American economy. By the late 1980s, over 20,000 major defense contracting corporations and an additional 100,000 subcontractors were working on Pentagon projects.[54] The military share of total goods consumption was more than 10 percent during the Reagan-Bush years. The military-industrial complex had swelled to such monstrous proportions that if it were a separate nation, it would rank as the world's thirteenth-largest power. In the 1980s the United States spent more than $2.3 trillion on military security. Nearly $46 out of every $100 of new capital went to the military economy.[55]

Even with the addition of a permanent military-industrial complex, the postwar boom was threatened by continued technological unemployment in the 1950s and 1960s resulting from breakthroughs in automation. New products—especially television and consumer electronics—helped cushion the blow and provide jobs for workers displaced by machines in other industries. The service sector also grew significantly, in part to fill the vacuum left by millions of women leaving the home to work in the economy. Government spending continued to provide jobs as well, dampening the effect of technological unemployment. In 1929 government spending was only 12 percent of the gross national product. By 1975 total government spending was more than 33.2 percent of the nation's GNP.[56]

The National Defense Highway Act of the 1950s, the most costly public-works project in history, spawned a new highway and suburban culture and opened up new employment opportunities in every region of the country. The Great Society programs in the 1960s provided jobs for many of the nation's poor, again mitigating the negative impact of rising productivity and growing technological unemployment. The Cold War and the Vietnam War led to an accelerated flow of government dollars into defense industries, insuring an expanding economy and employment for many who might otherwise have been displaced by new technologies. Finally, by the mid-1970s more than 19 percent of all U.S. workers had jobs in the public sector, making the government the largest employer in the United States.[57]

NEW REALITIES

The new economic realities of the coming century make it far less likely that either the marketplace or public sector will once again be able to rescue the economy from increasing technological unemployment and weakened consumer demand. Information and telecommunication technologies threaten a loss of tens of millions of jobs in the years ahead and the steady decline of work in many industries and employment categories. The technological optimists counter that the new products and services of the high-technology revolution will generate additional employment, and point to the fact that earlier in the century the automobile made the horse and buggy obsolete but generated millions of new jobs in the process. Although it is true that many of the products and services of the Information Age are making older products and services obsolete, they require far fewer workers to produce and operate. Take, for example, the highly touted information superhighway—a revolutionary new form of two-way communications that can bring a range of information and services directly to the consumer, bypassing traditional channels of transportation and distribution. The new data superhighway will employ an increasing number of computer scientists, engineers, producers, writers, and entertainers—to program, monitor, and run the networks. Nonetheless, their numbers will pale in contrast to the millions of employees in the wholesale and retail sectors whose jobs will be made redundant and irrelevant by the new medium.

Dennis Chamot, formerly of the Department for Professional Employees of the AFL-CIO, cites still another equally compelling example, the emerging biotechnology industry, one of the new growth industries of the high-technology revolution. The Clinton administration, and especially Vice President Al Gore, often single out biotechnology as the kind of new industry that is creating whole new jobs, many of which were unimaginable just a decade ago. While the types of jobs may be new, the number of jobs are few because of the capital-intensive nature of the industry. The biotech industry has generated fewer than 97,000 jobs in the last ten years. Chamot reminds us that "double that number of jobs were eliminated through downsizing last year [1993] alone." To reduce unemployment by a single percentage point, says Chamot, "we would have to overnight create something like eleven biotech industries," a feat well beyond the current scientific, technological, and economic capacity of our society.[58]

Many in the business community acknowledge that some of the new high-technology innovations and industries create far fewer jobs than they replace. They continue to believe, however, that the losses in the domestic market will be checked by an increase in foreign demand and the opening up of new markets abroad. Today's global corporations are engaged in a fierce battle to lower trade barriers and push into new untapped regions in search of markets for the expanding production of goods and services. They hope that new markets can be created at a fast enough pace to absorb the increased productive potential of the new technology revolution. Murray Weidenbaum, formerly chairman of the Council of Economic Advisors under President Reagan, among others argues that new markets opening up in Asia and the Pacific will likely provide a wellspring of new consumer purchasing power for American-made goods.[59]

Corporate efforts to create new markets, however, are being met with only marginal success for the simple reason that the same technological and economic forces at work in America are affecting much of the global economy. In Europe, Japan, and in a growing number of developing nations, re-engineering and automation are replacing human labor at an ever-accelerating rate, reducing effective demand in scores of countries.

Faced with anemic markets, both at home and abroad, many companies have turned to new laborsaving technology as a way of cutting costs and squeezing more profits out of an ever shrinking revenue base. "American companies, being very cost sensitive, are really trying to substitute machinery for labor rather than purchase more machinery and more labor," says David Wyss, chief economist for the consulting firm of DRS/McGraw-Hill. While U.S. companies spent more than $592 billion in 1993 on new capital, the Commerce Department reports that less than $120 billion went into the construction of new factories and buildings that require more workers. The rest went to upgrading the efficiency of existing facilities, allowing companies to produce the same output at less costs and with

fewer workers. Of course, the savings prove to be only temporary. Fewer workers translates into less purchasing power for the
economy as a whole, further shrinking potential markets and revenues.[60]

With demand seriously weakened by rising unemployment and
underemployment in most of the industrial world, the business community has turned to extending easy consumer credit in an effort to
stimulate purchasing power. Installment buying, loans, and credit card
purchases have become a way of life in many industrial countries. In
the United States alone, private consumer debt increased 210 percent
in the 1960s and 268 percent during the 1970s. Today it is more than
$4 trillion.[61] According to a 1994 report from the Federal Reserve
Board, middle-class families are paying nearly a quarter of their income to creditors, a substantially higher level than in previous periods
of economic recovery. The disquieting figures led Reserve Board
member Lawrence B. Lindsey to comment that "what seems to be one
of the best times financially for our country as a whole stands in
contrast to what is arguably one of the riskiest times that large parts of
the household sector have faced in many years."[62] The report went on
to say that middle-class wage earners may be nearing the limits of their
borrowing capacity.

In the past, when a technology revolution threatened the wholesale loss of jobs in an economic sector, a new sector emerged to absorb
the surplus labor. Earlier in the century, the fledgling manufacturing
sector was able to absorb many of the millions of farmhands and farm
owners who were displaced by the rapid mechanization of agriculture.
Between the mid-1950s and the early 1980s, the fast growing service
sector was able to re-employ many of the blue collar workers displaced
by automation. Today, however, as all these sectors fall victim to rapid
restructuring and automation, no "significant" new sector has developed to absorb the millions who are being displaced. The only new
sector on the horizon is the knowledge sector, an elite group
of industries and professional disciplines responsible for ushering
in the new high-tech automated economy of the future. The new
professionals—the so-called symbolic analysts or knowledge workers—come from the fields of science, engineering, management, con-
sultancy, teaching, marketing, media, and entertainment. While their
numbers will continue to grow, they will remain small compared to the
number of workers displaced by the new generation of "thinking
machines."

RETRAINING FOR WHAT?

The Clinton administration has pinned its hopes on retraining millions of Americans for high-tech jobs as the only viable means of reducing technological unemployment and improving the economic well-being of American workers. The White House is seeking more than $3.4 billion in federal funds to upgrade existing training programs and initiate new projects to retrain the more than 2 million Americans who lose their jobs each year.[63] Robert Reich, the Secretary of Labor, has been barnstorming the country, garnering support for a massive retraining effort. In speech after speech, Reich warns his audiences that the United States is entering a new, highly competitive global economy and that "to succeed in the new economy, our workers must be better educated, highly skilled, and adaptable, as well as trained to world-class standards."[64] While the White House is pleading for more job retraining, a growing number of critics are beginning to ask the question, "Retraining for what?" With the agricultural, manufacturing, and service sector all automating their operations and re-engineering millions of Americans out of their jobs, the question of where these displaced workers will find alternative employment, once they've become retrained, becomes paramount. A 1993 study by the Department of Labor found that less than 20 percent of those who were retrained under federal programs for dislocated workers were able to find new jobs paying at least 80 percent of their former salary.[65]

The few good jobs that are becoming available in the new high-tech global economy are in the knowledge sector. It is naive to believe that large numbers of unskilled and skilled blue and white collar workers will be retrained to be physicists, computer scientists, high-level technicians, molecular biologists, business consultants, lawyers, accountants, and the like. To begin with, the gap in educational levels between those needing jobs and the kind of high-tech jobs available is so wide that no retraining program could hope to adequately upgrade the educational performance of workers to match the kind of limited professional employment opportunities that exist. Charles F. Albrecht, Jr., President of Drake Beam Morin Human Resource Consulting, says that "a large majority of the people [being displaced by the new information and telecommunication technologies] will not have the skill bank or the capacity to be retrained." The hard reality, says Albrecht, is that "the thought processes and initiatives that are necessary to manage these machines and make them work are beyond their grasp."[66]

According to a study on "Adult Literacy in America," sponsored by the Department of Education, upwards of 90 million Americans are so poorly educated that they cannot even "write a brief letter explaining an error on a credit card, figure out a Saturday departure on a bus schedule or use a calculator to determine the difference between a sale price and a regular price."[67] Currently, one out of every three adults in the United States is functionally, marginally, or completely illiterate. More than 20 million Americans are either unable to read or have less than a fifth-grade reading level. An additional 35 million have less than a ninth-grade reading level. As educator Jonathan Kozol points out, "employment qualifications for all but a handful of domestic jobs begins at the ninth-grade level."[68] For these Americans, the hope of being retrained or schooled for a new job in the elite knowledge sector is painfully out of reach. And, even if re-education and retraining on a mass scale were implemented, not enough high-tech jobs will be available in the automated economy of the twenty-first century to absorb the vast numbers of dislocated workers.

THE SHRINKING PUBLIC SECTOR

For the past sixty years, increased government spending has been the only viable means "to cheat the devil of ineffective demand" says economist Paul Samuelson.[69] Technological innovation, rising productivity, growing technological unemployment, and ineffective demand have characterized the American economy since the 1950s, forcing the federal government to adopt a strategy of deficit spending to create jobs, stimulate purchasing power, and boost economic growth. As a result, the federal budget has run in the red every single year but one since President Kennedy took office in 1961.[70]

In 1960 the federal deficit exceeded $59 billion and the national debt stood at $914.3 billion. By 1991 the deficit was running over $300 billion and the debt was approaching a staggering $4 trillion. The deficit for 1993 exceeded $255 billion. The U.S. government currently borrows one dollar for every four dollars that it spends. Interest payments on the national debt are nearly $300 billion per year, or more than 20 percent of government spending.[71]

Increased federal deficits and an astronomical rise in the national debt have focused public attention on the need to cut spending. Concerns over deficit spending and mushrooming debt are being heard in other countries as well. All over the world, nations are beginning to cut their budgets in order to address the problem of deficits and national debts.

In the United States many of the cuts are occurring in defense. The military-industrial complex, which played a critical role in maintaining the economic prosperity of the country for more than half a century, is now being downsized in the aftermath of the Cold War. The dismantling has occurred suddenly, largely in response to the dissolution of the Soviet Union.

In the 1980s the Pentagon budget was still growing by 5 percent a year, reaching a high of $371 billion in 1986. During the Reagan years, the number of Americans working in defense industries or employed directly in the armed forces totaled 6.7 million, or 5.6 percent of the labor force. In just the past five years, however, military spending has declined by 26 percent to $276 billion in expenditures in 1993.[72]

Between 1989 and 1993, more than 440,000 defense workers were laid off. An additional 300,000 uniformed employees of the armed services and more than 100,000 civilian defense employees have also been let go. It is estimated that by 1997 the Pentagon budget will have slipped to less than $234 billion or 3 percent of the gross domestic product. That represents the smallest portion of national output on defense since Pearl Harbor. A Federal Reserve study projects that defense cuts between 1987 and 1997 could result in an overall loss of 2.6 million jobs.[73]

Cuts in defense are being matched by significant cuts in other government programs. At the beginning of the 1980s, government employment accounted for 17.9 percent of total employment in the United States. By the end of the decade, it had declined to 16.4 percent.[74] The number of government employees is likely to be reduced even more in the remainder of the decade as federal, state, and local governments downsize their operations and automate their services.

The Clinton administration has already announced its intention to "re-engineer" the government, utilizing many of the same management practices and new information technologies that have markedly increased productivity in the private sector. The goal, in the first round of restructuring, is to eliminate some 252,000 workers, or more than 12 percent of the current federal workforce. The plan also calls for the introduction of sophisticated new computer systems to streamline procurement practices and better serve constituent needs. The Administration has placed particular emphasis on thinning the ranks of middle-management personnel and hopes that the re-engineering effort will save the government and taxpayers more than $108 billion in the process.[75] Anxious not to be left behind, state and local governments have announced their own intention to hop aboard the re-engineering bandwagon, promising increased productivity and significant cuts in personnel in the years immediately ahead.

Much of the current fervor to cut government spending and reduce the deficit comes from the conviction that deficit reduction will help lower interest rates, which will in turn spur new consumer spending and business investment. While lower interest rates will encourage some additional home construction and increased automobile sales, the effect is likely to be dampened by the increased unemployment and loss of purchasing power resulting from a slash in government spending. As to the prospect that lower interest rates will encourage business investment, a number of economists believe that "job-creating investment is influenced more by market demand and profit prospects than by interest rates."[76] Low interest rates become increasingly irrelevant if there are insufficient customers to buy the products.

A few economists continue to argue against the conventional wisdom, warning that further reductions in government spending are likely to throw the economy into even greater turmoil, from which it may not recover. They would agree with a recent study on long-term economic growth that concludes that "there have been no extended periods of rapid economic growth in this century without rapid growth in government purchases."[77] Gar Alperovitz, economist and president of the National Center for Economic Alternatives, notes that although the U.S. deficit is currently running at about 4.8 percent of the gross national product, Britain ran up a deficit of 4.4 percent of its GNP in 1983, while Japan ran one of 5.6 percent in 1979. In the two world wars the U.S. deficit rose precipitously, reaching a peak of 27.7 percent of GNP in 1919 and 39 percent of GNP by the end of World War II. Alperovitz's point is that the deficit is not to be feared as much as current political rhetoric would suggest. On the contrary, looking at recent wartime booms, he argues that "A very substantial (rather than token) increase in the near-term deficit which stimulates strong growth can be recouped in the out years by increasing taxes when businesses are booming and people are working full-time jobs." Alperovitz acknowledges that while "such a policy has many expert advocates, it has little political feasibility at the moment."[78]

Despite mounting evidence of the destabilizing impacts of the new high-technology revolution, government leaders continue to champion the idea of trickle-down technology, believing, against all evidence to the contrary, that technological innovations, advances in productivity, and falling prices will generate sufficient demand and lead to the creation of more new jobs than are lost. During the Reagan-Bush era, supply-side economists like George Gilder and David Stockman were quick to embrace the concept of trickle-down technology, arguing that the key to growth lay in policies designed to stimulate production. In 1987 The National Academy of Sciences issued a report on the future of "Technology and Employment," reiterating the trickle-down arguments.

> By reducing the costs of production and thereby lowering the price of a particular good in a competitive market, technological change frequently leads to increases in output demand; greater output demand results in increased production, which requires more labor, offsetting the employment impacts of reductions in labor requirements per unit of output stemming from technological change. Even if the demand for a good whose production process has been transformed does not increase significantly when its price is lowered, benefits still accrue because consumers can use the savings from the price reductions to purchase other goods and services. In the aggregate, therefore, employment often expands. . . . Historically, and, we believe, for the foreseeable future, reduction in labor requirements per unit of output resulting from new process technologies have been and will continue to be outweighed by the beneficial employment effects of the expansion in total output that generally occurs.[79]

Although the Clinton administration does not openly use the term trickle-down technology, it continues to pursue an economic agenda based squarely on its underlying assumptions. Those assumptions are becoming increasingly suspect, even dangerous. In a world where technology advances promise to dramatically increase productivity and material output while marginalizing or eliminating millions of workers from the economic process, trickle-down technology appears naive, even foolish. Holding on to an old and outmoded economic paradigm in a new postindustrial, postservice era could prove disastrous for the global economy and for civilization in the twenty-first century.

While the idea of trickle-down technology has dominated the thinking of business leaders and elected officials for the better part of a century, another very different perspective on the role of technology has captured the imagination of the public. If the market entrepreneurs have always viewed new technologies as a means to generate increased production, greater profit, and more and more work, the public has long entertained an alternative vision—that one day technology will replace human labor and free them for a life of increasing leisure. Their inspiration has not been the dry writings of political economists but rather the millennial tracts of America's popular writers and essayists. Their vivid descriptions of a future techno-paradise, free of work and toil, has acted like a visionary magnet, drawing successive generations of pilgrims to what they hoped would be a new heaven on earth.

Now, these two very different ideas about technology's relation to work are coming into increasing conflict with one another on the eve of the new high-technology revolution. The question is whether the technologies of the Third Industrial Revolution will fulfill the economists' dream of endless production and profit or the public's dream of greater leisure. The answer to that question depends to a great extent on which of these two visions of humanity's future is compelling enough to enlist the energy, talent, and passion of the next generation. The vision of the entrepreneurs keeps us locked in to a world of market relations and commercial considerations. The second vision, the one championed by many of America's best-known utopian thinkers, brings us into a new era in which the commercial forces of the marketplace are tempered by the communitarian forces of an enlightened society.

Today, many people are at a loss to understand how the computer and the other new technologies of the information revolution that they had so hoped would free them have instead seemed to turn into mechanical monsters, depressing wages, subsuming jobs, and threatening livelihoods. American workers have long been made to believe that by being more and more productive, they would eventually free themselves from endless work. Now, for the first time, it is dawning on them that productivity gains often lead not to more leisure, but to unemployment lines. To understand how a dream of a better tomorrow could have overnight metamorphosed into a technological nightmare, it is necessary to revisit the utopian roots of America's other technological vision, the one that promised a future free from want and toil and from the unrelenting demands of the marketplace.

· 3 ·

Visions of
Techno-Paradise

E VERY SOCIETY CREATES an idealized image of the future—a
vision that serves as a beacon to direct the imagination and
energy of its people. The ancient Jewish nation prayed for deliverance
to a promised land of milk and honey. Later, Christian clerics held out
the promise of eternal salvation in the heavenly kingdom. In the
modern age, the idea of a future technological utopia has served as the
guiding vision of industrial society. For more than a century utopian
dreamers and men and women of science and letters have looked to a
future world where machines would replace human labor, creating a
near-workerless society of abundance and leisure.

Nowhere has the techno-utopian vision been more passionately
embraced than in the United States. It was in the fertile intellectual soil
of the young America that two great philosophical currents came
together to create a unique new image of the future. The first of those
currents focused on the heavens and eternal redemption, the second
on the forces of nature and the pull of the market. From the first
century of American nationhood, these two powerful philosophical
orientations worked hand-in-hand to conquer a continent. With the
official closing of the frontier in 1890, the millennial and utilitarian
energies that had so distinguished the frontier character were redirected to a new frontier—modern science and technology. The new
focus coincided with the vast economic changes after the Civil War
that were turning America from a rural to an urban society and from an
agricultural to an industrial economy.

The last quarter of the nineteenth century saw the rapid development of a spate of new scientific discoveries that were to reshape the American landscape and consciousness. None proved more important than the harnessing of electricity. If the westward pioneers' great accomplishment lay in traversing a continent and converting a wilderness to a civilized plain, the new pioneers—the scientists and engineers—claimed to tame an even more primordial force of nature—electricity. One hundred years after Ben Franklin first wrestled with the primitive forces of electricity, Alexander Graham Bell and his disciples successfully harnessed the powerful and enigmatic current and colonized it for the advancement of the new technological frontier. With electricity, distances could be traversed in an instant. Duration could be compressed to near simultaneity. The telegraph and telephone, the electric dynamo, the cinema, and, later, the radio, were bold extensions, providing human beings with godlike powers over time, space, and nature.

In 1886 electricity lit up the first shop windows in New York department stores. The effect on the public was mesmerizing. The *Electrical Review* recalled the reaction of passersby to the brilliant illumination: "They clustered and fluttered about it as moths do about an oil lamp . . . the demand for the light spread apace until now, when as soon as the electric light appears in one part of a locality in an American city it spreads from store to store and street to street."[1]

So powerful was the new medium that scientists and engineers of the day predicted that its widespread use would make the cities green, heal the breach between the classes, create a wealth of new goods, extend day into night, cure age-old diseases, and bring peace and harmony to the world.[2] Their unguarded optimism reflected the tenor of the times. The United States was fast becoming a leader of the emergent Industrial Revolution. In small makeshift tool and die shops scattered across the country, tinkerers, many without formal education, were busy experimenting with countless mechanical and electrical contraptions, hoping to speed commerce and improve manufacturing performance. Machines, once a novelty, were becoming a ubiquitous and essential component of the new "modern" way of life.

The machine, already a significant commercial force, was transformed into a cultural icon in the last quarter of the nineteenth century. The mechanical world view had long since been enthroned as the essential cosmic metaphor by men of science. René Descartes, the French mathematician and philosopher, was the first to advance the radical idea of nature as a machine. In Descartes' utilitarian world,

God, the benevolent and caring shepherd of Christendom, was replaced with God, the remote and cold technician who created and set in motion a machinelike universe that was orderly, predictable, and self-perpetuating. Descartes stripped nature of its aliveness, reducing both creation and creatures to mathematical and mechanical analogues. He even described animals as "soulless automata" whose movements were little different from those of the automated puppetry that danced upon the Strasbourg clock.[3]

Although a popular scientific metaphor, the mechanical world view held little influence with the American public during the first three quarters of the nineteenth century. Far more popular were organic metaphors that spoke to America's romanticized agricultural past, and religious metaphors that spoke to its long-anticipated millennial future. The transition from a rural to an industrial way of life provided the new social context for the flourishing of the mechanical view of the world.

Technology became the new secular God, and American society soon came to refashion its own sense of self in the image of its powerful new tools. Scientists, educators, writers, politicians, and businessmen began to recast the human image and nature in mechanistic terms, thinking of the human body and all of creation as intricate machines whose operating principles and performance mirrored those of the most sophisticated machines of modern commerce. Many Americans no doubt shared the view of the English social critic Thomas Carlyle, who, nearly a hundred years earlier, had written of the new machine culture, "Were we required to characterize this age of ours by any single epithet we should be tempted to call it, not an heroical, philosophical, or moral age, but above all others the mechanical age. It is the age of machinery in every outward and inward sense of that word. . . . Men have grown mechanical in head and heart, as well as in hand."[4]

The "technological frame of reference" became a permanent feature of American life, locking successive generations into a world view that glorified the machine culture and made everything that was alive and part of the organic world appear technological in nature. In the new age, human beings began thinking of themselves as tools—as mere instruments of production. The new self-image reinforced the modus operandi of an emerging industrial economy whose first order of business was to be productive. In less than a half a century, the technological vision had succeeded in converting the American masses from foot soldiers for the Lord to factors of production and from sentient beings created in the likeness of God to tools fashioned in the image of machines.

ENGINEERING UTOPIA

The proselytizers of the new technological vision of the world were popular science-fiction writers of the day. Between 1883 and 1933, dozens of homegrown American authors pumped out dimestore pulp novels extolling the virtues of a future kingdom on earth, a technological utopia of material pleasures and unlimited leisure. Overnight, a hungry populace embraced the new secular theology. The age-old Christian vision of eternal salvation was tempered by the new belief in an earthly paradise. The new gods were scientists and technicians who, by reason of their ingenuity and expertise, could work miracles and help usher in a millennial reign governed by rigorous mathematical calculation and scientific experimentation. In return for their hard work and an abiding faith in the principles of science and the miraculous powers of machine technology, the public could look forward to the day, in the not-too-distant future, when they could gain entrance to the new utopia—a technologically mediated world where their hopes and dreams would finally be realized.

The leading apostle of the new technological kingdom was Edward Bellamy, whose book *Looking Backward: 2000–1887*, published in 1888, became a bestseller and single-handedly converted millions of Americans to the new gospel of technological salvation. Other popular science-fiction writers included George Morrison and Robert Thurston, both civil engineers by profession. The carriage maker Charney Thomas and the prominent inventor King Camp Gillette were also among the more popular writers in the new science fiction genre. Many of the titles of the new books had a millennial ring, suggesting a close affiliation with the Christian evangelical tradition that had inspired two great religious awakenings in American history and helped provide the energy to colonize a great continent. Charles Woolridge's *Perfecting the Earth*, George Morrison's *The New Epoch*, Albert Mervill's *The Great Awakening*, and Fred Clough's *The Golden Age* are among the more celebrated titles. Other titles were cast more in the commercial vein, suggesting a link with America's other great tradition of utilitarianism. They included Albert Howard's *The Mill-*

tillionaire, Paul Devinne's *The Day of Prosperity,* and Harold Loeb's *Life in a Technocracy.*[5]

The technological utopians successfully melded the Christian notion of eternal salvation and the American utilitarian ethos into a new and powerful cultural synthesis. The idea that science and technology—harnessed by a nation of dedicated and faithful laborers steeped in the modern work ethic—would direct us into an earthly kingdom of great wealth and leisure continues to serve as a governing social and economic paradigm to the present day.

The images of the future presented by the early science-fiction writers remain compelling and surprisingly unaffected by the passage of nearly a century. Many of the writers envisioned the new earthly garden as a series of megalopolises—massive urban-suburban tracts that radiate out from a central core in large concentric circles covering up to 700 miles. In *The Milltillionaire,* Albert Howard divided the United States into twenty such megalopolises, each run "by the all potent power of electricity."[6]

At the center of these great cities, hundreds of giant skyscrapers reach up into the heavens like so many cathedral towers. One visitor to utopia tells of seeing a city of 36,000 buildings, marble palaces surrounded by wide avenues adorned with beautiful flowers and foliage. "Can you imagine the endless beauty of a conception like this?" he asked.[7]

These grand megalopolises were viewed by their creators as social machines, methodically planned, rationally organized, and efficiently run to the betterment of all of their inhabitants. Like the mathematical principles they were constructed on, the megalopolises were neat and orderly. Their surroundings were clean, even antiseptic, befitting the synthetic nature of the new enclosed artificial environment. Electricity, the clean, silent, invisible source of all power, animates the social machine. An inhabitant of utopia describes the conditions: "Our sanitary arrangements and laboratories are the best, and easily accessible; our roads are well paved; smoke, cinders, and ashes are unknown because electricity is used now for all purposes for which formerly fires had to be built; our buildings and furniture, made of lacquered aluminum and glass, are cleansed by delicately constructed machinery that operates automatically. The very germs of unclean matter are removed by the most powerful of disinfectants, electrified water, that is sprayed over our walls, and penetrates into every crack and crevice."[8]

Everything in the new technological utopia is brought under the watchful eye of science. Even the climate is technologically controlled by powerful machines. "We have absolute control of the weather," says one utopian.[9]

Production has been automated in the new utopias. In *The Golden Age*, Fred Clough describes a visit to a near-workerless factory. "On the tour of inspection the sights they [visitors to utopia] saw were something wonderful to behold; acres of wonderful machinery running noiseless and doing perfect work."[10] In these future worlds "nearly every calling . . . is industrial."[11] Children are trained in the practical arts from an early age and are groomed to be the scientists, engineers, and technicians of the new technological order.

The technological utopians wrote about what everyday life would look like in the new Eden. Virtually all of their accounts include descriptions of the many new labor- and time-saving machines that will free people for a life of increasing leisure. Of course, all are powered by the miracle of electricity. They correctly predicted electric clothes washers and dryers, vacuum cleaners, air conditioners, refrigerators, garbage disposals, even electric razors. Underground pneumatic tubes would connect factories, wholesalers, distributors, and customers and provide a twenty-four-hour pipeline for shipping goods to every household and to the far corners of the megalopolises. The pneumatic underground, says one citizen of utopia, is "like a gigantic mill, into the hopper of which goods are being constantly poured by the trainload and shipload, to issue at the other end in packages of pounds and ounces, yards and inches, pints and gallons, corresponding to the infinitely complex personal needs of half a million people."[12]

All of these inventions, claimed the new technological utopians, would mean freedom from "all of the annoyances" of housekeeping and work. The goal of the new order was to use increasingly sophisticated technologies to provide "everything for comfort, economy, convenience and freedom from care that a corporate intelligence could think of."[13]

Most of the technological utopians thought their visions of the future would be realized in the United States and elsewhere within one hundred years. They were convinced that science and technology would replace divine inspiration and intervention, creating a new secular theology more powerful than any conceived by the men of the Church. In one of the novels, the protagonist declares, "Eternity is here. We are living in the midst of it." Another citizen of utopia boldly proclaims: "Heaven will be on earth."[14]

While the pulp novelists did much to spread the "good word," converting countless readers to their technological vision, it was the staging of elaborate world fairs that most excited the masses of Americans. Several world fairs were held in the United States, beginning with the Columbian Exposition in Chicago in 1893 and culminating in the New York World's Fair in New York City in 1939–40. The fairs attracted millions of visitors to their gates. All of them played heavily on the themes advanced by the science fiction writers of the period. The cardinal message was that science and technology were continually pushing forward into new frontiers, taming the wild, domesticating the forces of nature, redirecting the talents of human beings, and reconditioning the culture to the demanding standards of the engineering credo. Corporate and government sponsored exhibits gave people their first three-dimensional glimpse of the breathtaking technological future that awaited them. The sights and insights captivated several generations of Americans, making them true believers in the Age of Progress.

During the depression years of the 1930s, the fairs took on an even more important role. Concerned about growing unemployment and social unrest, fair organizers were anxious to rekindle the flagging spirits of the American public, and used the fairs to sell the idea that the new utopia was within reach. At the New York World's Fair, promoters chose the theme "The World of Tomorrow" to highlight the imminence of the new technological society. The many exhibits featured prototypes of new household products, streamlined forms of transportation, and new modes of communication, including television, which would soon be available in the marketplace. Their objective was to instill renewed hope in the fairgoers, excite their yearnings for a better tomorrow, and re-invigorate them with the spirit of technological progress that had served so well as a motivating tool and secular catechism for more than two generations.

Printed on the archway overlooking the front gate of the New York World's Fair were the words SCIENCE EXPLORES, TECHNOLOGY EXECUTES, MAN CONFORMS. For the price of admission, visitors could be dazzled by the technological vistas that lie ahead. Their faith and belief in science and technology would be rewarded with a future society of abundance and leisure—technology would be the new slaves, freeing humanity to play, loaf, or pursue a higher calling.

Anticipating the automation revolution of the 1950s and 1960s, Chrysler treated fairgoers to an experimental film entitled *In Tune with Tomorrow*, showing a Plymouth automobile assembling itself. Done in animation and in 3-D, the film showed dancing springs and valves, a crankshaft that fit itself into the engine block, and "four tires that sashayed in singing 'my body is in the plant somewhere' to the tune of 'My Bonnie Lies Over the Ocean.'"[15] Although designed to be humorous and entertaining, the clear message was that automation of the production line was soon to be a reality, changing forever the way we view work.

For Americans in the early decades of the twentieth century, the new vision of a technological utopia proved a powerful rallying cry. Immigrants and native born alike were eager to join the march to the new promised land, the utopia that awaited them just over the scientific horizon. By the 1920s, Walter Lippmann was writing that "the miracles of science seem to be inexhaustible." The new Moses who would deliver the chosen people to the land of milk and honey would not be a man of God, but rather a man of science. "It is not surprising," said Lippmann, "that men of science should have acquired much of the intellectual authority which churchmen once exercised. Scientists do not, of course, speak of their discoveries as miracles. But to the common man they have much the same character."[16]

THE CULT OF EFFICIENCY

All of the technological utopians shared an obsession with the creative and redeeming power of efficiency, a once obscure English time value cloaked in religious significance that metamorphosed into a powerful new secular time value in the new machine culture. More efficient machines and more efficient use of time, they believed, would lead to a workerless future of vast material abundance and unlimited free time.

The modern notion of efficiency emerged in the nineteenth century in the wake of experiments in the new scientific field of thermodynamics. Engineers, experimenting with power-driven machinery, began to use the term "efficiency" to measure energy flows and entropy losses. "Efficiency" came to mean the maximum yield that could be produced in the shortest time, expending the least amount of energy, labor, and capital in the process.

The man most responsible for popularizing the notion of efficiency in the economic process was Frederick W. Taylor. His principles of "scientific management," published in 1895, became the standard reference for organizing the workplace—and were soon used to organize much of the rest of society. Economic historian Daniel Bell says of him, "If any social upheaval can ever be attributed to one man, the logic of efficiency as a mode of life is due to Taylor."[17]

Using a stopwatch, Taylor divided each worker's task into the smallest visibly identifiable operational components, then measured each to ascertain the best time attainable under optimal performance conditions. His studies calibrated worker performance to fractions of a second. By calculating the mean times and best times achieved in each component of the worker's job, Taylor could make recommendations on how to change the most minute aspects of performance in order to save precious seconds and even milliseconds. Scientific management, says Harry Braverman, "is the organized study of work, the analysis of work into its simplest elements and the systematic improvement of the worker's performance of each of these elements."[18]

Efficiency came to dominate the workplace and the life of modern society, in large part, because of its adaptability to both the machine and human culture. Here was a time value designed to measure the input/output ratio of energy and speeds in machines that could easily be applied to the work of human beings and the workings of all of society. Within its grasp, every force and activity became instrumental to utilitarian and productive goals. From now on, human beings and machines would be measured and assigned worth based on their relative efficiencies. In 1912 the editors of *Harper's Magazine* wrote, "Big things are happening in the development of this country. With the spreading of the movement toward greater efficiency, a new and highly improved era in national life has begun."[19]

The efficiency craze swept America in the second and third decades of the twentieth century. It was thought by many that by becoming more efficient, they could shorten the amount of personal labor required to perform a job and thereby gain more wealth and free time. Efficiency societies were established in offices, factories, schools, and civic institutions across the country.

Reformers urged a more rational approach to the workings of the market, predicated on the principles of scientific management. Economists of the day began to think of the corporate mission as much in terms of advancing technological progress and the goals of efficiency as in making profits for the stockholders. Years later, John Kenneth

Galbraith would crystallize the new bent toward technological profi-
ciency and productive efficiency in his book *The New Industrial State*.
He announced that power in the giant corporations had passed from
the stockholders to the "techno-structure." Galbraith argued that the
growing complexity of the modern corporation, coupled with the
introduction of increasingly sophisticated technology, required "specialized talent" and a new breed of scientific-minded managers who
could run the institutions more like the efficient machines they were
becoming.[20]

Progressives of the period called for the depoliticizing of government and the introduction of scientific management principles into
local, state, and federal government programs. New regulatory agencies, including the Federal Communications Commission and the
Securities and Exchange Commission, were created in the 1930s in
an effort to shield what many reformers considered to be purely
administrative matters from the manipulations and intrigues of traditional politics. Reformers hoped that a new generation of professional
managers would replace political appointees throughout the administrative structure, making government more scientific and efficient.
New professional schools were established to teach students how to
apply the principles of scientific management to governance, with the
aim of replacing the art of politics with the science of administration.

At the local level, city planning became popular. Hundreds of
cities created planning commissions and agencies to more efficiently
coordinate commercial and residential development and operate municipal utilities and services.[21] Many cities replaced mayors with city
planners and commissioners—generally architects, engineers, and
other specialists whose job was to substitute the old system of political
patronage and pork barrel politics with swift, efficient management of
services.

The efficiency crusade reached into every area of American life,
remaking society to the exacting temporal standards of the industrial
machine culture. It wasn't long before popular magazines and journals
began to turn the heat up on the American educational system, charging the nation's teachers and administrators with gross inefficiency and
with wasting the potential productive contribution of the next generation of workers. The *Saturday Evening Post* warned that "there is
inefficiency in the business management of many schools such as
would not be tolerated in the world of offices and shops."[22] In the
summer of 1912, the *Ladies' Home Journal* ran a scathing article

entitled "Is the Public School a Failure?" laying the blame for increased unemployment, starvation, incestuousness, and debauchery on inefficient methods of instruction that had failed to prepare the nation's youth to be productive, efficient citizens.[23] That same year, at the annual meeting of the nation's school superintendents, the attendees were told that "the call for efficiency is felt everywhere throughout the length and breadth of the land, and the demand is becoming more insistent every day." They were admonished that "the schools as well as other business institutions must submit to the test of efficiency."[24]

The efficiency dogma was even carried into the most private parts of daily life. In 1912 the craze reached into the home with the publication of an article in *Ladies' Home Journal* entitled "The New Housekeeping." The author, Christine Frederick, informed housewives across America that it was time to make homemaking more efficient and productive. Frederick confided with her readers that she had been unknowingly wasting precious time by continuing to use inefficient approaches to housework. "For years I never realized that I actually made 80 wrong motions in the washing alone, not counting others in the sorting, wiping and laying away."[25] The author asked her readers, "Do we not waste time by walking in poorly arranged kitchens? . . . Could not the housework train be dispatched from station to station, from task to task?"[26]

FROM DEMOCRACY TO TECHNOCRACY

Engineering values invaded and remade American culture in the opening decades of the twentieth century. The closing of the Western frontier and the opening of the technological frontier was greeted with excitement and anticipation by the nation's boys, who quickly traded in their toy pistols and cowboy hats for Erector sets. The Erector instruction manual of 1915 claimed that "Erector is the only builder with girders that resemble the real structural material used in the great sky-scrapers, offices, factories, and public buildings." The company invited the nation's youngsters to "build derricks, machine shops, battleships, aeroplanes, duplicates of celebrated bridges, arches etc, that can be operated with the electric motor."[27]

The cowboy, the hero of post–Civil War America, was now joined by a new hero—the civil engineer of the technological age. The engineer appeared as a hero in more than one hundred silent movies as well as in scores of bestselling novels. Tom Swift novels, aimed at the nation's young boys, were full of references to the wizardry of science and the wonders of new technologies. By 1922 a national survey of 6,000 high school seniors showed over 31 percent of the boys choosing engineering as their occupational choice.[28]

The engineer, equipped with the tools of efficiency, was the new empire builder. His majestic handiwork was everywhere. Great skyscrapers and mighty bridges and dams were being erected across the country. Author Cecilia Tichi writes, "The engineer renewed the spiritual mission embedded for over two and a half centuries in the national experience. He promised, so it seemed, to lead industrial America directly into the millennium."[29]

The nation's love affair with engineering and the ideology of efficiency caught the attention of a number of social critics. H. L. Mencken quipped that the whole country was becoming engineers. The mattress manufacturers were becoming "sleep engineers," beauticians had metamorphosed into "appearance engineers," garbagemen now referred to themselves as "sanitation engineers."[30] If fierce independence, daring, and common sense were the values most prized on the American frontier, organizational ability and efficiency were the new coveted values of an increasingly industrialized, urban America. By 1928 the nation was ready to elect its first engineer to the White House: Herbert Hoover.

So effective was the mass conversion to the new engineering values that even when the depression hit in 1929, Americans continued to defend the technological vision. They chose instead to vent their anger and fear against greedy businessmen who, in their mind, had undermined and thwarted the lofty aims and goals of the nation's new heroes—the engineers. Quite a few Americans agreed with the earlier criticism of economist and social theorist Thorstein Veblen, who, in 1921, penned a caustic frontal attack on the nation's businessmen. Veblen contended that commercial avarice and the irrationality of the marketplace were undermining the technological imperative and creating waste and inefficiencies on a monumental scale. He argued that only by entrusting the nation's economy to the professional engineers—whose noble standards stood above pecuniary and parochial concerns—could the economy be saved and the country transformed into a new Eden. Veblen believed that "if the country's productive industry were competently organized as a systematic whole, and was then managed by competent technicians with an eye . . . to maximum production of goods and services instead of, as now, being mishandled by ignorant businessmen with an eye . . . to maximum profits, the resulting output of goods and services would doubtless exceed the current output by several hundred per cent."[31]

Veblen envisioned a country run by professional engineers who, using the most rigorous standards of efficiency, would root out inefficiencies and operate the country like a finely tuned megamachine. Later, during the worst of the depression, a group of would-be reformers calling themselves the Technocrats took up Veblen's call, urging America to grant near-dictatorial power to the engineers. The technocrats were brazen in their disdain for popular democracy, arguing that "all philosophical concepts of human democracy and political economy have . . . been found to be totally lacking and unable to contribute any factors of design for a continental technological control."[32] The proponents of technocracy favored "rule by science" rather than "rule by man" and advocated the establishment of a national body—a technate—that would be empowered to marshal the nation's resources and make decisions governing production and distribution of goods and services with the aim of assuring maximum efficient use of natural, human, and machine capital.

The Technocrats came the closest of any political movement of the time in attempting to integrate the vision of a technological utopia directly into the political process. The leaders of the new movement asked the American people to transform their dream of a better tomorrow into a working reality in the here-and-now: "In technocracy we see science banishing waste, unemployment, hunger, and insecurity of income forever . . . we see science replacing an economy of scarcity with an era of abundance . . . [and] we see functional competence displacing grotesque and wasteful incompetence, facts displacing guesswork, order displacing disorder, industrial planning displacing industrial chaos."[33]

The technocracy movement captured the imagination of the country in 1932. The *Literary Digest* proclaimed that "Technocracy is all the rage. All over the country it is being talked about, explained, wondered at, praised, damned."[34] Its success was to be short-lived. Internal bickering among its leaders led to a splintering of the movement into warring factions. Then too, Hitler's meteoric rise to power and the Third Reich's fanatical obsession with technological efficiency gave many social thinkers, and not a few voters, second thoughts about the

Technocrats' call for a technological dictatorship in the United States. The technological world view suffered an even more critical setback in 1945 when U.S. airplanes dropped atomic bombs on Japanese cities: the entire world was abruptly forced to look at the dark side of the techno-utopian vision. The postwar generation was the first to live with the constant reminder of modern technology's awesome power to destroy as well as create the future.

The launching of the Russian space satellite and the Cold War race into space in the 1950s and 60s provided the impetus for a rekindling of the technological vision. Youngsters all over the world began to emulate the new heroes of the space age. Little boys and girls dreamed of one day being astronauts at the controls of a spaceship, careening through the farthest reaches of the universe. When the *Challenger* crew plummeted to their death in a fiery crash, as millions of schoolchildren looked on in disbelief, the great promise of modern science and technology was put into doubt as never before, and with it some of the hopes and dreams of a generation that, up to then, had believed wholeheartedly in the vision of a future techno-paradise.

Other technological mishaps in recent years have added to the general skepticism, muting the once boundless enthusiasm for the techno-utopian world view. Nuclear power, long heralded as the answer to humanity's search for a source of cheap, efficient energy, turned menacing and threatening in the aftermath of the accident at the Three Mile Island nuclear power plant and the catastrophic meltdown and explosion of the nuclear power plant in Chernobyl. The growing threat of global pollution has further weakened the technological vision, as people all over the world have become increasingly aware of the terrible environmental toll modern technologies have exacted in the name of progress.

While the threats and disappointments attendant to modern technologies have mounted in recent years, tarnishing the once invincible image of a technologically mediated future, the dream that one day science and technology would free humanity from a life of hardship and toil and usher in an earthly kingdom of abundance and leisure remains alive and surprisingly vibrant among many in the younger generation. Our children dream of traveling at nanosecond speeds along powerful information superhighways, entering into the worlds of virtual reality and cyberspace, where they can transcend traditional earthly bounds and limitations and become masters of a technologically enclosed universe. For them, the techno-utopian dream is

as real and compelling as it was for their great-grandparents' generation more than one hundred years ago when their thoughts first turned
to visions of a technologically constructed future world of convenience and ease.

Today, the century-old utopian dream of a future techno-paradise
is within sight. The technologies of the information and communication revolution hold out the long-anticipated promise of a near-
workerless world in the coming century. Ironically, the closer we seem
to come to the technological fruition of the utopian dream, the more
dystopian the future itself appears. That's because the forces of the
marketplace continue to generate production and profit, with little
thought of generating additional leisure for the millions of working
people whose labor is being displaced.

The high-tech Information Age is now on our doorsteps. Will its
arrival lead to a dangerous replay of the operating assumptions of
trickle-down technology, with continued emphasis on endless production, consumption, and work? Or will the high-tech revolution lead to
the realization of the age-old utopian dream of substituting machines
for human labor, finally freeing humanity to journey into a post-market
era? This is the great issue at hand for a world struggling to make the
transition into a new period of history.

PART II

THE THIRD
INDUSTRIAL REVOLUTION

· 4 ·

Crossing into the
High-Tech Frontier

T HE TRANSITION to a near-workerless, information society is the
third and final stage of a great shift in economic paradigms,
marked by the transition from renewable to nonrenewable sources of
energy and from biological to mechanical sources of power. Over the
long stretches of history, human survival was intimately tied to the
fecundity of the soil and the changing seasons. Solar flow, climate, and
ecological succession conditioned every economy on the earth. The
pace of economic activity was set by harnessing the energy of wind,
water, animal, and human power.

Several developments in the late Medieval Era set the basis for the
wholesale conversion of economic life to machine power. In England,
the opening up of new trade routes, a growing population, the emergence of cities, and a market economy increased the flow of economic
activity, placing strains on the country's ecological carrying capacity.
The cutting down of large swaths of trees to build ships for the royal
navy and to provide potash, building materials, and heat for a growing
population left forests bare, hastening an energy crisis for all of England. The energy shortage forced a shift to a new source of untapped
energy—coal. At about the same time an Englishman named Thomas
Savory invented a steam-driven pump to flush excess water from
underground mines. The coming together of coal and machines to
produce "steam" marked the beginning of the modern economic era
and the first leg in a long journey to replace human labor with mechanical power.

In the First Industrial Revolution, steam power was used to mine ore, produce textiles, and manufacture a wide range of goods that had previously been crafted by hand. The steamship replaced the sailing schooner, and the steam locomotive replaced horse-driven wagons, vastly improving the process of moving raw materials and finished goods. The steam engine was a new kind of work slave—a machine whose physical prowess exceeded by a magnitude the power of both animals and human beings.

The Second Industrial Revolution occurred between 1860 and World War I. Oil began to compete with coal, and electricity was effectively harnessed for the first time, creating a new source of energy to run motors, light up cities, and provide instant communication between people. As was the case with the steam revolution, oil, electricity, and the accompanying inventions of the Second Industrial Revolution continued to shift the burden of economic activity from man to machine. In mining, agriculture, transport, and manufacturing, inanimate sources of power combined with machines to augment, amplify, and eventually replace more and more human and animal tasks in the economic process.

The Third Industrial Revolution emerged immediately after World War II, and is just now beginning to have a significant impact on the way society organizes its economic activity. Numerically controlled robots and advanced computers and software are invading the last remaining human sphere—the realm of the mind. Properly programmed, these new "thinking machines" are increasingly capable of performing conceptual, managerial, and administrative functions and of coordinating the flow of production, from extraction of raw materials to the marketing and distribution of final goods and services.

Machines That Think

Many computer scientists have come to regard their new mechanical creations in almost mythical terms. Edward Fredkin, a prominent computer scientist, goes so far as to claim that the new technology represents the third great event in the whole of cosmic history. Fredkin gushes, "Event one is the creation of the universe. . . . Event two is the appearance of life. . . . And third, there's the appearance of artificial intelligence."[1]

The term artificial intelligence was coined at the first AI conference, held at Dartmouth College in 1956. Today, when scientists talk of artificial intelligence, they generally mean "the art of creating machines that perform functions which require intelligence when performed by people."[2] Although scientists, philosophers, and social critics often disagree as to what constitutes "genuine" intelligence as opposed to rote computation, there is no doubt that computers are taking on tasks of increasing complexity and, in the process, changing our concepts of self and society in fundamental ways.

Although most computer scientists would hesitate to put artificial intelligence on the same par as the creation of the universe and the appearance of life on earth, they are nearly unanimous in their belief that by sometime in the next century this powerful new technological force will be able to out-think the average human mind. The Japanese government has recently launched a ten-year research project to develop computers that can mimic the most subtle functions of the human brain. The ambitious effort, which has been dubbed the Real-World Program, will attempt to develop what the Japanese call "flexible information processing" or "Soft Logic," the kind of intuitive thinking that people use when they make decisions.[3] Using new computers equipped with massive parallel processing, neural networks, and optical signals, the Japanese hope to create a new generation of intelligent machines that can read text, understand complex speech, interpret facial gestures and expressions, and even anticipate behavior.

Intelligent machines equipped with rudimentary speech recognition already exist. Companies like BBN Systems and Technologies of Cambridge, Massachusetts, and Dragon Systems of Newton, Massachusetts, have developed computers with vocabularies of up to 30,000 words.[4] Some of the new thinking machines can recognize casual speech, carry on meaningful conversations, and even solicit additional information upon which to make decisions, provide recommendations, and answer questions.

There are currently more than 100 million computers in the world, and computer companies predict that more than one billion will be in use by the turn of the century.[5] Many computer scientists look to the day when intelligent machines will be sophisticated enough to evolve on their own—creating, in effect, their own consciousness—without the need of constant human intervention. Daniel Hillis, of the Thinking Machines Corporation, says that "the machines will get good enough at dealing with complexity that they can start dealing with their own complexity, and you'll get systems that evolve."[6] Nicholas Negroponte, of the MIT Media Lab, envisions a new generation of computers so human in their behavior and intelligence that they are thought of more as companions and colleagues rather than mechanical aids. In his book *The Architecture Machine,* Negroponte writes, "Imagine a machine that can follow your design methodology and at the same time discern and assimilate your conversational idiosyncrasies. The same machine, after observing your behavior, could build a predictive model of your conversational performance. . . . The dialogue would be so intimate—even exclusive—that only mutual persuasion and compromise would bring about ideas; ideas unrealizable by either conversant alone."[7]

In the future, scientists hope to humanize their machines, creating lifelike computer-generated images of human faces that can converse with the user from a video display screen. By the end of the first half of the twenty-first century, scientists believe it will be possible to create life-size holographic images of computer-generated human beings capable of interacting with real human beings in real time and space. These three-dimensional images, says Raymond Kurzweil, CEO of Kurzweil Applied Intelligence, will be so lifelike that they will be "indistinguishable from real people."[8]

Several of the leading lights in the fast-evolving computer field view their creations less as machines in the old-fashioned sense of mechanical appendages and more as newly evolved intelligent beings worthy of respect and deference. Negroponte says that the partnership between human beings and computers is "not one of master and slave but rather of two associates that have a potential and a desire for self-fulfillment."[9] Hillis personalizes his relationships with the computer even further, saying, "I would like to build a machine that can be proud of me."[10]

THE PLUGGED-IN SPECIES

The dream of creating a machine surrogate for human beings dates back to antiquity. More than two thousand years ago, Hero of Alexandria described automata that could mimic animals, birds, and human beings. In the early industrial era, when notions of mechanism and machine principles captured the imagination of philosophers and craftsmen alike, the construction of automata became popular throughout Europe. Engineers built little mechanical boys who wrote out poems and prose, petite mechanical maidens who danced to music, and animals of every kind and description performing wondrous feats. The toys, which became a favorite of princes and kings, were toured and put on exhibition throughout Europe. The most elaborate of the automata were the brainchildren of a brilliant and imaginative French engineer, Jacques de Vaucanson. In 1738 Vaucanson amazed his fellow countrymen with the introduction of a fully automated flutist. The mechanized miniature of a human being "possessed lips that moved, a moving tongue that served as the airflow valve, and movable fingers whose leather tips opened and closed the stops of the flute." Voltaire was so taken by the sight of the lifelike, remarkable little creature that he dubbed Vaucanson "Prometheus's rival." Vaucanson's greatest work was a mechanical duck, an automaton of such great versatility that it has not been surpassed in design to this day. The duck could drink puddle water with its bill, eat bits of grain, and within a special chamber, visible to admiring spectators, duplicate the process of digestion. "Each of its wings contained four hundred moving pieces and could open and close like that of a living duck."[11]

While many craftsmen toyed with lifelike automata, trying to mimic the physical characteristics and movements of sentient creatures, other machine enthusiasts wrestled with the idea of creating complex mechanisms that could mimic the human mind and even solve complex problems requiring intelligence. The first automatic calculating machine was invented by Blaise Pascal in 1642. His machine quickly became the talk of Europe and led Pascal to muse that "the arithmetic machine produces effects which appear nearer to thought than all the actions of animals." The philosopher and inventor muted his enthusiasm by observing that his invention "does nothing which would enable us to attribute will to it, as to the animals."[12]

Gottfried Wilhelm Leibniz augmented Pascal's feat by adding multiplication to the calculating machine's repertoire. Then, in 1821, Charles Babbage wrote a paper entitled "Observations on the Application of Machinery to the Computation of Mathematical Tables," which is still regarded as the first theoretical work on modern computation. Later, Babbage conceived of a new type of machine, an Analytical Engine, that could be programmed to solve logical or computational problems. Although Babbages's machines were never made fully operational, in part because the technology did not yet exist to fulfill his vision, his anticipation of the many salient features of modern computation was uncanny. Babbage included punch cards in his design and even a printer—fifty years before typesetting machines and typewriters were invented. Babbage even included a storage unit for housing programs and developed a machine language not too dissimilar from those used in today's modern computers.[13]

The first fully functional modern calculating machine was invented by William Burroughs in the late nineteenth century. Although Burroughs' machine was not programmable, its commercial success helped lay the groundwork for the introduction of computational machines in the business life of the nation.

In 1890 the U.S. Census Bureau held a competition to find new, more innovative ways of tabulating the national census. The country, by that time, had become so big and the demographics so unwieldy that it took upwards of seven or eight years just to tabulate the data from the previous census. The winner of the competition was an engineer named Herman Hollerith, who worked for the Census Bureau. The young inventor used punch cards similar to the ones envisioned by Babbage. He also created a keypunch machine for encoding information and a card reader called a pin press. Hollerith's electromechanical information machine completed the 1890 census in less than two and one-half years, cutting the time required for tabulation of data by two-thirds. The inventor set up his own firm, the Tabulating Machine Company, to market the amazing new machine. In 1924 the company's name was changed to International Business Machines, or IBM.[14]

The first programmable digital computer was invented in 1941 by a German civil engineer, Konrad Zuse. His machine was designed to ease the burden of civil engineers in making their calculations. At about the same time, British Intelligence invented its own computer—a nonprogrammable model—to help it decode German military messages. The machine, called Robinson, became the centerpiece of a massive intelligence-gathering operation involving more than 10,000 people. The Ultra Team, as it was called, successfully cracked the German code, providing the Allies with critical information on German strategic plans and troop movements during the war.[15]

In 1944 scientists from Harvard and MIT invented their own programmable computer, the Mark I. The machine was more than fifty feet in length and eight feet high and was nicknamed "the monster" by its inventors.[16] Just two years later, scientists at the University of Pennsylvania's Moore School of Engineering unveiled an even more advanced computing machine. The Electronic Numerical Integrator and Computer, or ENIAC, was made up of 18,000 radio tubes,

70,000 resistors, 10,000 capacitors, 6,000 switches, was forty feet long and over twenty feet high, and weighed more than thirty tons.[17] Though complex and gangly, the machine was a marvel of modern technology. ENIAC was the first fully electronic general-purpose (programmable) digital computer. It was said that the giant thinking machine was so powerful that the lights of Philadelphia dimmed when its creators first switched it on.[18] Yoneji Masuda, the Japanese computer savant, summed up the historical importance of the new invention, observing that "for the first time a machine was made to create and supply information."[19]

ENIAC's inventors, J. Presper Eckert and John W. Mauchly, sold their machine to Remington-Rand, which in turn rechristened it the Universal Automatic Computer, or UNIVAC. The Census Bureau became the first commercial customer, purchasing UNIVAC to help calculate the 1950 census.[20] By 1951 six electronic computers were running. When CBS television used the UNIVAC to successfully predict President Eisenhower's landslide victory over Senator Adlai Stevenson, the nation took notice of the strange new machine for the first time.[21]

IBM, which had scoffed at the commercial potential of computers just two years earlier—predicting a worldwide market of no more than twenty-five machines—suddenly embraced the new technology. In 1953 IBM came out with the Model 650, a machine that could be rented for $3,000 a month. Again, the company underestimated the potential market, believing it to be no more than a few hundred machines. American businesses were more bullish, grabbing up thousands of IBM computers in the next few years.[22]

The early computers were cumbersome, required high-voltage inputs, and generated a great deal of heat. Complex and costly to make, they were continually breaking down. It wasn't long, however, before scientists were able to substitute the more expensive vacuum-tube component with small solid-state semiconductors, or transistors. These second-generation computers revolutionized the industry, dramatically reducing the size and cost of computers while increasing both their efficiency and capacity. A third generation of computers emerged in the late 1950s with the introduction of integrated circuitry in a single manufacturing process. In the early 1970s, fourth-generation computers based on microtechnology and microchips emerged, once again reducing costs and streamlining processes, making the computer a ubiquitous part of daily life in every industrial country.[23]

PUTTING COMPUTERS TO WORK

The emergence of the programmable computer in the 1950s proved propitious. Industry was already engaged in a radical restructuring of operations designed to fully automate as much of the production process as possible. In April 1947 Ford Motor Company vice president Del Harder set up an "automation department." It was the first time that the noun "automation" had ever been used.[24] Harder had not anticipated the fledgling developments in the computer industry that would soon make automation and computerization synonymous in most people's minds. Rather, his new unit hoped to increase the use of existing technologies—hydraulic, electromechanical, and pneumatic—to speed up operations and enhance productivity on the assembly line.

Talk of the "automatic factory" was in the air. Just six months earlier *Fortune* announced that "the threat and promise of laborless machines is closer than ever."[25] The magazine ran a provocative article by two Canadians entitled "Machines Without Men," in which the authors, J. J. Brown and E. W. Leaver, imagined workerless factories in the future, run automatically. The authors pointed to the many breakthroughs in mechanization and the revolutionary potential of the electronics revolution and concluded that the day of the workerless factory was at hand. The authors disparaged human labor as at best a "makeshift" and argued that the new control technologies being developed "are not subject to any human limitations. They do not mind working around the clock. They never feel hunger or fatigue. They are always satisfied with working conditions and never demand higher wages based on the company's ability to pay. They not only cause less trouble than humans doing comparable work, but they can be built to ring an alarm bell in the central control room whenever they are not working properly."[26]

The article, and others that followed, offered a grand new vision—the prospect of a Third Industrial Revolution. The theme of the automatic factory fell on receptive ears. The end of World War II brought a wave of labor unrest. Angry over wage freezes imposed during the war and anxious to make up for ground lost in collective bargaining because of the no-strike pledge during the conflict, organized labor began to challenge management on a wide front. Between 1945 and 1955, the United States experienced over 43,000 strikes in the most concentrated wave of labor/management confrontations in industrial history.[27]

Management were growing concerned over what they perceived as organized labor's invasion of their traditional terrain. Issues of hiring and firing, promotions, discipline actions, health benefits, and safety concerns were brought into the collective bargaining process in every industry. *Business Week* warned that "the time has come to take a stand . . . against the further encroachment into the province of management."[28]

Menaced by the increasing intensity of labor's demands and determined to maintain its long-standing control over the means of production, America's industrial giants turned to the new technology of automation as much to rid themselves of rebellious workers as to enhance their productivity and profit. The new corporate strategy succeeded. In 1961 a U.S. House of Representatives subcommittee published statistics on the impact of automation on jobs in the preceding half decade. The Steel Workers Union reported a loss of 95,000 jobs, while production increased 121 percent. The United Auto Workers (UAW) reported more than 160,000 members displaced by automation. The International Union of Electricians (IUE) claimed a loss of 80,000 jobs in the electrical industry, while productivity increased by more than 20 percent.[29] Between 1956 and 1962, more than 1,500,000 lost their jobs in the manufacturing sector in the United States.[30]

Management's dream of a workerless factory came a step closer to reality in the early 1960s with the introduction of the computer on the factory floor. The new "thinking" machines were capable of managing a far greater range of tasks than could have been conceived by Del Harder when he set up the first automation division at the Ford Motor Company after the war. The new approach to computer-aided automation was called numerical control (N/C). With numerical control, instructions on how a piece of metal should be rolled, lathed, welded, bolted, or painted are stored in a computer program. The computer program instructs the machine tool on how to produce a part, and instructs robots on the line to shape or assemble parts into a product. Numerical control has been called "probably the most significant new development in manufacturing technology since Henry Ford introduced the concept of the moving assembly line."[31] From the management perspective, numerical control greatly enhanced efficiency and productivity while at the same time diminishing the need for human labor on the factory floor.

All of the skills, knowledge, and expertise that were heretofore embedded in the minds of the workers were effectively transferred onto a tape, allowing the manufacturing process to be controlled from a distance, with far less need of direct supervision or intervention at the point of production. With numerical control, many of the decisions affecting the factory floor and the manufacturing process passed from human workers to programmers and management. The advantages of the new automation technology were not lost on management. From now on, tighter control could be exercised over every aspect of production, including the pace of the manufacturing process itself. Business leaders, especially in the manufacturing sector, were buzzing with excitement over the new automation revolution. The Chicago management consulting firm of Cox and Cox published its report on numerically controlled machine tools, declaring a "management revolution is here . . . the management of machines instead of the management of men."[32] Alan A. Smith of Arthur D. Little Inc. summed up the feelings of many of his colleagues. Shortly after the first demonstrations of numerical control took place at MIT, he wrote to James McDonough, one of the project coordinators, to express his enthusiasm for the project. Smith proclaimed that the new generation of computer-driven numerical control tools marks our "emancipation from human workers."[33]

As automation spread across whole industries and worked its way through the country, its effects on people and communities began to be felt. The first group to be impacted was the American "Negro." The story of automation's effect on African-Americans is one of the least-known yet most salient episodes in the social history of the twentieth century. The experience of the black community needs to be properly analyzed, for it provides a much-needed historical backdrop for understanding the likely impact that re-engineering and the new automation technologies are going to have on the lives of working people around the world.

· 5 ·

Technology and the African-American Experience

A T THE BEGINNING of the twentieth century more than 90 percent of the black population of the United States still lived below the Mason-Dixon line.[1] The vast majority of blacks were tied to a form of agriculture that had changed little since the first slaves were brought to America. While the Civil War had given black Americans their political emancipation, they still remained yoked to an exploitative economic system that kept them in a state of near servitude.

After the Civil War and a short period of reconstruction, in which blacks made significant political gains, the white plantation owners were able to reassert control over their former slaves by instituting the sharecropper system. Near starvation, landless, and desperate for work, black Americans became reluctant pawns in the new sharecropping scheme. Under the new system, they were leased farmland and provided housing, seed, farm tools, and mules. In return, 40 percent of their harvest had to be given over to the landowner. Although in principle the remaining harvest was to go to the sharecropper, it seldom worked out that way. The monthly stipend, or "finish," provided to the sharecroppers to cover monthly expenses was always too little, forcing tenants to borrow on credit from the plantation general store. Goods were often marked up, and interest rates on credit were generally exorbitant. As a result, by the time the harvest was in and counted, the sharecroppers inevitably found that they owed the landlord more money than their share of the harvest was worth, forcing them into further debt and dependency. More often than not, planters fixed the bookkeeping records, cheating the sharecropper still further. A system of rigid segregation laws backed up by a reign of terror ensured white supremacy and a docile workforce.

Most black sharecroppers planted cotton, one of the most labor-intensive field crops. Picking cotton bolls at harvest was a grueling exercise. Laborers had to crawl on their knees or stoop over as they worked the cotton fields. The soft puff of cotton was surrounded by a tough stem that constantly pierced the hands. Cotton was picked and put into seventy-five-pound sacks that were dragged on a strap around the shoulder. Cotton picking lasted from sunup to sundown. In that time a seasoned picker could pick more than 200 pounds.[2]

Plantation housing was primitive, lacking heating and plumbing. Children were little schooled and generally helped out in the fields. The sharecropping system amounted to little more than slavery by another name.

A growing number of blacks began migrating to northern cities during and immediately after World War I, to escape the impoverishment of the rural South. With foreign immigration cut off during the war years, northern manufacturers desperately needed unskilled labor and began recruiting heavily among southern blacks. For many African-Americans, the prospects of earning a living wage in northern factories was sufficient to pick up stakes and leave families and friends behind in search of a better life. Most blacks, however, chose to stay, preferring not to risk the uncertainties of life in the northern cities.

Then, in October 1944, an event took place in the rural Mississippi Delta that was to forever change the circumstances of African-Americans. On October 2 an estimated 3,000 people crowded onto a cotton field just outside of Clarksdale, Mississippi, to watch the first successful demonstration of a mechanical cotton picker. Nicholas Lemann, in his book *The Promised Land*, describes what took place. "The pickers, painted bright-red, drove down the white rows of cotton. Each one had mounted in front a row of spindles, looking like a wide mouth, full of metal teeth, that had been turned vertically. The spindles, about the size of human fingers, rotated in a way that stripped the cotton from the plants, then a vacuum pulled it up a tube and into the big wire basket that was mounted on top of the picker."

The crowd of onlookers was awed by the sight. In an hour, a laborer could pick twenty pounds of cotton. The mechanical pickers could pick a thousand pounds of cotton in the same length of time. Each machine could do the work of fifty people.[3]

The arrival of the mechanical cotton picker in the South was timely. Many black servicemen, recently back from the war, were beginning to challenge Jim Crow laws and segregation statutes that had kept them in virtual servitude since Reconstruction. Having fought for their country and been exposed to places in the United States and overseas where segregation laws did not exist, many veterans were no longer willing to accept the status quo. Some began to question their circumstances; others began to act. In Greenville, Mississippi, four black veterans walked to the country courthouse and asked to register to vote. After repeated rejections they filed a complaint with the FBI which in turn sent agents to Greenville to help register the four men to vote in the state of Mississippi.[4]

Whites in Mississippi, and elsewhere in the South, were worried. The rumblings of change were getting louder and threatened to undermine the precarious arrangement that had maintained the plantation economy for so long. A prominent planter in the Delta wrote to the local Cotton Association with a suggestion that was to be taken up, in short order, by white landowners all over the South. His name was Richard Hopson, the brother of Howard Hopson, whose land was used to demonstrate the marvels of the new mechanical cotton picker. In his letter, Hopson reflected on the growing racial tension in the Delta and wrote, "I am confident that you are aware of the serious racial problem which confronts us at this time and which may become more serious as time passes. . . . I strongly advocate the farmers of Mississippi Delta changing as rapidly as possible from the old tenant or sharecropper system of farming, to complete mechanized farming. . . . Mechanized farming will require only a fraction of the amount of labor which is required by the sharecropper system thereby tending to equalize the white and negro population which would automatically make our racial problem easier to handle."[5]

In 1949 only 6 percent of the cotton in the South was harvested mechanically; by 1964, it was 78 percent. Eight years later, 100 percent of the cotton was picked by machines.[6]

For the first time since they had been brought over as slaves to work the agricultural fields in the South, black hands and backs were no longer needed. Overnight, the sharecropper system was made obsolete by technology. Planters evicted millions of tenants from the land, leaving them homeless and jobless. Other developments hastened the process. Federal programs forced a 40 percent reduction in cotton acreage in the 1950s.[7] Much of the land was converted to timber or pasture, which required little labor. Restrictions on tractor production were lifted after the war, greatly accelerating the substitution of tractors for manpower in the fields. The introduction of chemical defoliants to kill weeds reduced the workforce still further—black workers had traditionally been used to chop down weeds. When the federal government extended the minimum wage to farm laborers, most southern planters found it more economical to substitute chemical defoliants for hand chopping, leaving blacks with no source of employment.[8]

The push of mechanization in southern agriculture combined with the pull of higher wages in the industrial cities of the North to create what Nicholas Lemann called "One of the largest and most rapid mass internal movements of people in history." More than 5 million black men, women, and children migrated north in search of work between 1940 and 1970.[9] The migration routes ran from Georgia, the Carolinas, and Virginia along the Atlantic Seaboard to New York City and Boston; from Mississippi, Tennessee, Arkansas, and Alabama north to Chicago and Detroit; and from Texas and Louisiana west to California. By the time the migration was over, more than half of all black Americans had moved from South to North and from an entrenched rural way of life to become an urban industrial proletariat.[10]

The mechanization of farming deeply affected the whole of agriculture, forcing millions of farmers and farm laborers off the land. Its effect, however, on African-Americans was more dramatic and immediate because of their greater concentration in the cotton-growing region of the South, where mechanization spread more quickly and forcibly than was the case with other farm technology. Equally important, unlike most other farmers, the vast majority of blacks did not own the land they worked. Since most were sharecroppers at the mercy of the planters, and existed largely outside the money economy, they had no capital at their disposal and therefore no means by which to weather the technological storm that swept over their communities. The Reverend Martin Luther King tells of his surprise in visiting a plantation in Alabama in 1965, meeting sharecroppers who had never before seen U.S. currency.[11]

The mechanical cotton picker proved far more effective than the Emancipation Proclamation in freeing blacks from a plantation economy. It did so, however, at a terrible price. The forced eviction from the land and subsequent migration of millions of destitute black Americans to the North would soon unleash social and political forces of unimaginable proportions—forces that would come to test the very soul of the American compact. Writing in 1947, southern lawyer and businessman David Cohn implored the nation to take heed of the storm clouds on the political horizon. He warned:

> The country is upon the brink of a process of change as great as any that has occurred since the industrial revolution. . . . Five million people will be removed from the land within the next few years. They must go somewhere. But where? They must do something. But what? They must be housed. But where is the housing?
>
> Most of this group are farm negroes totally unprepared for urban industrial life. How will they be industrially absorbed? What will be the effect of throwing them upon the labor market? What will the effect be upon race relations in the United States? Will the victims of farm mechanization become the victims of race conflict?
>
> There is an enormous tragedy in the making unless the United States acts, and acts promptly, upon a problem that affects millions of people and the whole structure of the nation.[12]

CAUGHT BETWEEN TECHNOLOGIES

Although African-Americans were unaware of it at the time of their trek north, a second technological revolution had already begun in the manufacturing industries of Chicago, Detroit, Cleveland, and New York that once again would lock them out of gainful employment. This time the economic displacement created in its wake a new and permanent underclass in the inner cities and the conditions for widespread social unrest and violence for the remainder of the century.

At first, blacks found limited access to unskilled jobs in the auto, steel, rubber, chemical, and meat-packing industries. Northern industrialists often used them as strikebreakers or to fill the vacuum left by the decline in immigrant workers from abroad. The fortunes of black workers in the North improved steadily until 1954 and then began a forty-year historical decline.

In the mid-1950s, automation began taking its toll in the nation's manufacturing sector. Hardest hit were unskilled jobs in the very industries where black workers were concentrated. Between 1953 and 1962, 1.6 million blue collar jobs were lost in the manufacturing sector.[13] Whereas the unemployment rate for black Americans had never exceeded 8.5 percent between 1947 and 1953, and the white rate of unemployment had never gone beyond 4.6 percent, by 1964 blacks were experiencing an unemployment rate of 12.4 percent while white unemployment was only 5.9 percent. Ever since 1964 black unemployment in the United States has remained twice that of whites.[14] Writing on *The Problem of the Negro Movement* in 1964, civil rights activist Tom Kahn quipped, "It is as if racism, having put the Negro in his economic place, stepped aside to watch technology destroy that place."[15]

Beginning in the mid 1950s, companies started building more automated manufacturing plants in the newly emerging suburban industrial parks. Automation and suburban relocation created a crisis of tragic dimensions for unskilled black workers. The old multistoried factories of the central cities began to give way to new single-level plants that were more compatible with the new automation technologies. The limited availability of land and rising tax rates of the cities were a powerful disincentive, pushing manufacturing businesses into the newly emerging suburbs. The newly laid interstate highway system and the ring of metropolitan expressways being built around northern cities increasingly favored truck over train transport of goods, providing a further incentive to relocate plants to the suburbs.[16] Finally, employers anxious to reduce labor costs and weaken the strength of unions saw relocation as a way to draw distance between plants and militant union concentrations. Eventually the same anti-union feelings pushed companies to locate plants in the South, Mexico, and overseas.

The new corporate strategy of automation and suburbanization became immediately apparent in the automotive industry. Ford's River Rouge complex in Detroit was long the flagship plant of the company's far-flung operations. The Rouge plant was also the home of the UAW's most vocal and militant local union, whose membership was over 30 percent black. So powerful was Local 600 of the UAW, that it could cripple Ford's entire operation with a single strike action.[17]

Despite the fact that the Rouge complex had plenty of room for expansion, Ford management made the decision to move much of the production away from the site to new automated plants in the suburbs, in large part to weaken the union and regain control over its manufacturing operations. In 1945 the Rouge plant housed 85,000 workers. Just fifteen years later the employment rolls had plummeted to less than

30,000. Historian Thomas J. Sugrue notes that from the late 1940s through 1957, Ford spent more than $2.5 billion on automation and plant expansion. Ford initiatives were matched by General Motors and Chrysler. Together, the Big Three auto companies constructed twenty-five new, more automated plants in the suburbs surrounding Detroit."[18]

Satellite businesses that serviced the automotive industry also began to automate production in the 1950s—especially companies manufacturing machine tools, wire, car parts, and other metal products. Many auto-parts manufacturers like Detroit's Briggs Manufacturing and Murray Auto Body were forced to close up their shops in the mid- to- late 1950s as the giant automakers began to integrate their production processes, taking over more and more of the manufacturing of component parts in newly automated production lines.[19]

The number of manufacturing jobs in Detroit fell dramatically beginning in the mid-1950s as a result of the automation and suburbanization of production. Black workers, who just a few years earlier were displaced by the mechanized cotton picker in the rural South, once again found themselves victims of mechanization. In the 1950s, 25.7 percent of Chrysler workers and 23 percent of General Motors workers were African-American. Equally important, because the black workers made up the bulk of the unskilled labor force, they were the first to be let go because of automation. In 1960 a mere twenty-four black workers were counted among the 7,425 skilled workers at Chrysler. At General Motors, only sixty-seven blacks were among the more than 11,000 skilled workers on the payroll.[20] The productivity and unemployment figures tell the rest of the story. Between 1957 and 1964, manufacturing output doubled in the United States, while the number of blue collar workers fell by 3 percent.[21] Again, many of the first casualties of the new automation drive were black workers, who were disproportionately represented in the unskilled jobs that were the first to be eliminated by the new machines. In manufacturing operations across the entire northern and western industrial belt, the forces of automation and suburbanization continued to take their toll on unskilled black workers, leaving tens of thousands of permanently unemployed men and women in their wake.

The introduction of computers and numerical control technology on the factory floor in the 1960s accelerated the process of technology displacement. In the nation's four largest cities, New York, Chicago, Philadelphia, and Detroit, where blacks made up a large percentage of the unskilled blue collar workforce—more than a million manufacturing, wholesale, and retail jobs were lost, many the result of technology displacement. Author James Boggs voiced the concern of many in the black community when he declared that "cybernation . . . is eliminating the 'Negro jobs.'"[22]

As businesses fled to the suburbs, millions of white middle and working class families followed suit, relocating in new suburban sub-divisions. The central cities became increasingly black and poor in the 1960s and 1970s. Sociologist William Julius Wilson notes that "the proportion of blacks living inside central cities increased from 52 percent in 1960 to 60 percent in 1973, while the proportion of whites residing inside central cities decreased from 31 percent to 26 percent." Wilson blames the exodus for a spiraling decline in the inner-city tax base, a precipitous drop in public services, and the entrapment of millions of black Americans in a self-perpetuating cycle of permanent unemployment and public assistance. In New York City in 1975, more than 15 percent of the residents were on some form of public assistance. In Chicago it was nearly 19 percent.[23]

In the 1980s many of the nation's northern cities partially revived by becoming hubs for the new information economy. Scores of downtown areas made the transition from "centers of production and distribution of material goods to centers of administration, information exchange and higher order service provision."[24] The emerging knowledge-based industries have meant increased jobs for high-skilled white collar and service workers. For large numbers of African-Americans, however, the new urban renaissance has only served to accentuate the ever widening employment and income gap between highly educated whites and poor unskilled blacks.

The only significant rise in employment among black Americans in the past twenty-five years has been in the public sector: more than 55 percent of the net increase in employment for blacks in the 1960s and 1970s occurred there.[25] Many black professionals found jobs in the federal programs spawned by the Great Society initiatives of President Lyndon Johnson. Others found employment at the local and state levels, administering social service and welfare programs largely for the black community that was being displaced by the new forces of automation and suburbanization. In 1960, 13.3 percent of the total employed black labor force was working in the public sector. A decade later more than 21 percent of all black workers in America were on public payrolls.[26] By 1970 government employed 57 percent of all black male college graduates and 72 percent of all black female college graduates.[27]

AUTOMATION AND THE MAKING OF
THE URBAN UNDERCLASS

The corporate drive to automate and relocate manufacturing jobs split the black community into two separate and distinct economic groups. Millions of unskilled workers and their families became part of what social historians now call an underclass—a permanently unemployed part of the population whose unskilled labor is no longer required and who live hand-to-mouth, generation-to-generation, as wards of the state. A second smaller group of black middle-class professionals have been put on the public payroll to administer the many public-assistance programs designed to assist this new urban underclass. The system represents a kind of "welfare colonialism" say authors Michael Brown and Steven Erie, "where blacks were called upon to administer their own state of dependence."[28]

It is possible that the country might have taken greater notice of the impact that automation was having on black America in the 1960s and 1970s, had not a significant number of African-Americans been absorbed into public-sector jobs. As early as 1970, sociologist Sidney Willhelm observed that "As the government becomes the foremost employer for the working force in general during the transition into automation, it becomes even more so for the black worker. Indeed, if it were not for the government, negroes who lost their jobs in the business world would swell the unemployment ratio to fantastic heights."[29]

The public image of an affluent and growing black middle class was enough to partially deflect attention away from the growing plight of a large new black underclass that had become the first casualty of automation and the new displacement technologies.

Technological unemployment has fundamentally altered the sociology of America's black community. Permanent joblessness has led to an escalating crime wave in the streets of America's cities and the wholesale disintegration of black family life. The statistics are chilling. By the late 1980s one out of every four young African American males was either in prison or on probation. In the nation's capital, Washington DC, 42 percent of the black male population between eighteen and twenty-five years of age is either in jail, on parole, awaiting trial, or being sought by the police. The leading cause of death among young black males is now murder.[30]

In 1965 Daniel Patrick Moynihan, now a U.S. senator, published a controversial report on "Employment, Income, and the Ordeal of the Negro Family" in which he argued rather forcefully that "The under-employment of the negro father has led to the break-up of the Negro family."[31] When that report was written, 25 percent of all black births were out of wedlock and nearly 25 percent of all black families were headed by women. Single-parent households headed by women are typically locked into a cycle of welfare dependency that is self-perpetuating generation after generation, with a high number of teenage pregnancies out of wedlock, a disproportionate school drop-out rate, and continued welfare dependency. Today, 62 percent of all black families are single-parent households.[32]

These statistics are likely to rise in the remainder of the decade, as an increasing number of unskilled black workers are let go in the current wave of re-engineering and downsizing. According to a report issued by the Equal Employment Opportunity Commission, black wage earners made up nearly one third of the 180,000 manufacturing jobs lost in 1990 and 1991.[33] Blacks also suffered disproportionately in the loss of white collar and service jobs in the early 1990s. The reason for the heavy losses in black employment, according to *The Wall Street Journal*, is that "blacks were concentrated in the most expendable jobs. More than half of all black workers held positions in the four job categories where companies made net employment cuts: office and clerical, skilled, semi-skilled and laborers."[34] John Johnson, the director of labor for the National Association for the Advancement of Colored People (NAACP), says that "what the whites often don't realize is that while they are in a recession, blacks are in a depression."[35]

More than forty years ago, at the dawn of the computer age, the father of cybernetics, Norbert Weiner, warned of the likely adverse consequences of the new automation technologies. "Let us remember," he said, "that the automatic machine . . . is the precise economic equivalent of slave labor. Any labor which competes with slave labor must accept the economic consequences of slave labor."[36] Not surprisingly, the first community to be devastated by the cybernetics revolution was black America. With the introduction of automated machines, it was possible to substitute less costly, inanimate forms of labor for millions of African-Americans who had long toiled at the bottom of the economic pyramid, first as plantation slaves, then as sharecroppers, and finally as unskilled labor in northern factories and foundries.

For the first time in American history, the African-American was no longer needed in the economic system. Sidney Willhelm summed up the historical significance of what had taken place in his book *Who Needs the Negro?* "With the onset of automation the Negro moves out of his historical state of oppression into one of uselessness. Increasingly, he is not so much economically exploited as he is irrelevant. . . . The dominant whites no longer need to exploit the black minority; as automation proceeds, it will be easier for the former to disregard the latter. In short, White America, by a more perfect application of mechanization and a vigorous reliance upon automation, disposes of the Negro; consequently, the Negro transforms from an exploited labor force into an outcast."[37]

Writing from his prison cell in the Birmingham jail, the Reverend Martin Luther King lamented the ever-worsening self-image of black Americans who were "forever fighting a degenerating sense of 'nobodiness.'"[38] Marx's reserve army of exploited labor had been reduced to Ralph Ellison's specter of the "invisible man." Automation had made large numbers of black workers obsolete. The economic constraints that had traditionally kept black Americans "in line" and passively dependent on the white power structure for their livelihoods, disappeared. Vanquished and forgotten, thousands of urban black Americans vented their frustration and anger by taking to the streets in urban ghettos across the country. The rioting began in Watts in 1965 and spread east to Detroit and other northern industrial cities over the remainder of the decade. After the Watts riots, one of the local residents delivered a terse postmortem warning to the nation that spoke directly to the pent-up rage that had led to the outbreak. "The whites," he declared, "think they can just bottle people up in an area like Watts and then forget about them. It didn't work."[39]

It should be noted that not all civil rights leaders at the time accurately diagnosed the problem at hand. Many traditional leaders in more mainstream black organizations continued to perceive the black plight in strictly political terms, arguing that social discrimination was at the root of the crisis and that antidiscrimination laws were the appropriate cure. A few, however, saw what was taking place in the economy as a precursor of a more fundamental change in black-white relations, with ominous consequences for the future of America. In the conclusion to his poignant book on the subject, Sidney Willhelm wrote, "An underestimation of the technological revolution can only lead to an underestimation of the concomitant racial revolution from exploitation to uselessness; to misjudge the present as but a continuation of industrialization rather than the dawn of a new technological era, assures an inability to anticipate the vastly different system of race relations awaiting the displaced Negro"[40]

Willhelm's prediction proved correct. Today, millions of African-Americans find themselves hopelessly trapped in a permanent underclass. Unskilled and unneeded, the commodity value of their labor has been rendered virtually useless by the automated technologies that have come to displace them in the new high-tech global economy.

· 6 ·

The Great
Automation Debate

WHILE CIVIL RIGHTS LEADERS, as early as the 1960s, began to
warn of the consequences of automation on the African American community, others began to draw broader implications for society
as a whole. A national debate on the probable effects of automation on
the economy and employment emerged in the early 1960s, fueled, in
large part, by the increasing loss of jobs in the black community.

In March 1963 a group of distinguished scientists, economists, and
academicians led by J. Robert Oppenheimer, the director of the Institute for Advanced Studies at Princeton University, published an
open letter to the President in *The New York Times*, warning of the
dangers of automation on the future of the American economy and
calling for a national dialogue on the subject. The Ad Hoc Committee
on the Triple Revolution—whose name was derived from its analysis of
three new revolutionary changes taking place in society—the Cybernation Revolution, the Weaponry Revolution, and the Human Rights
Revolution—argued that the new cybernetic technologies were forcing a fundamental change in the relationship between income and
work. The authors pointed out that until the present moment in history
"economic resources had always been distributed on the basis of
contributions to production." That historic relationship was now being
threatened by the new computer-based technologies. They warned
that, "A new era of production has begun. Its principles of organization
are as different as those of the industrial era were different from the
agricultural. The cybernation revolution has been brought about by

81

the combination of the computer and the automated self-regulating machine. This results in a system of almost unlimited productive capacity which requires progressively less human labor."[1]

The Committee reiterated that "The Negroes are the hardest hit of the many groups being exiled from the economy by cybernation," but predicted that, in time, the new computer revolution would take over more and more of the productive tasks in the economy, leaving millions of workers jobless.[2] The Committee urged the President and Congress to consider guaranteeing every citizen "an adequate income as a matter of right" as a way of distributing funds to the millions of people made redundant by the new laborsaving technologies.[3]

The warnings of the Ad Hoc Committee caught the attention of the White House. In July 1963 President Kennedy called for the establishment of a National Commission on Automation.[4] Six months later, in his State of the Union message, President Lyndon Johnson proposed the creation of a Commission on Automation, Technology, and Economic Progress. That spring, public hearings were held in Congress and legislation enacted to set up the commission.[5]

THE GOVERNMENT STEERS A MIDDLE COURSE

The Commission report, published in 1965, attempted to steer a middle course between those who argued that the cybernetic revolution required an immediate government response and those, especially in the business community, who argued that technology displacement was a normal outgrowth of economic progress and would eventually be absorbed by a robust economy: "According to one extreme view, the world—or at least the United States—is on the verge of a glut of productivity sufficient to make our economic institutions and the notion of gainful employment obsolete. We dissent from that view. . . . However, we also dissent from the other extreme view of complacency that denies the existence of serious social and economic problems related to the impact of technological change."[6]

Curiously, although the authors of the government report attempted to draw distance between themselves and critics and establish a centrist approach to the issue, many of their findings reinforced the arguments advanced by the Oppenheimer Committee on the Triple Revolution. For example, they acknowledged the destructive impact of the new technology revolution on black America. The report stated:

> Modern farm technology—ranging from the cotton picker and huge harvesting combines, to chemical fertilizers and insecticides—has resulted in rapid migration of workers to the cities and has contributed to serious urban problems.
>
> The technological revolution in agriculture has compounded the difficulties of a large section of our Negro population. Pushed out of rural areas, many of them have migrated to cities in search of livelihood. But many arrived just when . . . advancing technology has been reducing the numbers of the semi-skilled and unskilled manufacturing jobs for which they could qualify. Despite improvements in the past 2 years, there are 700,000 fewer factory production and maintenance jobs than at the close of the Korean War.[7]

The government commission argued that "technology eliminates jobs, not work," in effect making the same argument that Oppenheimer and the authors of the Triple Revolution had made. If the economy was producing work without workers, as both sides seemed to suggest, then some form of government intervention would be necessary to provide a source of income and purchasing power for the increasing numbers of workers displaced by laborsaving technologies and increased productivity. The commission conceded the point: "It is the continuous obligation of economic policy to match increases in productive potential with increases in purchasing power and demand. Otherwise, the potential created by technical progress runs to waste in idle capacity, unemployment and deprivation."[8]

In the end, the Presidential Commission backpedaled on the questions raised by automation, concluding that technology displacement is a necessary and temporary condition engendered along the road to economic progress. Their measured optimism was given a lift by a recent upturn in the economy and a lowering of the unemployment figures brought on, in large measure, by the buildup for the Vietnam conflict. The commission admitted as much. "With the intensification of the war in Vietnam, the prospects are for still further cuts in unemployment."[9] In a prescient aside, the authors of the report warned that "The nation should not be lulled into forgetfulness by a short-run need for increased defense expenditures."[10] The warning was drowned out by the drums of war and a massive buildup of the military economy.

LABOR'S CAPITULATION

After years of growing concern over technology displacement, the long overdue debate on automation fizzled in the mid-1960s. Charles Silberman, writing in *Fortune*, declared that "the effects of automation on employment have been wildly and irresponsibly exaggerated, principally by social scientists who seem to be engaged in a competition in ominousness."[11]

The failure to adequately address the question of technological unemployment is partially the fault of organized labor. The voice of millions of working Americans, the labor movement waffled repeatedly on the issue of automation, only to eventually cast its lot with management, to the detriment of its own constituency.

The father of cybernetics, Norbert Weiner, who perhaps more than any other human being was in a position to clearly perceive the long-term consequences of the new automation technologies, warned of the dangers of widespread and permanent technological unemployment. He wrote, "If these changes in the demand for labor come upon us in a haphazard and ill-organized way, we may well be in for the greatest period of unemployment we have yet seen."[12]

Weiner became so fearful of the high-tech future he and his colleagues were creating that he wrote an extraordinary letter to Walter Reuther, president of the United Auto Workers, pleading for an audience. He warned Reuther that the cybernetic revolution "will undoubtedly lead to the factory without employees." Weiner predicted that "In the hands of the present industrial set-up, the unemployment produced by such plants can only be disastrous," and promised Reuther his full backing and personal loyalty in any concerted national campaign by organized labor to address the issue.[13]

Reuther was initially sympathetic and began to faintly echo Weiner's concerns before congressional committees and in public addresses. He warned that "The economy has failed to generate the purchasing power necessary to absorb the volume of goods and services which we have the technologies . . . to produce," and urged the federal government to "create the necessary demand."[14]

Other union leaders spoke out cautiously against the new technological forces that were threatening millions of jobs. George Meany, the powerful president of the AFL-CIO, warned that the new labor-saving technologies were "rapidly becoming a curse to this society . . . in a mad dash to produce more and more with less and less labor, and without feeling [as to] what it may mean to the economy as a whole."[15]

Despite all of the public rhetoric, however, organized labor proved far more conciliatory behind closed doors in the collective bargaining process. As historian David Noble documents in *The Forces of Production*, the unions for the most part capitulated to management on the issues surrounding automation. Fearful of being branded as modern-day Luddites and obstacles to progress, labor leaders were forced on the defensive. Many, including Reuther's own union, openly embraced the new laborsaving technologies. In 1955 the UAW issued a resolution at its annual convention amounting to a ringing endorsement of the very forces of automation that were beginning to seriously erode their membership rolls: "The UAW welcomes automation [and] technological progress. . . . We offer our cooperation . . . in a common search for policies and programs . . . that will insure that greater technological progress will result in greater human progress."[16]

Having accepted both the inevitability and even desirability of laborsaving technology, labor began to lose the momentum it had enjoyed since the end of World War II. Boxed into a corner, the union made a hasty retreat, shifting their collective bargaining demands from the issue of control over production and work processes to the call for job retraining. On the eve of the historic transition from mechanization to automation of production, the labor movement made a calculated decision to push for retraining, in the belief that while a vast number of unskilled jobs would be eliminated by the new computer technologies, the number of skilled and technical jobs would be increased. The CIO laid out the new strategy in a pamphlet issued in 1955, entitled "Automation."

> The introduction of automated machines and electronic computers will likely result in lay-offs and in the upgrading of the level of skills required in the workforce. . . . The prospect of labor displacement can be eased, in part, by joint consultation between companies and unions and by management planning to schedule the introduction of automation in periods of high employment, to permit attrition, reduce the size of the labor force, and to allow time for the retraining of employees.[17]

The AFL-CIO passed a number of resolutions at its annual conventions in the 1960s, calling for retraining provisions in collective bargaining agreements. Employers were more than willing to concede to labor's new demands. The costs of introducing retraining programs was far less onerous than the prospect of a long and protracted battle with labor over the introduction of new automated technologies on the shop floor. Between 1960 and 1967, the percentage of collective bargaining agreements containing provisions for job retraining increased from 12 percent to more than 40 percent.[18] Labor also lent its political muscle to federal legislation to promote job retraining. In 1962 the AFL-CIO mobilized rank-and-file support behind the passage of the Manpower Development Training Act, which was designed to provide retraining for workers displaced by automation.

By abandoning the question of control over the technology in favor of calls for retraining, the unions lost much of their effective bargaining power. Had control issues remained a strong priority, labor might have successfully negotiated collective bargaining agreements with management that would have ensured labor participation in productivity gains brought on by automation. Shorter workweeks and increased wages could have been tied to increases in productivity. Instead, labor capitulated, contenting itself with defensive agreements that provided job security for older workers, phased attrition of the existing workforce, and limited retraining opportunities for its members as ways of dealing with automation.

While the unions were correct in their belief that automation would shrink the ranks of the unskilled labor force, they grossly overestimated how many high-skilled jobs would be created by the new technologies. They failed to come to grips with the central dynamic of the automation revolution—management's single-minded determination to replace workers with machines wherever possible, and, by so doing, reduce labor costs, increase control over production, and improve profit margins. Some workers were retrained and found better high-skilled jobs; most did not. There were simply too many displaced workers and too few new high-tech jobs being created. The result was that the unions began to lose members and clout. Eventually, automation destroyed their most important single weapon—the strike. The new technologies allowed management to run plants with skeletal crews during strikes, effectively undermining the unions' ability to win significant concessions at the collective bargaining table.

To their credit, many unions did fight back, attempting to forestall "the inevitable" and win as many concessions for their rank and file as possible. The longshoremen, refinery workers, printers' unions, and others used strikes, slowdowns, and various means at their disposal to protect their members from the onslaught of automation. The International Typographers Union was one of the more militant unions in regard to automation. In 1966 its New York local was able to secure a labor agreement with New York newspaper publishers that "gave the union absolute authority over the types of technology which could be brought into the composing room." For eight years the ITU was able to stave off the shift from hot metal printing to cold type and forestall the automation of the composing room. The Big Three newspapers—*The New York Times*, the *Daily News*, and the *New York Post*—had agreed to the 1966 contract giving the ITU control over the introduction of new technology on the shop floor in the hope that the unions' resistance to cold type would eventually bankrupt their competitors. That is exactly what happened. In that period, New York's six smallest newspapers folded, in part because they could no longer afford the increasing labor costs associated with hot type. By 1974 the union was widely viewed as responsible for the bankruptcy of the smaller publishers and the loss of hundreds of jobs. The national media and the business community accused the ITU of being antiprogress and, worse yet, to blame for the loss of the very jobs the union had fought so hard to protect.[19]

Public pressure on the union increased, and in 1974 its leaders capitulated to management and public perception, signing an agreement to rescind their veto power over the introduction of new technologies in the composing room. In return, the union was guaranteed lifetime employment for currently employed typesetters and a handsome early retirement program. The agreement also called for systematic reductions of the workforce, phased in over a period of time. The publishers were willing to make short-term wage and benefit concessions, knowing that the historic agreement would mean the death knell for the union in the long run. The union, for its part, felt trapped by the increasing pressures of automation and public opinion and was determined to secure the best terms it could for its remaining members, while resigning itself to eventual extinction. Years later, former *New York Times* labor reporter A. H. Raskin reflected on what had taken place. He wrote, "The New York publishers' willingness to be so generous in negotiating the 1974 contract stemmed from an awareness of both sides that the packet represented the last hurrah for the typographical union. The union had strength enough to exact a high price for removing its veto power over automated processes, but the advent of automation effectively stripped it of future power. All that the union can now look forward to is a precipitous decline, as old-timers retire or die off and the traditional composing room disappears."[20]

In the end, the technological forces sweeping through the economy proved too powerful a foe. Their ranks thinned by wave after wave of new technological innovation, as well as by losses suffered at the hands of foreign competition, the nation's blue collar unions began their historic retreat and now exist as little more than a hollow reminder of their once pre-eminent role in American economic life.

Today, the concerns over automation are being heard once again. This time, however, the field upon which the battle over technology is being fought has grown dramatically to encompass the whole United States economy and much of the global marketplace. Issues surrounding technological unemployment, which a generation ago touched primarily the manufacturing sector of the economy, affecting poor black workers and blue collar laborers, are now being raised in every sector of the economy, and by virtually every group and class of workers.

The bitter experience of black laborers and blue collar workers in the traditional manufacturing industries over the past quarter century is an augur of what lies ahead as millions of additional workers are idled by massive technological displacement. America's underclass, which is still largely black and urban, is likely to become increasingly white and suburban as the new thinking machines relentlessly make their way up the economic pyramid, absorbing more and more skilled jobs and tasks along the way.

The world has changed dramatically in the three decades since the National Commission on Automation, Technology and Economic Progress issued its report. Norbert Weiner's premonition of a world without workers is fast becoming an issue of public concern in the industrialized nations. The Third Industrial Revolution is forcing a worldwide economic crisis of monumental proportions as millions lose their jobs to technological innovation, and global purchasing power plummets. As in the 1920s, we find ourselves dangerously close to another great depression, yet not a single world leader seems willing to entertain the possibility that the global economy is moving inexorably toward a shrinking labor market with potentially profound consequences for civilization.

Politicians everywhere have failed to grasp the fundamental nature of the changes taking place in the global business community. In corporate boardrooms, on plant floors, and in retail stores around the world, a quiet revolution has been going on. Businesses have been busy restructuring their organizations, in effect reinventing themselves, to create new management and marketing structures that can work effectively alongside the extraordinary array of new information and telecommunication technologies being hurried on-line. The result is a radical transformation in the way the world does business that threatens to bring into question the very role of the mass worker in the coming century.

The emerging world of lean management, high-technology production, and global commerce had its beginnings in the mid-1960s. The ink barely had time to dry on the report issued by the National Commission on Automation, when the world economy began to make its historic shift into the post-Fordist era, laying the organizational groundwork for a workerless future.

· 7 ·

Post-Fordism

IN THE MID-1960s few Americans were aware of the sweeping changes taking place in management practices inside Japanese companies that would, in less than a generation, force the United States and the world to rethink the very way they do business. In 1965 the United States was the most powerful nation on the face of the earth. Its military might, though shaken by the Russian advances in nuclear weaponry and outer space, was still unassailable. American technology was the envy of the world.

U.S. companies dominated international trade and commerce in the mid-1960s. Millions around the world looked for the "Made in America" label when they purchased products, convinced that U.S. goods meant top-of-the-line quality. On the domestic front, salaries and wages were rising and millions of Americans were enjoying the benefits that go with middle-class status.

Nineteen sixty-five was also the year that American corporations saw their after-tax profits rise to a postwar high of 10 percent. Although no one could have foreseen it at the time, that was to be the high-water mark for American business—the last great year of steadily rising profits for the corporate community. By the 1970s corporate profit had shrunk to less than 6 percent. A combination of domestic and international factors contributed to the decline.[1]

The U.S. consumer market had become saturated with consumer goods. By 1979 there was one car for every two Americans, and more than 90 percent of American households were equipped with refrigerators, washing machines, vacuum cleaners, radios, electric irons, and toasters. At the same time that demand was tapering off, foreign competition for American markets was increasing. Cheap imports flooded the U.S., dramatically cutting the market share of American companies. Between 1969 and 1979, the value of manufactured imports relative to domestic products rose from 14 percent to 38 percent. By the mid 1980s, for every dollar spent on goods produced in the United States, American families and businesses were spending 45 cents on imported goods.[2]

Increases in both corporate taxes and wage benefits to American workers reduced corporate profits still further. The OPEC oil embargo increased the cost of energy, driving corporate profits lower in the late 1970s and early 1980s. The decision to deregulate protected U.S. industries during the Reagan years—especially the airlines, telecommunications, and trucking—heightened competition for market share between traditional corporate giants and newcomers anxious to expand their niche. Again profits declined.

Old-line companies that had become complacent during the boom years began to take stock of the new circumstances confronting them. Faced with increasing competition from abroad and greater competition within each industry at home, companies searched for new ways to cut costs and improve market share and profits. They turned to the new computer and information technologies in hopes of increasing productivity in lean times. In the 1980s, U.S. businesses invested more than one trillion dollars in information technology.[3] More than 88 percent of the total investment was made in the service sector, to help improve efficiency and reduce costs. By 1992 virtually every white collar worker in the country had access to $10,000 in information-processing hardware.[4] Despite the large investments, productivity continued to limp along, increasing at about 1 percent a year. Economists began talking about the "productivity paradox." Some, like Harvard's Gary Loveman, spoke openly about the utter failure of the highly touted technological revolution to whom so many had looked for their salvation. "We simply can't find evidence that there has been a substantial productivity increase—and in some cases any productivity increase—from the substantial growth in information technology," Loveman told his colleagues.[5]

Just as corporate CEOs began to sour on the new information technologies, the productivity paradox suddenly disappeared. In 1991 output per hour increased by 2.3 percent. In 1992 productivity soared to nearly 3 percent, the best performance of any year in more than two decades.[6] MIT's Sloan School of Management published productivity data collected over a five-year period from 1987 to 1991 for more than 380 giant firms that together generated nearly $2 trillion in output per year. The gains in productivity were impressive, suggesting that the vast amount of money invested in information technology for more than a decade had begun to pay off.

The authors of the study, Erik Brynjolfsson and Lorin Hitt, found that between 1987 and 1991, return on investment (ROI) for computer capital averaged 54 percent in manufacturing and 68 percent for manufacturing and service combined. Brynjolfsson said that computers not only "added a great deal to productivity," but also contributed markedly to downsizing and the decline in the size of firms.[7] Morgan Stanley's Stephen Roach who, along with others on Wall Street, had raised the issue of a productivity paradox, dropped his earlier reservations, proclaiming that "The U.S. economy is now entering its first productivity-driven recovery since the 1960s, courtesy of efficiency gains being realized through the use of information technology." Much of the gain in productivity, says Roach, is coming in white collar areas and in the service industries.[8]

It became increasingly apparent to Roach and everyone else concerned that the failure to achieve productivity gains faster lay not with the new laborsaving, timesaving information technologies, but rather with outmoded organizational structures that were not able to accommodate the new technologies. Michael Borrus, of the Berkeley Roundtable on the International Economy, went directly to the heart of the matter, saying, "It simply isn't good enough to spend money on new technology and then use it in old ways." Borrus opined that "for every company using computers right, there is one using them wrong—and the two negate each other."[9]

American corporations and companies around the world had been structured one hundred years earlier to produce and distribute goods and services in an age of rail transport and telephone and postal communication. Their organizational apparatus proved wholly inadequate to deal with the speed, agility, and information-gathering ability of computer-age technology.

OLD-FASHIONED MANAGEMENT

Modern management had its birth in the railroad industry in the 1850s. In the early years, railroads ran their trains along a single track. Keeping "track" of train movements became critical to maintaining safe passage along the line. When the Western Railroad experienced a series of accidents on its Hudson River rail, culminating in a head-on crash on October 4, 1841, that killed a passenger and conductor, the company responded to the growing safety problem by instituting elaborate changes in its organizational management, including a more systematic process of data collection from its roadmasters and faster dissemination of vital scheduling information to its train crews. The innovations in management, says historian Alfred Chandler, made Western Railroad "the first modern, carefully defined, internal organizational structure used by American business enterprise."[10]

The invention of the telegraph in 1844 greatly facilitated communications, allowing the railroads to expand across the continent. Together, the rail and telegraph provided the critical transportation and communication infrastructure to serve a national market stretching some 3,000 miles. To meet the needs of this new market, other businesses began to adopt their own increasingly sophisticated managerial schemes. By the time Alfred Sloan of General Motors introduced the multidivisional organizational model in the 1920s, the modern managerial corporation had grown to maturity and was the driving force behind the American economy.

The defining characteristic of the modern corporation is its hierarchical management structure. Virtually every modern corporation chart appears as a pyramid, with field staff and production workers at the bottom of the hierarchy and an ascending staff of professional managers rising up the hierarchy, with a chief executive officer perched on top of the pyramid. Employees at each rung of the corporate ladder have assigned tasks and are held accountable for their work to those immediately on top of them on the corporate pyramid. Vital information concerning production, distribution, and marketing flows up the chain of command, where it is processed at each level and then carried to the next until it eventually reaches top management which, in turn, use that information to make command decisions that are then transmitted down the hierarchy and implemented at each descending level of the corporate structure. The organizational chart of the giant modern corporation contains hierarchies within hierarchies. Departments like finance and accounting, research and development, and marketing and advertising, each has its own chain of command embedded inside the larger structure.

At the very bottom of the corporate hierarchy is the unskilled and semiskilled workforce whose job is to make and move things or perform the hands-on services that are the company's trademark. Their tasks are for all intents and purposes rigidly routinized along the classical lines of scientific management first espoused by efficiency expert Frederick Taylor at the turn of the century.

For the better part of the twentieth century, this form of managerial capitalism dominated the American and European economies. The organizational arrangement relied heavily on the increasingly bloated ranks of middle management to both process the flow of information up and down the corporate hierarchy and coordinate and control the many functions of the company.

Robert Reich, the Secretary of Labor, has compared the modern corporation to a military bureaucracy. In both instances, the chain of command runs from the top down, with less and less room for independent decision-making at the lower levels of the command structure. In the era of mass production and distribution, with its emphasis on increasing division of labor and standardized goods, the need for "absolute control was necessary," says Reich, "if plans were to be implemented exactly."[11]

The managerial system of corporate organization was like a lumbering giant, a powerful producer able to turn out a large volume of standardized goods but lacking the flexibility to make the kind of rapid changes necessary to adjust to sudden fluctuations in the domestic or global market. At their apex of power in the late 1950s and early 1960s, five hundred giant corporations produced half of the nation's industrial output and nearly one quarter of the industrial output of the noncommunist world. They employed more than 12 percent of the nation's workforce. General Motors, the world's largest corporation, had earnings in 1955 equivalent to 3 percent of the GNP of the country.[12]

By the 1980s, however, American corporate power was being challenged by new global competitors armed with a very different organizational arrangement better equipped to take advantage of the new technologies of the information revolution. The new form of management emerged first in the Japanese automobile industry after World War II. The new approach to making cars diverged so radically from the kind of management used in Detroit that industry observers began to refer to the Japanese method as post-Fordist production.

In their book *The Machine That Changed the World*, James Womack, Daniel Jones, and Daniel Roos examine the revolutionary changes in the manufacturing of automobiles that have occurred over the past century. They recount the story of the Honorable Evelyn Henry Ellis, a well-to-do member of the British Parliament, who in

1894 paid a visit to the Paris machine tool company of Panhard and Levassor to "commission" an automobile. The company's owners, Panhard and Levassor, met with Ellis, soliciting his ideas about the kind of automobile he wanted. Their skilled craftsman then set about the task of designing the vehicle and ordering materials to be made by other machine and tool shops in Paris. The custom-ordered parts and components were brought together in the Panhard and Levassor shop, where they were assembled by hand to make the automobile. Ellis's car, like the few hundred other automobiles made each year by Panhard and Levassor, was unique and drawn up to meet the very exacting standards of an individual customer. Ellis became the first Englishman to own an automobile.[13]

Less than twenty years later Henry Ford was producing thousands of identical cars each day at a fraction of the cost Ellis paid for his handcrafted vehicle. Ford was the first automaker to mass produce a standardized product using interchangeable parts. Because the individual components were always cut and shaped exactly the same, they could be attached to each other quickly and simply, without requiring a skilled craftsman to put them together. To quicken the process of attachment, Ford introduced a moving assembly line to the factory floor—an innovation he first observed in the giant slaughterhouses of the Chicago stockyards. By bringing the car directly to the worker, he shaved precious time off the production process and was able to control the pace of movement in the factory.

By the 1920s Ford was mass producing more than 2 million automobiles a year, each one identical in every detail to the one before and after it on the assembly line.[14] Ford once quipped that his customers could choose any color they wanted for their Model T as long as it was black. This principle of mass-produced standardized products set the norm for manufacturing for more than a half a century.

Like other giant manufacturing concerns, Ford and the Detroit automakers were organized along rigid hierarchical lines with a command structure running from top management down a descending line to the shop floor. In strict Tayloresque style, the workforce assembling the cars was stripped of any kind of skilled knowledge and denied independent control over the pace of production. Design and engineering skills and all production and scheduling decisions were placed in the hands of management. The organizational hierarchy was divided into departments, each with responsibility over a specific function or activity and all accountable up the chain of command, with the ultimate authority resting in the hands of top management.

THE SWITCH TO LEAN PRODUCTION

The mass-production system spread from the auto industry to other industries and became the unchallenged standard around the world for how best to conduct the affairs of business and commerce. While the "American method" was enjoying an unqualified success in world markets in the 1950s, a Japanese auto company, struggling to recover from World War II, began experimenting with a new approach to production—one whose operating assumptions were as different from those of mass production as the latter was from the earlier craft methods of production. The company was Toyota, and its new managerial process was called *lean production*.

The guiding principle behind lean production is to combine new management techniques with increasingly sophisticated machinery to produce more output with fewer resources and less labor. Lean production differs significantly from both craft and industrial production. In craft production, highly skilled workers, using hand tools, craft each product to the design specifications of the buyer. Items are made one at a time. In mass production, "skilled professionals . . . design products made by unskilled or semi-skilled workers tending expensive, single purpose machines. These turn out standardized products in very high volume."[15] In mass production the machinery is so expensive that downtime has to be avoided at all costs. As a result management adds "buffers" in the form of extra inventory and workers to make sure of not running out of inputs or slowing down the production flow. Finally, the high cost of investment in machinery precludes quick retooling for new product designs. The customer benefits from cheap prices but at the expense of variety.

Lean production, in contrast, "combines the advantage of craft and mass production, while avoiding the high cost of the former and the rigidity of the latter."[16] To meet these production objectives, management brings together teams of multiskilled workers at every level of the organization to work alongside automated machines, producing high volumes of goods with a great degree of variety to choose from. Lean production is "lean," say Womack, Jones, and Roos, because "It uses less of everything compared with mass production— half the human effort in the factory, half the manufacturing space, half the investment in tools, half the engineering hours to develop a new product in half the time. Also, it requires keeping far less than half the needed inventory on site, results in many fewer defects, and produces a greater and ever growing variety of products."[17]

The Japanese form of lean production starts by doing away with the traditional managerial hierarchy and replacing it with multiskilled teams that work together at the point of production. In the Japanese lean factory, design engineers, computer programmers, and factory workers interact face-to-face, sharing ideas and implementing joint decisions directly on the factory floor. The classical Taylor model of scientific management, which favored the separation of mental from physical labor and the retention of all decision making in the hands of management, is abandoned in favor of a cooperative team approach designed to harness the full mental capabilities and work experience of everyone involved in the process of making an automobile. For example, in the older mass-production model, research and development is separated from the factory and housed in a laboratory. Scientists and engineers design new models and the machinery to produce them in the laboratory and then introduce the changes to the factory floor along with a complete set of detailed instructions and schedules for mass producing the product. Under the new system of lean production, the factory floor becomes in effect the research and development laboratory, a place where the combined expertise of everyone in the production process is utilized to make "continual improvements" and refinements in the production process and the final product.

Workers from every department are even invited to take part in the design of new cars, a process always under the tight control of an engineering elite in the older U.S. auto companies. Concurrent engineering, as it has come to be known, is based on the principle that everyone affected by the design, scale-up, production, distribution, marketing, and sales of a new automobile should participate as early as possible in the development of a new car to ensure that each department's specific needs and requirements are taken into consideration and to help pinpoint potential trouble spots before full-scale production is set. Studies over the years suggest that up to 75 percent of a product's cost is determined at the conceptual stage. A delay of just six months in getting a new product to market can cut profits by up to 33 percent.[18] Japanese companies have found that by including everyone in at the design stage, crucial bottom-line costs can be held to a minimum.

The notion of continual improvement is called *kaizen* and is considered the key to the success of Japanese production methods. Unlike the older American model, in which innovations are made infrequently and often in a single changeover, the Japanese production system is set up to encourage continued change and improvement as part of day-to-day operations. To achieve *kaizen*, management harnesses the collective experience of all of its workers and places value on joint problem-solving.

Work teams on the factory floor are given much greater latitude over the production process. If a machine breaks down or a line slows, the workers themselves often repair the equipment and clear any bottlenecks in the process—a far different approach than that of the Detroit auto manufacturers, where machine breakdowns require notification of supervisors, who, in turn, summon technicians to the floor to fix the equipment. The result is far fewer breakdowns and a more smoothly running line because the workers closest to the production process are better prepared to anticipate problems, and when they do come up, resolve them quickly and efficiently. Again, the data is telling. According to a study conducted by James Harbour on the automotive industry, U.S. equipment was inoperative more than 50 percent of the time while machines in Japanese auto factories were down less than 15 percent of the time.[19]

The team-based model of work creates greater efficiencies by encouraging the development of multiskilled workers. Being well versed in a number of tasks on the production floor gives individual workers a far better understanding of the overall manufacturing process—knowledge that can be used effectively within team settings to pinpoint problems and make suggestions for improvements. To assist workers in seeing how their work fits into the larger production process, Japanese companies provide employees with access to all computerized information generated within the company. One Japanese manager explained the importance his company attached to sharing information with workers: "One of our most important jobs is to make all of our employees willing to cooperate fully, and to make them want to continually improve themselves. To achieve this, it is necessary for us to provide all kinds of information equally to everyone. . . . Every employee has the right of access to 'all' computerized information within the company."[20]

Unlike the older corporate model of management, where decision making is continually being pushed up higher on the managerial hierarchy, the Japanese teamwork model attempts to push decision-making authority as far down the managerial ladder as possible so as to be closer to the point of production. This creates a more egalitarian atmosphere within the factory and far less friction between management and workers. In most Japanese automotive factories, workers and management share a common cafeteria and parking lot. Managers as

well as workers wear company uniforms. To encourage further open-
ness and a closer working relationship, managers sit at open desks on
the factory floor next to the production facility. Because most managers are recruited directly from the workforce, they are far more
likely to understand the special needs of the employees in their work
teams and better prepared to cement strong personal bonds with
members of their work teams. In the Japanese system workers even
meet in special "quality circles" before or after regular work hours to
discuss improvements in the production process. In a recent survey,
76 percent of Japanese workers were found to take part in quality
circles.[21]

The Japanese production model also places a high priority on what
is called "just-in-time" production, or stockless production. The idea
behind just-in-time came from a visit to the United States by Taiichi
Ohno of Toyota Motors in the 1950s. Ohno was far more impressed
with America's giant supermarkets than with its automotive plants. He
later recounted his surprise at the speed and efficiency by which the
supermarkets kept shelves stocked with exactly the products customers desired in just the amount needed: "A supermarket is where a
customer can get (1) what is needed, (2) at the time needed, (3) in the
amount needed. . . . We hoped that this would help us approach our
just-in-time goal and, in 1953, we actually applied the system in our
machine shop at the main plant."[22]

Womack, Jones, and Roos tell of being stunned by the difference in
physical appearance on the factory floor at a General Motors plant they
visited in Framingham, Massachusetts, and a Toyota plant in Japan. At
the General Motors facility, parts of the production line were down,
workers were milling around with nothing to do, weeks' worth of
inventory were piled up in the aisles, and trash cans were filled with
defective parts. In stark contrast, at the Toyota plant the aisles were
clear and "the workers were all at their workstations performing their
tasks. No workstation had more than an hour's worth of inventory piled
up. As soon as defective parts were discovered they were immediately
tagged and sent off to a quality control center for replacement."[23]

The American manufacturing philosophy is based on "just-in-
case" production. Automobile manufacturers store large and redundant inventories of materials and equipment along the entire production line in anticipation of having to replace defective parts or faulty
equipment. This process is viewed by Japanese management as costly
and unnecessary. The Japanese system of just-in-time production is
based on exacting standards of quality control and crisis management

designed to ferret out potential problems before they force a major breakdown in the production process.

The radical differences in production philosophy at General Motors and Toyota showed up in the bottom-line figures for both companies. In a MIT study of the two plants, researchers found that at the Toyota facility, "It took 16 hours to build a car in 4.8 square feet of work space per vehicle per year, with .45 defects per car. At GM-Framingham it took nearly thirty-one hours in 8.15 square feet with 1.3 defects."[24] Toyota was able to build a car quicker, in less space, with fewer defects, and with half the labor.

In recent years, Japanese manufacturers have combined the new lean-management techniques with increasingly sophisticated computer and other information technologies to create the "factory of the future"—automated production facilities with few workers, which more nearly resemble a laboratory than a factory. Social scientists Martin Kenney and Richard Florida talk of the new lean factories that are more cerebral than physical in appearance: "Under past forms of industrial production, including mass-production Fordism, much of work was physical. . . . The emergence of digitization increases the importance of abstract intelligence in production and thus requires that workers actively undertake what were previously thought of as intellectual activities. In this new environment, workers are no longer covered with grease and sweat, because the factory increasingly resembles a laboratory for experimentation and technical advance."[25]

The operating assumptions of lean management, with their strong emphasis on "process" rather than "structure and function," made Japanese manufacturers ideally suited to take advantage of the new computer-based information technologies.

RE-ENGINEERING THE WORKPLACE

Womack, Jones, and Roos predicted that the lean-production method of management developed by the Japanese would spread beyond the automotive industry and "change everything in almost every industry."[26] Their optimistic forecast is now becoming a reality. Borrowing from the Japanese model of lean production, American and European companies have begun to introduce their own changes in organizational structure to accommodate the new computer technologies. Under the broad rubric of re-engineering, corporations are flattening traditional organizational pyramids and transferring more and more decision-making responsibilities to networks and teams. The re-engineering phenomenon is forcing a fundamental overhaul in the way business is handled, and, in the process, deeply cutting into employment rolls, eliminating millions of jobs and hundreds of job categories. While unskilled and semiskilled jobs continue to be cut by the introduction of new information and communication technologies, other positions in the corporate hierarchy are also being threatened with extinction. No group is being harder hit than middle management. Traditionally, middle managers have been responsible for coordinating the flow up and down the organizational ladder. With the introduction of sophisticated new computer technologies, these jobs become increasingly unnecessary and costly.

The new information and communication technologies have both increased the volume and accelerated the flow of activity at every level of society. The compression of time requires quicker responses and faster decision making to remain competitive. In the emerging nano-second culture, the traditional control and coordination functions of management are woefully slow and utterly incapable of responding, in real time, to the speed and volume of information coming into the organization. In the information era, "time" is the critical commodity, and corporations bogged down by old-fashioned hierarchical management schemes cannot hope to make decisions fast enough to keep up with the flow of information that requires resolution.

Today, a growing number of companies are deconstructing their organizational hierarchies and eliminating more and more middle management by compressing several jobs into a single process. They are then using the computer to perform the coordination functions previously carried out by many people often working in separate departments and locations within the company. Gary Loveman says that the restructuring of the corporation is fast eliminating middle management from the organizational chart. He points out that while better jobs are being created for a fortunate few at the top levels of management, the men and women in "garden variety middle management jobs" are "getting crucified" by corporate re-engineering and the introduction of sophisticated new information and communication technologies.[27]

Departments create divisions and borders that inevitably slow down the decision-making process. Companies are eliminating those borders by reassigning personnel into networks or teams that can work together to process information and coordinate vital decisions, thus bypassing the long delays that invariably accompany the shuffling of paper reports and memoranda between various divisions and levels of authority. The computer has made all of this possible. Now, any employee at any location within the company can access all of the information being generated and directed through the organization.

Instant access to information means that the control and coordination of activity can be exercised quickly and at lower levels of command that are "closer to the action." The introduction of computer-based technologies allows information to be processed horizontally rather than vertically, in effect collapsing the traditional corporate pyramid in favor of networks operating along a common plane. By eliminating the slow climb up and down the old-fashioned decision-making pyramid, information can be processed at a speed commensurate with the capabilities of the new computer equipment.

Michael Hammer and James Champy, whose book *Re-engineering the Corporation* helped focus public attention on the current restructuring phenomenon, use the example of IBM Credit to explain how re-engineering works in practice. IBM Credit finances the computer equipment purchased by IBM customers. Before re-engineering, customer requests for financing had to go through several departments and levels of decision making, often taking many days to process. An IBM salesperson would call in with a request for financing. One of fourteen people would take down the information on a piece of paper. The slip of paper was then delivered upstairs to the credit department, where a second person logged the information into a computer and did a background check on the customer's creditworthiness. The credit check information was attached to the original sales request form and then delivered to the business practices department. Using its own computer, the department modified the terms of the agreement to match the customer's request and then attached the special terms to the request form. The paper form then went to a pricer, who, using his or her own computer, determined the appropriate interest rate to charge the customer. The information was written onto the paper form and sent to a clerical group. At that department all the information that had been collected along the way was reworked and put into a quote letter, which was then delivered to IBM's sales representatives by way of Federal Express.[28]

Sales representatives were frustrated over the slow response time in processing customer requests for financing, and complained about customers canceling orders or finding alternative financing with other companies. Concerned over the delays, two IBM senior managers walked a customer request through all five departments, asking each to process the information without the usual delay that results from request forms backing up for days on people's desks. They found that the actual time it took to process the entire order was less than ninety minutes. The remainder of the seven days was used up in "handing the form off from one department to the next."[29] IBM management eliminated the five separate offices and handed over the task of handling a customer's request for financing to a single "case worker" called a "deal structurer." One generalist, armed with a computer, now handles the entire process. According to Hammer and Champy, when IBM looked closely at the old management scheme, "they found that most of it was little more than clerical: finding a credit rating in a database, plugging numbers into a standard model, pulling boiler plate clauses from a standard file. These tasks fall well within the capability of a single individual when he or she is supported by an easy-to-use computer system that provides access to all the data and tools the specialist would use."[30]

IBM Credit reduced the time it took to process a request for financing from seven days to less than four hours, using less labor in the process. Hammer and Champy report that a caseworker or case team approach to production operates ten times faster than the older hierarchical approach to management activity, with its reliance on separate departments and vertical chains of command.[31]

Hammer believes that "re-engineering is going to have a massive impact on jobs in the next several decades." The former MIT professor says that "a very large amount of productivity gains still remain" to be achieved even during this first wave of re-engineering. "I don't think that we've come close, in fact, to squeezing out what's available to be squeezed," says Hammer. Re-engineering the economy, according to Hammer, could result in an unofficial unemployment figure of as much as 20 percent by the time the current re-engineering phenomenon runs its course.[32]

The re-engineering revolution has achieved some of its most dramatic successes in the retail sector. Quick-response systems are cutting both time and labor from the entire distribution process. Bar coding allows retailers to keep a continuously updated record of exactly what items are being sold, and in what quantities. Point of sale (POS) data eliminates pricing and cashier errors and greatly reduces the time spent on ticketing products. Bar-code marking on shipping containers (SCM) allows the customer to log in and verify the contents of packages without having to open them for inspection. Electronic data interchange (EDI) allows companies to substitute electronic transmission of information like purchase orders, invoices, and payment for paper correspondence, reducing the need for both transportation and clerical handling. Together, all of these information tools allow companies to bypass traditional channels of distribution and communication and deal instantaneously and directly with warehouses and suppliers, ensuring just-in-time inventories to meet customer needs.

The giant discount chain Wal-Mart owes some measure of its success to its pioneering role in harnessing these new information technologies. Wal-Mart uses information gathered by scanners at the point of sale and transmits it by electronic data interchange directly to its suppliers like Procter & Gamble, who, in turn, make the decision on what items to ship and in what quantities. Suppliers ship directly to the stores, bypassing the warehouse altogether. The process eliminates purchase orders, bills of lading, large inventories on hand, and reduces clerical costs by eliminating the labor needed at each step of the traditional process to handle orders, shipping, and warehousing.[33]

Saturn auto retailers use computer terminals in showrooms to punch in the specific options and colors a customer would like for his or her car and transmit the information electronically directly to the production plant. The manufacturer then makes the automobile to the customer's requirements. "Made-to-order" rather than "made to inventory" is becoming increasingly common as businesses compete for each and every customer's loyalty while attempting to hold down the costs of keeping large inventories on hand.[34]

Japan's National Bicycle Company is even more advanced in its quick-response, made-to-order operations. A customer is measured on a machine in the showroom and fitted to an appropriate size and shape of bicycle with the help of a computer-aided design system. The customer then picks the make and model of brakes, chain, tire, derailer, and color. He or she can even choose to have a personalized name put on the bike. The information is electronically transmitted to the company's factory, and the finished, made-to-order bicycle can be manufactured, assembled, and shipped within less than three hours. Ironically, the company has discovered through its marketing studies that its response is too quick and dampens the enthusiasm of its customers, so it purposely delays delivery for a week so that the customer can experience "the joy of anticipation."[35]

Companies across the country are discovering countless new ways to use re-engineering to compress time and reduce labor costs. Increasingly, computers are providing needed information and helping to structure the coordination and flow of activity in the economic process, eliminating the need for salespersons, account executives, truck drivers, warehouse handlers, shipping department personnel, and billing department people. While the new information and telecommunication technologies are eliminating jobs at every rung of the corporate hierarchy, the impact on middle management has been particularly unsettling to many in the business community. Authors William Davidow and Michael Malone sum up the growing consensus: "Computers can gather most information more accurately and cost-effectively than people. They can produce summaries with electronic speeds, and they can transmit the information to decision makers at the speed of light. Most interesting . . . is that, frequently, this information is so good and the analysis so precise that an executive decision is no longer required. A well-trained employee dealing directly with the situation can now make the decision faster and in a more responsive fashion than the remote manager miles away."[36]

Franklin Mint has cut its management layers from six to four and doubled sales. Eastman Kodak has reduced its management levels from thirteen to four. Intel has cut its management hierarchy in some of its operations from ten to five levels.[37] John D. O'Brien, vice president for human resources at Borg-Warner, predicts the very term "'staff function' will become extinct some time in the 1990s."[38]

The re-engineering of work is eliminating jobs of all kinds and in greater numbers than at any time in recent memory. In Japan, NIKKO Research estimates that there are more than one million "redundant" employees in Japanese companies that could be replaced by re-engineering and the new information technologies.[39]

Corporate re-engineering is only in its infancy, and already unemployment is rising, consumer purchasing power is dropping, and domestic economies are reeling from the aftershocks of flattening giant corporate bureaucracies. All of these problems are likely to accelerate dramatically in the years ahead as companies, faced with more intense global competition, use increasingly sophisticated technologies to raise productivity and reduce labor force requirements. The prospect of farms, factories, offices, and retail stores producing, marketing, and selling goods with fewer and fewer workers at the helm is no longer unthinkable. A survey of recent technological developments and trends in the agricultural, manufacturing, and service sectors suggests that a near-workerless world is fast approaching and may arrive well before society has sufficient time to either debate its broad implications or prepare for its full impact.

PART III

THE DECLINE OF THE GLOBAL LABOR FORCE

· 8 ·

No More Farmers

THE HIGH-TECHNOLOGY REVOLUTION is not normally associated with farming. Yet some of the most impressive advances in automation are occurring in agriculture. While public attention of late has focused on the effects of technology displacement on the manufacturing and service sectors, an equally profound technology revolution is changing the nature of modern agriculture and, in the process, raising serious questions about the future of farm labor in countries around the world.

Nearly half the human beings on the planet still farm the land. Now, however, new breakthroughs in the information and life sciences threaten to end much of outdoor farming by the middle decades of the coming century. The technological changes in the production of food are leading to a world without farmers, with untold consequences for the 2.4 billion who rely on the land for their survival.[1]

The mechanization of agriculture began more than one hundred years ago. In 1880 it took more than twenty man-hours to harvest an acre of a wheatland. By 1916 the number of man-hours was reduced to 12.7. Just twenty years later only 6.1 man-hours were required.[2] The productivity gains in agriculture were so swift and effective that by the late 1920s economic instability was no longer fueled by crop failures but, rather, by overproduction. The mechanization of the agricultural sector was heralded as a triumph of industrial society. One leading agriculturalist of the day boasted, "We no longer raise wheat here, we manufacture it. . . . We are not husbandrymen, we are not farmers. We are producing a product to sell."[3]

The technological changes in American agriculture transformed the country from a largely agricultural society to an urban, industrial nation, in little more than one hundred years. In 1850, 60 percent of the working population were employed in agriculture. Today, less than 2.7 percent of the workforce is engaged directly in farming. Since World War II, more than 15 million men and women have left the farm in the United States.[4]

The decline in the farm population has left fewer and bigger farms. Between 1935 and 1987 the average size of farms rose from 139 to 462 acres.[5] The high cost of machine capital and increases in productivity resulting from economies of scale have favored the large over the small producer. Currently, 32,023 large-scale farms account for more than 38 percent of total product sales in the United States.[6] Although the farm population is less than 3 million, it sustains a food industry employing more than 20 million.[7] In our highly industrialized urban culture, most people would probably be surprised to learn that the food and fiber industry is the single largest industry in the United States. More than 20 percent of the GNP and 22 percent of the workforce is dependent on crops grown on America's agricultural lands and animals raised on feedlots and in factory farms.[8]

Farm mechanization, which began with the horse-drawn steel plow in the mid-1850s, is nearing completion today with the introduction of sophisticated computerized robots in the fields. The short history of farm mechanization provides an object lesson of the tremendous potential of modern technology to replace and eventually eliminate human beings from the production process.

The replacement of handcrafted wood plows with mass-produced cast-iron plows in the last century greatly improved farm productivity. John Deere, of Illinois, produced the first iron plow with a steel cutting edge in 1837. It was so effective at cutting through the heavy, sticky soils of Illinois farmland that it became known as the "singing plow." By the mid-1850s the John Deere Company was producing more than 10,000 iron plows a year. The lighter plows allowed farmers to shift from oxen to horses, quickening the speed of plowing fields and reducing the labor time in preparing the soil for seeding.[9]

While the new iron-steel plows quickened the spring seeding, the introduction of mechanical reapers, at about the same time, greatly increased the speed of harvesting. As late as the 1840s, farmers were still using hand tools to cut the fall harvest. The horse-drawn mechanical reaper cut the work time required to harvest grain by more than half. Cyrus McCormick's reaper gained widespread acceptance in the 1850s and became synonymous with farm equipment over the remaining decades of the nineteenth century. Grain-threshing machines also became popular. In the West, giant grain combines, weighing up to fifteen tons and pulled by forty horses, cut swaths of grain up to thirty-five feet wide.[10]

The first gasoline-powered tractor was built in 1892 by John Froehlich in Iowa. By 1910, 25,000 tractors were in use in the United States. In 1917 Henry Ford introduced the Fordson, a cheap mass-produced tractor. Overnight, tractor sales soared. By 1920, 246,000 tractors were in use on the nation's farms.[11] Two decades later, more than 1.6 million were being used for a wide range of tasks on the farm, and by 1960 more than 4.7 million of them were working the agricultural fields.[12] The horse, mule, and oxen, once the primary sources of power on the farm, had been eclipsed and virtually eliminated by the internal combustion engine. The workhorse disappeared from American farms in the early 1950s.

Motor trucks also increased on the farms during the same time period. In 1915 there were 25,000 trucks being used for farm work. By 1980 more than 3.5 million trucks were in use. The gasoline engine, harnessed to tractors, trucks, and harvesting machines, now does all the heavy work on the farm.[13]

Mechanization of agriculture went hand-in-hand with new plant-breeding techniques designed to introduce varieties and strains that were more uniform and easier to manipulate by machines. We already described the mechanical cotton picker. The first mechanical picker proved ineffective because cotton bolls opened irregularly over a period of many weeks, making it difficult to run a machine through partially unharvestable fields. Plant breeders were finally able to develop a strain of cotton in which the bolls grew higher up on the stalks and opened up more quickly, making the machine picker feasible for the first time.[14]

Tomatoes offer still another example of the symbiotic relationship that developed between breeders and engineers in agriculture. A new variety of tomato was introduced in the 1960s that would ripen at the same time and be strong enough to withstand machine handling. A new harvesting machine was designed specifically for harvesting the new variety, and within less than twenty-four years—from 1963 to 1987—the harvesting of tomatoes in California went from hand picking by Mexican immigrant labor to automated machine handling.[15]

Aside from being more uniform and easier to manipulate, virtually all of the new varieties being developed by plant biologists were high-yield crops. The early hybrid corn varieties often tripled the yield per acre.[16] The introduction of industrial quantities of nitrogen fertilizer onto the soil greatly increased crop yields and allowed for more intensive farming practices. Fields no longer had to be left fallow to restore fertility but could be used over and over again with the introduction of increasing amounts of artificial chemicals. Greater productivity meant that fewer farm workers and farms were necessary to produce an expanded output.

The introduction of high-yield monoculture crops also led to the widespread use of chemical pesticides and herbicides. Monocultures were found to be more susceptible to pest infestation and disease, and more vulnerable to weeds. The use of insecticides, herbicides, and fungicides greatly reduced the number of farm laborers needed to tend the fields.

Animal husbandry practices also became increasingly mechanized and industrialized over the course of the current century. Innovative breeding technologies, specialized feeds, and new animal-based pharmaceuticals greatly improved the growth and productivity of farm animals. Factory feedlots of cattle and swine and factory farming of poultry allowed large-scale operators to produce meat, dairy, and other animal-derived products in record volume with a greatly reduced labor force. By the 1980s, giant cattle feedlots in the Midwest were handling upwards of 50,000 head of cattle at a time. Today, some fifteen poultry companies produce more than 3.7 billion chickens a year, using streamlined factory methods that differ little from those used in the manufacture of inanimate products.[17]

The mechanical, biological, and chemical revolutions in agriculture have put millions of farm laborers out of work. Between 1940 and 1950, human labor on the farm declined by 26 percent. In the following decade it declined again, this time by more than 35 percent. The decline was even more dramatic in the 1960s. Nearly 40 percent of the remaining agricultural workforce was replaced by machinery in that single decade.[18] At the same time, farm productivity has increased more in the past 100 years than at any time since the dawn of the Neolithic Revolution. In 1850 a single farm worker produced enough food to feed four people. Today, in the United States, a single farmer supplies enough to feed more than seventy-eight people.[19] Agricultural productivity has registered remarkable gains over the past half century. Output increased by 25 percent in the 1940s, 20 percent in the 1950s, and 17 percent in the 1960s. In the 1980s agricultural productivity grew by more than 28 percent.[20]

The spectacular gains in productivity have had a devastating impact on the family farm. Higher yields and greater output have created a crisis of oversupply for most of the current century, continually pushing prices down for farmers. Depressed prices in turn have forced farmers to produce even more in order to cover fixed costs and overhead, only perpetuating the cycle of overproduction and falling prices. Ever since the depression years of the 1930s, price and commodity supports have been used to both artificially prop up the price of farm commodities and pay farmers not to produce in order to curtail production. Again, Say's law, that supply creates its own demand, has proven wrong. Agricultural production, even more than manufacturing production and service, has been stymied by ever-increasing output pitted against ineffective demand, with terrible consequences for farm families and rural communities.

The massive displacement and dislocation of farm labor over the past century has deprived millions of people of a livable wage. There are currently more than 9 million persons living under the poverty line in depressed rural areas across the United States—all casualties of the great strides in farm technology that have made the United States the number-one food producer in the world and made American agriculture the envy of every nation.[21]

SOIL AND SOFTWARE

The decline in the number of farms is likely to accelerate in the coming years with advances in agricultural software and farm robotics. Agricultural software is already being developed to assist farmers in monitoring the environment, locating problem areas, devising intervention strategies, and implementing action plans. In the near future, computerized "expert systems" will collect data on weather changes, soil conditions, and other variables from computer-based sensors located on the land and use the information to make specific recommendations to the farmer. Highly specialized robots will be instructed, in turn, to carry out many of the computer-generated action plans.

Many expert systems are currently being tested around the country. Virginia Tech has developed the Crop Rotation Planning System (CROPS) to assist farmers in evaluating the risk of soil erosion and nutrient and pesticide leaching and runoff. The farmer enters data on soil type, topography, land use, and field size into the computer. The computer then uses the information to devise an overall program of farm production, balancing acreage targets and profit objectives with the need to reduce environmental risks to an acceptable level.[22] Expert systems are currently being developed to assist farmers in a range of integrated crop-management decisions covering irrigation, fertilization, nutrition, weed and insect control, and herbicide application.

The Department of Agriculture has an expert system on-line for managing cotton. Called GOSSYM/COMAX, it uses a simulation model that collects weather data and then forecasts "when to irrigate and fertilize to achieve optimal agronomic goals." The system is already being used by more than 500 cotton farms in fifteen states. The USDA Agriculture Research Service has developed its own expert system for determining "whether insects will become a problem [in stored wheat] and helps select the most appropriate prophylactic or remedial actions." Pennsylvania State University has designed a similar system, called GRAPES, to help farmers assess the risks of insects and diseases in vineyards and make recommendations for abating the problem. The University of Manitoba has created an expert system that acts as a Fertilization Selection Advisor, helping farmers choose the right mix of fertilizers for different soil bases and moisture contents.[23]

Expert systems are also being developed and used in animal husbandry management. The University of Minnesota has created expert software to diagnose herd mastitis (an infection of the udder). By analyzing DHI somatic cell data, the computer can make expert evaluations and suggest appropriate remedial action. The university has developed several other expert systems for dairy, including one that assists in manure management. Other expert systems tell farmers when to keep or cull commercial beef cows and how to manage sheep and swine. XLAYER, an expert system used in poultry production, can diagnose and make recommendations for over eighty separate production management problems that affect the profitability of flocks.[24]

In addition to individual expert systems, agricultural software companies are beginning to develop full-text retrieval systems allowing individual farmers instant access to journal articles and other relevant agricultural data from anywhere in the world. By the end of the current decade, industry analysts hope to integrate many of these separate systems, providing the farmer with the information to make complex decisions governing a wide range of production problems and financial matters.

Currently, only 15 to 27 percent of farm managers are using computers as management tools. Still, scientists are predicting that within less than twenty years virtually every aspect of farming will have come under the control of computers—monitoring, analyzing, and making recommendations in every conceivable area of farm management.[25]

A new generation of sophisticated computer-driven robots may soon replace many of the remaining manual tasks on the land, potentially transforming the modern farm into an automated outdoor factory. Israel's farmers are already well along the way to advanced robotized farming. Concerned over the potential security risks involved in employing Palestinian migrant labor, the Israelis turned to the Institute of Agricultural Engineering for help in developing mechanical farm laborers. In a growing number of kibbutzim, it is not unusual to see self-guided machines traveling on tracks laid out between rows of plants, spraying pesticides on the crops. "We turn the machines on and then go to eat lunch," says one Israeli farmer.[26]

The Israelis are currently experimenting with a robotic melon picker developed jointly by the Institute of Agricultural Engineering and Purdue University researchers. The robotic harvester can be used to transplant, cultivate, and harvest round or "head" crops including melons, pumpkins, cabbage, and lettuce. Named ROMPER (Robotic Melon Picker), the robot is mounted on a trailer frame and equipped with cameras that scan the rows of plants while a fan blows leaves aside "to expose hidden produce." An on-board computer "analyzes the images, looking for a round bright spot and identifying it as the crop to be picked." Even more impressive, the ROMPER is able to confirm whether or not the crop is ripe to pick by "smell." Special sensors measure ethylene levels—the naturally occurring hormone that causes fruit to ripen—and can "judge" ripeness of the crop to within one day.[27]

During harvesting season more than 30,000 Palestinians are employed by Israeli farmers. The introduction of the ROMPER and other automated machinery is going to dramatically affect their economic prospects. "If we mechanize," says Ezra Sadan, head of the Volcani Research Center, which oversees the Institute of Agricultural Engineering, "we need to accept the fact that many Palestinians will go hungry."[28] In the United States, Purdue University scientists say they expect to see the ROMPER in use in "every Indiana county by the end of the decade."[29] Similar R & D efforts are under way in Western Europe, where scientists hope to introduce automated robots equipped with artificial intelligence and sophisticated sensors, to plow and seed fields.[30]

Robots are also being readied for use in livestock management. The Australian Wool Corporation has been experimenting with a robotized shearing machine that can replace the high cost of professional shearers. The sheep is picked up off the ground and placed in a fixture that resembles an iron cage. The robot is equipped with a computer and a software program for shearing a "generic" sheep. Once in the fixture, the sheep is probed by the robot and the data is fed into the generic program, which then creates a sheep-specific program, to ensure that the robot shearers cut exactly to the girth of the animal being sheared. The automated shears are programmed to "ride just a half centimeter off the quivering sheep's body." An observer explains what comes next: "At this point the sheep is somewhat distraught, breathing heavily, heaving and wriggling around. There is a preferred shearing pattern that involves taking two swipes down the sheep's back and then proceeding to strip the body sides from shorn back to belly. The robot arms must position the shears on a bouncing target and make clean cuts right next to the sheep's skin without inflicting wounds or leaving a punk rocker's hairdo."[31] The robotized sheep shearer is likely to be perfected and fully operational before the end of the decade.

Computerized systems with robotized extensions are already being used to feed dairy cows. Each cow wears a necklace pendant around her neck identifying her. The dairyman enters into a computer each cow's ration number and the amount of grain to be given each day. The cow goes to a feeding station. Her pendant makes contact with a metal plate on the feeder, allowing the computer to identify the specific cow. The computer checks to see if the cow has already eaten her food allotment. If not, the computer activates a motor switch which runs an auger. The auger turns, delivering the grain to the cow.[32]

Scientists are working on even more advanced monitoring systems and computer-controlled handling systems. Researchers say the day is not far off when sensors will be implanted on the skin of the animals to monitor external environmental conditions. Any changes, for example, in the outside environment picked up by the sensors could trigger automated systems to turn on and off lights, fans, water misters, and the like. Changes in blood, milk, and urine content could also be automatically monitored and analyzed by a computer that would in turn dispense the appropriate drug in the feed ration during the animal's next visit to the automated feed station.[33]

Writing in the journal *Science*, Donald A. Holt, associate dean of the University of Illinois College of Agriculture, envisioned a fully automated farm of the future, running virtually by computers and robots much like the new workerless factories coming on-line in Japan. The scene is a Midwest farm on a June morning.

> During the night, the farm computer automatically dialed several local and national databases to obtain information on current fertilizer, seed, fuel, and pesticide supplies and prices, weather, markets, insect and disease predictions, and buyer offers . . . information gathered and processed by the computer during the night appears on the bedroom monitor.
>
> Sensors in nose rings, ear tags, and implanted devices have been scanned to assess the physiological conditions of the farm's animals.
>
> The automatic feed grinders and mixers functioned satisfactorily during the night. All animals were automatically fed and watered, the quantities of feed distributed, recorded, and the amounts consumed by each animal estimated and registered. . . . Environmental conditions in all farm buildings and facilities . . . were monitored continuously during the night and automatically checked against acceptable standards and schedules. Actions to illuminate, darken, heat, cool, dry, humidify, ventilate, and move animal wastes to digesters were initiated by computer. . . . The computer has been scanning by telemetry a number of miniature portable weather stations placed in the fields. . . . On this particular day it anticipates low soil moisture in sands near the river and has activated the pivot irrigation system in that field. . . . One simulator has identified this day as the optimum time in terms of weather conditions and plant growth stage for dealing with foxtail infestation in the soybean field . . . by treating it with a photo-activated herbicide. The herbicide will be applied . . . by high-clearance ground equipment with precise micro-processors control and monitoring of steering, ground speed, pump pressure . . . and application rate of the active ingredient.[34]

Holt goes on to detail other automated production processes on the farm, including the use of computerized harvesting equipment and expert systems designed to assist the farmer with up-to-the-minute financial data and recommendations. Many of the technologies in this scenario already exist and others are in the prototype stage. Researchers predict that the fully automated factory farm is less than twenty years away.

MOLECULAR FARMING

While the new information technologies and robotics are changing the nature of farm management, replacing machines for human labor in virtually every area of activity, the new gene-splicing technologies are changing the very way plants and animals are produced. Genetic engineering is the application of engineering standards to the manipulation of genes. Those engineering standards include quality controls, quantifiable standards of measurement, accuracy, efficiency, and utility. The long-term impacts of the new biotechnologies are likely to be as significant as the impact of "pyrotechnologies" over the course of the first five millennia of recorded history. For thousands of years human beings have been using fire to burn, solder, forge, and melt metallic ores, creating a range of useful materials. Now, for the first time, molecular biologists are able to add, delete, recombine, insert, stitch, and edit together genetic materials across biological boundaries, creating novel new microorganisms, plant strains, and animal breeds that have never before existed in nature. The shift from pyrotechnologies to biotechnologies is epochal, with potentially profound consequences to the way future generations will reshape their relationship to the biosphere.

Although some in the scientific community continue to perceive gene-splicing technology as merely a sophisticated extension of classical breeding techniques, others acknowledge its qualitative break from any known procedures for manipulating nature. We need cite only three examples to illustrate the vast differences that exist between classical breeding and the new gene-splicing techniques.

At the University of Pennsylvania, Dr. Ralph Brinster and a team of researchers inserted human growth-hormone genes into the biological code of mice embryos in vitro. The embryos were implanted into a female mouse and gestated. At birth, the mice contained fully functioning human genes in their biological makeup. The mice with human growth-hormone genes grew to be nearly twice as large as ordinary ones, and passed the human gene into successive generations of their offspring. In a second experiment, scientists inserted the gene that emits light in a firefly into the genetic code of a tobacco plant, forcing the plant to glow twenty-four hours a day. In a third experiment, scientists at the University of California at Davis, using cell-fusion technology, combined the embryonic cells of a sheep and a goat—two unrelated species—and transplanted the embryo to a surrogate sheep that gave birth to a geep. The strange new animal chimera has the head of a goat and the body of a sheep.[35]

None of these experiments could have been accomplished through classical breeding technologies. Although it is possible to use traditional breeding to cross some biological boundaries—for example, crossing a horse and a donkey to create a mule—nature places limits on what is possible. The new gene-splicing and cell-fusion techniques allow scientists to cross virtually all biological boundaries, recombining genes from totally unrelated species. Species are no longer viewed in organismic terms as indivisible entities, but more as mainframes containing programmed genetic cassettes that can be reedited, resequenced and recombined by proper manipulation in the laboratory.

From a production perspective, the importance of gene splicing lies in the ability to manipulate living entities, for the first time, on the level of their component parts—to treat life as an assemblage of individual genetic traits. By eliminating the constraints imposed by biological boundaries, and by reducing microorganisms, plants, and animals to their constituent building blocks, scientists can begin to organize life as a manufactured process.

The tremendous economic potential of biotechnology has drawn chemical, pharmaceutical, agribusiness, and medical companies together into a new life-science complex whose commercial clout is likely to equal or surpass that of the petrochemical complex of the past century. In 1980 the U.S. Supreme Court awarded the first patent on a genetically engineered creature—a microorganism created in the laboratories of General Electric—that was designed and manufactured to eat up oil spills on the high seas. In 1987 the Patent and Trademark Office extended patent protection to any "man-made" creature, recognizing life, for the first time, as a manufacture. Today, thousands of microorganisms and plants have been patented as well as six animals. More than 200 genetically engineered animals are awaiting patent approval at the Patent and Trademark Office. By granting broad patent protection over genetically engineered life forms, the government is giving its imprimatur to the idea that living creatures are reducible to the status of manufactured inventions, subject to the same engineering standards and commercial exploitation as inanimate objects.

The global agribusiness complex hopes to make the transition from petrochemical-based agriculture to gene-based agriculture in the coming century. Toward this end, researchers and corporations are engineering thousands of new plant varieties and animal breeds in the laboratory. As in other manufacturing processes, the primary goal is to increase productivity and lessen labor requirements.

To eliminate the cost of insecticides and the labor required to monitor and spray crops, scientists are engineering pest-resistant genes directly into the biological codes of plants. Researchers have isolated and cloned the gene that codes for the toxin in a spore-forming bacterium called *Bacillus thuringiensis* (Bt) and inserted it into the biological makeup of tobacco, tomatoes, cotton, and other plant crops. The transgenic plants produce a continuous supply of the Bt toxin that kills invading insects.[36]

Scientists have also successfully inserted genes into plants that make them resistant to common herbicides. Monsanto has created genetically engineered plants that are resistant to the company's own herbicide—Roundup. The company has patented the new genetic strains and hopes to market both the patented seeds and the herbicide together as a single package.[37]

Other companies are experimenting with transferring genes into plants that make them better able to tolerate drought or extreme heat and cold. Scientists have implanted a frost-resistant gene from a fish into the genetic code of a tomato plant in hopes of conferring frost resistance. The ability to insert specific genes into plants to improve their tolerance to drought, heat, and cold could save billions of dollars in equipment and labor costs by reducing the need to build, install, and manage expensive irrigation systems and frost-protection equipment. Researchers have even transferred nitrogen-fixing genes to non-nitrogen-fixing crops. Molecular biologists look to the day when such genetically engineered crops will substantially reduce the need for nitrogen fertilizers as well as the labor required to manufacture, transport, and apply the chemicals on the soil.[38]

Genetic engineering is also being used to increase animal productivity and reduce labor requirements in animal husbandry. Bovine Growth Hormone (also known as Bovine Somatotropin) is a naturally occurring hormone that stimulates the production of milk in cows. Scientists have successfully isolated the key growth-stimulating gene and cloned industrial portions in the laboratory. The genetically engineered growth hormone is then injected back into the cow, forcing the animal to produce between 10 and 20 percent more milk. Four companies, Monsanto, American Cyanamid, Eli Lilly and Upjohn, have spent more than a billion dollars in research and development to bring the controversial product to market.

By greatly increasing the productivity of dairy cows, genetically engineered BGH threatens the livelihood of thousands of dairy farmers in North America, Europe, and elsewhere. Most industrial nations are already overproducing milk. Faced with a milk glut, depressed prices, and ineffective demand, the United States and other industrial nations have long pursued a policy of price supports and subsidies to keep dairy farmers in business. Now, with the commercial introduction of BGH in the United States, even more milk will be produced, requiring even greater price supports. According to a report prepared by the Office of Management and Budget (OMB) for the Clinton administration, the government's milk-support program will increase by more than $116,000,000 a year in 1995 because of the introduction of BGH into the market.[39] Another study conducted several years ago predicted that within three years of the introduction of BGH into the marketplace, upwards of one third of all remaining U.S. dairy farmers may be forced out of business because of overproduction, falling prices, and dwindling consumer demand.[40]

Many industry analysts argue that BGH will benefit the giant corporate dairy farms in California at the expense of small family farms in states like Wisconsin and Minnesota. The large operations are highly automated and can produce more milk with fewer cows, significantly reducing the amount of human labor required to get the milk to market. To increase productivity even further, researchers are currently experimenting with insertion of a revved-up growth-hormone gene directly into the biological code of the animal at the embryonic stage of development so that the adult animal will produce more milk without needing injections.

Swine producers are experimenting with a porcine growth hormone (PST) designed to increase feed efficiency and weight gain in pigs. According to a recent report published by the Office of Technology Assessment (OTA), "Pigs administered porcine somatotropin (PST) for a period of 30 to 77 days show increased average daily weight gains of approximately 10 to 20 percent, improved feed efficiency of 15 to 35 percent, decreased adipose (fat) tissue mass and lipid formation rates of as much as 50 to 80 percent . . . without adversely affecting the quality of the meat."[41]

At the University of Adelaide in Australia, scientists have succeeded in producing genetically engineered pigs that are 30 percent more efficient and brought to market seven weeks earlier than normal pigs. A faster production schedule will mean less labor is required to produce a pound of flesh. The Australian Commonwealth Scientific and Industrial Research Organization has produced genetically engineered sheep that grow 30 percent faster than normal ones, and are currently working on transplanting genes into the genetic code of sheep to make their wool grow faster.[42] Scientists have even transferred human and bovine genes to fish to create faster-growing transgenic salmon, carp, and trout. In one study, the trout somatotropin gene was transferred to other fish, increasing their growth by 22 percent.[43]

In 1993 researchers at the University of Wisconsin announced a successful attempt to increase the productivity of brooding hens by deleting the gene that codes for the protein prolactin. Scientists were concerned that mother hens were spending too much time sitting on their eggs. Brooding hens lay one quarter to one third fewer eggs than nonbrooding ones. Since up to 20 percent of an average flock is made up of brooding hens, "broodiness disrupts production and costs producers a lot of money." By eliminating the prolactin hormone, researchers were able to curtail the natural brooding instinct in hens. The new genetically engineered hens no longer exhibit the mothering instinct. They do, however, produce more eggs.[44]

Transgenic animals are also being created in the laboratory to serve as chemical factories, producing useful drugs in their milk and blood. A new field, "pharming," has emerged over the past decade and promises to revolutionize the way drugs are made. Researchers have successfully inserted human genes into sheep embryos that will cause the mature adult sheep to produce the human protein alpha-1-antitrypsin. Antitrypsin is used to fight emphysema and is normally extracted from human blood serum, but in such small amounts that it cannot meet the demand. At Pharmaceutical Proteins Limited (PPL) in Edinburgh, Scotland, scientists have produced transgenic sheep that can churn out antitrypsin at levels fifteen times what can be produced by blood plasma. The productivity gains are so spectacular that a flock of 1,000 ewes "could match the entire world production of the protein."[45]

Scientists at Virginia Polytechnic and State University have created transgenic pigs that produce protein C in their milk—protein C is an anticoagulant that has medical promise as a pharmaceutical to help stroke and heart attack victims.[46] Other transgenic pharm animals are being created in laboratories around the world. Pharmaceutical companies hope to raise productivity, increase their profit margins, and significantly reduce their laboratory workforce by shifting over, where possible, to pharm husbandry.

All of the breakthroughs in gene splicing depend on the efforts of computers and sophisticated information technologies. The computer and its software are the means used to decipher, isolate, and analyze genetic information and are indispensable in the creation of new transgenic farm animals and plants. The computer, then, is the critical tool used to manipulate "living systems" on both the macro and micro level and will be increasingly relied on to assist in farm management as well as in the engineering of new farm crops and animal breeds.

THE END OF OUTDOOR AGRICULTURE

The coming together of the computer revolution and the biotechnology revolution into a single technological complex foreshadows a new era of food production—one divorced from land, climate, and changing seasons, long the conditioning agents of agricultural output. In the coming half century, traditional agriculture is likely to wane, a victim of technological forces that are fast replacing outdoor farming with manipulation of molecules in the laboratory. While the first technological revolution in agriculture replaced animal power and human labor with machinery and chemicals, an emerging biotechnology revolution is soon going to replace land cultivation with laboratory cultures, changing forever the way the world views the production of food. Authors David Goodman, Bernardo Sorj, and John Wilkinson sum up the historical significance of the changes occurring in worldwide agricultural production:

> The emerging nexus between biotechnology and automation increasingly will transform the food industry into a high-technology sector, facilitating its incorporation within a larger generic raw materials transformation industry. . . . The farmer will give way to the 'bio-manager' and observation will be replaced by "software." Biotechnology and information technologies therefore go hand in hand to create the new production process in agriculture. In this perspective, biotechnology and micro-electronics mark the end of the pre-history of the food industry and its incorporation within the broader dynamics of the industrial system and post-industrial society.[47]

Chemical companies are already investing heavily in indoor tissue-culture production in the hope of removing farming from the soil by the early decades of the twenty-first century. Recently, two U.S.-based biotechnology firms announced they had successfully produced vanilla from plant-cell cultures in the laboratory. Vanilla is the most popular flavor in America. One third of all the ice cream sold in the United States is vanilla. Over 98 percent of the world's vanilla crop is grown in the small island countries of Madagascar, Reunion, and Comoros. In Madagascar alone, which produces more than 70 percent of the world's harvest, 70,000 peasant farmers rely on this single crop for their livelihood.[48] Vanilla, however, is expensive to produce. The vanilla orchard has to be hand-pollinated and requires special attention in the harvesting and curing process. Now, the new gene-splicing technologies allow researchers to produce commercial volumes of vanilla in laboratory vats—by isolating the gene that codes for the vanilla protein and cloning it in a bacterial bath—eliminating the bean, the plant, the soil, the cultivation, the harvest, and the farmer.

Pat Mooney, of the Rural Advancement Fund International (RAFI), and Cary Fowler, of the United Nations Food and Agriculture Organization (FAO), who have written extensively on the potential impact that the new biotechnologies will have on third-world economies, explain how the tissue-cell process works: "The basic technique used to produce vanilla flavor by means of tissue culture technology involves the selection of high-yielding cell tissue from the vanilla plant. The cell tissues are then propagated in suspended cultures. Careful regulation of culture conditions, nutrient mediums, and metabolic regulators are then used to induce the production of the desired chemical flavored compound—vanilla."[49]

Escagenetics, a start-up biotechnology company headquartered in San Carlos, California, has produced vanilla in tissue culture at a fraction of the cost of producing natural vanilla. While natural vanilla sells on the world market for about $1,200 per pound, Escagenetics says it can sell its genetically engineered version for less than $25 per pound. The company has recently applied for patent protection on its laboratory-produced vanilla. With the worldwide market for vanilla approaching $200 million, companies like Escagenetics are eager to bring their product to market, convinced that it will drive farm-grown vanilla out of business.[50]

For the tiny island nations of the Indian Ocean, the indoor farming of vanilla is likely to mean economic catastrophe. The export of vanilla beans accounts for more than 10 percent of the total annual export earnings of Madagascar. In Comoros, vanilla represents two thirds of the country's export earnings. Altogether, more than 100,000 farmers in the three vanilla-producing countries are expected to lose their livelihood over the next several decades.[51]

Vanilla is only the beginning. The global market for food flavors is hovering near $3 billion and is expected to grow at a rate of 30 percent or more a year.[52] Eager to cash in on new biotechnologies that promise to greatly reduce operating costs and raise productivity and profits, other companies are looking to tissue-cell-culture food-production practices. Several biotechnology firms are currently concentrating on the laboratory production of thaumatin—a sweetener derived from the fruit of the thaumatin plant, grown in West Africa. Thaumatin is the sweetest substance yet discovered in nature, and in its pure form is 100,000 times sweeter than sugar. In the mid-1980s the gene that codes for the thaumatin protein was successfully cloned by scientists at Unilever in the Netherlands and at Ingene in Santa Monica, California.[53]

The laboratory production of thaumatin and other sweeteners is likely to further weaken the worldwide sugar market, which has already been hurt by the introduction of corn sweeteners and sugar substitutes like NutraSweet. Sugar imports to the United States declined from $686 million in 1981 to $250 million in 1985.[54] According to a Dutch study, upwards of 10 million farmers in the third world may face a loss of livelihood as laboratory-produced sweeteners begin invading world markets in the next several years.[55]

Scientists are just beginning to explore the great potential of tissue-culture production in the laboratory. Researchers have successfully grown orange and lemon vesicles from tissue culture, and some industry analysts believe that the day is not far off when orange juice will be grown in vats, eliminating the need for planting orange groves.[56]

Recently, researchers at the Department of Agriculture "tricked" loose cotton cells into growing by immersing them in a vat of nutrients. Because the cotton is grown under sterile conditions, free of microbial contamination, scientists say it could be used to make sterile gauze.[57] Although the production of cotton in vitro did not use gene-splicing technology, it provides still another example of the potential of reducing agricultural commodities to their component parts and then mass-producing them.

Tissue culture is seen by many as the inevitable next stage of a process that has continued to reduce the market share of farming in the food-production system. For the better part of the twentieth century, farming has declined in importance as an increasing number of its activities have been expropriated by the input sector on the one end and the marketing sector on the other. For example, chemical fertilizers have replaced animal manuring on the farm. Commercial pesticides have replaced crop rotation, mechanical tillage, and hand weeding. Tractors have replaced horses and manual labor. Today only a handful of farmers package their own produce or transport it to retail markets. These functions have been increasingly taken over by agri-business companies.

Now, chemical and pharmaceutical companies hope to use genetic-engineering technologies to eliminate the farmer altogether. The goal is to convert food production into a wholly industrial process by bypassing both the organism and the outdoors, and "farming" at the molecular level in the factory. Martin H. Rogoff and Stephen L. Rawlins, biologists and research administrators with the Department of Agriculture, envision a food-production system in which fields would be planted only with perennial biomass crops. The crops would be harvested and converted to sugar solution by the use of enzymes. The solution would then be piped to urban factories and used as a nutrient source to produce large quantities of pulp from tissue cultures. The pulp would then be reconstituted and fabricated into different shapes and textures to mimic the traditional forms associated with "soil-grown" crops. Rawlins says that the new factories would be highly automated and require few workers.[58]

Indoor tissue-culture food production will eliminate millions of jobs along the entire agricultural grid. In addition to making most farmers redundant—a small percentage of them will still be required to manage biomass crops—continuous-process food production will eliminate jobs in auxiliary industries related to the farm sector, including the manufacturers of farm equipment and long-distance haulers.

The advantages, argue the proponents of tissue-culture farming, include reduced use of land, less soil erosion, less agrichemicals, and reduced energy and transportation costs. Continuous-process production in the laboratory also means that production can be regulated to daily market demand and not be dependent on the uncertainties of climate, seasonal disruptions, and political influences. With the new laboratory processes, multinationals will be able to exert far greater economic control over world markets, with far less risks to themselves. Controlling genes in the laboratory is far less troublesome than controlling climate, land, and workers in a third-world country. *Food Technology* magazine summed up the economic and political advantages of the revolutionary new approach to food production: "Many of our flavors and other products come from remote parts of the world, where the political instability of governments or the vagaries of weather yield inconsistent supply, cost, and product quality from season to season. In a plant tissue culture process, all parameters . . . can be controlled."[59]

The era of whole-commodities food production is likely to decline in the decades ahead as chemical, pharmaceutical, and biotech companies are able to increasingly substitute tissue-culture production, significantly lowering the price of food products on world markets. The economic impact on farmers, especially in the third world, could be catastrophic. Many third-world nations rely on the sale of one or two key export crops. Tissue-culture substitution could mean the near collapse of national economies, unprecedented unemployment, and default on international loans, which, in turn, could lead to the destabilization of commercial banking and to bank failures in first-world nations.[60]

The recent technological breakthroughs in world agriculture promise increased productivity and reductions in labor requirements more spectacular than any comparable technology revolution in world history. The human price of commercial progress is likely to be staggering. Hundreds of millions of farmers across the globe face the prospect of permanent elimination from the economic process. Their marginalization could lead to social upheaval on a global scale and the reorganization of social and political life along radically new lines in the coming century.

The specter of the world's farmers being made redundant and irrelevant by the computer and biotechnology revolutions is deeply troubling. Even more unsettling, the manufacturing and service sectors, which have traditionally absorbed displaced rural workers, are undergoing their own technology revolution, shedding millions of jobs to make room for re-engineered, highly automated work environments. Transnationals are entering a new era of fast communications, lean-production practices, and just-in-time marketing and distribution operations relying increasingly on a new generation of silicon-collar workers. Much of the human workforce is being left behind and will likely never cross over into the new high-tech global economy.

· 9 ·

Hanging Up
the Blue Collar

IN HIS AUTOBIOGRAPHY, America's first great labor leader, Samuel Gompers, recalled an experience in early childhood that was to have a profound effect in shaping his lifelong efforts on behalf of working men and women. "One of my most vivid early recollections is the great trouble that came to the silk weavers when machinery was invented to replace their skill and take their jobs. No thought was given to these men whose trade was gone. Misery and suspense filled the neighborhood with a depressing air of dread. The narrow streets echoed with the tramp of men walking in groups with no work to do."[1]

From the very beginning of the Industrial Revolution, machines and inanimate forms of energy have been used to boost production and reduce the amount of labor required to make a product. As early as the 1880s, manufacturers such as the American Tobacco Company, Quaker Oats, Pillsbury, Diamond Match, Campbell Soup, Procter & Gamble, H. J. Heinz, and Eastman Kodak began experimenting with "continuous-process" machinery in manufacturing. This machinery required little human tending and turned out a massive volume of goods more or less automatically. Workers merely fed materials into it and let the equipment shape, mold, and package the product.

In 1881 James Bonsack patented a cigarette machine that rolled cigarettes automatically without human labor. The machine "swept the tobacco onto the 'endless tape,' compressed it into a round form, wrapped it with tape and paper, carried it to a 'covering tube' which shaped the cigarette, pasted the paper, and then cut the resulting rod into the length of cigarette desired." By the late 1880s the continuous-process machine was producing 120,000 cigarettes per day. Most skilled hand-workers were only able to make at best some 3,000 cigarettes per day. So productive was the new equipment that fewer than thirty machines could fulfill the entire national demand for cigarettes in 1885, using only a handful of workers.[2]

The Diamond Match Company introduced continuous-process machinery in 1881, and was soon producing billions of matches automatically. About the same time, Procter & Gamble introduced continuous manufacturing into the production of soap, making its new product, Ivory, a household name within less than a decade. George Eastman invented a continuous-process method for making photographic negatives, propelling his company to national prominence. Pillsbury and other grain companies introduced continuous-process machinery into milling, producing high-quality flour in large volume and at a low cost, again using far less labor in the process.[3]

The continuous-process technologies introduced a radical new approach to manufacturing. The idea of automatic machinery producing goods with little or no human input was no longer just a utopian dream. Today, the new information and communication technologies are making possible far more sophisticated continuous-process manufacturing.

AUTOMATING THE AUTOMOBILE

Some of the most dramatic breakthroughs in re-engineering and technology displacement are occurring in the automotive industry. As noted earlier, post-Fordism is rapidly transforming the automobile industry around the world. At the same time, post-Fordist restructuring is resulting in massive layoffs of blue collar workers on the assembly line. The world's largest manufacturing activity, auto manufacturers produce more than 50 million new vehicles each year. Peter Drucker once christened auto manufacturing "the industry of industries."[4] The automobile and its related industrial enterprises are responsible for generating one out of every twelve manufacturing jobs in the United States and are serviced by more than 50,000 satellite suppliers. One enthusiastic supporter in the 1930s exclaimed, "Think of the results to the industrial world of putting on the market a product that doubles the malleable iron consumption, triples the plate-glass consumption, and quadruples the use of rubber. . . . As a consumer of raw material, the automobile has no equal in the history of the world."[5]

The importance of the automobile to the global economy and jobs is unquestionable. From the time Henry Ford installed the first moving assembly line, automakers have experimented with thousands of innovations to increase production and reduce labor in the production process. Ford himself took pride in his company's ability to substitute technology for physical labor, and was continually engaged in finding new ways to reduce tasks to simple effortless operations. He claimed in his autobiography, *My Life and Work,* that while producing a Model T required 7,882 distinct tasks, only 949 of those tasks required "strong able bodied, and practically physically perfect men." As to the rest of the tasks, Ford claimed that "670 could be filled by legless men, 2,637 by one legged men, two by armless men, 715 by one-armed men, and ten by blind men."[6]

Ford's vision of an assembly line is advancing rapidly, and the Japanese are leading the way. Industry experts predict that by the end of the current decade, Japanese-owned factories will be able to produce a finished automobile in less than eight hours.[7] The shortening of production time means far fewer workers are required on the line.[8]

Following Japan's lead, U.S. automakers are beginning to re-engineer their own operations in the hope of increasing productivity, reducing labor rolls, and improving on their market share and profit margin. In 1993 General Motors president John F. Smith, Jr., announced plans to implement much-needed re-engineering reforms at GM plants and estimated that the changes in production practices could eliminate as many as 90,000 auto jobs, or one third of its workforce, by the late 1990s. These new cuts come on top of the 250,000 jobs GM has already eliminated since 1978.[9]

Other global automakers are also re-engineering their operations and eliminating large numbers of workers. Mercedes-Benz announced in September of 1993 that it would seek to increase efficiency in its facilities by 15 percent in 1994, and would cut more than 14,000 jobs. By 1995 industry analysts predict that German automakers could eliminate as many as one in seven jobs. This in a country where 10 percent of the entire industrial workforce is either in the automotive industry or services it.[10]

Automakers view labor-displacing technology as their best bet to reduce costs and improve profit performance. Despite the fact that labor costs are less than 10 to 15 percent of total costs, they represent a larger percentage of sales than do profits, and are easily reducible with the substitution of new information technologies. The International Labor Organization of the United Nations estimates that by reducing labor costs in half, global automakers could triple their profits. GM hopes that by eliminating one fourth of its workforce and re-engineering its operations, it can save more than $5 billion a year by 1995.[11]

Robots are becoming increasingly attractive as a cost-cutting alternative to human labor on the automobile assembly line. The Japanese, far ahead of other automakers, have robotized much of their production lines. Mazda Motor Corporation announced in 1993 that it was targeting a 30 percent automation of final assembly at its new Hofu Japan plant. The company hopes to have a 50 percent automated final assembly line by the year 2000.[12] As the new generation of "smart" robots, armed with greater intelligence and flexibility, make their way to the market, automakers are far more likely to substitute them for workers because they are most cost effective. The trade journal *Machinery and Production Engineering* stated the corporate view in blunt terms: "The payment of higher wages to workers who cannot be described by any standards as anything more elevated than machine minders is rapidly becoming unattractive, and where a man is employed solely for unloading one machine and loading another . . . the substitution of a robot is not only a glaringly obvious course but also increasingly easy to justify financially. Moreover a robot is not subject to the random variations in performance . . . and is for all practical purposes working as hard, as conscientiously, and as consistently at the end of the shift as it is at the beginning."[13]

Industrial engineers are currently developing even more advanced machine surrogates "with such capabilities as voice communication, a general purpose programming language, learning from experience, three-dimensional vision with color sensitivity, multiple hand to hand coordination, walking and self-navigating skills, and self-diagnostic and correction skills." The goal, says sociologist Michael Wallace, "is to approach, as closely as possible, the human capabilities to process environmental data and to solve problems, while avoiding the problems (e.g. absenteeism and turnover) presented by human agents."[14]

It is estimated that each robot replaces four jobs in the economy, and if in constant use twenty-four hours a day, will pay for itself in just over one year.[15] In 1991, according to the International Federation of

Robotics, the world's robot population stood at 630,000. That number is expected to rise dramatically in the coming decades as thinking machines become far more intelligent, versatile, and flexible.[16]

COMPUTING STEEL

While the global auto industry is quickly re-engineering its operations and investing in new labor-displacing information technologies, related industries are doing the same, eliminating more and more jobs in the process.

The steel industry's fortunes are so closely linked to those of the automotive industry that it is not surprising to see the same sweeping changes in organization and production taking place in steel as are occurring in the car business. The steel industry is the heart and soul of industrial power. The great steel mills of England, Germany, and the United States provided the material infrastructure for the modern industrial economy. Giant blast furnaces in industrial towns like Sheffield, Essen, and Pittsburgh converted massive amounts of iron ore into smooth rolled steel that was used to make rails, build frames for locomotives and later automobiles, cast girders for giant sky-scrapers and factories and, in the United States, roll barbed wire to fence the great plains of the Western range.

By the 1890s the United States was the leader in steel production. Andrew Carnegie's furnaces, the largest in the world, were producing 2,000 tons per week. At the turn of the century, a modern American rolling mill was producing as much steel in a day as a midcentury mill produced in a year.[17]

Steel was king of the smokestack industries and the price of entry for every country that desired to become part of the industrial club. America enjoyed pre-eminence in steel production by dint of its superior technologies and organizational methods and its access to cheap raw materials and continent-wide markets. Today, that competitive edge has been seriously eroded, in large part because of the failure of U.S. companies to keep up with the new technologies of the information revolution that have remade the steel industry.

Authors Martin Kenney and Richard Florida contrast two very different steel factories located within an hour of each other in America's rust belt. The first is a sprawling complex of old rusted buildings and sheds housing hundreds of workers toiling in near-Dickensian conditions. Caked with grease and grime, they tend aged steel furnaces, transforming molten metal into steel slabs. The muddied floors are cluttered with rusted-out parts, abandoned tools, and chemical containers. The noise is deafening. The steel is moved by overhead chains across the cavernous factory, as supervisors shout commands to each other, often amidst the confused coming and going of material and men. Outside the factory, broken-down machines and trucks are visible and piles of rusted steel slabs and coils litter the property.

The second mill is a gleaming white structure that looks more like a laboratory than a factory. Inside are brightly colored machines turning out sheets of steel. In the center of the factory is a glass-enclosed booth full of computer and electronic equipment. Workers in clean, crisp uniforms program and monitor the computers that oversee and control the production process. None of the men handle the steel directly. The process itself is nearly fully automated and produces cold rolled steel in less than one hour. The same process in an older integrated steel mill used to take as much as twelve days.[18]

The computerized mill belongs to Nippon Steel, which, along with other Japanese steel manufacturers like Kawasaki, Sumitomo, and Kobe, are opening up plants in the United States, some in partnership with American steel companies. The new high-technology mills have successfully transformed steelmaking from a batch process to a highly automated continuous operation by combining formerly separated procedures into a single operation that is similar to the production of rolls of paper in a paper factory.[19]

In the traditional cold-rolling process, thick steel coils are taken through a number of discrete steps and transformed into thinner sheet steel for use in automobiles, refrigerators, washing machines, and other household appliances. First, the steel coils are taken to a machine that scrapes the rust and oxidation off the surface. Then the steel is carried to another machine that bathes it in a chemical solution to complete the cleaning process. From there, the steel is taken to a machine for drying, after which it is sent to still another machine for pressing to the desired thickness. Finally, the steel is cut and prepared.[20]

Nippon and other Japanese steel producers have collapsed all of these discrete stages into a uniform flow and in so doing revolutionized steelmaking. They began by combining the entry and scraping processes. They then combined the cleaning and drying processes. Computer controls were added to automate production. Nippon's new

$400 million cold rolling mill near Gary, Indiana—a joint venture with Inland Steel—is run by a small team of technicians. By reducing production time from twelve days to one hour at the new automated facility, Inland's management was able to significantly reduce its work-force, closing down two older mills and laying off hundreds of workers.[21]

Employment in the steel industry has also been dramatically affected by the introduction of mini-mills. These new computerized, highly automated factories use electric arc furnaces to convert scrap steel into wire rods and bar products. Much cheaper to operate than integrated steel mills, the new mini-mills are already producing one third of all the steel in the United States. The high-tech workforce in the mini-mills is few in number and skilled in chemistry, metallurgy, and computer programming. With its computerized manufacturing process, the mini-mill can produce a ton of steel with less than one twelfth the human labor of a giant integrated steel mill.[22]

The increasing automation of steel production has left thousands of blue collar workers jobless. In 1980 United States Steel, the largest integrated steel company in the United States, employed 120,000 workers. By 1990 it was producing roughly the same output using only 20,000.[23] These numbers are projected to fall even further in the next ten to twenty years as new, even more advanced, computerized opera-tions are introduced into the manufacturing process.

The new, highly automated manufacturing methods are being combined with radical restructuring of the management hierarchy to bring steelmaking into the era of lean production. Job classifications in the steel industry have become so complex and labyrinthine over the years that even those responsible for overseeing the process aren't exactly sure how many separate categories and demarcations exist. In some companies there are between 300 and 400 different job classi-fications. Japanese companies, with joint ventures in United States, have re-engineered traditional plant operations and slashed job clas-sifications in the process. At the LTV-Sumitomo plant, the job catego-ries have been reduced from one hundred to three. The new classifica-tions are "entry-level," "intermediate," and "advanced."[24] Workers have been taken off hourly wages and put on salaries. New self-managing work teams have been given greater control over the shop floor, significantly reducing the number of managers on the payroll. Management hierarchies have also been flattened. Inland Steel has reduced its management layers from ten to six.[25] The same re-engineering process is at work in steel plants around the world.

According to the International Labor Organization, finished steel output from 1974 to 1989 dropped only 6 percent in the Organization for Economic Cooperation and Development (OECD) countries while employment fell by more than 50 percent. More than one million jobs were lost in the steel industry in OECD nations during this fifteen-year period. "In up to 90 percent of the cases," says the ILO, "the basic explanation for the reduction in employment is therefore not changes in the level of output but improvement in productivity."[26]

Other industries that use steel to make products are also undergoing a fundamental overhaul, reflecting the new emphasis on lean-production practices. The metalworking-machinery industry is a good case in point. Just three decades ago the International Association of Machinists posted a sign over the front door of their union's headquarters in Washington, D.C., saying ONE MILLION STRONG. Over the subsequent years the sign remained, while the number of machinists in the country dwindled to less than 600,000.[27]

William Winpisinger, the former president of the IAM, catalogues the many revolutionary changes in materials and technologies that have shrunk the ranks of skilled machinists around the world. He cites the example of bars of raw steel that have traditionally been cut, ground, deburred, and polished by expert machinists to make components for aircraft engines. Today, powderized metals are merely poured from bags—like cement mix—into pressurized molds which shape the component parts. In some instances lightweight ceramics and plastics are substituted for powderized metals and put through the same mold process.[28] Making precision-made parts from molds and casts has eliminated the jobs of thousands of skilled machinists.

The metalworking-machinery industry encompasses a range of subindustries including metal-forming machine tools, rolling-mill machinery, welding apparatus, metal-cutting machine tools, special dies, jigs, and fixtures.[29] In all of these industries computerized, numerically controlled machine tools; computer-aided design, manufacturing and engineering systems; flexible manufacturing cells; and automated sensor-based inspection equipment have reduced the need for skilled machinists. Winpisinger says that while we shouldn't "stand in the way of advances which make work easier . . . we have to prepare to take care of those workers who may be displaced by the new technology."[30]

Between 1979 and 1990, employment in the metalworking industry declined by an average annual rate of 1.7 percent. The Bureau of Labor Statistics predicts an overall loss of an additional 14,000 workers by the year 2005. For operators, fabricators, and laborers the decline in employment is expected to be even higher, reaching 14 percent between now and the first decade of the coming century.[31] In countries such as Germany, where skilled machinists are a national treasure and much revered for their expert craftsmanship, the new automated processes are likely to have a powerful psychological as well as economic impact on the national economy.

THE SILICON-COLLAR WORKFORCE

In industry after industry, companies are replacing human labor with machinery, and in the process changing the nature of industrial production. One of the industries most affected by re-engineering and the new information-based technologies is rubber. Kenney and Florida recount the story of a Firestone Tire facility in La Vergne, Tennessee. Conditions in the plant were so poor, said one union official, that it "made it difficult to believe that tires could actually be produced there."[32] Although this plant was one of Firestone's most technologically advanced facilities, poor management-labor relations had so poisoned the work environment over the years that production had nearly ground to a halt. The factory floor was so disorganized and unclean that foreign materials like cigarette butts, nails, and paper cups would become embedded in tires.

In 1982 Bridgestone, a Japanese rubber producer, acquired the Firestone facility and immediately began re-engineering the operations to conform with its own high standards of lean production. It introduced work teams, flattened the organizational hierarchy from eight to five levels, reduced job classifications, instituted job-retraining programs to improve quality control, and invested $70 million in new equipment designed to automate the production process. In less than five years, the production increased from 16,400 to 82,175 tires per month. In the same time period, the production of tires with blemishes declined by 86 percent.[33]

Goodyear, a company long associated with quality tires in the United States, claims a similar success story. Goodyear earned a record $352 million in 1992 on sales of $11.8 billion. The company is producing 30 percent more tires than in 1988 with 24,000 fewer employees.[34]

The Bridgestone and Goodyear experience is being duplicated in other tire plants around the world. In the United Kingdom, Sumitomo, another Japanese tire producer, acquired Dunlop facilities and converted them to lean-production practices. Today, productivity has increased by more than 40 percent with 30 percent fewer workers.[35]

The extractive industries have also been affected by automation. In 1992, 45,000 jobs were eliminated in mining in the United States.[36] Mining, like agriculture, has been undergoing a steady process of technology displacement for nearly seventy years. In 1925, 588,000 men, nearly 1.3 percent of the nation's entire workforce, mined 520 million tons of bituminous coal and lignite. In 1982 fewer than 208,000 men and women produced more than 774 million tons of coal.[37] With the use of advanced computer technology, faster excavating and transportation equipment, improved blasting technologies, and new processing methods, mining companies have been able to increase output at an average annual rate of 3 percent since 1970.[38]

The increasing automation of the mining industry has resulted in the loss of tens of thousands of jobs in the coal producing regions of the country. By the first decade of the coming century, fewer than 113,200 people—a labor force 24 percent smaller than at present—will produce all of the coal needed to meet both domestic and overseas demand.[39]

Like mining, the chemical refining industry has also been substituting machines for human labor. Texaco's Port Arthur refinery was the first chemical facility to introduce digital computer control in 1959. Between 1959 and 1964, productivity soared and the number of workers in the chemical industry declined from 112,500 to 81,900 as companies like Monsanto and Goodrich turned their operations over to digital computer control. The dramatic changes in production practices brought about by computerization and continuous-process operations became apparent to the Oil, Atomic and Chemical Workers Union when their members struck oil-refining facilities in the early 1960s. Walkouts failed to significantly slow production at the new automated factories. The plants virtually ran themselves.[40] In the succeeding years, the chemical industry continued to automate its production facilities, laying off more and more workers. From 1990 to mid-1992, productivity increased while the number of production and supervisory personnel declined by 6 percent of the industry's entire workforce. Today, as Harry Braverman points out, "the work of the chemical operator is generally clean," and it has to do with "reading instruments" and "keeping charts."[41]

Not surprisingly, some of the most significant strides in

re-engineering and automation have occurred in the electronic industry. General Electric, a world leader in electronic manufacturing, has reduced worldwide employment from 400,000 in 1981 to less than 230,000 in 1993, while tripling its sales. GE flattened its managerial hierarchy in the 1980s and began to introduce new highly automated equipment on the factory floor. At the GE Fanuc Automation Plant in Charlottesville, Virginia, new high-technology equipment "places electronic components into circuit boards in half the time of the older technology."[42]

At the Victor Company in Japan, automated vehicles deliver camcorder components and materials to sixty-four robots which in turn perform 150 different assembly and inspection tasks. Only two human beings are present on the factory floor. Before the introduction of intelligent machines and robots, 150 workers were required to manufacture the camcorders at Victor.[43]

In the household appliance industry new high-technology equipment, including computer-aided design, engineering, and manufacturing systems, robots and automated conveyors and transport systems are increasing productivity and eliminating jobs at every stage of the production process. Between 1973 and 1991, output in the household appliance industry in the United States increased at an annual rate of 0.5 percent. In the same time period, output per employee-hour increased at an average rate of 2.7 percent. As in other industries, productivity gains resulting from the introduction of new labor- and time-saving technologies has meant a decline in employment. Between 1973 and 1991, employment declined sharply from 196,300 to 117,100, and the Bureau of Labor Statistics expects it to continue to shrink. By the year 2005, a mere 93,500 workers—fewer than half the number employed in 1973—will be producing the nation's total output of home appliances.[44]

The loss of production workers by product category in the appliance industry is staggering. In 1973, 49,000 workers were employed in the refrigeration and freezer industry. By 1991 the number had fallen to 25,700, for an average annual decline of 3.5 percent. Laundry equipment manufacturers reduced their workforce from 28,300 in 1973 to 20,600 in 1991. In the electric housewares and fans industry, employment declined in the same period from 56,300 to 31,000. According to the Department of Labor, "Virtually none of this employment decline has resulted from growing imports or falling demand."[45] In a detailed study of the home appliance industry, the department found that, "despite these employment declines, the electrical housewares and fans industrial segment is a major success story in manufacturing. The continuing strength of demand for housewares and fans reflect attractive prices and a significant expansion in the number of products available to consumers."[46]

No industry is more associated with the Industrial Revolution than textiles. More than 200 years ago the first steam-powered machines were applied to the spinning of wool in England, launching a revolution in the way goods are produced. Today, while other industries have raced ahead into the age of automation, textiles has lagged behind, in large part because of the labor-intensiveness of the sewing process.

A study of the garment industry found that it takes upwards of sixty-six weeks for a garment style to move from design and fiber production to retail distribution. The long lead times and slow delivery schedules cost the industry more than $25 billion a year in lost potential sales. Most of the losses occur at the retail end, when stores are forced to mark down goods because of changes in fashion or changing seasons. Lost sales potential also results from out-of-stock items.[47]

In recent years, however, textile manufacturing has begun to catch up with other manufacturing industries by introducing lean-production practices and advanced computer automation systems. The goal is to introduce flexible manufacturing and just-in-time delivery so that orders can be "tailor-made" to individual consumer demand. Some companies, like England's Allied Textile Co., Parkland Textile Co., and Courtaulds, have begun to introduce robotization into their manufacturing process. Computer-aided design (CAD) has reduced the design time for a garment from weeks to minutes. Computerized dying and finishing systems have also been introduced. Computerized systems are also streamlining the storage, handling, packing, and shipping of garments.[48]

Although the sewing of garments still remains labor-intensive, companies have been able to cut production time in other areas of the manufacturing process. Some now use computerized automated cloth laying and cutting machines. Microelectronic sewing machines have also been introduced into the sewing rooms, helping deliver a preprogrammed number of stitches accompanied by an automatic cutoff upon completion.[49] Jack Sheinkman, president of the Amalgamated Clothing and Textile Workers Union, says that textile is fast becoming "a high-tech industry." According to Sheinkman, "the labor component has been reduced significantly" in recent years and accounts for little more than 30 percent of the production process. The rest of the process is automated."[50]

The new technologies are beginning to make garment manufacturing in the industrial nations cost-competitive with firms operating in low-wage countries. As more and more of the manufacturing process bends to re-engineering and automation, even third-world exporters, like China and India, will be forced to shift over from current labor-intensive manufacturing processes to cheaper and faster methods of mechanized production.

The automation of "high end" manufacturing—the making of fine garments—is already resulting in a record loss of jobs. In the textile companies surveyed in a recent English study, productivity and profits were found to be rising while employment rolls were declining. For example, at Allied Textile Company, pretax profit increased by 114 percent between 1981 and 1986 while employment shrank from 2,048 workers to 1,409.[51]

In virtually every major manufacturing activity, human labor is being steadily replaced by machines. Today, millions of working men and women around the world find themselves trapped between economic eras and increasingly marginalized by the introduction of new laborsaving technology. By the mid-decades of the coming century, the blue collar worker will have passed from history, a casualty of the Third Industrial Revolution and the relentless march toward ever greater technological efficiency.

· 10 ·

The Last
Service Worker

F OR MORE THAN FORTY YEARS, the service sector has been absorbing the job losses in the manufacturing industries. Until recently, most economists and business leaders remained confident that
the trend would continue. Their hopes are now being tempered as new
information technologies begin to make major inroads in the service
sector itself, raising productivity and displacing labor across the entire
expanse of service-related industries.

In February 1994, *The Wall Street Journal* ran a front page story
warning that a historic shift was occurring in the service sector, with
growing numbers of workers being permanently replaced by the new
information technologies. According to the *Journal,* "Much of the huge
US service sector seems to be on the verge of an upheaval similar
to that which hit farming and manufacturing, where employment
plunged for years while production increased steadily. . . . Technological advances are now so rapid that companies can shed far more
workers than they need to hire to implement the technology or support expanding sales."[1]

AT&T has announced that it is replacing more than 6,000 long-
distance operators with computerized voice-recognition technology.
In addition to eliminating one third of its long-distance operators, the
company said it would close down thirty-one offices in eleven states
and cut 400 management jobs. The new robotic technology, pioneered
by AT&T Bell Laboratories in New Jersey, is able to distinguish key
words and respond to callers' requests. For example, once the caller is
on the line, the silicon operator asks if he or she would like to make a

collect or person-to-person call, or charge the call to a third number. When the call is put through, the computer system tells the called party, "I have a collect call from Mr. So-and-So. Do you accept the call?" AT&T expects to replace more than half of its long-distance operators with robotized voice-recognition technology over the next several years.[2]

The new silicon operators are the latest in a string of technological advances that have allowed AT&T to handle 50 percent more calls with 40 percent fewer workers in recent years. Between 1950 and the early 1980s, AT&T led the service industries in introducing labor-replacing technology. In that period of time, the firm eliminated more than 140,000 operators across the country.[3] Many of the remaining ones are destined for pink slips by the end of the current decade.

Recent technology innovations, including fiber-optic cable networks, digital switching systems, digital transmission, satellite communications, and office automation have kept the telephone industry's output per employee increasing at nearly 5.9 percent a year, making it one of the key pace-setters in the new high-tech economy. Dramatic gains in productivity have led to the elimination of jobs in virtually every area of the telephone industry. Between 1981 and 1988, employment declined by 179,800.[4]

Many of the unemployed are installers and repairers who have been laid off as a result of recent technological innovations. The introduction of modular preassembled equipment makes for easier repairs and requires less maintenance. Plug-in phones have eliminated the need for constant installation visits. Buried cable with "quick connect" functions means fewer and faster repairs. Digital switching systems, using advanced computers and software, greatly increase the volume of telephone service while significantly lowering unit labor requirements. This means fewer installers and repair personnel are needed in central offices. The number of workers employed in central office repair is expected to decline by more than 20 percent by the year 2000.[5]

Equally dramatic developments are taking place in the United States postal service. In 1991 Postmaster General Anthony Frank announced that he would be replacing more than 47,000 workers by 1995 with automated machines capable of sight recognition. The new silicon sorters can read street addresses on letters and cards and automatically sort them faster than postal workers, who often spend up to four hours a day hand-sorting mail for their routes. Frank predicts that the new automation technologies will effect greater changes in the way mail is delivered in the next six years than in the past 200 years of U.S. postal operations.[6]

AT YOUR SERVICE

Computers that can understand speech, read script, and perform tasks previously carried out by human beings foreshadow a new era in which service industries come increasingly under the domain of automation. The computerization and automation of the service sector has barely begun, but is already having a deep effect on the state of the economy, impacting both productivity and employment. Economist Stephen Roach of Morgan Stanley says that "the service sector has lost its role as America's unbridled engine of job creation" and cautions that we have yet to see the emergence of any new industries to replace it.[7] Global service centers like New York City have been the first to feel the economic aftershocks of the new electronic innovations.

New York City's economy rebounded in the 1990s and is prospering despite growing unemployment and rising poverty. Re-engineering and the new information technologies are transforming the nature of work in the premier service center of the world. While service industries are experiencing rapid gains in productivity and profit, they are doing so with fewer workers. Nine out of ten jobs in New York City are in the service sector. Many of them are being lost as scores of New York employers—from Merrill Lynch and Grey Advertising to Arthur Andersen and NYNEX—are "making quantum leaps in learning how to produce ever more work with ever fewer people." From 1989 to 1993, productivity gains in industries like banking, insurance, accounting, law, communication, airlines, retailers, and hotels surpassed the expectations of even the most bullish forecasters. In the same time period, the city lost more than 350,000 jobs. The good news, according to *The New York Times*, is that "Ultimately this remarkable innovation could help . . . increase [New York's] competitiveness in the intensifying battle for global markets." The price for global success, however, is likely to be costly for New York's workforce. The city's former comptroller, Elizabeth Holtzman, painted the employment picture in stark contrasts. "What we may be moving towards here," she said, "is a tale of two cities: growth in higher paying jobs and a shrinking in lower-paying jobs." Holtzman warned that unless new low-skilled jobs can be found to fill the vacuum created by the new displacement technologies, the city will face "turmoil—more social dislocation, more crime, more poverty."[8]

The economic problems facing New York City are occurring throughout the country and in every developed nation with an advanced service sector. Routine personal services and an increasing number of more complex service functions are being taken over by intelligent machines.

The nation's banking and insurance industries have already begun making the transition to the Third Industrial Revolution. The number of banks in the United States will likely decline by 25 percent by the year 2000, and more than 20 percent of bank employees will lose their jobs by the twin processes of re-engineering and automation. In a study of the nation's banking sector, Andersen Consulting concluded that "the application of automation and process simplification can result in productivity gains of 20 to 30 per cent."[9]

At Cleveland's Society National Bank, more than 70 percent of customer service calls are handled by a voice-mail system, greatly reducing the amount of time representatives have to spend answering inquiries. At Fleet Financial Corp. in Providence, a customer service center, operating twenty-four hours a day, processes 1.5 million calls a month, 80 percent of which are entirely handled by computer. The new automated computer system has allowed Fleet to reduce its customer service workforce by 40 percent.[10]

Automatic teller machines, once a rarity, have become ubiquitous in U.S. cities and suburbs, significantly reducing the number of human tellers. The machines reduce transaction times, are available twenty-four hours a day, and operate at a fraction of the cost of employing human tellers. "A human teller can handle up to 200 transactions a day, works 30 hours a week, gets a salary anywhere from $8,000 to $20,000 a year plus fringe benefits, gets coffee breaks, a vacation and sick time. . . . In contrast, an automated teller can handle 2,000 transactions a day, works 168 hours a week, costs about $22,000 a year to run, and doesn't take coffee breaks or vacation."[11]

Between 1983 and 1993, banks eliminated 179,000 human tellers, or 37 percent of their workforce, replacing them with automated teller machines. By the year 2000, upwards of 90 percent of banking customers will use automated teller machines.[12]

Debit and point-of-sale banking are also gaining wider use. A growing number of supermarkets and other retailers are installing debit machines at the cash register, allowing customers to pay by way of electronic check, which automatically and instantly debits the bank account at the point of sale—eliminating check writing, credit clearance, handling, posting, record entry, and the many other steps involved in processing paper checks. By the year 2000, 30 to 40 percent of all bank customers will probably be using on-line debit cards at point of sale.[13]

Many of the back-office functions of banks are routine and mathematical and therefore easily amenable to automation. Increasingly, banks are outsourcing the processing of checks and loans—that is, contracting with other companies to perform services that used to be handled in-house. By the year 2000 more than one third of the banks in the country will be outsourcing their data center operations.[14]

The insurance industry is also making a quick transition into the new high-tech era. Mutual Benefit Life (MBL) was among the first of the nation's giant insurance companies to re-engineer its operations. Under its old system of processing applications, as many as thirty separate steps involving five departments and nineteen different people were required. Most claims took upwards of twenty-two days to process, although the actual work time expended on the application was less than seventeen minutes. The rest of the time was eaten up in the transfer of information from person to person and department to department. MBL did away with the slow, cumbersome, multilayered process and installed a single case-manager to process applications. Armed with a sophisticated PC-based workstation and programmed with an "expert system" to help answer questions, the caseworker can process an application in less than four hours. The average turnaround now at MBL is only two to five days. The savings in labor have been as dramatic as the savings in time. MBL has been able to eliminate 100 field office staff, while the new reduced workforce of caseworkers can process twice the volume of applications as before.[15]

Aetna Life and Casualty Co. enjoyed similar success in its re-engineering reforms. In 1992 Aetna's business centers had mushroomed to twenty-two offices with a staff of more than 3,000. By flattening the organizational hierarchy and replacing supervisors and agents with work teams and computers, Aetna compressed the time it takes to process an application from fifteen days to five. Today, the operations have been reduced to four business centers staffed by just 700 workers. Aetna has now reorganized all of its major divisions, cutting 5,000 employees, or nearly 9 percent of its workforce. It expects to save more than $100 million annually from its re-engineering changes.[16]

Imaging technology, expert systems, and mobile computing are key tools in the new re-engineering arsenal. Imaging systems digitize documents and store them on optical disks, making them immediately accessible to any employee with a desktop computer. Expert systems contain the stored knowledge of insurance experts that can be instantly accessed in handling insurance applications and claims. Mobile computing allows agents to answer clients' questions, draw up applications, and process claims on-site, bypassing the long delays experienced in forwarding information back and forth between the field and headquarters. Aetna's Hartford-based small-business market group uses laptops with sophisticated software "to enroll prospective members at the customer's site," even printing out ID cards instantly. The application process, which used to take two months and involve volumes of paperwork and labor, is now performed in less than four hours.[17]

THE VIRTUAL OFFICE

The technological changes taking place in the banking and insurance industries are indicative of the kinds of sweeping reforms that are redefining every aspect of white collar and service work. At the heart of these changes is the transformation of the traditional office from a paper-handling to an electronic-processing operation. The paperless electronic office has now become a goal of modern business.

The changes in office technologies and operations over the course of the Industrial Revolution have been extraordinary. We need only recall that blotting paper, pencils with erasers, and steel pens were introduced less than 150 years ago. Carbon paper and the keyboard typewriter were first introduced into offices in the 1870s. The keyboard calculator and punchcard tabulator followed in the late 1880s. The mimeograph was invented in 1890.[18] Together with the telephone, these advances in office technology greatly increased the productivity of business and commerce during the growth stage of industrial capitalism. Now, as the global economy metamorphoses into a Third Industrial Revolution, the office is evolving to better coordinate and control the accelerating flow of economic activity. The electronic office will eliminate millions of clerical workers by the end of the decade.

Each business day in the United States, 600 million pages of computer printouts are produced, 76 million letters are generated, and 45 sheets of paper are filed per employee. American businesses consume nearly one trillion pages of paper annually, enough to cover the earth's entire surface. A single optical disk stores more than 15 million pages of paper. Today 90 percent of all information is still stored on paper, while 5 percent is on microfiche and another 5 percent in electronic media.[19] With new image-processing equipment, however, businesses are now beginning to convert their offices to electronic workrooms. Image processing, as *Business Week* wryly observes, allows employees "to move digital pictures of documents through their offices at the speed of electrons, rather than at the speed of the guy from the mailroom."[20] Industry analysts expect the U.S. imaging market to grow dramatically between now and the opening decades of the twenty-first century.

Nordstrom, the Seattle-based department store chain, is already saving more than $1 million a year in paper costs by changing over from internal reports produced on paper to electronic reports accessible only on computers. Aetna, mentioned earlier, has made even more impressive gains. The giant insurance company found that it had 435 separate manuals that had to be continually updated. Management decided to eliminate the printed page in favor of electronically stored information. John Loewenberg, who heads up information services for the company, says, "Paper in a service business is like cholesterol in the bloodstream . . . bad paper is the internal stuff that clogs up the arteries." Now, when a change in a manual has to be made, it can be done electronically and be made instantly available to all of the 4,200 field staff—bypassing the need for typesetting, proofreading, printing, collating, binding, shipping, and filing. Aetna has saved more than $6 million a year by changing over to the electronic manual. Over 100 million pages of addenda and updates costing 4.5 cents a sheet are no longer sent out. Less paperwork means fewer employees. Aetna closed up its warehouse facility where employees "did nothing but update manuals."[21] Loewenberg says that Aetna is moving quickly toward a paperless office "because it's a more efficient way of delivering and maintaining information."[22]

Many in the computer software industry compare the paperless office to the cashless society and predict that most companies will convert to the new way of doing business well before the second decade of the next century. Nirex, a UK company, already processes its mail electronically. When paper-based correspondence arrives in the mailroom, an electronic image of the letter appears on a screen. The postal clerk enters key information about the letter—author, date of delivery, address—into an on-line database. The image is then transmitted to a workstation where it is electronically routed to the appropriate office and electronically filed.[23]

In 1993 Microsoft teamed up with fifty other global companies, including Xerox, Hewlett-Packard, Canon, and Compaq, to announce a joint venture to integrate all of the existing computer systems into a single network. Called "Microsoft at Work," the ambitious effort is designed to usher in the era of the fully digitized electronic office. In the very near future, companies will be able to receive incoming E-Mail, have it logged, entered into an on-line database, filed, and even printed out in multiple paper copies, collated and shipped without ever touching human hands.[24]

Microsoft is already at work on an even more sophisticated electronic office system that will allow an executive to take written reports on trips. He or she will be able to make cuts and add handwritten notes on the margin. The report can then be faxed directly to another machine in the home office that will read the report and even translate the scribbled notes, preparing a clean revised copy for electronic transmission to other employees, suppliers, and customers.[25]

The dazzling new array of high-tech electronic office equipment is bringing the fully electronic office closer to reality. "In the long run," says Paul Saffo, a director of the Institute for the Future, "we are going to become paperless in the same way we became horseless . . . horses are still around, but they're just ridden by little girls and hobbyists."[26] Corporate management expects to save untold billions of dollars in productivity gains and labor savings with the new silicon-collar office workforce. For millions of clerical workers, the electronic office spells the end of the career line.

The nation's secretaries are among the first casualties of the electronic office revolution. Secretaries currently spend more than 45 percent of their time filing papers, delivering messages, posting letters, making photocopies, and waiting for assignments.[27] Economists Wassily Leontief and Faye Duchin estimate that the conversion from a paper-handling to an electronic-processing office will save 45 percent of all secretarial time and between 25 percent and 75 percent of all office-related activities.[28] The number of secretaries has been steadily declining as personal computers, electronic mail, and fax machines replace manual typewriters, paper files, and routine correspondence. Between 1983 and 1993, the country's secretarial pool shrank by nearly

8 percent to about 3.6 million, according to Harvard economist James Medoff.[29]

Receptionists are also being reduced in number and in some firms eliminated altogether. Bellcore, the research division of the regional Bell companies, is currently developing an "electronic receptionist," a fully automated computer system that can answer calls, record messages, and even hunt down the party being phoned. Once located, the computer can deliver a short message on the name of the caller and the nature of the call and ask the recipient if he'd like to be connected. If he chooses not to accept the call, the electronic receptionist will get back to the caller and route him to voice mail, where he can leave a longer message. The new electronic receptionists can also be programmed to screen callers based on their phone numbers, putting some through to their intended parties while directing others to voice mail.[30]

The intelligent machine is steadily moving up the office hierarchy, subsuming not only routine clerical tasks but even work traditionally performed by management. In perhaps the unkindest cut of all, high-tech computerized hiring systems have been installed in hundreds of companies to screen job applications. Resumix Inc., a California-based company, recently installed a computerized hiring system at United Technologies Corporation. An optical scanner stores the images of 400 incoming résumés each day in a computer database the size of a small file cabinet. The Resumix can scan a résumé in less than three seconds and generate the appropriate acknowledgement letter to the applicant. Then, using "spatial text understanding and extraction," Resumix looks over each résumé, reviewing the applicant's educational history, skills and proficiencies, and past-employment record. Using a sophisticated logic process built into the program, Resumix decides which job category the applicant is best suited for. Field tests comparing Resumix to human personnel directors shows the silicon worker to be at least as skilled in making evaluations and much quicker in processing applications.[31]

The new information and telecommunication technologies are also making offices less relevant as centers of operations. Portable fax machines, modems, and wireless laptop computers allow business to be conducted either on location or from home. Between 1992 and 1993, the number of telecommuters grew by an estimated 20 percent. Nearly 8 million people now telecommute. In the year 2000, according to one study, upwards of 20 percent of the U.S. workforce will be working, at least part of the time, from home.[32]

By compressing time and collapsing space, the new electronic wizardry has transformed the very idea of an office from a spatial to a temporal concept. Companies such as AT&T have begun to introduce the idea of the "virtual office." Employees are provided with a mobile office, complete with laptop, fax, and cellular phone, and literally sent home. Companies, anxious to increase the productivity of their workers, see telecommuting as the wave of the future. Russell Thomas, a telecommuting specialist at AT&T, says that "Before we adopted telecommuting we had situations that people would drive one and a half hours to the office, stay for a few hours, drive an hour to visit a client, come back to the office, then leave for the day. Obviously, there was a big loss in productivity going on."[33]

Telecommuting not only increases employee productivity, but also reduces the amount of office space necessary to conduct business. Dun & Bradstreet Software cut its real estate costs by 30 percent by implementing a telecommuting plan.[34]

Some companies are taking the concept of a virtual office even further, introducing the idea of "hoteling." Any employee who needs to use an office to meet clients or hold a meeting can reserve a desk in advance by calling in his or her request to a small staff of "hoteling managers." Before the employee arrives, the managers will attach the employee's name plate on the door and even place family photos on the desk to make him or her feel comfortable.

Ernst and Young, a New York–based accounting firm, recently pared down its office space in Chicago from 377,000 to 300,000 square feet and instituted a hoteling program. Everyone below the senior manager level became "deskless." Now, if they want to use an office they have to make a reservation. IBM has taken away the desks of more than 5,000 of its employees and told them to work at home, in their car, or at their clients' offices. It expects to save 15 to 20 percent in space requirements.[35] While some employees welcome the new freedom that comes with less supervision, others say they miss the camaraderie and social interaction that comes with face-to-face office operations.

Steve Patterson, vice president of Gemini Consulting Company, says that in a growing number of companies today, workers interact less with each other face-to-face in a traditional office setting. Patterson cautions that the cost savings in reducing office-space requirements need to be weighed against the less tangible, equally significant, psychological costs of less-frequent interaction, including the potential weakening of corporate bonds and feelings of loyalty to the firm.[36] A small group of account executives at AT&T have attempted to salvage their former social ties by creating the "virtual water cooler," a tongue-in-cheek metaphor they use to describe their once-a-week evening get-togethers to talk business and socialize.[37]

To help ease the psychological trauma that comes with spatial disengagement, companies like Olivetti Research Laboratory in Cambridge, England, are experimenting with computers that will allow up to five people to converse and perform work together in an electronic version of face-to-face communications. Each computer screen is equipped with five separate windows so that the participants can see each other on the screen as they share information and work together. With video desktop computers, corporate management says it hopes "to recapture some of the flexibility and human warmth that electronic communication has lacked."[38]

DOWNSIZING THE WHOLESALE AND RETAIL SECTORS

While the office is being revolutionized by intelligent machines, so too is every other area of the service economy. The changes have been dramatic in the wholesale and retail sectors. Wholesalers, like middle management, are becoming increasingly redundant in the age of instant electronic communication. As we noted in chapter 7, retailers like Wal-Mart are now bypassing wholesalers altogether, preferring to deal directly with manufacturers. With computerized monitoring and scanning equipment at the point of sale, retailers can transmit shipping orders directly to manufacturers' warehouses by way of electronic data interchange (EDI). At the other end, automated warehouses staffed by computer-driven robots and remote-controlled delivery vehicles fill orders in a matter of minutes without the assistance of human physical labor. An increasing number of warehouses are operated by "silicon supervisors" and overseen by a skeleton human workforce whose primary task is to monitor the equipment and serve as traffic controllers. Automated guided vehicles are being integrated with microprocessor-controlled conveyor systems, robotized vertical lifts, and other equipment "creating a completely automated storage and retrieval system." Automated warehousing can reduce labor requirements by at least 25 percent or more.[39]

Andersen Consulting recently published a study of the productivity gains and labor savings in more than a thousand companies that successfully re-engineered their warehouse operations. The statistics are impressive. Epson Australia Limited, makers of personal computers and printers, in Sydney, showed a customer-service lead-time reduction of 66 percent, space savings of 50 percent, labor savings of 43 percent, and operating costs savings per receipt of 25 percent in their warehouse operations. Sevel Argentina, in Buenos Aires, dealing in Fiat and Peugeot automobiles, showed space savings of 28 percent and labor savings of 26 percent. IME Excavators, in Eslöv, Sweden, working with excavator components and raw materials, realized labor savings of 30 percent after re-engineering. Entertainment U.K. in Hayes Middy, United Kingdom, producers of entertainment software, showed operating costs savings per transaction of 19 percent and labor savings of 26 percent. Hernandez Perez in Murcia, Spain, dealing in canned vegetables, showed a customer service lead-time reduction of 80 percent, space savings of 50 percent, and labor savings of 37 percent.[40]

The new information technologies allow retailers and manufacturers to come together in a single continuous-flow process, leaving little need for wholesalers. In 1992 the wholesale trade industry lost 60,000 jobs. Since 1989 the wholesale sector has dropped more than a quarter million jobs.[41] By early in the next century most wholesaling, as we have come to know it, will have been eliminated, a victim of the revolutionary innovations in electronic transmission control and coordination.

Retail establishments are also quickly re-engineering their operations, wherever possible, introducing intelligent machines to improve productivity and reduce labor costs. Modern mass retailing emerged in the United States in the 1870s and 1880s. Today, chain department stores dominate an industry that employs more than 19.6 million or 22 percent of the total private nonagricultural workforce.[42]

Employment in retailing increased dramatically in the decades after World War II, as postwar consumers, with money to burn, went on a forty-year buying binge. Beginning in the late 1980s, however, employment in the retail sector began to slow down as rising unemployment in other sectors dampened purchasing power. In an effort to cut costs and improve their profit margins, companies began to replace their workers with computerized systems and automated processes. While annual employment growth in the retail sector averaged close to 3.0 percent between 1967 and 1989, the Bureau of Labor Statistics projects a dramatic slowdown in employment growth to 1.5 percent or less in the 1990s.[43]

Typical of the new trend is Sears, Roebuck, one of the giants in the retail sector. Sears eliminated a staggering 50,000 jobs from its merchandising division in 1993, reducing employment by 14 percent. The cutbacks came in a year when Sears' sales revenues rose by more than 10 percent. "We are asking a fundamental question," says Anthony Rucci, executive vice president of merchandising. "Are our workers adding value?" Rucci says, "There is a very strong commitment to get rid of needless staff work and tasks that don't add value."[44]

In most retail outlets, the use of electronic bar codes and scanners at the point of sale has greatly increased the efficiency of cashiers and as a result significantly reduced labor requirements. In 1992 the National Retail Federation surveyed retailers and found that more than 80 percent of them would be using bar codes by the end of 1993. The increased use of point-of-sales computing equipment and other intelligent machines, says Stephen Roach of Morgan Stanley, "helps explain why retail employment is still down some 400,000 from its 1990 peak."[45]

Cashiers are the third-largest clerical group after secretaries and bookkeepers, with nearly 1.5 million employed in the United States alone. According to a survey prepared by the Bureau of Labor Statistics, the new electronic scanning equipment "permits a 30 percent increase in ringing speed and a possible overall 10 to 15 percent reduction in unit labor requirements for cashiers and baggers."[46]

Some retailers are eliminating the cashier altogether. In the Crystal Court Shopping Mall in Minneapolis, customers entering the Robot Music Store are greeted by a single employee—a 400-pound robot. Rotating in a circular glass enclosure in the center of the store, the robot is equipped with keyboards that allow customers to punch up any one of 5,000 CDs in stock for a thirty-second sample listening. Once a CD is selected, the robot's video display is used to process the payment. The robot's arm then selects the CD from the shelves and delivers it to the customer along with his or her receipt. A twenty-three-year-old who shops regularly at the store says he prefers the robot to a human salesperson. "It's easy to use and it can't talk back to you."[47] More sophisticated robots equipped with speech recognition and conversational abilities will likely be commonplace in department stores, convenience stores, fast-food restaurants, and other retail and service businesses by the early part of the next century.

A large European super-discounter is experimenting with a new electronic technology that allows the customer to insert his or her credit card into a slot on the shelf holding the desired product. There is no shopping cart. Instead, the customer finds the items she purchased already packaged and waiting for her when she leaves the store. She merely signs a prepared credit slip and leaves without ever having her items rung up on a cash register.[48]

The retail sector has long acted as an unemployment sponge, absorbing countless numbers of displaced blue-collar workers let go by the automation of manufacturing industries. Now, with retail industries undergoing their own automation revolution, the question becomes one of where will all the workers go.

Many economists look to the food industry to rescue the workers cast adrift by technological innovations in other sectors. Even here, though, employment is sluggish, suggesting hard times ahead for unskilled and semiskilled service workers. The food and drink industry led the service sector in the creation of new jobs in the 1980s. More than 2 million new workers were hired in the past decade to service a growing consumer market. Now the employment boom appears to be over. Although corporate profits are expected to increase in the 1990s as a result of new labor- and time-saving technologies, fewer workers will be needed in the food industry. The Department of Labor projects the growth rate in employment to be cut in half over the next 15 years.[49]

In many restaurants, computer systems allow waiters to transmit orders electronically, avoiding unnecessary trips back to the kitchen. The same electronic transmission can be used by the computer to prepare a check for the customer and alert the store manager or suppliers to replenish the stocks being depleted. Automated order taking, check preparation, and inventory stocking significantly reduce labor requirements.

A new state-of-the-art cooking method—sous vide—allows food to be cooked under a vacuum in heat-resistant pouches in steam-injected air-convection ovens in large centralized commissaries. The food is then chilled at 30 degrees Fahrenheit and shipped to local restaurants, where it remains refrigerated until the customer places his or her order. Being a chef today often means emptying a pouch of already prepared frozen food into hot water or placing it under a microwave for three to seven minutes. Sous vide reduces labor costs in most restaurants by 20 percent or more.[50]

Some fast-food drive-through restaurants are beginning to replace human order takers with touch-sensitive screens that list the items on the menu. To place an order, all the customer has to do is lean out her window and touch the appropriate symbol representing the item. The transmission is sent instantly by an on-line database to the kitchen, where it appears on a video screen and is subsequently filled, eliminating human intermediaries in the ordering process. Drive-through restaurants have now become so highly automated and efficient that six to eight employees can serve as many customers at peak hours of operation as twenty employees working in a sit-down fast-food restaurant.[51]

Automated beverage-control systems are also being installed, lessening the need for experienced bartenders. The system is controlled by a microcomputer that transmits a request for a drink to a dispensing cart, which delivers the drink as ordered in less than three seconds. A computerized check is prepared simultaneously and handed to the customer. The automated beverage-control system reduces labor costs by 20 to 40 percent.[52]

The retail sector still operates largely alongside a road and highway culture. Customers travel to the store to buy things. Recently, however, the fledgling information highway has begun to fundamentally alter the way people shop, lessening the need for entire categories of retail workers whose jobs are tied to moving goods to market and serving customers face-to-face in a retail setting.

In May 1993 IBM and Blockbuster Video announced a new joint venture, the NewLeaf Entertainment Corporation, which will provide instant made-to-order audio compact disks, video games, and videocassettes through Blockbuster's 3,500 retail outlets. The store will bypass the highway culture, with its warehouses, shippers, truckers, and loading docks, and transport products electronically to the customer by way of the information highway. Each store will have a kiosk where customers can order selections by touching a computer screen. The information will be transmitted to a central computer that will make an electronic copy of the item required and transmit it back to the store within minutes. Machines in the store will copy the electronic information into recordings, CDs, and cassettes. Color laser printers in the kiosk will reproduce the jacket pictures with the same clarity and resonance as exists now on pre-existing stock. The new electronically distributed goods assure the customer that what he or she wants will never be out of stock or unavailable. David Lundeen, vice president of Blockbuster's technology division, is enthusiastic over the potential of the new electronic distribution system: "If a seven-year-old comes in on a Friday night and wants the latest hot video game, the chances are high now that it's sold out. But with this system it's never sold out—you can get another one electronically in a couple of minutes."[53]

The company says it will save three to four dollars in transportation and handling costs for each electronically distributed CD or cassette. Other retailers are expected to follow Blockbuster's lead. Jack McDonald, vice president for business development at NewLeaf, foresees "a nationwide network of digital servers on which movies, software games, music, and virtually any other kind of entertainment you can think of, will be stored digitally, and transmitted over telecommunication links to retail stores and eventually right into your living room."[54] Electronic transmission of products will likely mean the loss of tens of thousands of jobs in the warehousing and transportation industries in the coming years.

Electronic shipping is only a small part of the revolutionary changes taking place in retailing. Electronic shopping is also quickly penetrating the retail market, threatening the jobs of tens of thousands of sales clerks, managers, stock personnel, maintenance crews, security guards, and others who make up the retail employment complex. Electronic shopping is already a $2-billion-a-year industry and is growing at a rate of 20 percent a year. The laying down of a nationwide information superhighway and the opening up of hundreds of new cable channels with interactive capabilities promises a flood of home-shopping services. Companies are investing huge sums of money in the new home-shopping television networks, convinced that shopping without a store is likely to be the next growth market in retail sales.[55]

Many industry analysts are predicting that electronic home shopping will take over more and more of the nation's one-trillion-dollar-a-year retail market and point to the convenience it offers to customers, many of whom are working women with less leisure time to "go shopping" at a mall. Electronic shopping is also a tremendous cost-cutting approach to retailing, says Peter Suris, an analyst for UBS Securities. "It's a low cost distribution system," and "you don't need thousands of stores, and you don't need thousands of pieces of inventory in each location."[56]

Some of the nation's largest retailers have announced plans to enter the electronic shopping market. R. H. Macy and Company will go on air in 1994 with a twenty-four-hour shopping channel. Myron E. Ullman III, Macy's chairman and chief executive, says that "TV Macy's will be a twenty-four-hour-a-day, seven-day-a-week department store in your living room." Macy's hopes to reach 20 million subscribers, and projects revenues in excess of $250 million over the first four years. Don Hewitt, the executive producer of the television news magazine *60 Minutes*, who holds a financial interest in the company, says that the new Macy's channel will attempt to re-create the visual appearance of being in the department store by designing sets that duplicate the departments.[57]

Home TV shopping, with its just-in-time retailing, is going to pose a significant challenge to the nation's highway-oriented retail culture. *Forbes* calls the new revolution in retailing "a serious threat to the country's traditional retail industry and to the nineteen million people it employs."[58] Since 1989, more than 411,000 retail jobs have been eliminated, a trend that "can only accelerate," says *Business Week*, "as the TV tube becomes the salesperson." All of the indices point to a steady decline in traditional retail shopping and increased sales for the home-shopping networks. In 1982 shoppers averaged more than 1.5 hours per visit at the shopping mall. By 1992 the average time had dropped to 71 minutes, and the number of stores visited declined from 3.6 to 2.6. Retail sales in shopping centers declined by 3 percent between 1988 and 1992. At the same time, purchases by credit card at home totaled $42 billion in 1992, a 30 percent jump over home-sales figures in 1988. For the growing number of consumers who are "getting plain tired of the parking, schlepping, crime and other hassles involved in going to shop," home TV shopping is a welcome alternative.[59]

Many companies are using on-line computer services to draw business away from traditional retail markets. For $39 a customer can become an on-line customer of CUC International and for a slightly larger sum of $49 a consumer can become a phone member for a year. The company offers discounted prices on more than 250,000 brand-name products, from luggage to home appliances. In 1992 CUC posted revenues of $644 million and had millions of members in its telephone and computer buying clubs.[60]

During the heyday of the highway culture, retailers and real-estate developers built more than 39,000 shopping centers across the United States. "When shopping at home really takes off," says the editor of *Forbes*, "many of these malls will be obsolete." Their steady decline will mean a significant drop in employment in the retail sector.[61]

DIGITIZING THE PROFESSIONS, EDUCATION, AND ART

As the brief survey of retail shopping suggests, the electronic-information superhighway is going to change employment patterns even more radically than did the U.S. highway system when it was constructed in the late 1950s and early 1960s. Whole categories of workers will dwindle in number and in some instances disappear altogether. Information technologies are going to get smarter and cheaper in the years to come, and far more capable of integrating a wide range of mental and physical activities.

Intelligent machines are already invading the professional disciplines and even encroaching on education and the arts, long considered immune to the pressures of mechanization. Doctors, lawyers, accountants, business consultants, scientists, architects, and others regularly use specially designed information technologies to assist them in their professional endeavors. For example, computerized robots are now being used in complex human surgery. Robodoc is a 250-pound robot developed by researchers at the University of California at Davis. On November 7, 1992, Robodoc assisted in the first operation on a human being. The surgery was performed on a sixty-four-year-old patient in need of a hip replacement. The robot is equipped with a CT scanner that can generate three-dimensional images of the thighbone and a robotic arm to drill the hole: "The surgeon calls up a live image of the patient's thighbone and uses a mouse (an electronic pointer) to designate an ideal cavity. Then, after opening up the patient and guiding the robot to the bone, he gives a go-ahead, and the robot drills the hole with a high-speed drill."[62] Researchers are currently experimenting with the use of surgical robots in eye, ear, and brain surgery.

In the field of education, the nation's 152,000 librarians are growing increasingly concerned over electronic data systems that are able to search, retrieve, and electronically transmit books and articles over information highways in a fraction of the time spent in performing the same task with human labor. Data networks like Internet can provide abstracts from thousands of journals and books within a matter of minutes. Project Gutenberg is one of many programs designed to digitize and download onto computer disks the entire contents of books, manuscripts, and journals. With advanced scanning technology, books can be removed from their bindings and fed into a machine that reads the script and translates it to disk form, ready for instant transmission anywhere in the world. Full-text retrieval, according to industry analysts, is "just around the corner. When it arrives, the local library as we know it all but disappears."[63]

Even the art of book writing is falling victim to intelligent machines. In 1993 the publishing industry was taken aback when the first computer-generated novel was released. Using software equipped with artificial intelligence, Scott Finch was able to program an Apple Macintosh computer to pump out nearly three quarters of the prose in a torrid potboiler entitled *Just This Once*. The prose is simple and intelligible: "Her heart leapt into her throat and she jumped involuntarily as the stranger appeared in front of her. Then it all came back in a rush. No wonder she thought she had been dreaming."

The first printing, which received decent reviews, sold more than 15,000 copies. While the book's publisher, Steven Schraggs, of the Carol Publishing Group, muted his praise for the silicon author, he said he was sure that this kind of pioneering effort would lead to more significant literary contributions in the future. "I'm not saying this a great work of literary distinction," Schraggs confessed, "but it is as good as a hundred other romance novels being published this year." The publisher said he was proud to be involved in a project that "was at the cutting edge of literary artificial intelligence."[64]

Although novelists may have little to fear in the short run from silicon authors, musicians have every reason to be alarmed by the new generation of high-tech synthesizing machines that are fast redefining the way music is made. In 1993 the Bechstein piano factory filed for bankruptcy. The handmade pianos, which composer Richard Strauss once called "The most beautiful and most refined in the world," were no longer in demand. Piano sales worldwide have dropped by one third to one half in recent years, while digital keyboards have increased in sales by 30 percent or more in the same period.[65]

Synthesizers, as they have come to be called, are silicon musicians. A synthesizer reduces musical sound to digitized form. Once digitized, the sounds can be stored and, when needed, be combined with other digitized sounds to create an entire symphony orchestra. In a process called "sampling," the computer might record a single note or a combination of notes by great musicians like violinist Jascha Heifetz. The individual notes can then be rearranged into wholly different performances that were never performed by the artist. Buell Neidlinger, a string bass player, describes a recording session where he was asked to play "every note of the chromatic scale." After the session, Neidlinger noticed that a sampling machine had been hidden in the corner of the room behind a coffee machine. "He had stolen my sound," Neidlinger later recounted. Henceforth, the studio could use the notes to compose and produce any piece it desired.[66]

Sampling originated in 1980, when a New York composer, Charles Dodge, successfully digitized the voice of Enrico Caruso off old records and used the sounds to create new recordings. Today, synthesizers make more than 50 percent of all the music on television commercials. The silicon musicians are also used as background for rock recordings, TV shows, and movies. Much of the music used on *Miami Vice* and in movies like *The Right Stuff, Risky Business,* and *Desperately Seeking Susan* was composed and recorded by a musician named Jon Harness, working out of a house in upstate New York filled with computerized musical technology. In the music industry, the new silicon-age musicians are referred to as "synths" while traditional artists using instruments are called "acoustic musicians."[67]

Vince Di Bari, former vice president of the Los Angeles local of the American Federation of Musicians, estimates that recording jobs for acoustic musicians have dropped off by 35 percent or more because of synthesizers.[68] Silicon musicians are replacing human musicians in theaters, clubs, and even opera houses around the country. Recently, the Washington Opera Company's production of *Don Carlo* was put on with just the conductor, two pianos, and a synthesizer player in the pit. On Broadway, management replaced eight string players in the orchestra with synthesizer players for the production of *Grand Hotel.* In Long Beach, a dispute with the musicians union led to the replacement of musicians with two keyboard players for the production of *Hello, Dolly!*[69] Because keyboard players or "synths" can produce the sounds of multiple instruments without compromising the quality of the work, costs are slashed and profit margins are improved.

Many musicians compare their circumstances with those of auto workers replaced by automation in Detroit. Bill Peterson, a professional trumpet player in Hollywood and president of the Los Angeles local chapter of the AFM, blames synthesizers for a loss of work and expresses the anger of many of his colleagues when he says, "These machines are monsters."[70] John Glasel, president of New York's Local 802 of the American Federation of Musicians, like others in the music business is worried about the future job security of his members. "As these machines take over jobs once done by studio musicians, we're talking about the loss of a lot of people's livelihood," says Glasel.[71] Musicians are no less worried by the artistic implications of substituting "virtual music" for "real" music. "A day could come," lamented one musician, "when a whole generation of Americans will never know what a real piano sounds like."[72]

Even more troubling than synthesized music is the new technology of "morphing," which allows movie and television producers to isolate, digitize, and store every visual expression, movement, and sound of an actor and then reprogram them in virtually any new combination, effectively creating new roles and performances for the artist. Hollywood studios are already beginning to digitize some of the thousands of films stored in their libraries in anticipation of using many of the actors—some long dead—in new productions. Nick de Martino, who heads the American Film Institute's computer lab, says that with the new computer technologies it is possible to eliminate soundstages, sets, even actors, and replace them with "synthespians," "created from libraries of gestures and expressions housed in a computer bank." For example, it is now technically possible—although expensive—to extract the thousands of gestures, facial expressions, movements, and voice inflections of Dr. Spock and Captain Kirk from the seventy-eight episodes of *Star Trek*, and using sophisticated computer technology, reprogram the actors to perform in wholly new episodes.[73]

In 1986 Ted Turner bought MGM for $1.7 billion, largely to acquire its library of 3,600 feature films. Turner realized, early on, the great potential commercial value of using the thousands of reels of film footage as digital source material for new movies, television shows, commercials, and computer and video games. Turner's acquisition led *Forbes* editors to quip that "James Cagney may soon be working harder than ever."

Digitized imagery is even being used to clone extras for movies, allowing studios to save millions of dollars in the hiring of background actors for scenes. In the film *The Babe*, one thousand extras were turned into a cast of thousands "by digitizing their images frame by frame, cutting out individuals, and randomly pasting their images in the stands jigsaw-style similar to cut-and-paste in word processing— except they end up as live, moving images."[74]

Studios anxious to cut costs are likely to turn increasingly to film libraries for casting for new productions. Already, Humphrey Bogart, Louis Armstrong, Cary Grant, and Gene Kelly have been digitized and put back to work in new television commercials.[75] Live actors and entertainers are going to be increasingly competing for parts against their digitized and stored past images as well as those of actors long deceased. The age of the synthespian means even less employment for an industry already suffering from underemployment.

Although still in its formative stage, the Third Industrial Revolution has led to the casting aside of tens of millions of workers in the agricultural, manufacturing, and service sectors. The new technologies have paved the way for a revamping of the global economic system along high-tech lines with a concomitant decline in the global workforce required to produce goods and services. Still, the current wave of re-engineering and automation is only the very beginning of a technological transformation that is destined to greatly accelerate productivity in the years ahead while making increasing numbers of workers redundant and irrelevant in the global economy.

Management consultants, scientists, and engineers are quick to point out that today's information technologies are primitive compared to what will be coming on-line in the next two to three decades. Physicist Gordon Moore, the chairman of Intel, points out that raw computing power is now doubling every eighteen months, setting a blistering pace for technological change.[76] In the future, advanced parallel computing machines, high-tech robotics, and integrated electronic networks spanning the globe are going to subsume more and more of the economic process, leaving less and less room for direct hands-on human participation in making, moving, selling, and servicing.

PART IV

THE PRICE OF
PROGRESS

· 11 ·

High-Tech
Winners and Losers

VIRTUALLY EVERY BUSINESS LEADER and most mainstream economists continue to assert that the dramatic technological advances
of the Third Industrial Revolution will have a trickle-down effect,
reducing the costs of products, stimulating increased consumer demand, creating new markets, and putting more and more people to
work in better-paying, new high-tech jobs and industries. For a growing number of working people, however, who find themselves either
unemployed or underemployed, the concept of trickle-down technology is of very little solace.

At USX Corporation, employees experienced the effects of
trickle down technology first hand. On March 26, 1991, USX, one of
the nation's leading steel producers, announced that it was laying off
2,000 at its Fairless works plant on the Delaware River in Pennsylvania.
The news of the shutdown was tucked inside the second paragraph
of a company statement outlining "a number of restructuring actions . . . intended to enhance USX's future market competitiveness."
One of the laid-off workers was Joe Vandegrift, a forty-six-year-old mill
mechanic who had been with the company for more than twenty-five
years. Vandergrift, who is now a counselor in a dislocated workers'
center, is helping other laid-off workers apply for one of the eighty
demolition jobs made available by the company. USX plans to disman-
tle furnaces, buildings, and machines in what was once one of the great
open-hearth steel mills in the world. The steel infrastructure will be
shipped to other more efficient USX plants, where it will be melted
down and recast into high-quality steel. One former employee at the

plant says she would like to be on the demolition team if for no other reason than to finally convince herself that the way of life she had known for so long was truly coming to an end. Rochelle Connors, who worked as a bricklayer, then added, "Maybe it would be good therapy for me. If I saw it go down, I'd be able to tell myself: yes, it's done. It's gone. It's over with."[1]

Most of the laid-off workers from USX's Fairless plant are having a difficult time finding work. Many lack even the most basic reading and math skills necessary to retrain for the dwindling number of low-paying service jobs still available in the region. In their forties, with children in college and mortgages and car payments due, they are in desperate search for any kind of employment just to make ends meet. Men and women who just a few short years ago were taking home wages in excess of $30,000 consider themselves lucky to find jobs as janitors and security guards for $5 an hour. For them and their families, the post–World War II dream of being part of the middle class is over. In its place is growing frustration and anger over a company and an industry they feel abandoned them. Alcoholism, drug abuse, and crime are on the rise in communities like Fairless. So are the incidences of spouse abuse and divorce. Looking out of his window at the nine smokestacks rising majestically out of the now-silent blast furnace, Vandergrift mourned the loss. "My *Titanic*," he said, "that's my ship that went down."[2]

Vandergrift and Connors are just two unemployed workers in an industry that has eliminated more than 220,000 jobs, or half of its routine workforce, in just fourteen years.[3] Both the manufacturing and service sectors are trimming down their employment rolls and scaling up their capital investments to become globally competitive in the new high-tech world of the twenty-first century. The re-engineering revolution is paying off. In the 1980s American corporations posted a 92 percent increase in the level of profits before taxes. (These figures are adjusted for inflation.) Many stockholders have seen their dividends quadruple in less than a decade.[4]

SQUEEZING THE LITTLE GUY

Although stockholders have greatly profited from new technologies and advances in productivity, benefits have not "trickled down" to the average worker. During the 1980s, real hourly compensation in the manufacturing sector alone decreased from $7.78 to $7.69 an hour.[5] By the end of the decade nearly 10 percent of the American work-force was unemployed, underemployed, or working part time because full-time work was unavailable, or were too discouraged to even look for a job.[6]

Between 1989 and 1993, more than 1.8 million workers lost their jobs in the manufacturing sector, many of them victims of automation, either at the hands of their American employers or by foreign com-panies whose more highly automated plants and cheaper operating costs forced domestic producers to downsize their operations and lay off workers. Of those who have lost their jobs to automation, only a third were able to find new jobs in the service sector, and then at a 20 percent drop in pay.[7]

Government figures on employment are often misleading, mask-ing the true dimensions of the unfolding job crisis. For example, in August 1993 the federal government announced that nearly 1,230,000 jobs had been created in the United States in the first half of 1993. What they failed to say was that 728,000 of them—nearly 60 per-cent—were part-time, for the most part in low-wage service industries. In February 1993 alone, 90 percent of the 365,000 jobs created in the United States were part time, and most of them went to people who were in search of full-time employment.[8] Increasingly, American workers are being forced to settle for dead-end jobs just to survive. Craig Miller, a former sheetmetal worker in Kansas City, represents the growing frustration of millions of American workers. Miller lost his job at TWA, where he was making $15.65 an hour. Now he and his wife hold down four jobs between them and make less than half what he made in his former job at TWA. When Miller hears the Clinton administration boast of creating new jobs, he responds with a forced chuckle, "Sure—we've got four of them. So what?" Miller asks what good it is to have several low-paying jobs that pay a fraction of the wages he used to receive when he had one decent job at a livable wage.[9] According to a Senate Labor Committee report in 1991, 75 percent of American workers are accepting lower wages than they would have ten years ago. Dean Baker, a research economist at the Economic Policy Institute, says that the people who once enjoyed high-paying secure jobs with ample benefits are now "going to work in 7-11s and McDonald's."[10]

Many of the new part-time jobs are found in the so-called pink-collar ghetto—work concentrated in service and white collar areas such as secretaries, cashiers, and waitresses that are occupied largely by women. But even many of these low-paying jobs are likely to vanish in the next decade.

The mounting statistics reveal a workforce in retreat in virtually every sector. Forced to compete with automation on the one hand and a global labor pool on the other, American workers find themselves squeezed ever closer to the margins of economic survival. In 1979 the average weekly wage in the United States was $387. By 1989 it had dropped to $335. In the twenty-year period from 1973 to 1993, American blue collar employees lost 15 percent of their buying power.[11]

The decline in average wages is attributable in part to the waning influence of unions. Wage freezes and pay cuts were unheard of in the unionized sector of the economy in the 1960s and 1970s. During the 1981–1982 recession, however, unions began to lose ground for the first time. More than 44 percent of the unionized workforce that engaged in collective bargaining in the single year of 1982 accepted wage freezes or cuts, establishing a precedent for the remainder of the decade.[12] By 1985 one third of all workers covered by new labor agreements were submitting to wage freezes or a reduction in wages. With union representation falling in relationship to the total workforce, American workers were left with no effective voice to represent their interests with employers. The Economic Policy Institute estimates that in the manufacturing sector alone, de-unionization has meant a lowering of wages by 3.6 percent or more.[13]

Behind the many lofty pronouncements of the merits of downsizing and lean-production practices lies a far different reality—one little discussed in the public arena. In the 1980s, manufacturers were able to shave $13 million an hour in wages by eliminating more than 1.2 million jobs. The non-durable goods industries saved nearly $4.7 million an hour in wages by cutting 500,000 jobs. An additional $3.1 million an hour was saved by lowering real hourly wages from $10.75 to $10.33 an hour in manufacturing. Overall, American wage earners were earning $22 million an hour less than a decade earlier.[14] Economist Jared Bernstein, of the Economic Policy Institute, argues that "Cutting labor costs . . . has led to a disinvestment in the labor force," with untold consequences to the economy and society. With downsizing and re-engineering, says Bernstein, you're "essentially meeting employer's rather than employee's needs." He says that hourly wages are "continuing to fall as we come close to the half-way mark of the 1990s" and that the trend is likely to continue well into the future.[15]

For many workers, lean production has meant a fall into near-abject circumstances. In a 1994 report, the Census Bureau released figures showing that the percentage of Americans working full time but earning less than a poverty level income for a family of four—about $13,000 a year—rose by 50 percent between 1979 and 1992. The study, which the bureau called "astounding," provided further dramatic evidence of the downward slide of the American workforce. Economists blamed much of the decline on the loss of manufacturing jobs and the globalization of the world economy.[16] The forced redistribution of wealth away from American workers and to corporate management and stockholders led conservative economist Scott Burns to remark that "the 80s will be known as the decade of the fat cats, a time when entrepreneurial pieties were used to beat the average worker into cowed submission while America's corporate elite moved yet higher on the hog."[17]

Some of the blame for the current plight of American workers can be traced to the emergence of a single global marketplace in the 1970s and 80s. The postwar recovery of Japan and Western Europe presented American companies with formidable new trading competitors in the international arena. New developments in information and telecommunication technology made it increasingly easier to do business everywhere in the world. The emergence of a common global market and labor pool served as a prod and incentive for American companies to undermine the uneasy truce they had made with organized labor since the 1950s.

Recall that immediately after World War II organized labor and corporate management engaged in a bitter series of strikes over wages, benefits, and working conditions. In the mid-1950s an informal accommodation of sorts was reached which was to last, more or less intact, until the mid-1970s. Labor was to share, at least in part, in the gains in productivity—enjoying better wages and benefits—in return for the promise of labor peace and cooperation. For nearly twenty-five years real wages of American workers grew between 2.5 and 3 percent a year. Benefits also grew. The number of workers covered under corporate pension plans increased from 10 percent in 1950 to more than 55 percent in 1979.[18] Health benefits, sick leave, and paid vacations also improved.

The hard-won benefits and the "accommodation" between management and labor began to unravel in the late 1970s and early 1980s. Facing stiff competition abroad and armed with an increasingly sophisticated array of new labor-displacing technologies at home as well as a cheap labor pool in other countries to draw upon, American corporations began a concerted drive to weaken organized labor's influence and reduce the cost of the labor component in the economic process. During the 1980s, the hourly wages of 80 percent of the American workforce declined by an average of 4.9 per cent.[19] "Back in the early 1970s," observes labor economist Frank Levy, "the average guy with a high school diploma was making $24,000 in today's dollars. Today a similar guy is making about $18,000."[20] Worker benefits also declined. The percentage of the workforce covered by a pension plan dropped from 50 percent in 1979 to 42.9 percent in 1989.[21] Health-care coverage has also been weakened. A study by a consulting firm, Foster Higgins, found that 80 percent of American companies require their employees "to pay an average of $103 a month for family coverage, up from $69 in 1989."[22] Paid days off have declined by 2.3 days for manufacturing workers in the past decade.[23]

THE DECLINING MIDDLE

While the first automation wave had its greatest impact on blue collar workers, the new re-engineering revolution is beginning to affect the middle echelons of the corporate community, threatening the economic stability and security of the most important political group in American society—the middle class. The newest victims of re-engineering are likely to live in affluent suburbs and have been laid off from a management job paying upwards of six figures in yearly compensation. Ten years ago, the sight of a white male between the ages of forty and fifty at home in the yard or walking a dog down a suburban street at midday would have been considered strange. Today, thousands of laid-off middle managers and executives find themselves at home, waiting for the phone to ring with a potential job offer. For many, the call they hoped for never comes.

Recently, *The Wall Street Journal* profiled the new suburban unemployed. John Parker, who lives in a wealthy suburban community along Philadelphia's Main Line, lost his job at IBM during corporate restructuring. For months he remained cloistered in his six-bedroom home printing out résumés and checking out job leads. Parker says that, "At first I didn't even want to step outside during business hours." The forty-three-year-old executive said he feared "neighbors would look at me and wonder why I was playing hooky." His isolation ended one day when he heard a loud crash and rushed outside where a road-paving gang was working. He looked up from the curve and was shocked to see two of his friends looking on. "We gawked at each other," said Parker, "as if to say, so it's two in the afternoon and you aren't at the office either!"[24]

A local librarian, Ann Kajdasz, says she started noticing middle-aged businessmen coming into the library in the middle of the day three years ago. They would read business publications or scan the Dow Jones *National Business Employment Weekly*. "At first, they always come in all spiffy in shirts and ties," says Kajdasz. "After a while, however, they become scruffier and scruffier and sometimes they talk about their fear of never finding work again."[25]

An increasing number of the new unemployed give up altogether. Some retreat behind closed doors, spending more and more of their time in darkened living rooms, shades drawn, watching television. A few turn to alcohol. Others begin taking on chores as househusbands, ferrying children to and from school and to extracurricular activities. A few volunteer as chaperons or coaches.

A number of communities have established support groups for the new middle-class unemployed. In Bryn Mawr, Pennsylvania, Executives in Transition brings together unemployed executives every Monday morning at nine to talk about their feelings and share the concerns. The question of finding a job and living with the uncertainty of being without employment always dominates the discussion.[26]

Parker is part of a new demographic category called "the declining middle." In the 1980s more than 1.5 million midlevel management jobs were eliminated. In the 1990s their ranks are swelling to include upper-middle-management executives as well. Peter Drucker says that the managerial class is beginning to "feel like slaves on an auction block."[27] Many are being let go with little chance of finding an equivalent job with comparable benefits. Those that do find work often accept a dramatic reduction in pay and job assignments. Jerry Scott, one of the participants in Executives in Transition, recently found a new job at a 45 percent reduction in pay. Some end up in temp jobs at places like H&R Block, preparing tax returns for $5 an hour.[28]

All over America, middle-income jobs are disappearing in the wake of the re-engineering revolution. Tens of thousands of families living in suburban tracts along the country's highway culture are putting up For Sale signs on the front lawns, selling possessions, and packing their bags. For the first time since the Great Depression, they are moving down the income ladder, the victims of lean production, fast-track automation, and global market competition. According to the Census Bureau, the number of Americans living on middle incomes fell from 71 percent of the population in 1969 to less than 63 percent at the beginning of the 1990s.[29]

The decline in the middle class would have been far greater had not more wives entered the workforce in the past decade. At the beginning of the 1980s, there were more couples with the wife at home than at work. By the end of the decade 45.7 percent of all married couples were working to support their families, and only 33.5 percent were still one-earner married couples.[30] The statistics show the salaries of individual wage earners declining throughout the 1980s. Were it not for the extra paychecks, many families would have been dropped from the ranks of the middle class. By 1989 even the additional family income was not enough to make up for the wage cuts in individual salaries. The average American family experienced an income loss of 2 percent between 1989 and 1990.[31]

The declining fortunes of the American middle class show up most dramatically among the college educated. Between 1987 and 1991, the real wage of college educated workers fell 3.1 percent.[32] The college educated make up the bulk of management-level positions in the American economy, and it is these jobs that are being wiped out by the new technology advances and re-engineering practices. More than 35 percent of recent graduates have been forced to take jobs that don't require a college degree, up from 15 percent just five years ago. According to figures compiled by the Michigan State University College Employment Research Institute, the job market for college graduates is now the poorest since World War II.[33] Corporate recruiting is down on the nation's campuses. What positions are available are hotly contested. It is not unusual for thousands of college graduates to apply for a single opening. With Fortune 500 companies scaling down their workforces and quickly replacing human management with silicon management, the prospects are dim for many college graduates aspiring to become part of a dwindling American middle class.

THE NEW COSMOPOLITANS

Although the information-technology revolution has seriously undermined the fortunes of middle-class wage earners and foreclosed opportunities for a younger generation of college educated workers entering the labor force, it has been a boon to the small number of top executives who run the nation's businesses. Much of the productivity gains and increased profit margins of the past half century since automation and numerically controlled equipment were first introduced have gone into the coffers of top management. In 1953 executive compensation was the equivalent of 22 percent of corporate profit. By 1987 it was 61 percent. In 1979 CEOs in the United States made 29 times the income of the average manufacturing worker. By 1988 the average CEO was making 93 times the earnings of the average factory worker. To put these figures in perspective, consider the fact that when John F. Kennedy came into office, the typical CEO of a Fortune 500 company was earning $190,000 a year. In 1992 the average compensation topped $1.2 million. Between 1977 and the beginning of the current decade, salaries of top executives in American corporations rose by 220 percent. Had the nation's manufacturing workers shared in the productivity gains and profits to the same extent as management, the average factory laborer today would be earning more than $81,000 a year.[34] Even the editors of *Business Week* were forced to acknowledge that "executive pay is growing out of all proportion to increases in what many other people make—from the worker on the plant floor to the teacher in the classroom."[35]

The growing gap in wages and benefits between top management and the rest of the American workforce is creating a deeply polarized America—a country populated by a small cosmopolitan elite of affluent Americans enclosed inside a larger country of increasingly impoverished workers and unemployed persons. The middle class, once the signature of American prosperity, is fast fading, with ominous consequences for the future political stability of the nation.

The concentration of wealth in the United States remained fairly steady between 1963 and 1983. In the 1980s, however, the income gap began to dramatically widen. By the end of the decade, the richest 0.5 percent of families owned 30.3 percent of household net worth, an increase of 4.1 percent from 1983. In 1989 the top 1 percent of families earned 14.1 per cent of the total income in the United States, and owned 38.3 percent of the total net worth and 50.3 percent of the net financial assets of the country.[36]

In dollar terms, the top 5 percent of the nation's wage earners increased their incomes from $120,253 in 1979 to $148,438 in 1989, while the poorest 20 percent of the population experienced a decline in income from $9,990 to $9,431 a year.[37] The rich became super rich in the 1980s, largely at the expense of the rest of the American workforce, who saw their wages cut, their benefits shrink, and their jobs eliminated.

The number of millionaires jumped to a record high in the 1980s, as did that of billionaires. In 1988 more than 1.3 million people reported incomes in excess of one million dollars, up 180,000 from 1972. The number of billionaires increased from twenty-six families in 1986 to fifty-two families just two years later. The net worth of the nation's 834,000 richest families now totals over $5.62 trillion. In contrast, the net worth of the bottom 90 percent of American families is only $4.8 trillion.[38]

Less than half of 1 percent of the American population now exerts unprecedented power over the American economy, affecting the lives of some 250 million Americans. This small elite owns 37.4 percent of all corporate stocks and bonds and 56.2 percent of all U.S. private business assets.[39]

Below the super rich is a slightly larger class consisting of 4 percent of the working population of the United States. Their ranks are made up largely of the new professionals, the highly trained symbolic analysts or knowledge workers who manage the new high-tech information economy. This small group, numbering fewer than 3.8 million individuals, earns as much as the entire bottom 51 percent of American wage earners, totaling more than 49.2 million.[40]

In addition to the top 4 percent of American income earners who make up the elite of the knowledge sector, another 16 percent of the American workforce also consists mostly of knowledge workers. Altogether, the knowledge class, which represents 20 percent of the workforce, receives $1,755 billion a year in income, more than the other four fifths of the population combined. The incomes of this class continue to increase by 2 to 3 percent a year after inflation, even as the income of other American wage earners continues to decline.[41]

The knowledge workers are a diverse group united by their use of state-of-the-art information technology to identify, process, and solve problems. They are the creators, manipulators, and purveyors of the stream of information that makes up the postindustrial, postservice global economy. Their ranks include research scientists, design engineers, civil engineers, software analysts, biotechnology researchers, public relations specialists, lawyers, investment bankers, management consultants, financial and tax consultants, architects, strategic planners, marketing specialists, film producers and editors, art directors, publishers, writers, editors, and journalists.[42]

The importance of the knowledge class to the production process continues to grow while the role of the two traditional groups of the industrial era—laborers and investors—continues to diminish in importance. In 1920, for example, 85 percent of the cost of manufacturing an automobile went to production workers and investors. By 1990 these two groups were receiving less than 60 percent, and the remainder was being allocated "to designers, engineers, stylists, planners, strategists, financial specialists, executive officers, lawyers, advertisers, marketers, and the like."[43]

Semiconductors offer an even more telling example. Today, less than 3 percent of the price of a semiconductor chip goes to the owners of raw materials and energy, 5 percent to those who own the equipment and facilities, and 6 percent to routine labor. More than 85 percent of the cost goes to specialized design and engineering services and for patents and copyrights.[44]

In the early industrial era, those who controlled finance capital and the means of production exercised near-total control over the workings of the economy. For a while, during the mid-decades of this century, they had to share some of that power with labor, whose critical role in production assured it some influence in decisions governing both the ways and means of doing business and the distribution of profits. Now that labor's clout has significantly diminished, the knowledge workers become the more important group in the economic equation. They are the catalysts of the Third Industrial Revolution and the ones responsible for keeping the high-tech economy running. For that reason, top management and investors have had increasingly to share at least some of their power with the creators of intellectual property, the men and women whose knowledge and ideas fuel the high-tech information society. It is no wonder, then, that intellectual-property rights have become even more important than finance in some industries. Having a monopoly over knowledge and ideas ensures competitive success and market position. Financing that success becomes almost secondary.

In the high-tech automated world of the 1990s, the new elite of knowledge workers are emerging with critical skills that elevate them to center stage in the global economy. They are fast becoming the new aristocracy. As their fortunes wax, the economic circumstances of the vast numbers of low-level service workers wane, creating a new and dangerous division between the haves and have-nots in every industrial nation. The changing social geography of cities like New York, Berlin, London, and Paris provides visible evidence of the new class markers. Social historians Bennett Harrison and Barry Bluestone describe the social dynamic that is unfolding: "The upper tier of the labor market includes the managers, lawyers, accountants, bankers, business consultants, and other technically trained people whose daily duties lie at the heart of the control and co-ordination of the global corporation and the corporate services that are clearly linked to them. . . . At the bottom of the labor market is the other, less fortunate, pool of urban residents whose collective function is to provide services to the workers in the upper tier. . . . They are the ones who wait tables, cook meals, sell everything from office supplies to clothing, change beds and bath linen in the dozens of new hotels, provide custodial service and child care and find lower-level employment in the city's hospitals, health clinics, schools, and municipal government itself."[45]

Peter Drucker has warned his business colleagues that the critical social challenge facing the emergent information society is to prevent a new "class conflict between the two dominant groups in the post-capitalist society: knowledge workers and service workers."[46] Drucker's concerns are likely to become even more pronounced in the years ahead, as an increasing number of service jobs now performed by the working class are replaced by machines, forcing even more workers into the growing urban underclass.

Although many of the professionals who make up the new elite of symbolic analysts work in the world's great cities, they have little or no attachment to place. Where they work is of far less importance than the global network they work in. In this sense, they represent a new cosmopolitan force, a high-tech nomadic tribe who have more in common with each other than with the citizens of whatever country they happen to be doing business in. Their expertise and services are sold all over the world. This emergent new group of high-tech international workers, who will account for more than 60 percent of the income earned in the United States by 2020, are likely to retreat from civic responsibilities in the future, preferring not to have to share their earnings and income with the country as a whole. Secretary of Labor Robert Reich says it is possible that

> symbolic analysts will withdraw into ever more isolated enclaves, within which they will pool their resources rather than share them with other Americans or invest them in ways that improve other Americans' productivity. An even smaller proportion of their incomes will be taxed and thence redistributed or

invested on behalf of the rest of the public. . . . Distinguished from the rest of the population by their global linkages, good schools, comfortable lifestyles, excellent health care, and abundance of security guards, symbolic analysts will complete their secession from the union. The townships and urban enclaves where they reside, and the symbolic-analytical zones where they work, will bear no resemblance to the rest of America.[47]

THE OTHER AMERICA

Two very different Americas are emerging as we make the turn into the twenty-first century. The new high-technology revolution is likely to exacerbate the growing tensions between rich and poor and further divide the nation into two incompatible and increasingly warring camps. The signs of social disintegration are everywhere. Even conservative political pundits are beginning to sit up and take notice. Author and political analyst Kevin Phillips worries about the emergence of "dual economies" and points to states like Pennsylvania and North Carolina, where high-tech, postservice cities like Philadelphia and Durham are prospering in the new global economic web, while other areas of the states are losing steel mills and textile plants, forcing thousands of workers onto the relief rolls.[48]

Paul Saffo echoes Phillips' concerns. He notes that in high-tech enclaves like Telluride, Colorado, "You've got people living in electronic cottages making New York–scale salaries, while right next door there's someone else who's a hamburger flipper at the local fast food joint and he's making a rural Colorado salary." Saffo says that when "you get the ultra wealthy and the ultra poor cheek to cheek . . . it's absolute political dynamite . . . and could lead to a social revolution."[49]

The 1993 Census Bureau report on poverty in America provided statistical evidence of the growing gap between rich and poor. According to the study, the number of Americans living in poverty in 1992 is greater than at any other time since 1962. In 1992, 36.9 million Americans were living in poverty, an increase of 1.2 million over 1991 and 5.4 million more than in 1989. More than 40 percent of the nation's poor are children. The poverty rate among African-Americans now exceeds 33 percent and for Hispanics, 29.3 percent. Nearly 11.6 percent of all white Americans live in poverty.[50]

Despite the fact that more than 40 percent of the nation's poor worked during 1992, they were not able to make ends meet with low-paying, often part-time employment.[51] Their paltry incomes had to be supplemented with government-assisted relief efforts, just to survive. In 1992 more than 1 in 10 Americans depended on food stamps—the largest percentage since the federal program was launched in 1962. Nine million people have joined the food stamp program in just the past four years, bringing the number of Americans on food stamp assistance to 27.4 million. Some experts estimate that another 20 million are currently eligible for food stamps but have failed to apply.[52] Many of the new recipients are working people whose depressed wages and part-time employment are inadequate to feed their families. Others are the recently unemployed, the victims of global competition, corporate restructuring, and technology displacement.

In addition to government food-assistance programs, more than 50,000 private food banks, pantries, and soup kitchens are distributing food to the nation's hungry. In Chicago the Greater Chicago Food Repository distributed more than 22 million pounds of food in 1992, including 48,000 meals every single day of the year.[53]

Many of the nation's hungry are older Americans. Upwards of a million senior citizens are undernourished, and reports indicate that more than 30 million older people are forced to regularly skip meals. Hunger strikes most often among the nation's young. One child in four growing up in the United States goes hungry, according to studies prepared by Bread for the World, a Washington-based relief organization.[54] Don Reeves, an economic policy analyst for Bread for the World, says that the globalization of the economy and rapid technology displacement are "principal factors" in the growing numbers of American families who are going hungry.[55]

Chronic hunger is a major contributing factor to escalating health-care costs. Low-birth-weight infants and malnourished children often grow up with serious long-term health problems, adding billions of dollars to the health-care bill. Many of the nation's poorest citizens have little or no access to adequate health-care. According to the 1992 census, 28.5 percent of the poor have no health insurance of any kind.[56]

The recently unemployed are especially vulnerable to illness and disease. A study conducted by economists Mary Merva and Richard Fowles of the University of Utah found that a one percentage point rise in unemployment leads to a 5.6 percent increase in death from heart attacks and a 3.1 percent increase in death from strokes. Unemployed workers are more likely to experience increased levels of stress and depression, consume more alcohol and cigarettes, and eat less healthy diets, all contributing to the increased likelihood of heart attacks and strokes. Merva and Fowles studied thirty major metropolitan areas with a total population of nearly 80 million. Based on the 1990–1992 unemployment rate, which averaged 6.5 percent, the economists estimate that more than 35,307 additional deaths by heart attack and 2,771 additional deaths by strokes were attributed to higher unemployment. Fowles says that given the striking correlation between job loss and the rising incidence of disease, the government should step in and provide an adequate social safety net for workers who find themselves unemployed for extended periods of time.[57]

Those Americans still holding down a job often suffer from long-term health problems because employers have either provided a health-care package that is too limited to cover full medical needs or have failed to provide benefits at all. The Census Bureau reports that 35.4 million Americans were without health-care coverage in 1992, up by 2 million in one year.[58] Many employers have reduced or eliminated benefits altogether to save on overhead. Others have reduced their workforce, substituting machines for human labor to save on health-care programs. Still others have switched over to part-time or temporary labor and outsourcing of work to avoid paying for health-care coverage. The result is a nation of workers and unemployed people increasingly vulnerable and at risk without adequate health-care coverage to insure them even a minimum amount of care. Today, millions of families live with the constant fear that a single major medical crisis might force them into increased debt, bankruptcy, and a free fall into the permanent underclass.

The growing chasm between the haves and the have-nots is seen in the disquieting statistics on home ownership and housing. In the 1980s the average American had to give over 37.2 percent of his or her income to purchase a first home—up from 29.9 percent the preceding decade.[59] With the cost of homes rising and real wages dropping, fewer Americans are able to purchase their own house. In the 1980s the percentage of people between the ages of twenty-five and twenty-nine able to afford a house of their own dropped from 43.3 percent to 35.9 percent. For persons in the thirty-to-thirty-four age bracket, the rate of home ownership dropped from 61.1 percent to 53.2 percent. And, in the thirty-five-to-thirty-nine group, home ownership declined from 70.8 percent to 63.8 percent.[60]

Of those "fortunate" enough to have a roof over their head, 17.9 percent live in deficient structures. Many others are homeless, living on the streets and in emergency shelters across the urban landscape. A survey of twenty-five cities taken in 1991 found that requests for emergency shelters had increased by 13 percent over a twelve-month period. Currently more than 600,000 Americans, including as many as 90,000 children, are homeless in any given month.[61] Congressman Henry Gonzales, chairman of the House Committee on Banking, Finance, and Urban Affairs, charges that "we have made Americans nomads in their own land." Gonzales warns his colleagues that we have "families roaming this land, some of them living in cars and under bridges," and their ranks are growing daily.[62]

The nation's poor are concentrated in rural areas and in inner-city cores, the two regions hardest hit by technology displacement over the past two decades. More than 42 percent of the country's poor live in inner cities, up from 30 percent in 1968. The costs to society of "providing" for the nation's urban underclass now exceeds $230 billion a year, a staggering figure especially at a time when the nation is concerned about mounting debt and increased federal deficits.[63]

A growing number of industry analysts fix the blame for the escalating poverty on intense global competition and changes in technology. Light-manufacturing industries employing urban workers cut employment by upwards of 25 percent or more in recent years. The editors of *Business Week* note that, "For urban workers who counted on steady factory jobs that required little education, the losses have been devastating." Low-skilled white males in their twenties had their earnings drop by 14 percent, after adjusting for inflation, between 1973 and 1989. Black males fared worse. Their earnings fell by 24 percent in the same time period.[64]

While millions of urban and rural poor languish in poverty, and an increasing number of suburban middle-income wage earners feel the bite of re-engineering and the impact of technological displacement, a small elite of American knowledge workers, entrepreneurs, and corporate managers reap the benefits of the new high-tech global economy. They enjoy an affluent lifestyle far removed from the social turmoil around them. The frightening new circumstance the United States finds itself in led Secretary of Labor Robert Reich to ask, "What do we owe one another as members of the same society who no longer inhabit the same economy?"[65]

· 12 ·

Requiem for the
Working Class

W E LIVE IN A WORLD of increasing contrasts. Before us looms the
specter of a gleaming high-tech society with computers and
robots effortlessly channeling nature's bounty into a stream of sophisticated new products and services. Clean, quiet, and hyperefficient, the
new machines of the Information Age place the world at our fingertips,
giving us a measure of control over our surroundings and the forces of
nature barely imaginable just a century ago. On the surface, the
streamlined new information society seems to bear little resemblance
to the Dickensian conditions of the early industrial period. With its
powerful new mind machines, the automated workplace appears an
answer to humanity's age-old dream of a life free of toil and hardship.
In many communities, the poorly lit factories of the Second Industrial
Age have disappeared. The air is no longer cloaked with industrial
fumes; the floors, machines, and workers are no longer caked in grease
and grime. The hissing of live furnaces and the incessant clanking of
giant machines is now a distant echo. In their place can be heard the
soft whir of computers, speeding information along circuits and path-
ways, transforming raw materials into a cornucopia of goods.

This is the reality most often spoken of in the media, among
academicians and futurists, and within the councils of government.
The other side of the emerging techno-utopia—the one littered with
the casualties of technological progress—is only faintly hinted at in
official reports, in statistical surveys, and in occasional anecdotal tales
of lost lives and abandoned dreams. This other world is filling up with
millions of alienated workers who are experiencing rising levels of

stress in high-tech work environments and increasing job insecurity as the Third Industrial Revolution winds its way into every industry and sector.

HIGH-TECH STRESS

Much has been said and written about quality-control circles, team-work, and greater participation by employees at the worksite. Little, however, has been said or written about the de-skilling of work, the accelerating pace of production, the increased workloads, and the new forms of coercion and subtle intimidation that are used to force worker compliance with the requirements of post-Fordist production practices.

The new information technologies are designed to remove whatever vestigial control workers still exercise over the production process by programming detailed instructions directly into the machine, which then carries them out verbatim. The worker is rendered powerless to exercise independent judgment either on the factory floor or in the office, and has little or no control over outcomes dictated in advance by expert programmers. Before the computer, management laid out detailed instructions in the form of "schedules," which workers were then expected to follow. Because the execution of the task lay in the hands of the workers, it was possible to introduce a subjective element into the process. In implementing the work schedule, each employee placed his or her unique stamp on the production process. The shift from scheduling production to programming production has profoundly altered the relationship of workers to work. Now, an increasing number of workers act solely as observers, unable to participate or intervene in the production process. What unfolds in the plant or office has already been pre-programmed by another person who may never personally participate in the automated future as it unfolds.

When numerically controlled equipment was first introduced in the late 1950s, management was quick to appreciate the increased element of control it provided over work on the factory floor. In an address before the Electronic Industries Association in 1957, Air Force Lieutenant General C. S. Irvine, Deputy Chief of Staff for Materiel, noted that "heretofore, regardless of how carefully drawn and specified on paper, a finished piece [of machinery] could not be any better than the machinist's interpretations." The advantage of numerical control, argued Irvine, is that "since specifications are converted to objective digital codes of electronic impulses, the element of judgment is limited to that of the design engineer alone. Only his interpretations are directed from the tool to the workplace."[1] Others shared Irvine's enthusiasm for numerical control. In the late 1950s, Nils Olesten, general supervisor of Rohr Aircraft, stated publicly at the time what was privately on every manager's mind. "Numerical control," said Olesten, "gives maximum control of the machine to management . . . since decision making at the machine tool has been removed from the operator and is now in the form of pulses on the control media."[2] The quick adoption of numerical control was inspired as much by management's desire to consolidate greater control over decision making on the shop floor as to boost productivity.

A machinist at a Boeing plant in Seattle at the time numerical controls were first introduced voiced the frustration and anger of many semiskilled and skilled workers whose expertise was being transferred onto a magnetic tape: "I felt so stifled, my brain wasn't needed any more. You just sit there like a dummy and stare at the damn thing [a four-axis N/C milling machine]. I'm used to being in control, doing my own planning. Now, I feel like someone else has made all the decisions for me."[3]

Of course, it is true that re-engineering and the new information technologies allow companies to collapse layers of management and place more control in the hands of work teams at the point of production. The intent, however, is to increase management's ultimate control over production. Even the effort to solicit the ideas of workers on how to improve performance is designed to increase both the pace and productivity of the plant or office and more fully exploit the full potential of the employees. Some critics, like German social scientist Knuth Dohse, contend that Japanese lean production "is simply the practice of the organizational principles of Fordism under conditions in which management prerogatives are largely unlimited."[4]

A wealth of statistics collected over the past half decade bring into serious question the merits of many of the "new" management techniques being introduced into factories and offices around the world. In Japanese factories, for example, where working hours are 200 to 500 hours longer each year than in the United States, life on the assembly line is so fast-paced and stressful that most workers experience significant fatigue. According to a 1986 survey by the All Toyota

Union, more than 124,000 of the company's 200,000 member workers suffered from chronic fatigue.[5]

It should be pointed out that the principles of scientific management have long been known in Japan. Japanese automakers began using them in earnest in the late 1940s. By the mid-1950s, Japanese companies had created a hybrid form of Taylorism uniquely suited to their own circumstances and production goals. As noted in chapter 7, in post-Fordist production, work teams made up of staff and line employees participate in planning decisions in order to improve productivity. Once a consensus has been reached, however, the plan of action is automated into the production process and carried out unflaggingly by everyone on the line. Workers are also encouraged to stop the production line and make on-the-spot quality-control decisions, again with the intent of increasing the pace and predictability of operations.

Unlike traditional scientific management practiced in the United States, which denied workers any say in how the work is to be done, Japanese management decided early on to engage its workers in order to more fully exploit both their mental and physical labor, using a combination of motivational techniques and old-fashioned coercion. On the one hand, workers are encouraged to identify with the company, to think of it as their home and security. As noted earlier, much of their life outside of work is involved with company-related programs, including quality circles and social outings and trips. The companies become "total institutions," say Kenney and Florida, "exerting influence over many aspects of social life." In this regard, "they bear some resemblance to other forms of total institutions such as religious orders or the military."[6] On the other hand, in return for their loyalty, workers are guaranteed lifetime employment. Japanese workers often remain with the same company for their entire career.

Management often relies on its work teams to discipline members. Peer-review committees continually pressure recalcitrant or slow workers to perform up to par. Because the work teams are not supplied with additional help to make up for absentee workers, the remaining members must work even harder to catch up. As a result, tremendous peer pressure is exerted on employees to be at work on time. Japanese management is unyielding on the issue of absenteeism. In many plants all absences, even documented illnesses, are put on the employee's record. If a worker at Toyota misses five days of work a year, he or she is subject to dismissal.[7]

Authors Mike Parker and Jane Slaughter, who studied the Toyota-GM joint venture in California to make Toyota Corollas and Chevrolet Novas, characterize Japanese lean-production practices as "management by stress." The Toyota-GM plant has succeeded in greatly improving productivity, reducing the work time required to assemble a Nova from twenty-two hours to fourteen.[8] They have accomplished this by introducing an overhead visual display, called an Andon board. Each worker's station is represented by a rectangular box. If a worker falls behind or needs help, he pulls a cord and his rectangular area lights up. If the light remains on for one minute or more, the line stops. In a traditional plant the desired goal would be to keep the light off and production running smoothly. In management by stress, however, unlit warning lights signal inefficiency. The idea is to continually speed up and stress the system to find out where the weaknesses and soft spots are, so that new designs and procedures can be implemented to increase the pace and performance.

According to Parker and Slaughter, "stressing the system can be accomplished by increasing the line speed, cutting the number of people or machines, or giving workers more tasks. Similarly, a line can be 'balanced' by decreasing resources or increasing the work load at positions that always run smoothly. Once problems have been corrected, the system can be further stressed and then balanced again. . . . The ideal is for the system to run with all stations oscillating between lights on and lights off."[9]

Parker and Slaughter believe that the team concept of lean production is as far removed from enlightened management practices as is possible to conceive and that from the workers' perspective is merely a new, more sophisticated way to exploit them. While the authors acknowledge the limited participation of workers in planning and problem solving, they say it serves only to make workers willing accomplices in their own exploitation. Under management by stress, when the workers are able to identify weak points on the line and make recommendations or take remedial action, management simply increases the pace of production and further stresses the system. The key is to continually locate weak spots in a never-ending process of continuous improvement or *kaizin*. The effect on the workers of this Draconian method of management is devastating: "As the line goes faster and the whole system is stressed, it becomes harder and harder to keep up. Since tasks have been so painstakingly charted, refined, and recharted, management assumes any glitch is the workers' fault.

chimes and lights of the Andon board immediately identify the person who is not keeping up."[10]

The pace of production in Japanese-managed plants often results in increased injuries. Mazda reported three times the number of injuries per hundred than in comparable General Motors, Chrysler, and Ford auto plants.[11]

Worker stress under lean-production practices has reached near-epidemic proportions in Japan. The problem has become so acute that the Japanese government has even coined a term, *karoshi,* to explain the pathology of the new production-related illness. A spokesperson for Japan's National Institute of Public Health defines karoshi as "a condition in which psychologically unsound work practices are allowed to continue in such a way that disrupts the worker's normal work and life rhythms, leading to a buildup of fatigue in the body and a chronic condition of overwork accompanied by a worsening of pre-existing high blood pressure and finally resulting in a fatal breakdown."[12]

Karoshi is becoming a worldwide phenomenon. The introduction of computerized technology has greatly accelerated the pace and flow of activity at the workplace, forcing millions of workers to adapt to the rhythms of a nanosecond culture.

BIORHYTHMS AND BURNOUT

The human species, like every other species, is made up of myriad biological clocks that have been entrained, through the long period of evolution, to the rhythms and rotation of the earth: Our bodily functions and processes are timed to the larger forces of nature—the circadian day, lunar and seasonal cycles. Until the modern industrial era, bodily rhythms and economic rhythms were largely compatible. Craft production was conditioned by the speed of the human hand and body and constrained by the power that could be generated by harnessing animals, wind, and water. The introduction of steam power and later electrical power vastly increased the pace of transforming, processing, and producing goods and services, creating an economic grid whose operating speed was increasingly at odds with the slower biological rhythms of the human body. Today's computer culture operates on a nanosecond time gradient—a unit of duration that is so small that it cannot even be experienced by the human senses. In a snap of the fingers more than 500 million nanoseconds have elapsed. Author Geoff Simons draws an analogy that captures the awesome speed of computer time: "Imagine . . . two computers conversing with each other over a period. They are then asked by a human being what they are talking about, and in the time he takes to pose the question, the two computers have exchanged more words than the sum total of all the words exchanged by human beings since Homo sapiens first appeared on earth 2 or 3 million years ago."[13]

In the industrial era, workers became so enmeshed in the rhythms of mechanical machinery that they often described their own fatigue in machine terms—complaining of being "worn-out" or experiencing a "breakdown." Now, a growing number of workers are becoming so integrated with the rhythms of the new computer culture that when they become stressed, they experience "overload" and when they feel unable to cope they "burn out" and "shut down," euphemisms that reflect how closely workers have come to identify with the pace set by computer technology.

Psychologist Craig Brod, who has written extensively on stress induced by the high-tech computer culture, says that the increased pace of the workplace has only increased the impatience of workers, resulting in unprecedented levels of stress. In office situations, clerical and service workers become accustomed to "interfacing" with computers and "accessing" information at lightning speeds. In contrast, slower forms of human interaction become increasingly intolerable and a source of growing stress. Brod cites the example of the office worker who "becomes impatient with phone callers who take too long to get to the point."[14] Even the computer itself is becoming a source of stress as a growing number of impatient users demand faster and faster responses. One study found that a computer response time of more than 1.5 seconds in duration was likely to trigger impatience and stress on the part of the user.

Computer monitoring of employee performance is also causing high levels of stress. Brod recounts the experience of one of his patients, a supermarket cashier. When Alice's employer installed electronic cash registers, built into the computer-run machines was a counter that "transmits to a central terminal a running amount of how many items each cashier has run up that day." Alice no longer takes the time to talk with customers, as it slows down the number of items she can scan across the electronic grid and might jeopardize her job.[15]

A repair service company in Kansas keeps a running computer

tally of the number of calls its employees process and the amount of information collected with each telephone call. One stressed employee explains that "if you get a call from a friendly person who wants to chat, you have to hurry the caller off because it would count against you. It makes my job very unpleasant."[16]

According to a 1987 report published by the Office of Technology Assessment, entitled *The Electronic Supervisor,* between 20 and 35 percent of all clerical workers in the United States are now monitored by sophisticated computer systems. The OTA report warns of an Orwellian future of "electronic sweatshops" with employees doing "boring, repetitive, fast paced work that requires constant alertness and attention to detail, where the supervisor isn't even human" but an "unwinking computer taskmaster."[17]

The critical factor in productivity has shifted from physical to mental response and from brawn to brain. Companies are continually experimenting with new methods to optimize the "interface" between employees and their computers. For example, in an effort to speed up the processing of information, some visual display units are now being programmed so that if the operator does not respond to the data on the screen within seventeen seconds it disappears. Researchers report that operators experience increasing stress as the time approaches for the image to disappear on the screen. "From the eleventh second they begin to perspire, then the heart rate goes up. Consequently, they experience enormous fatigue."[18]

Even small, subtle changes in office routine have increased the stress level of workers. Brod recalls the experience of Karen, a typist. Before the shift from typewriters to word processors Karen would "use the physical cue of removing the paper from her typewriter to remind her to take a break." Now, sitting in front of the computer display terminal, Karen processes an unending stream of information. There is never a natural point to signal an end and a break. According to Brod, Karen "no longer takes time to chat with the other secretaries in the office pool," because they are similarly glued to their screens, processing their own incessant flow of information. "At the end of the morning," says Brod, "she is exhausted, and wonders how she'll find the energy to complete the day's work."[19]

The new computer-based technologies have so quickened the volume, flow, and pace of information that millions of workers are experiencing mental "overload" and "burnout." The physical fatigue generated by the fast pace of the older industrial economy is being eclipsed by the mental fatigue generated by the nanosecond pace of the new information economy. According to a study conducted by the National Institute of Occupational Safety and Health (NIOSH), clerical workers who use computers suffer inordinately high levels of stress.[20]

The hyperefficient high-tech economy is undermining the mental and physical well-being of millions of workers around the world. The International Labor Organization says that "stress has become one of the most serious health issues of the 20th century."[21] In the United States alone, job stress costs employers in excess of $200 billion a year in absenteeism, reduced productivity, medical expenses, and compensation claims. In the United Kingdom, job stress costs up to 10 percent of the annual gross national product. According to an ILO report, published in 1993, the increased levels of stress are a result of the fast pace set by new automated machinery both on the factory floor and in the front offices. Of particular concern, says the ILO, is computer surveillance of workers. The UN agency cites a University of Wisconsin study that found that "electronically monitored workers were 10 to 15 percent more likely to suffer depression, tension and extreme anxiety."[22]

High stress levels often lead to health-related problems, including ulcers, high blood pressure, heart attacks, and strokes. Increased stress also results in alcohol and drug abuse. The Metropolitan Life Insurance Company estimated that an average of one million workers missed work on any given day because of stress-related disorders. Another study commissioned by the National Life Insurance Company found that 14 percent of the workers sampled had quit or changed jobs in the previous two years because of workplace stress. In recent surveys, more than 75 percent of American workers "describe their jobs as stressful and believe that the pressure is steadily increasing."[23]

More than 14,000 workers die from accidents on the job each year and another 2.2 million suffer disabling injuries. Although the ostensible cause of the accidents can vary from faulty equipment to the pace of production, investigators say that stress is most often the trigger that precipitates the errors. Says one ILO investigator, "of all the personal factors related to the causation of accidents, only one emerged as a common denominator, a high level of stress at the time the accident occurred. . . . A person under stress is an accident about to happen."[24]

The increased stress levels from working in high-tech, automated work environments is showing up in worker's compensation claims. In 1980 less than 5 percent of all claims were stress related. By 1989, 15 percent were related to stress disorders.[25]

THE NEW RESERVE ARMY

While the conditions of work in re-engineered, automated facilities are increasing the stress and compromising the health of workers, the changing nature of work is also contributing to their economic insecurity. Many workers are no longer able to find full-time employment and long-term job security.

In February 1993, BankAmerica Corporation—the nation's second-largest bank—announced that it was turning 1,200 full-time jobs into part-time employment. The bank estimates that less than 19 percent of its employees will be full-time workers in the near future. Nearly six out of ten BankAmerica employees will work fewer than twenty hours a week and receive no benefits. The company, which experienced record profits over the past two years, says the recent decision to turn more jobs into part-time work was made to make the company more flexible and to reduce overhead costs.[26]

BankAmerica is not alone. Across the country U.S. corporations are creating a new two-tier system of employment, composed of a "core" staff of permanent full-time employees augmented by a peripheral pool of part-time or contingent workers. At Nike's distribution facility in Memphis, 120 permanent employees, each earning more than $13 an hour in wages and benefits, work side-by-side with 60 to 255 temporary workers. The temps are provided by Norrell Services, one of the nation's leading temporary services. The temp agency receives $8.50 an hour for each worker—two dollars goes to Norrell, leaving each worker $6.50 an hour, half of the hourly compensation of Nike's permanent employees. The large wage differential exists despite the fact that the permanent employees "do the same work as the temps."[27]

Temporary agencies like Norrell provide American companies with 1.5 million temps every day. Manpower, the nation's largest temp agency, is now the country's single largest employer, with 560,000 workers. In 1993 more than 34 million Americans were "contingent" workers—working as temps on a part-time basis or as contractors or freelancers.[28]

In the last fifteen years, says Mitchell Fromstein of Manpower, "there has been greater growth in contingent work . . . than there has been in the permanent work force."[29] Between 1982 and 1990, temporary-help employment grew ten times faster than overall employment. In 1992 temporary jobs accounted for two out of every three new private-sector jobs. Temporary, contract, and part-time workers now make up more than 25 percent of the U.S. workforce.[30] Those figures are expected to rise appreciably in the remainder of the current decade. Richard Belous, vice president and chief economist at the National Planning Association, predicts that upwards of 35 percent of the U.S. workforce will be contingent workers by the year 2000.[31] The movement toward contingent workers is part of a long-term strategy by management to cut wages and avoid paying for costly benefits like health care, pensions, paid sick leave, and vacation. All told, employee benefits account for nearly 45 percent of the total reimbursement for time worked by permanent full-time employees.[32] Belous likens contingent work to a one-night stand and warns, "that's not how you build long-term relationships." He worries that contingent work may "diminish employee loyalty" in the future, with potentially serious consequences to the business community.[33]

Faced with a highly competitive and volatile economy, many companies are paring down their core labor pool and hiring temps in order to be able to add and delete workers quickly in response to seasonal and even monthly and weekly trends in the market. Nancy Hutchens, a human resources consultant, draws an analogy between the new contingent workforce emerging in the 1990s and the just-in-time inventory revolution that swept the business community in the 1980s. "The revolution in the 1990s," says Hutchens, "is toward just-in-time employment . . . companies will use people only as they need them." "The ramifications are staggering," says Hutchens, who warns that the nation has not yet "come to terms" with the impact just-in-time employment is likely to have on the economic well-being and emotional security of the workforce."[34]

Part-time temporary workers earn on average 20 to 40 percent less than full-time workers doing comparable work.[35] According to the Department of Labor, part-time workers averaged $4.42 per hour in 1987 compared to $7.43 an hour for full-time workers. While 88 percent of full-time workers received health coverage through their employers, less than 25 percent of the temporary workforce was covered either by temp agencies or the companies they were leased out to. Similarly, while 48.5 percent of full-time workers were covered by employee pension plans, only 16.3 percent of part-time workers received pension benefits.[36]

Companies are also cutting labor costs by contracting with outside suppliers for goods and services traditionally handled in-house. Outsourcing allows companies to bypass unions. Many of the outsource suppliers are smaller companies paying low wages and providing few benefits to their workers. Outsourcing has become a permanent feature in the Japanese economy and has become increasingly popular in the United States and Europe. In the information sector, the outsourcing market for services topped $12.2 billion in 1992 and is expected to grow to more than $30 billion by 1997.[37] Chrysler procures more than 70 percent of the value of its final products from outside suppliers. According to a study conducted by Paine Webber, upwards of 18 percent of the workforce in the steel industry is now made up of employees working for subcontractors.[38] Typical is the case of a former pipe fitter employed by U.S. Steel at the Gary Works. He earned $13 an hour and enjoyed a generous company benefits package. After being laid off, he was only able to find a job for a small subcontractor at $5.00 an hour with no benefits. His new job was making parts for his former employer.[39]

Although the public perception of temp workers is still the Kelly girl—part-time receptionists, secretaries, and other pink collar clerical workers—the reality is that temps are being used as a substitute for permanent workers in virtually every industry and sector. In 1993 temporary agencies leased more than 348,000 temporary workers a day to the nation's manufacturing companies, up from 224,000 in 1992.[40]

Professional employment is also becoming temporary. The *Executive Recruiter News* reports that more than 125,000 professionals work as temps every day. "Professionals are the fastest growing group of temporary workers," says David Hofrichter, managing director of the Chicago office of the Hay Group compensation consultants. Many companies, according to Dr. Adela Oliver, president of Oliver Human Resources Consultants, are eliminating entire departments because they know they can quickly pick up experts in different areas on a contract basis."[41]

Dick Ferrington, an employee-training expert, is typical of the new professional temps. Now forty-eight, Ferrington has been temping for seven of the last nine years, earning close to $100,000 per year without benefits. He is currently serving as an interim vice president for human resources at Scios Nova, a Silicon Valley biotechnology company. His contract is for six months. When between temp jobs,

Ferrington hunts for new temp assignments from his house, which is equipped with a computer, modem, and fax.[42]

Not all professionals are as fortunate as Ferrington in securing temporary work at high wages. Many professional temps are more likely to face the kind of hardships experienced by Arthur Sultan, a former financial services executive at Xerox making $200,000 a year. Sultan was laid off when his division was closed. After searching for permanent work for more than two years, Sultan settled for temp assignments, just to pay the mortgage and keep some income coming in. Unable to find a job in his professional field, Sultan was forced, at one point, to take on three part-time jobs, working an eighty-hour week as a driver for a car service, a camera salesman at Caldor's department store, and a credit manager for Pepperidge Farm. For the past nine months Sultan has been working for the Federal Deposit Insurance Corporation as a temporary financial analyst, making $21 an hour. While he enjoys his current job, he worries constantly about whether he will have a job to report to tomorrow morning. "It's worse than being out of work," says Sultan. "You can't even make plans for the future."[43]

Even scientists, who, by virtue of their expertise, are widely thought to be immune to job insecurity in the high-tech knowledge economy are being reduced to temp work. On Assignment Inc, a temporary agency specializing in leasing scientists to companies ranging from Johnson & Johnson to Miller Brewing Company, has more than 1,100 chemists, microbiologists, and lab technicians ready to lease around the country. Recently Frito Lay requested a college-trained technician to test the crunchiness of its newest tortilla chip and was sent one of On Assignment's professional technicians within forty-eight hours—saving the company the cost of hiring a full-time permanent employee for the job.[44]

The federal government has begun to follow the lead of the private sector, replacing more and more full-time civil servants with temps to save on overhead and operating costs. Nearly 157,000 government workers, or 7.2 percent of the workforce, are currently temps. The Department of Defense, the Agriculture Department, and the Interior Department each employs nearly 50,000 temporary workers. Many agencies fire their temps just short of a year's service and then rehire them days later, says Robert Keener, president of the National Federation of Federal Employees, in order to avoid paying health and retirement benefits that automatically kick in after one year's service. The shoddy treatment of temp workers by federal government agencies led the director of the Office of Personnel Management to warn a House subcommittee that the federal workforce is being made into "a public service sweat shop."[45]

Temporary workers and outsourcing make up the bulk of today's contingent workforce—millions of Americans whose labor can be used and discarded at a moment's notice and at a fraction of the cost of maintaining a permanent workforce. Their very existence acts to drive wages down for the remaining full-time workers. Employers are increasingly using the threat of temp hiring and outsourcing to win wage and benefit concessions from unions—a trend that is likely to accelerate in the years ahead. It is no wonder that in a study conducted in 1986, Bluestone and Harrison, along with Chris Tilly of the Policy and Planning Institute at the University of Massachusetts, found that 42 percent of the growth in inequality in wages and income was directly attributable to management's decision to create a two-tier labor force of well-paid core workers and poorly paid contingent workers.[46] "Working on the edge as a temporary employee doesn't give us much of a life," said one temp at an automotive plant. "They think of us as throw away people."[47]

Depressed wages, a frenetic pace set at the workplace, the rapid rise in part-time contingent work, increased long-term technological unemployment, a growing disparity in income between the haves and the have-nots, and the dramatic shrinking of the middle class are placing unprecedented stress on the American workforce. The conventional optimism that propelled generations of immigrants to work hard in the belief that they could better their lot in life and improve the prospects for their children has been shattered. In its place is a growing cynicism about corporate power and increased suspicion of the men and women who wield near total control over the global marketplace. Most Americans feel trapped by the new lean-production practices and sophisticated new automation technologies, not knowing if or when the re-engineering drive will reach into their own office or workstation, plucking them from what they once thought was a secure job and casting them into the reserve army of contingent workers, or, worse yet, the unemployment line.

A SLOW DEATH

The profound psychological impact on the American worker of the radical changes in the conditions and nature of work is being viewed with alarm by industry observers. Americans, perhaps more than any other people in the world, define themselves in relationship to their work. From early childhood, youngsters are constantly asked what they would like to be when they grow up. The notion of being a "productive" citizen is so imprinted on the nation's character that when one is suddenly denied access to a job, his or her self-esteem is likely to plummet. Employment is far more than a measure of income: for many it is the essential measure of self-worth. To be under-employed or unemployed is to feel unproductive and increasingly worthless.

The steady growth in long-term technological displacement has sparked interest among psychologists and sociologists in the mental-health problems of the unemployed. A spate of studies conducted over the past decade have found a clear correlation between rising tech-nological unemployment and increased levels of depression and psy-chotic morbidity.[48]

Dr. Thomas T. Cottle, a clinical psychologist and sociologist affili-ated with the Massachusetts School of Professional Psychology, has been meeting with the "hard-core" unemployed for more than fifteen years. The hard-core unemployed are what the government defines as "discouraged workers," men and women who have been out of work for six months or longer and are too demoralized to continue looking for employment. A growing number of them come from the ranks of the technologically dispossessed—men and women whose jobs have been eliminated by new laborsaving technologies and restructured work environments.

Cottle has observed that the hard-core unemployed experience symptoms of pathology similar to dying patients. In their minds, productive work is so strongly correlated with being alive that when employment is cut out from under them, they manifest all of the classic signs of dying. Cottle recalls the sentiments of one of the workers he interviewed, a forty-seven-year-old named George Wilkinson, who was once a manager of a small tool company. He told Cottle, "There's only two worlds: either you work every day in a normal nine-to-five job with a couple weeks vacation, or you're dead! There's no in-between. . . . Working is breathing. It's something you don't think about: you just do it and it keeps you alive. When you stop you die."[49] Cottle reports that a year after making these remarks, Wilkinson killed himself with a shotgun.

In his study of the hard-core unemployed, Cottle has found a common progression of symptoms. In the first stage of unemployment, the men he interviewed vented their anger and frustration at former co-workers and employers. In some places around the country, the workplace has become a virtual war zone, with laid-off employees shooting their fellow employees and employers with increasing frequency. Homicide is now the third major cause of death at the workplace. In 1992, reports the National Institute for Occupational Safety and Health, there were 111,000 incidents of workplace violence, including 750 fatal shootings. The murdering of employers has nearly tripled since 1989 and is the fastest-growing category of workplace violence.[50]

According to a study prepared by the National Safe Workplace Institute in Chicago, violence against employers is frequently triggered by downsizing and layoffs. Robert Earl Mack was fired from his job at the General Dynamics Convair plant in San Diego after twenty-five years on the payroll. At a reinstatement hearing, he pulled out a .38 caliber handgun and shot his former supervisor and the union negotiator. When asked why he had done it, Mack replied, "It's the only job I ever had . . . how can they take everything away from me?"[51]

Troubled over the escalating wave of violence at the workplace, some companies are setting up "threat management teams" to identify potential sources of violence and take appropriate preventive actions to deter shootings and bombings. "Rapid-response teams" are also being established to intervene during an attack and thwart the assailant. "Trauma teams" have even been set up to notify next-of-kin after a homicide, prepare witnesses, and counsel workers suffering post-traumatic syndrome.[52]

Cottle says that after nearly a year of being unemployed most former workers begin to turn their rage inward. Suspecting that they may never work again, they begin to blame themselves for their predicament. They experience an overwhelming sense of shame and worthlessness, punctuated by a loss of vitality. In the place of anger they become weary and resigned. Many turn away from their families, says Cottle. "Their masculinity and strength sapped, they appear shameful, childlike, as if they deserve to be the invisible, reclusive people they in fact have become."[53]

Psychological death is often followed by actual death. Unable to cope with their condition and feeling like a burden to family, friends, and society, many end up taking their own lives. Cottle remembers one of the unemployed workers he counseled. His name was Alfred Syre. One January night his wife called, "hysterical and screaming." Syre, who had never had an auto accident, had driven his car head-on into an embankment, killing himself instantly. Syre and Wilkinson are among a growing number of hard-core unemployed who have lost all hope and chosen suicide as their escape route.

The death of the global labor force is being internalized by millions of workers who experience their own individual deaths, daily, at the hands of profit-driven employers and a disinterested government. They are the ones who are waiting for pink slips, being forced to work part-time at reduced pay, or being pushed onto the welfare rolls. With each new indignity, their confidence and self-esteem suffer another blow. They become expendable, then irrelevant, and finally invisible in the new high-tech world of global commerce and trade.

· 13 ·

The Fate of Nations

T HE DESTABILIZING EFFECTS of the Third Industrial Revolution are being felt all over the world. In every advanced economy, new technologies and management practices are displacing workers, creating a reserve army of contingent laborers, widening the gap between the haves and the have-nots, and creating new and dangerous levels of stress. In the Organization for Economic Cooperation and Development (OECD) countries, 35 million people are currently unemployed and an additional 15 million "have either given up looking for work or unwillingly accepted a part-time job."[1] In Latin America, urban employment is over 8 percent. India and Pakistan are experiencing unemployment of more than 15 percent. Only a few East Asian nations have unemployment rates of below 3 percent.[2]

In Japan, where the term "unemployment" is barely uttered, fierce new global competition is forcing companies to tighten their operations, throwing workers into unemployment lines for the first time in recent memory. Although Japan claims an unemployment rate of only 2.5 percent, some analysts point out that if the high number of discouraged unemployed workers and unrecorded jobless is added to the totals, the figure might be as high as 7.5 percent.[3] *The Wall Street Journal* reported in September 1993 that "fears are spreading [in Japan] that major corporations will soon be forced to lay off workers— perhaps on a large scale."[4] Manufacturing job openings have fallen by 26 percent, and some Japanese economists predict two job applicants for every job in the next few years. Koyo Koide, a senior economist at the Industrial Bank of Japan, says, "the potential pressure of labor adjustment [in Japan] is the greatest since World War II."[5]

Employment prospects have dimmed in virtually every sector of the Japanese economy. Megumu Aoyana, a job placement officer at Toyo University in Tokyo, complains that corporate recruitment of college graduates is at a postwar low. Middle-management job openings in manufacturing firms are slowing, and some analysts claim that as many as 860,000 management jobs will likely be eliminated in the next wave of corporate re-engineering. In the past, says Aoyana, it was assumed that if manufacturing jobs were cut, the service sector would absorb the excess workers. Now, service-sector job offers have fallen by 34 percent, the largest drop of any sector. Aoyana believes that Japan's giant corporations "will never again hire a lot of people."[6]

In a recent article in the *Harvard Business Review*, Shintaro Hori, a director of the consulting firm of Bain and Company Japan, warned that Japanese companies would likely have to eliminate as much as 15 to 20 percent of their entire white collar workforce to match the low overhead of U.S.-based companies and remain competitive in world markets. Japanese employers, faced with the realities of a highly competitive global economy, are likely to feel increasing pressure to downsize their operations in the years immediately ahead, displacing millions of workers in the process.[7]

While concerns over unemployment are mounting in Japan, the same fears have reached a near fever pitch in Western Europe, where one in nine workers is currently without a job.[8] Every Western European nation is experiencing worsening unemployment. France's unemployment is at 11.5 percent. In England it has topped 10.4 percent. In Ireland unemployment is now over 17.5 percent. Italy's has reached 11.1 percent. In Belgium, unemployment stands at 11 percent. Denmark's unemployment is approaching 11.3 percent. In Spain, once among the fastest-growing countries in Europe, one out of five workers has no job.[9]

German unemployment now hovers at 4 million. More than 300,000 jobs in the auto industry alone are expected to be eliminated in the coming period.[10] Comparing the unemployment figures today with those in Germany in the early 1930s, Chancellor Helmut Schmidt recently made the chilling observation that "more people are unemployed in Chemnitz, Leuna or Frankfurt an der Oder than in 1933, when people there elected the Nazis." Schmidt warned the German people and the global community of dire consequences ahead. "If we cannot overcome this [problem]," said Schmidt, "we must be prepared for everything."[11] The German situation is sending shock waves through the European economy. Germany's 80 million citizens make up 23 percent of Europe's consumers, and its

$1.8 trillion economy accounts for 26 percent of the European Union's GNP.[12]

Industry observers claim that the number of unemployed in Europe will climb to 19 million by the beginning of 1995 and will probably continue to rise during the remainder of the decade. Drake, Beam, Morin, a consulting company, recently surveyed more than 400 European companies and reported that 52 percent intend to cut their workforce by 1995. (In a similar survey conducted in the United States, the consulting company found that 42 percent of the firms interviewed were planning further cuts in their workforce by 1995.) The firm's chairman, William J. Morin, warns that "the pressures of global competition and new technology are . . . beginning to hit hard in Europe."[13]

HIGH-TECH POLITICS IN EUROPE

The issue of technology displacement is fast moving to the fore in European political debate. By the beginning of the 1990s, only one in five European workers was employed in manufacturing, down from one in four in 1960.[14] The loss of manufacturing jobs is due in large part to the introduction of new laborsaving, time-saving technologies and the restructuring of production practices along lines already well advanced in the United States and Japan.

The European automotive-components industry is illustrative of the trend. The industry currently employs more than 940,000 workers in EC countries. According to a confidential report prepared for the European Commission, in order for European firms to remain competitive and regain their market position they will need to re-engineer their operations and reduce their workforce by 400,000 by 1999. That represents a 40 percent projected drop in employment in just one industry in less than six years.[15]

Manufacturing industries in Europe and the other OECD countries are expected to continue to eliminate increasing numbers of workers over the next several decades as they move inexorably toward the era of the workerless factory. Whatever hope economists and policy leaders had that the service sector would provide jobs for the unemployed, as it had done in the past, is now dwindling. While the service sector in OECD countries grew by 2.3 percent per year during the 1980s, by 1991 the rate of growth had dropped to less than 1.5 percent. In Canada, Sweden, Finland, and the United Kingdom, the service sector actually declined in 1991. The ILO places the blame for the downturn on the structural changes taking place in the service sector. In its *World Labour Report* of 1993, the ILO noted that "most services, from banking to retailing (with the possible exception of health care) are now restructuring in ways which the manufacturing industry adopted a decade ago."[16]

In Europe, the unemployment problem is likely to be further exacerbated by the drop in public employment. During the 1980s, public-sector jobs—totaling 5 million—accounted for most of the job growth in the European Union.[17] Now, with European nations thinning their budgets in an effort to lower government deficits and debt, the prospect of governments' hiring displaced manufacturing and service workers and acting as an employer of last resort is no longer politically feasible. Even more alarming is the fact that more than 45.8 percent of the unemployed workers in Europe have been without a job for more than a year—a staggering figure compared to the United States, where only 6.3 percent have been out of a job for more than twelve months.[18]

What employment opportunities do exist are largely limited to part-time work. As in the United States, European companies are increasingly turning to temps to save on labor costs. Just-in-time employment is becoming the norm in many European countries. Temps are concentrated in the service sector, where the re-engineering phenomenon is spreading rapidly, challenging traditional notions of job security. In the Netherlands, 33 percent of the workers are part-time, and in Norway more than 20 percent. In Spain, one out of every three workers is now part-time. In the United Kingdom, nearly 40 percent of the jobs are part-time.[19]

The evidence suggests that just-in-time employment is going to play a larger and even more expanded role in the new high-tech global economy of the twenty-first century.[20] Multinational companies, anxious to remain mobile and flexible in the face of global competition, are increasingly going to shift from permanent to contingent workforces in order to respond quickly to market fluctuations. The result is going to be increased productivity and greater job insecurity in every country of the world.

In Europe, in particular, the increasing reliance on a reserve army of contingent workers reflects the growing concern on the part of corporate management that the expensive social net erected in the EC countries in the postwar era is making their companies less competitive in the global arena. The average German manufacturing worker is much better paid than is his American counterpart. His hourly compensation costs employers approximately $26.89, with 46 percent going to benefits. Italian manufacturing workers make more than $21 an hour, and most of their compensation comes in the form of benefits. An American manufacturing worker costs his employer only $15.89 an hour and only 28 percent of it goes to benefits.[21]

Europeans also enjoy longer paid vacations and work fewer hours. In 1992 the average German worker put in 1,519 hours a year and received forty days of paid vacation. Government workers averaged 1,646 hours. American employees work an average of 1,857 hours a year while Japanese workers top the list, logging more than 2,007 hours of work every year. All in all, European labor is 50 percent more expensive than either U.S. or Japanese labor.[22]

Public spending in Europe is also higher than in any other industrial region of the world. Much of it goes to finance social programs to protect and enhance the well-being of workers and their families. Social security payments in Germany in 1990 were 25 percent of the gross domestic product, compared to only 15 percent in the United States and 11 percent in Japan. Financing social benefits for workers requires heavier taxes on corporations. The corporate tax burden in Germany now exceeds 60 percent, and in France is approaching 52 percent. In the United States it is only 45 percent.[23] When all of the costs of maintaining an adequate social net are added up—including the costs of taxes, social security, unemployment compensation, pensions, and medical insurance—they amount to about 41 percent of the total gross domestic product in Europe, compared to 30 percent in the United States and Japan.[24]

Corporate leaders have introduced a new term, "Euro-sclerosis," into the public dialogue in an effort to draw attention to what they consider to be bloated and unnecessary social welfare programs. In defense of their claims, they point to the United States, where the social net was stripped away during the Reagan-Bush years as part of a well-orchestrated campaign to rid companies of undue labor costs.[25]

In August 1993, Chancellor Helmut Kohl's government announced a $45.2 billion cut in social-benefit programs as part of an austerity drive designed to tame the escalating federal deficit.[26] Other European countries are following suit. In France, the new conservative government enacted measures to significantly cut social programs, including a reduction in retirement payments and reimbursement for medical expenses. The new government also shortened the number of weeks an unemployed worker can receive jobless benefits. Commenting on the changes, a French official remarked, "We can't have people working for eight months and then receiving 15 months of unemployment benefits, as they do today." In the Netherlands, the conditions governing disability benefits have been tightened up in the hope of saving more than $2 billion a year in public spending.[27] Some European officials, such as European Union (EU) Commissioner Padraig Flynn, are urging caution in the debate over lowering the social net. He warns that "you're going to see more low-wage jobs being created . . . and more part-time work." In both cases, says Flynn, "the key is to have a satisfactory level of social protection . . . so that you're not creating working poor and increased levels of poverty."[28]

The lowering of the social net, at a time when growing numbers of workers are being displaced by new technologies and management restructuring, is increasing tensions throughout Europe. In March 1994, tens of thousands of students took to the streets in cities across France to protest a government decree lowering the minimum wage for young people. With one out of four French youth already unemployed, the government is worried that increasing political unrest could lead to a repeat of the kind of violent protests that shook France in 1968, paralyzing the government. In Italy, where youth unemployment has reached 30 percent, and in England, where it now tops 17 percent, political observers watched the events taking place in France with keen interest, worried that their countries might be the next to be rocked by militant youth protests.[29]

Surveying the plight of European workers, researcher Heinz Werner said it's "like a treadmill for hamsters. Anyone who gets off the treadmill will find it hard to get back on." Once off, says labor expert Wilhelm Adamy, "the problem of each unemployed person will worsen," as they find themselves facing an ever shrinking social net.[30] More than 80 million people in the EC are already living in poverty. Their numbers are likely going to swell, perhaps to epidemic proportions, as more and more workers are displaced by new technologies and set adrift in an economic sea with fewer public lifeboats to rescue them.[31]

AUTOMATING THE THIRD WORLD

The Third Industrial Revolution is spreading quickly into the third world. Global companies are beginning to build sophisticated high-tech, state-of-the-art plants and facilities in countries throughout the southern hemisphere. "In the 1970s," says Harley Shaiken, Professor of Labor and Technology at the University of California at Berkeley, "capital intensive, highly automated production seemed to be linked to industrial economies like the United States, and the jobs that went off-shore were low-tech, low productivity jobs like sewing blue jeans and assembling toys." Now, says Shaiken, "with computers, telecommunications and new forms of cheap transport, highly advanced production has been successfully [transplanted] to third world countries.[32]

As noted earlier, the wage component of the total production bill continues to shrink in proportion to other costs. That being the case, the cost advantage of cheap third-world labor is becoming increasingly less important in the overall production mix. While cheap labor might still provide a competitive edge in some industries like textiles and electronics, the advantage of human labor over machines is fast diminishing with advances in automation. Between 1960 and 1987, "less than a third of the increase in output in developing countries . . . came from increased labor," according to a recent report by the United Nations Development Program. "More than two-thirds [came] from increases in capital investment."[33]

Many companies in third-world countries have been forced to invest heavily in automated technologies in order to ensure speed of delivery and quality control in an ever more competitive global market. Often, the decision to locate a plant in a developing nation is as much influenced by the desire to be close to a potential new market as by labor-cost differentials. Whether it be market performance or market location, say the editors of *Fortune*, "New technology and the continuing drive for higher productivity push companies to build in less developed countries plants and offices that require only a fraction of the manpower that used to be needed in factories back home."[34]

Consider the case of Mexico. Global companies based in the United States and Japan have been setting up plants along a 300-mile strip of border towns in northern Mexico since the late 1970s. The assembly plants, known as *maquiladoras,* include Ford, AT&T, Whirlpool, Nissan, Sony, and scores of other manufacturing giants. The newer plants are highly automated facilities requiring a much smaller workforce of skilled technicians to operate.[35]

Companies are quickly automating their plant production process in northern Mexico more in an effort to improve quality than to save labor costs. Like other global companies operating there, Zenith has automated its manufacturing facilities and reduced its workforce from

3,300 to 2,400. Elio Bacich, the director of Zenith's Mexican operations, says that "sixty per cent of what we once did by hand is now done by machinery."[36]

Machines are replacing workers in every developing country. Martin Anderson, vice president of the Gemini Consulting Firm, in New Jersey, says that when companies build new factories in developing countries they are generally far more highly automated and efficient than their counterparts back in the United States. "Some of the most Japanese-looking American plants are going up in Brazil," says Anderson.[37] The idea that transferring production facilities to poor countries is going to mean high levels of local employment and greater prosperity is no longer necessarily true. Shaiken agrees, arguing that "the kind of needs in the third world for jobs dwarf the number of jobs that are being created" by the new high-technology automated plants and businesses. He worries that the Third Industrial Revolution is going to mean a few high-tech jobs for the new class of elite knowledge workers and growing long-term technological unemployment for millions of others. The clear trend, says Shaiken, is "a continuation of the extensive polarization of incomes and the marginalization of millions of people."[38]

The substitution of machines for human labor is leading to increased labor unrest in the third world. On July 1, 1993, workers struck at the Thai Durable Textile Company, just outside of Bangkok, shutting down production. The strike was called to protest the layoff of 376 of the company's 3,340 workers, who were let go to make room for new laborsaving technology. With more than 800,000 workers—mostly women—employed in the Thai textile industry, both labor and management view the strike as a test case that is likely to decide the fate of tens of thousands of workers caught in the throes of a technology revolution that is moving the world ever closer to the workerless factory.[39]

In neighboring China, where cheap labor has long substituted for more expensive machine capital, government officials have announced an across-the-board restructuring of factories and upgrading of equipment to help give the world's most populous nation a competitive advantage in world markets. Chinese industry analysts predict that as many as 30 million will be let go in the current wave of corporate restructuring.[40]

Nowhere is the contrast between the high-tech future and the low-tech past more apparent than in Bangalore, India, a city of 4.2 million that is fast becoming known as that country's Silicon Valley. Global companies like IBM, Hewlett-Packard, Motorola, and Texas Instruments are flocking to this city located atop a 3,000-foot plateau some 200 miles west of Madras. In colonial times, the city, with its mild climate, tropical plants, and beautiful vistas, was a favorite vacationing spot for British civil servants. Today, it sports "gleaming office towers blazoned with Fortune 500 logos." In a country teeming with poverty and social unrest, Bangalore "is an island of relative affluence and social stability." Touting some of the best-trained scientists and engineers anywhere in the world, this Indian city has become a high-tech mecca for global electronic and computer firms eager to set up shop close to burgeoning new markets.[41]

Bangalore is just one of a number of new high-tech enclaves being established in key regional markets around the planet. Their very existence, amidst growing squalor and despair, raises troubling questions about the high-tech future that awaits us in the coming century. Historian Paul Kennedy asks whether countries like India can "take the strain of creating world competitive, high-tech enclaves . . . in the midst of hundreds of millions of their impoverished countrymen." Noting the growing disparity between the new symbolic analyst class and the declining middle and working poor in countries like the United States, Kennedy asks whether developing countries like India might fare even more poorly in the new high-tech world. "Given the even greater gap in income and lifestyles that would occur in India," says Kennedy, "how comfortable would it be to have islands of prosperity in a sea of poverty?"[42]

Kennedy's concerns become even more compelling in light of the rising number of workers projected to enter the labor force in developing countries in the years ahead. Between now and the year 2010, the developing world is expected to add more than 700 million men and women to its labor force—a working population that is larger than the entire labor force of the industrial world in 1990. The regional figures are equally striking. In the next thirty years the labor force of Mexico, Central America, and the Caribbean is expected to grow by 52 million, or twice the number of workers as currently exist in Mexico alone. In Africa, 323 million new workers will enter the labor force over the next three decades—a working-age population larger than the current labor force of Europe.[43]

Worldwide, more than a billion jobs will have to be created over the next ten years to provide an income for all the new job entrants in both developing and developed nations.[44] With new information and telecommunication technologies, robotics, and automation fast eliminating jobs in every industry and sector, the likelihood of finding enough work for the hundreds of millions of new job entrants appears slim.

Again, Mexico offers a good case in point. Even though Mexico is better off than most developing nations, 50 percent of the labor force is still unemployed or underemployed. Just to maintain the status quo, Mexico will need to generate more than 900,000 jobs a year during the remainder of the current decade to absorb the new workers entering the labor force.[45]

We are rapidly approaching a historic crossroad in human history. Global corporations are now capable of producing an unprecedented volume of goods and services with an ever smaller workforce. The new technologies are bringing us into an era of near workerless production at the very moment in world history when population is surging to unprecedented levels. The clash between rising population pressures and falling job opportunities will shape the geopolitics of the emerging high-tech global economy well into the next century.

· 14 ·

A More
Dangerous World

IN A GROWING NUMBER of industrialized and newly emerging nations, technology displacement and increasing unemployment are leading to a dramatic rise in crime and random violence, providing a clear portent of the troubled times ahead. Recent studies have shown a disturbing correlation between increases in unemployment and the rise in violent crime. In the Merva and Fowles study, cited earlier, the researchers found that in the United States, a one percent rise in unemployment results in a 6.7 percent increase in homicides, a 3.4 percent increase in violent crimes, and a 2.4 percent increase in property crime. In the thirty major metropolitan areas covered in their study, the University of Utah economists estimate that between mid-1990 and mid-1992 the rise in unemployment from 5.5 percent to 7.5 percent resulted in 1,459 additional homicides, 62,607 additional violent crimes (including burglary, aggravated assault, and murder), and 223,500 additional property crimes (including robbery, larceny, and motor vehicle theft).[1]

The Merva and Fowles study also showed a striking correlation between growing wage inequality and increased criminal activity. Between 1979 and 1988, the thirty metropolitan areas studied in the survey experienced a 5 percent increase in wage inequality. The growing gap between the haves and have-nots was accompanied by a 2.05 percent rise in violent crimes, a 1.87 percent increase in property crime, a 4.21 percent rise in murder, a 1.79 percent increase in robbery, a 3.1 percent rise in aggravated assault, a 1.95 percent increase in larceny and theft, and a 2.21 percent increase in motor vehicle theft. By the end of 1992, more than 833,593 Americans were incarcerated in state and federal prisons, up by 59,460 over the previous year.[2]

George Dismukes, who is currently serving a sixteen-year sentence for murder, expressed the anger and frustration of many in the prison population in a bitter indictment delivered in the pages of *Newsweek* in the spring of 1994. Dismukes reminded the rest of America:

> We, the imprisoned, are America's shame. The real crime here is that of your folly. Millions of people in this land languish wasted, underachieving. . . . Society has no use for them outside, so it pays to lock them out of sight, without opportunity or spiritual rehabilitation. . . . I say to you, the smug and contented: Watch out. . . . Our numbers are enlarging, our costs are rising swiftly. Building bigger and better . . . prisons does not begin to [resolve] the reasons behind the problems and madness. It only makes the gibbering louder and the eventual consequences more awful for everyone when they finally occur.[3]

Technology displacement and the loss of job opportunities have affected the nation's youth most of all, helping spawn a violent new criminal subculture. Unemployment rates among New York City's teenagers rose to 40 percent in the first quarter of 1993. The figures were double the number just two years earlier and the worst recorded in the twenty-five years statistics have been kept. In the rest of the country teenage unemployment was nearly 20 percent in 1993.[4] Much of the increase in youth joblessness is attributable to the introduction of new technologies that are replacing jobs traditionally held by teenagers.

Rising unemployment and loss of hope for a better future are among the reasons that tens of thousands of young teenagers are turning to a life of crime and violence. Police estimate that more than 270,000 students carry guns to school every day in the United States, and a recent study by the Harvard School of Public Health found that 59 percent of children in the sixth through twelfth grades said they "could get a handgun if they wanted one." Many children arm themselves out of fear. More than 3 million crimes occur every year on school grounds. Our nation's schools are fast turning into armed fortresses, with halls patrolled by security forces and monitored by high-tech surveillance equipment. Hidden cameras, X-ray machines, and metal detectors are becoming the norm in many schools. With stabbings and random killings rising sharply, some schools have begun to include "yellow-code alerts" alongside fire drills for classes ranging from kindergarten through grade twelve. "We have to teach students to hit the deck when the bullets fly," says one school security expert. The escalating costs of security are putting enormous strain on school budgets, already hard hit by budget deficits and shrinking tax revenues. The New York City school system now operates the eleventh-largest security force in the United States, with more than 2,400 officers.[5]

The current Attorney General, Janet Reno, has called youth violence "the greatest single crime problem in America today." Between 1987 and 1991, the number of teenagers arrested for murder in the United States increased by 85 percent. In 1992 nearly a million young people between the ages of twelve and fourteen were "raped, robbed or assaulted, often by their peers."[6]

In Washington, D.C., where several hundred young people have been shot in the past five years, and where random killings on school playgrounds and on the streets is a regular occurrence, a growing number of youngsters are planning for their own funerals—a macabre new phenomenon that has parents, school officials, and psychiatrists concerned. Eleven-year-old Jessica has already told parents and friends what she'd like to wear at her funeral. "I think my prom dress is going to be the prettiest dress of all," said the youngster in an interview with a *Washington Post* reporter. "When I die I want to be dressy for my family." School counselors and parents say that children as young as ten have provided detailed instructions on "what they want to wear and what songs they want played at their funerals." Some kids have even informed friends and relatives of what kind of funeral floral arrangements they would like to have. Douglas Marlowe, a psychiatrist at the Hahnemann University hospital in Philadelphia, says that "once they [the children] start planning their own funerals, they have given up."[7]

Occasionally, teenage criminal activity escalates from individual acts of terror to full-scale rioting, as was the case in Los Angeles in 1992. Many of the rioters, who set ablaze hundreds of houses and businesses, beat innocent bystanders, and scuffled with the police were members of teenage street gangs. It is estimated that more than 130,000 teenagers in greater Los Angeles are members of gangs.[8] Illiterate, unemployed, and on the streets, these youngsters have become a powerful social force, able to terrorize entire neighborhoods and communities.

Los Angeles has been hard hit by corporate restructuring, automation, plant relocation, and loss of defense contracting jobs. The South Central district, the epicenter of the riots, lost more than 70,000 jobs in the 1970s and 80s, forcing the poverty rate to a record high.[9] Unemployment now stands at 10.4 percent in Los Angeles County, while black unemployment is as high as 50 percent in some neighborhoods. Although the trigger for the L.A. riots was the not-guilty verdict handed down on four police officers in the infamous videotaped beating of African-American Rodney King, it was increasing unemployment, poverty, and hopelessness that ignited the collective fury of inner-city residents. As one political observer noted, "the nation's first multiracial riot was as much about empty bellies and broken hearts as it was about police batons and Rodney King."[10]

Teenage gangs have begun to proliferate in the nation's suburbs, and so too has the incidence of violent crimes. Once-safe communities are now becoming war zones, with reports of rapes, drive-by shootings, drug trafficking, and robberies. In generally affluent Westchester County, just outside of New York City, police report the emergence of more than seventy rival middle-class gangs in just the past few years.[11] Suburban youth gangs are popping up with increasing frequency across the country. The increase in crime has suburbanites worried. According to a 1993 Time/CNN poll, 30 percent of those surveyed "think suburban crime is at least as serious as urban crime—double the number who said that was true five years ago."[12]

Suburban homeowners are responding to the rise in crime with stepped-up security measures. In 1992 alone, more than 16 percent of all U.S. homeowners installed electronic security systems. Middle-class homeowners are even installing motion detectors and surveillance cameras, once considered expensive high-tech security items reserved for the homes of the very rich. Some are installing "video doorbells" to warn of intruders.[13]

Suburban architecture is also beginning to change, reflecting the new concern for personal security. "We are talking about the development of private fortresses," says Mark Boldassare, a professor of urban and regional planning at the University of California at Irvine. Boldassare and other architects say that steel and concrete are fast becoming the materials of choice, along with twelve-inch windows, twelve-foot fences, and swivel security camera systems. "Stealth buildings," homes whose façades are plain and even grim, masking an opulent interior, are also becoming popular among security-conscious residents.[14]

Many suburban communities are augmenting home security by hiring private security forces to monitor the neighborhoods. A growing number of subdivisions are being walled off from the outside, with only a single access road leading to a guardhouse. Residents have to show identification cards to gain entrance. In other neighborhoods, residents have literally purchased their streets from the city and blocked them off with iron gates and private security guards. In still other cities, residential neighborhoods are being fenced off by the building of concrete cul-de-sacs.[15]

Edward Blakely, a professor in the city and regional planning department at the University of California at Berkeley, estimates that between 3 and 4 million people already live inside walled residential communities. As many as 500,000 Californians are currently living in walled-in communities, and fifty new developments are currently under construction, according to Blakely. Many of the walled-in communities have installed state-of-the-art high-technology deterrence systems to keep out intruders. In Santa Clarita, California, just north of Los Angeles, any automobile attempting to speed through the guarded entryway into the community is stopped by metal cylinders shot from underground into the bottom of the car. Blakely says that the growth in walled-in communities reflects both a concern for personal safety and "a retreat from civic responsibility." For a growing number of wealthier Americans, living inside walled communities is a way of "internalizing their economic position and privilege and excluding others from sharing it."[16]

Reduced wages, steadily rising unemployment, and the increasing polarization of rich and poor is turning parts of America into an outlaw culture. While most Americans view unemployment and crime as the most pressing issues facing the country, far fewer are willing to acknowledge the inseparable relationship that exists between the two. As the Third Industrial Revolution spreads through the economy, automating more and more of the manufacturing and service sectors, forcing millions of blue and white collar workers out of work, crime, and especially violent crime, is going to increase. Trapped in a downward spiral, and with fewer safety nets to break their fall, a growing number of unemployed and unemployable Americans will of necessity turn to crime to survive. Locked out of the new high-tech global village, they will find ways of stealing their way back in to take by force what is being denied them by the forces of the marketplace.

Since 1987, according to the FBI's Uniform Crime Report, shoplifting is up by 18 percent, convenience store robberies are up by 27 percent, bank robberies are up by 50 percent, commercial business robberies are up by 31 percent, and violent crimes are up by 24 percent.[17] It is no wonder that the nation's security industry is among the fastest-growing sectors of the economy. With economic crime now approaching a staggering $120 billion a year, the nation's homeowners and industry find themselves shelling out billions for increased security.[18]

Today, the nation's private security force outspends public law enforcement by 73 percent and employs two and a half times the people. The private security industry is expected to grow at an annual rate of 2.3 percent during the remainder of the decade, or more than twice the rate of public law enforcement. The security industry currently ranks in the top ten among all service industries, along with electronic information systems, computer software, computer professional services, and data processing. By the year 2000, expenditures for private security are expected to exceed $100 billion.[19]

A GLOBAL PROBLEM

The increasing violence taking place on the streets of America is being played out in other industrialized nations throughout the world. In October 1990 in Vaux-en-Velin, a depressed working class town near Lyon, hundreds of youth took to the streets, clashing with police and later riot troops, for more than three days. Although the riot was triggered by the death of a teenager run over by a police car, local residents and government officials alike blamed increasing unemployment and poverty for the rampage. Youths stoned cars, burned down local businesses, and injured scores of people. By the time it was over, the damages had run to $120 million.[20]

In Bristol, England, in July 1992, violence erupted in the wake of an accident uncannily similar to the one that occurred in Vaux-en-Velin. A police car had run over and killed two teenagers who had stolen a police motorcycle. Hundreds of youth rampaged through the shopping area, destroying commercial property. Over 500 elite troops had to be called up to quell the disturbance.[21]

French sociologist Loic Wacquant, who has made an extensive study of urban rioting in first-world cities, says that in almost every instance the communities that riot share a common sociological profile. Most are formerly working class communities that have been caught up in and left behind by the transition from a manufacturing to an information-based society. According to Wacquant, "For the residents of flagging working class areas, the reorganization of capitalist economies—visible in the shift from manufacturing to education-intensive services, the impact of electronic and automation technologies in factories and offices, and the erosion of unions . . . have translated into unusually high rates of long-term joblessness and a regression of material conditions."[22] Wacquant adds that the increasing influx of immigrants into poor communities puts additional strain on job opportunities and public services, heightening tensions among residents who are forced to compete for a smaller slice of the economic pie.

A growing number of politicians and political parties—especially in Europe—have been playing off the concerns of working class and poor communities, exploiting their xenophobic fears of immigrants taking away precious jobs. In Germany, where 76 percent of the high school students in a recent survey said they were worried about being unemployed, young people are taking to the streets in violent political protests aimed at immigrant groups whom they accuse of taking away German jobs. Led by neo-Nazi youth gangs, the violence has steadily spread throughout Germany. In 1992, seventeen people were killed in 2,000 separate violent incidents, as neo-Nazi leaders blamed immigrants and Jews for the rising unemployment problem. In 1992 two neo-fascist parties on the right, the German People's Union and the Republikaner Party, whose leader was a former SS officer in Hitler's Third Reich, won seats for the first time in two state parliaments by appealing to xenophobic fears and anti-Semitism.[23]

In Italy, the neo-fascist National Alliance Party won an unexpected 13.5 percent of the vote in national elections in March 1994, becoming the third most powerful party in Italy. The party's mediagenic leader, Gianfranco Fini, was greeted with chants of "Duce! Duce! Duce!" by hundreds of young people at a postelection victory celebration, conjuring up dark images of the Mussolini era in the 1930s and 1940s. Political pollsters in Italy say that much of the party's support is coming from angry unemployed youth.[24]

In Russia, Vladimir Zhirinovsky's neo-fascist party, the Liberal

Democratics, won a surprising 25 percent of the vote in the first post-Soviet election to select a national parliament. In France, the followers of Jean-Marie Le Pen have made similar political gains, whipping up xenophobic fears of immigrants taking jobs away from native-born Frenchmen.[25]

Rarely, in their public statements, do any of the leaders of the extreme right broach the issue of technology displacement. Yet it is the forces of downsizing, re-engineering, and automation that are having the most effect on eliminating jobs in working class communities in every industrial country. The growing tide of immigration from east to west in Europe, and from south to north in the Americas, reflects in part the changing dynamics of the global economy and the emergence of a new world order that is forcing millions of workers to move across national borders in search of an ever-dwindling supply of manufacturing and service jobs.

The combination of technological displacement and population pressure continues to tax the carrying capacity of countless urban-core communities. The increased hardship and stress are leading to spontaneous upheavals and collective acts of random violence. Residents of inner-city cores in industrial nations now have more in common with the slum dwellers of the developing countries than they do with the new cosmopolitan workers who live in suburbs and exurbs just a few miles away.

Nathan Gardels, the editor of *New Perspectives Quarterly*, summed up the prevailing mood in terms remarkably similar to the arguments used to characterize the plight of urban blacks just thirty years ago, when they were uprooted first by new agricultural technologies in the South and then by mechanical and numerical-control technologies in northern factories. "From the standpoint of the market," says Gardels, "the ever swelling ranks of the [unemployed] face a fate worse than colonialism: economic irrelevance." The bottom line, argues Gardels, is that "we don't need what they have and they can't buy what we sell." Gardels foresees an increasingly lawless and foreboding future—a world populated by "patches of order and swaths of pandemonium."[26]

Some military experts believe that we are entering into a new and dangerous period of history increasingly characterized by what they call low-intensity conflict: warfare fought by terrorist gangs, bandits, guerrillas, and others. Military historian Martin Van Creveld says that the distinctions between war and crime are going to blur and even break down as marauding bands of outlaws, some with vague political

goals, menace the global village with hit-and-run murders, car bombings, kidnappings, and high-profile massacres.[27] In the new environment of low-intensity conflict, standing armies and national police
forces will become increasingly powerless to quell or even contain the
mayhem, and will likely give way to private security forces that will be
paid to secure safe zones for the elite classes of the high-tech global
village.

The transition into a Third Industrial Revolution throws into question
many of our most cherished notions about the meaning and direction
of progress. For the optimists, the corporate CEOs, professional futurists, and avant garde political leaders, the dawn of the Information Age
signals a golden era of unlimited production and rising consumption
curves, of new and faster breakthroughs in science and technology, of
integrated markets and instantaneous gratifications.

For others, the triumph of technology appears more a bitter curse,
a requiem for those who will be made redundant by the new global
economy and the breathtaking advances in automation that are eliminating so many human beings from the economic process. For them
the future is filled with dread, not hope, with growing rage, not
anticipation. They sense that the world is passing them by, and feel
increasingly powerless to intervene on their own behalf, to demand
their rightful inclusion in the new high-tech global order. They are the
outcasts of the global village. Shunned by the powers that be, and
forced to languish at the periphery of earthly existence, they are the
hordes whose collective temper is as unpredictable as the changing
political winds—a mass of humanity whose fortunes and destiny increasingly tend toward social upheaval and rebellion against a system
that has made them all but invisible.

On the eve of the third millennium, civilization finds itself pre-
cariously straddling two very different worlds, one utopian and full of
promise, the other dystopian and rife with peril. At issue is the very
concept of work itself. How does humanity begin to prepare for a
future in which most formal work will have passed from human beings
to machines? Our political institutions, social covenants, and economic relationships are based on human beings selling their labor as a
commodity in the open marketplace. Now that the commodity value of
that labor is becoming increasingly unimportant in the production and
distribution of goods and services, new approaches to providing income and purchasing power will need to be implemented. Alterna-

tives to formal work will have to be devised to engage the energies and talents of future generations. In the period of transition to a new order, the hundreds of millions of workers affected by the re-engineering of the global economy will have to be counseled and cared for. Their plight will require immediate and sustained attention if we are to avoid social conflict on a global scale.

Two very specific courses of action will need to be vigorously pursued if the industrialized nations are to successfully make the transition into a post-market era in the twenty-first century.

First, productivity gains resulting from the introduction of new labor- and time-saving technologies will have to be shared with millions of working people. Dramatic advances in productivity will need to be matched by reductions in the number of hours worked and steady increases in salaries and wages in order to ensure an equitable distribution of the fruits of technological progress.

Secondly, the shrinking of mass employment in the formal market economy and the reduction of government spending in the public sector will require that greater attention be focused on the third sector: the non-market economy. It is the third sector—the social economy—that people will likely look to in the coming century to help address personal and societal needs that can no longer be dealt with by either the marketplace or legislative decrees. This is the arena where men and women can explore new roles and responsibilities and find new meaning in their lives now that the commodity value of their time is vanishing. The partial transfer of personal loyalties and commitments away from the market and the public sector and to the informal, social economy foreshadows fundamental changes in institutional alignments and a new social compact as different from the one governing the market era as it, in turn, is different from the feudal arrangements of the medieval era that preceded it.

PART V

THE DAWN OF THE POST-MARKET ERA

· 15 ·

Re-engineering
the Work Week

NEARLY FIFTY YEARS AGO, at the dawn of the computer revolution, the philosopher and psychologist Herbert Marcuse made a prophetic observation—one that has come to haunt our society as we ponder the transition into the Information Age: "Automation threatens to render possible the reversal of the relation between free time and working time: the possibility of working time becoming marginal and free time becoming full time. The result would be a radical transvaluation of values, and a mode of existence incompatible with the traditional culture. Advanced industrial society is in permanent mobilization against this possibility."[1]

The Freudian scholar went on to say that "since the length of the working day itself is one of the principal repressive factors imposed upon the pleasure principle by the reality principle, the reduction of the working day . . . is the first prerequisite for freedom."[2]

Technological utopians have long argued that science and technology, properly harnessed, would eventually free human beings from formal work. Nowhere is that view more widely held than among the champions and advocates of the information revolution. Yoneji Masuda, one of the prime architects of Japan's computer revolution, envisions a future computopia where "free time" replaces "material accumulation" as the critical value and overriding goal of society. Masuda agrees with Marcuse that the computer revolution opens the door to a radical reorientation of society away from regimented work and toward personal freedom for the first time in history. The Japanese visionary argues that while the Industrial Revolution was primarily concerned with increasing material output, the information revolution's primary contribution will be the production of greater increments of free time, giving human beings the "freedom to determine voluntarily" the use of their own futures.

Masuda sees the transition from material values to time values as a turning point in the evolution of our species: "Time value is on a higher plane in human life than material values as the basic value of economic activity. This is because time value corresponds to the satisfaction of human and intellectual wants, whereas material values correspond to the satisfaction of physiological and material wants."[3]

In both industrial and developing nations there is a growing awareness that the global economy is heading toward an automated future. The information and communication technology revolutions virtually guarantee more production with less human labor. One way or another, more free time is the inevitable consequence of corporate re-engineering and technology displacement. William Green, the former president of the AFL, put the issue succinctly: "Free time will come," the labor leader said. "The only choice is unemployment or leisure."[4]

Economic historians point out that in the case of the first two industrial revolutions, the issue of rising unemployment versus greater leisure was eventually settled in favor of the latter, although not without a protracted struggle between labor and management over the productivity and hours question. The dramatic productivity gains of the first stage of the Industrial Revolution in the nineteenth century were followed by a reduction of work hours from eighty to sixty hours a week. Similarly, in the twentieth century, as industrial economies made the transition from steam technologies to oil and electric technologies, the steady increases in productivity led to a further shortening of the workweek from sixty hours to forty. Now, as we cross the divide into the third stage of the Industrial Revolution and reap the productivity gains of the computer and the new information and telecommunication technologies, a growing number of observers are suggesting the inevitability of reducing work hours once again to thirty and even twenty hours per week to bring labor requirements in line with the new productive capacity of capital.

Although in previous periods of history increases in productivity have resulted in a steady reduction in the average number of hours worked, the opposite has been the case in the four decades since the birth of the computer revolution. Harvard economist Juliet Schor points out that American productivity has more than doubled since

1948, meaning that we can "now produce our 1948 standard of living (measured in terms of marketed goods and services) in less than half the time it took in that year." Yet Americans are working longer hours today than forty years ago at the outset of the information-technology revolution. Over the past several decades, work time has increased by 163 hours, or one month a year. More than 25 percent of all full-time workers put in forty-nine or more hours on the job each week. The amount of paid vacation time and sick leave also declined over the past two decades. The average American worker now receives three and one half fewer paid vacation and sick days than he or she did in the early 1970s. With working hours now longer than they were in the 1950s, Americans report that their leisure time has declined by more than one third. If current trends in work continue, by the end of the century American workers will be spending as much time at their jobs as they did back in the 1920s.[5]

The productivity revolution, then, has affected the amount of time worked in two ways. The introduction of labor- and time-saving technologies has allowed companies to eliminate workers en masse, creating a reserve army of unemployed workers with idle time on their hands rather than leisure time at their disposal. Those still holding on to a job are being forced to work longer hours, partially to compensate for reduced wages and benefits. Many companies prefer to employ a smaller workforce at longer hours rather than a larger one at shorter hours to save the costs of providing additional benefits, including health care and pensions. Even with the payment of time and a half for overtime, companies still pay out less than they would if they had to pay for benefit packages for a larger workforce.

Barry Jones, former Minister of Technology for the Australian government, raises a question that is in the minds of many: if, as virtually every economist agrees, it was beneficial to significantly reduce the number of hours of work in both the nineteenth and early twentieth centuries to accommodate the dramatic increases in technological productivity, why isn't it just as beneficial, from a societal perspective, to cut the number of hours by a like proportion to accommodate the dramatic rise in productivity coming out of the information and telecommunication revolution?[6] Former senator and presidential candidate Eugene McCarthy says that unless we shorten the workweek and more equitably distribute the available work, "we're going to end up having to let 20 to 30 million more people slip into the poverty class where they will have to be maintained with food stamps and subsidies."[7]

TOWARD A HIGH-TECH WORKWEEK

Today the demand for the shorter workweek is being actively pro-moted, once again, by a growing number of labor leaders and econo-mists. With government less able or willing to intervene with tax-and-spend public-works projects, many see the shorter workweek as the only viable solution to technological displacement. Lynn Williams, past president of the United Steel Workers of America, says that, "We need to start thinking [now] about shorter hours . . . as a way to share in the improved productivity."[8] In 1993 Volkswagen, Europe's largest automaker, announced its intentions to adopt a four-day workweek to save 31,000 jobs that might otherwise have been lost to a combination of stiffening global competition and new work technologies and methods that had boosted productivity by 23 percent. The workers voted to support the management plan, making Volkswagen the first global corporation to move to a thirty-hour work week. While take-home pay will be cut by 20 percent, lower taxes and a spreading of the traditional Christmas and holiday bonuses over the entire work year is expected to soften the impact.[9] Peter Schlilein, a spokesman for Volks-wagen, said that both the company and the workers accepted the idea of a shorter workweek as an equitable alternative to mass permanent layoffs.[10]

The call for the shorter workweek is spreading quickly through Europe, where unemployment has reached record postwar highs. In Italy, trade unions are marching under the new slogan "Lavorare Meno, Lavorare Tutti"—Work Less, and Everyone Works. In France, the idea has galvanized popular support and won the endorsement of a majority of the Parliament. President François Mitterrand has spoken favorably of the idea of a four-day workweek, and Michel Rocard, the Socialist Party's presidential candidate in 1995, has pledged to cam-paign for shorter hours in the upcoming elections.[11]

The proposed four-day week in France is the brainchild of Pierre Larrouturan, a French consultant for the international accounting firm of Arthur Andersen. The Larrouturan plan calls for a switch from the current thirty-nine-hour week to a thirty-three-hour week, beginning in 1996. While the new shorter workweek would mean a 5 percent reduction in wages, it would increase employment by 10 percent, creating 2 million new jobs. To compensate for the loss of wages, companies would be required to introduce profit-sharing plans to allow workers to participate in and benefit from future gains in productivity. Employee costs would be offset by the national government's assuming the burden of financing unemployment insurance. Companies currently pay an 8.8 percent payroll tax. At the same time, the French government is not expected to suffer financially by abolishing the unemployment payroll tax, which amounts to $21.8 billion a year. According to the plan's proponents, with 2 million fewer people unemployed, the state will save $27.5 billion in payments that would have gone to unemployed workers in the form of various relief benefits, effectively canceling out the increased costs of abolishing the payroll tax and assuming the burden of paying for the unemployment insurance.[12]

The plan's advocates also believe that the rescheduling of the workweek will improve productivity and make French companies more competitive in the global economy. Aside from the traditional argument that the shorter workweek reduces fatigue and improves efficiency, the new emphasis on flexible hours, say proponents, has been shown to increase productivity by optimizing the use of capital and equipment.

Experiments with shorter workweek schedules by companies like Hewlett-Packard and Digital Equipment have convinced many skeptics in the business world of the potential benefits to management of the new approach to work. At Hewlett-Packard's Grenoble plant, management adopted a four-day workweek, but kept the plant running twenty-four hours a day, seven days a week. The company's 250 employees are now working a 26-hour-and-50-minute workweek on the night shift, a 33.5-hour workweek on the afternoon shift, and a 34-hour-and-40-minute workweek on the morning shift. They are paid the same wages as they received when they were working a 37.5-hour week, despite the fact that they are working on the average nearly six hours less a week. The extra compensation is viewed by management as a tradeoff for the worker's willingness to operate under a flexible-hours arrangement. Production has tripled at the Grenoble facility in large measure because the company is able to keep its plant in continual operation seven days a week rather than having it remain idle for two days, as was the case before the reorganization of the work schedule. Gilbert Fournier, an official of the French Confederation of Democratic Labor, says labor is "pleased by experiments like Hewlett-Packard." "We are convinced," says Fournier, "that shorter working weeks that also leave machinery functioning as long or longer represent a key to creating employment in Europe."[13]

Digital Equipment introduced a different scheme in its plants. The company offered its workers a four-day workweek with a 7 percent pay cut. Of the company's 4,000 workers, 530, or more than 13 percent of the workforce, opted for the shorter workweek. Their decision saved ninety jobs that would have otherwise been cut through re-engineering. "A large number of people were interested in working less and being paid less," said Robin Ashmal, a spokeswoman for Digital Management. "Young people want to divide their lives differently and have more leisure time."[14]

The Commission of the European Union and the European Parliament have both gone on record in favor of shortening the workweek to address the issue of unemployment. A Commission memorandum warned that it was "important to avoid the hardening of two distinct groups in society—those with stable employment and those without—a development which would have disruptive social consequences and would endanger the very foundations of all democratic societies in the longer run." The Commission statement made plain that the time had come for governments and industries "to maintain and create jobs through the reduction of working time in order to achieve greater [social] equity at a time of very high and rising unemployment."[15] Similarly, the European Parliament has lent its support to Community initiatives that "guarantee, in the short term, a significant reduction in daily, weekly and/or yearly working hours and in working life, in order to significantly slow down and subsequently halt the trend towards growing unemployment."[16]

The call for a shorter workweek is even making inroads in Japan, long the bastion of the industrial work ethic. The workweek has been steadily declining in Japan over the past three decades. The shortening of the workweek has accompanied dramatic increases in productivity and economic growth, belying the oft-heard claim that less work and more leisure undermines corporate competitiveness and profits.

Some Japanese economists and business leaders take a bottom-line approach, arguing that more leisure is necessary to stimulate the service economy and provide Japanese workers the time to purchase and use more goods and services. Others see the work and leisure issue as a quality-of-life concern and argue that workers need more time to be with their families, to take part in parenting, to engage in neighborhood and community activities, and to enjoy life.

In 1992 Prime Minister Kiichi Miyazawa announced that shorter hours would be a national goal and said the government would commit its resources to promoting the "quality of life" in Japan. In August 1992 the government announced the Economic Council's five-year plan to become "the lifestyle superpower." The plan will emphasize programs that create a more healthy, leisurely environment for Japanese citizens. At the top of the list of priorities is shortening the workweek from forty-four to forty hours.[17]

Shortening the workweek has taken on added importance in Japan, of late, with reports that Japanese companies are employing at least 2 million more workers than they need.[18] With the re-engineering and automation revolutions expected to further trim employment and payrolls in the next decade, many Japanese are beginning to see the shorter week as an answer to technological displacement and widespread future unemployment.

Despite the successful examples of companies like Hewlett-Packard, Digital Equipment, and others who have moved to a shorter workweek in their European plants without compromising productivity or profits, most American CEOs remain steadfastly opposed to the idea. A survey of 300 business leaders, conducted several years ago, soliciting their support for a shorter week did not receive a single positive response. One Fortune 500 CEO wrote back, "My view of the world, our country and our country's needs is dramatically opposite of yours. I cannot image a shorter workweek. I can imagine a longer one . . . if America is to be competitive in the first half of the next century."[19]

WORKERS' CLAIMS ON PRODUCTIVITY

The business community has long operated under the assumption that gains in productivity brought on by the introduction of new technologies rightfully belong to the stockholders and corporate management in the form of increased dividends and larger salaries and other benefits. Workers' claims on productivity advances, in the form of higher wages and reduced hours of work, have generally been regarded as illegitimate and even parasitic. Their contribution to the production process and the success of the company has always been viewed as of a lesser nature than those who provide the capital and take the risk of investing in new machinery. For that reason, any benefits that accrue to the workers from productivity advances are viewed not as a right, but rather as a gift bestowed by management.

More often than not, that gift comes in the form of grudging concessions to union representatives in the collective bargaining process.

Ironically, the conventional argument used by management to justify their claims on productivity gains has been stood on its head in recent years by the profound changes that have taken place in the capital market. Management's claim that gains in productivity ought to go to the investors who risk their capital to create the new technology has now become a potentially potent weapon in the hands of the workers. For, as it turns out, the investors by and large happen to be the workers. It is the deferred savings of millions of American workers that are being invested in the new information technologies. Pension funds are now the largest pool of investment capital in the U.S. economy. These funds, now worth more than $4 trillion, represent the savings of millions of working Americans. Pension funds account for 74 percent of net individual savings, over one third of all corporate equities, and nearly 40 percent of all corporate bonds. Pension funds hold nearly one third of the total financial assets of the U.S. economy. In 1993 alone, these funds made new investments of between $1 and $1.5 trillion. Pension assets now exceed the assets of commercial banks in the United States, making them a formidable investment tool.[20]

Unfortunately, workers have little or no say over how their deferred savings are invested. Consequently, for more than forty years, banks and insurance companies have been investing billions of dollars of workers' funds in new laborsaving technologies, only to eliminate the jobs of the very workers whose money is being used. For a long time, pension-fund managers argued that under the government's "prudent man" rule, their only obligation was to maximize the return on the portfolio. In recent years, partially in response to the prodding of organized labor, the federal government has broadened the concept of the prudent man principle to include investments that promote the overall economic well-being of the recipients. From the workers' perspective, it makes little or no sense for portfolio managers to simply maximize the return on pension investments if it means the wholesale elimination of their jobs in the process. Since it is their own hard-earned savings that are being used to advance productivity, American workers have a justifiable right to share in that productivity both as investors and as employees. Despite the American workers' just claim to a piece of the productivity pie, the business community has steadfastly held the line against any attempts to shorten the workweek and increase wages to accommodate the rapid gains in productivity.

MODEST PROPOSALS

The chances are that corporate resistance to the shorter workweek will soften in the years ahead as management becomes more aware of the need to bridge the gap between greater productive capacity and falling consumer purchasing power. Public pressure to shorten the workweek, as a means of more equitably distributing the available work, is also likely to have a significant impact both on the collective bargaining process and on legislative initiatives in the halls of Congress.

Economists such as Nobel Laureate Wassily Leontief are already preparing the ground for the transition to the shorter workweek. Leontief argues that the mechanization of the manufacturing and service sectors is similar to what took place earlier in the century in agriculture. In the case of agriculture, the government stepped in and established an income policy to help the farmers adjust to overproduction against ineffective demand. Today, says Leontief, industrial nations already have a well-established income policy for their labor forces in the form of social security benefits, unemployment benefits, medical insurance, and welfare payments. He concludes that what is needed is a broadening of the idea of income transfer to adjust to the tightening grip of technological displacement. He suggests that a first tentative step in that direction might include supplemental benefits to those who work less than the normal hours—already a widespread practice in Europe.

While Leontief believes that technological change is inevitable, he readily admits that the emerging knowledge sector will not be able to create enough new jobs to absorb the millions of workers displaced by re-engineering and automation. He says he favors a shortening of the workweek as a means of sharing the available work, but adds that it should be voluntary and not mandated, because enforcement is difficult.[21]

John Zalusky, head of Wages and Industrial Relations at the AFL-CIO, argues for an even more immediate and less complicated answer to the employment and hours question. Zalusky points out that each one of the 9.3 million unemployed workers in the United States costs the economy $29,000 in loss of revenue "because they become tax users; they are on public assistance rather than being tax payers."[22] He contends that new jobs could be created if measures were implemented to discourage overtime work and bring the workweek back to forty hours. The labor spokesman reminds us that the overtime premium was originally designed "to allow work on real emergencies like power outages but to deter employers from imposing more than 40 hours in 7 days."[23] In recent years—as mentioned earlier—employers have used overtime as an alternative to maintaining a larger workforce in order to save on the costs of providing additional fringe benefits. In 1993 factory overtime in the United States averaged 4.3 hours, the highest level ever recorded. Hours of work have increased by 3.6 percent since 1981, while the number of workers employed has steadily declined.[24]

Zalusky advocates increasing overtime compensation from time-and-one-half to double or even triple time to dissuade management from relying on it as an alternative to hiring additional workers. "Just getting the work week back to 40 hours per week for full-time workers," says Zalusky, "would mean 7 million additional jobs."[25] The AFL-CIO spokesman admits, however, that it will be extraordinarily difficult to pass corrective legislation, and points to the fact that the Fair Labor Standards Act provisions regarding overtime payment have not been amended since 1938.[26]

At the AFL-CIO convention in San Francisco in October 1993, the question of shorter hours was seriously discussed for the first time in several decades. Lynn Williams says the question of reduced hours "is becoming a higher and higher item on the agenda as we watch this alleged economic recovery unfold without creating enough jobs." Even more to the point is Thomas R. Donahue, secretary-treasurer of the AFL-CIO. He told his colleagues that "there is no question that the long-term salvation of work lies in reducing working hours."[27]

Dennis Chamot says that while many in organized labor believe that lowering the number of hours in the workweek is inevitable in the long run, "it's not going to be an easy sell." The reason is that politicians have been slow to grasp the extent of the transition taking place in the global economy. Up to now, says Chamot, elected officials have continued to hope that the current wave of re-engineering and technology displacement is a temporary phenomenon, not understanding "that this is part of a major restructuring of our economy in the way work is done."[28]

Bills have been introduced in Congress to mandate a shorter workweek. Congressman John Conyers, chairman of the powerful Government Operations Committee, introduced legislation more than a decade ago that would amend the Fair Labor Standards Act, reducing the number of hours worked from forty to thirty, phased in over an eight-year period. The Conyers bill would also increase overtime pay from time-and-a-half to double time to deter management from using it as an alternative to hiring additional workers. The bill also contains a provision that would outlaw mandatory overtime clauses in labor contracts. In a letter to his colleagues soliciting support for the reduced workweek bill, Conyers wrote, "One of the chief methods of keeping unemployment in check during the Depression was the adoption of the 40-hour workweek. During the past 30 years, however, the workweek has remained substantially unchanged despite the frequency of massive unemployment, large-scale technological displacement of human labor, and considerable gains in productivity. We ought to look at reducing the workweek and spreading employment among a greater number of workers, once again, as a means of reducing joblessness without sacrificing productivity."[29]

A second bill, introduced in October 1993 by Congressman Lucien E. Blackwell, calls for a government-mandated thirty-hour week. The bill includes a provision that would increase the federal minimum wage to $7 per hour. The legislation also includes automatic increases in the minimum wage tied to the consumer price index. Proponents of the legislation point to the savings in unemployment compensation and welfare payments that will result from putting millions back to work at a reduced weekly work schedule.[30]

With global competition tightening, many business leaders are reluctant to reduce the workweek for fear that the increased cost of wages would drive up the price of their product relative to foreign competition. Higher labor costs, so the argument goes, would put domestic producers at a marked disadvantage and result in the loss of market shares in the global economy. William McGaughey and former Senator Eugene McCarthy, in their book *Nonfinancial Economics,* partially refute the standard argument tying hours worked to global competitiveness, saying that between 1960 and 1984, United States manufacturers reduced their workweek by a smaller amount than any other industrial nation and provided the smallest increase in hourly compensation. Yet, even though U.S. companies' annual increases in per-unit labor costs were the smallest of the twelve leading industrial nations, the U.S. trade balance shifted from surpluses to deficits during that same period. Curiously, Japan's trade balance went from deficits to surpluses in the same years, even though it experienced large annual increases in labor costs.[31]

Still, the argument persists that fewer hours at existing pay could put companies at a competitive disadvantage globally. One way to address the concern is the proposed solution being advocated in France. As mentioned earlier, French business and labor leaders and politicians from several parties have embraced the idea of the government taking over the burden of paying for unemployment compensation, in return for an agreement by companies to shorten the workweek. French policymakers calculate that the hiring of additional workers will significantly reduce welfare and other relief payments, canceling out any additional costs the government might have to assume by absorbing the payroll tax for unemployment compensation. Companies might also be extended tax credits for shifting to a shorter workweek and hiring additional workers. The size of the tax credit could be determined by the number of workers hired and the total amount of the increased payroll. The loss of revenue up-front, some argue, would likely be made up for later on by the taxable revenue generated by more workers bringing home a paycheck. The Clinton administration has already floated the idea of providing tax credits to companies that hire welfare recipients, setting a precedent for a broader initiative that would cover the bulk of the workforce.

Finally, the government might consider mandating a profit-sharing plan at each firm—as is being suggested in France—to allow workers to directly participate in the productivity gains. In addition, Congress ought to consider providing a tax deduction for employees facing reduced workweeks and smaller take-home pay. By allowing a deduction for every hour of work eliminated, the government could help ease the burden on wage earners and make the shorter workweek more palatable to the nation's workforce.

Even with these innovations, many economists believe it will be necessary to negotiate multilateral agreements with other industrial and developing nations to ensure a fair playing field. Michael Hammer argues that "you can only [reduce the workweek] if everybody does it." Like many other industry analysts, Hammer contends that "if you're going to pay people the same amount for less hours of work, then you're basically raising the cost of your products, and you can only do that if everyone is willing to go along with it."[32] Some, like McCarthy and McGaughey, favor the development of a tariff system "to promote the worldwide advancement of labor standards." The tariff rates would be determined on the basis of an index measuring the level of wages and hours worked in the countries from which the products are exported.

"The purpose of such a system," say McCarthy and McGaughey, "would be to create an incentive for foreign producers to upgrade wages and reduce hours by allowing them cheaper access to U.S. markets."[33]

Regardless of the particular approaches used to shorten the workweek, the nations of the world will have no choice but to downshift the number of hours worked in coming decades to accommodate the spectacular productivity gains resulting from new labor- and time-saving technologies. As machines increasingly replace human beings in every sector and industry, the choice will be between a few being employed for longer hours while large numbers of people are jobless and on the public dole, or spreading the available work out and giving more workers the opportunity to share shorter weekly work schedules.

TRADING WORK FOR LEISURE

In the United States, interest in the shorter workweek has spread from labor leaders and policy analysts to the public at large. Harried by the stress of long work schedules and the burden of single-parent households, a growing number of Americans say they would trade some income gains for increased leisure in order to attend to family responsibilities and personal needs. According to a 1993 survey conducted by the Families and Work Institute, employees said they were "less willing to make sacrifices for work" and "want to devote more time and energy to their personal lives."[34] An earlier survey asked which of two career choices they would opt for: "One enabling you to schedule your own full-time work hours, and give more attention to your family, but with slower career advancement; and the other with rigid work hours and less attention to your family, but faster career advancement." Seventy-eight percent of the respondents said they would prefer more free time over career advancement. Surprisingly, 55 percent said they would be less "likely to accept a promotion involving greater responsibility if it meant spending less time with family."[35] On the question of the trade-off between income and leisure, a Department of Labor study found that the average American worker is prepared to give up 4.7 percent of his or her earnings in return for more free time.[36]

The new interest in trading income for leisure reflects a growing concern on the part of millions of Americans over family obligations and personal needs. Balancing work and leisure has become a serious parenting issue. With a majority of women now in the workforce, children are becoming increasingly unattended in the home. Upwards of 7 million kids are home alone during parts of the day. Some surveys have found that as many as one third of the nation's youngsters are caring for themselves. Between 1960 and 1986, according to one nationwide study, the amount of time parents were able to spend with their children declined by ten hours a week for white households and twelve hours for black ones.[37] The decline in parental supervision has created an "abandonment" syndrome. Psychologists, educators, and a growing number of parents worry about the dramatic increase in childhood depression, delinquency, violent crime, alcohol and drug abuse, and teen suicide, brought on in large part by the absence of parental supervision in the home.

The increased stress of extended work schedules has been particularly burdensome for women workers, who are, more often than not, forced to manage the household as well as hold down a forty-hour job. Studies indicate that the average working woman in the United States works in excess of eighty hours a week on the job and in the home.[38] It is not surprising, then, that women workers are more receptive to the possibility of shorter workweeks than men. Unions representing heavy concentrations of women, including the Communications Workers of America and the Service Employees International Union, have successfully negotiated reduced-work schedules for their members. Many progressive labor leaders believe that the rebirth of the American labor movement hinges on the prospect of organizing women workers and that "shorter hours hold the key to such organization."[39]

Challenging the business community for a more just distribution of the productivity gains of the Third Industrial Revolution will require a new crosscultural political movement based on the coalescing of communities of like-minded interests. Labor unionists, civil rights organizations, women's groups, parenting organizations, environmental groups, social justice organizations, religious and fraternal organizations, and neighborhood civic and service associations— to name just a few—all share a vested interest in shortening the workweek.

The call for a reduced workweek has many attractive features and will likely be implemented in countries around the world by the early years of the twenty-first century. If, however, the shift to a shorter week is not accompanied by an equally aggressive program to find work for the millions of unemployed whose labor is no longer needed in the global economy, many of the economic and social ills that currently threaten political stability will only heighten in intensity— especially if the growing underclass feels abandoned by the remainder of the workforce who are able to keep or reclaim jobs under a share-the-work strategy.

With millions of Americans facing the prospect of working fewer and fewer hours in the formal market sector in the coming years, and with increasing numbers of unskilled Americans unable to secure any work at all in the automated high-tech global economy, the question of the utilization of idle time is going to loom large over the political landscape. The transition from a society based on mass employment in the private sector to one based on non-market criteria for organizing social life will require a rethinking of the current world view. Redefining the role of the individual in a society absent of mass formal work is, perhaps, the seminal issue of the coming age.

· 16 ·

A New
Social Contract

THE HIGH-TECH GLOBAL ECONOMY is moving beyond the mass worker. While entrepreneurial, managerial, professional, and technical elites will be necessary to run the formal economy of the future, fewer and fewer workers will be required to assist in the production of goods and services. The market value of labor is diminishing and will continue to do so. After centuries of defining human worth in strictly "productive" terms, the wholesale replacement of human labor with machine labor leaves the mass worker without self-definition or societal function.

At the same time that the need for human labor is disappearing, the role of government is undergoing a similar diminution. Today, global companies have begun to eclipse and subsume the power of nations. Transnational enterprises have increasingly usurped the traditional role of the state, and now exercise unparalleled control over global resources, labor pools, and markets. The largest global corporations have assets exceeding the GNP of many countries.

The shift from an economy based on material, energy, and labor to one based on information and communication further reduces the importance of the nation-state as a critical player in guaranteeing the fortunes of the marketplace. A primary function of the modern nation-state is its ability to use military force to seize vital resources and capture and exploit local and even global labor pools. Now that energy, mineral resources, and labor are becoming less important than information, communications, and intellectual property in the production mix, the need for massive military intervention is less apparent. Information and communications, the raw material of the high-tech global economy, are impervious to physical boundaries. They invade physical spaces, cross political lines, and penetrate the deepest layers of national life. Standing armies cannot stop or even slow down the accelerating flow of information and communications across national frontiers.

The nation-state, with its fixed physicality and spatial grounding, is far too slow to initiate and react to the quick pace of global market forces. By contrast, the global corporations are, by their very nature, temporal rather than spatial institutions. They are not grounded in any specific community nor accountable to any given locale. They are a new quasipolitical institution that exercises tremendous power over people and places, by reason of control over information and communications. Their agility, flexibility, and above all mobility, allow them to transfer production and markets quickly and effortlessly from one place to another, effectively controlling the commercial agenda of every country.

The changing relationship between government and commerce is becoming increasingly apparent in the emergence of sweeping new international trade agreements that effectively transfer more and more political power away from the nation-state and to the global corporations. The General Agreement on Trade and Tariffs (GATT), the Maastricht Accord, and the North American Free Trade Agreement (NAFTA) are a sign of changing patterns of power in the global community. Under these trade agreements hundreds of laws governing the affairs of sovereign nation-states are potentially made null and void if they compromise the freedom of the transnational companies to engage in open trade. Voters and constituent groups in dozens of countries have mounted vigorous public protests aimed at blocking these trade agreements for fear that hard-won legislative victories governing labor standards, environmental safeguards, health regulations, and the like will be cast aside, clearing the way for the near-total control by the transnationals over the economic affairs of the planet.

While the geopolitical role of the nation-state is lessening in importance, so too is its role as employer of last resort. As mentioned earlier, governments hampered by mounting long-term debt and growing budget deficits are less willing to embark on ambitious public spending and public-works programs to create jobs and stimulate purchasing power. In virtually every industrial nation of the world, central governments are shrinking from their traditional tasks of guaranteeing markets, lessening both their economic influence over transnationals and their power to effect the well-being of their own citizenry.

The diminishing role of both the mass worker and central governments in the affairs of the marketplace is going to force a fundamental rethinking of the social contract. Recall that for most of the industrial era, market relationships took precedence over traditional relationships, and human worth was measured almost exclusively in commercial terms. Now that "selling one's time" is diminishing in value, the entire labyrinth of commercial relationships that has been built upon that arrangement is likewise threatened. Similarly, now that the role of the central government as a guarantor of markets is diminishing in importance, governing institutions find themselves adrift and will need to redefine their mission if they are to remain relevant to the lives of their citizens. Weaning the body politic away from a strictly market-centered orientation becomes the pressing task of every nation on earth.

Most people would find it difficult to imagine a society in which the market sector and the government play less of a role in day-to-day affairs. These two institutional forces have come to so dominate every aspect of our lives that we forget how limited their role was in the life of our society just one hundred years ago. Corporations and nation-states are, after all, creatures of the industrial era. Over the course of the current century, these two sectors have taken over more and more of the functions and activities previously carried on by neighbors working hand-in-hand in thousands of local communities. Now, however, that the commercial and public sectors are no longer capable of securing some of the fundamental needs of the people, the public has little choice but to begin looking out for itself, once again, by reestablishing viable communities as a buffer against both the impersonal forces of the global market and increasingly weak and incompetent central governing authorities.

In the coming decades, the shrinking role of the market and public sectors is going to affect the lives of working people in two significant ways. Those who remain employed will likely see a shortening of their workweek, leaving them with more leisure. Many on reduced work schedules are likely to be pressured by the marketplace to spend their leisure indulging in mass entertainment and stepped-up consumption.

The increasing number of unemployed and underemployed people, by contrast, will find themselves sinking inexorably into the permanent underclass. Desperate, many will turn to the informal economy to survive. Some will barter occasional work for food and lodging. Others will engage in theft and petty crime. Drug dealing and prostitution will continue to increase as millions of able bodied human beings, stranded by a society that no longer needs or wants their labor, try to better their lot in life. Their cries for help will be largely ignored as governments tighten their purse strings and shift spending priorities from welfare and job creation to beefed-up police security and the building of more prisons.

While this is the course many industrial countries are currently on, it is by no means inevitable. Another choice is available—one that could help provide a cushion against the increasingly harsh blows imposed by the technological juggernaught of the Third Industrial Revolution. With the employed having more free time at their disposal and the unemployed having idle time on their hands, the opportunity exists to harness the unused labor of millions of people toward constructive tasks outside the private and public sectors. The talents and energy of both the employed and unemployed—those with leisure hours and those with idle time—could be effectively directed toward rebuilding thousands of local communities and creating a third force that flourishes independent of the marketplace and the public sector.

LIFE BEYOND THE MARKETPLACE

The foundation for a strong, community-based third force in American politics already exists. Although much attention in the modern era has been narrowly focused on the private and public sectors, there is a third sector in American life that has been of historical significance in the making of the nation, and that now offers the distinct possibility of helping to reshape the social contract in the twenty-first century. The third sector, also known as the independent or volunteer sector, is the realm in which fiduciary arrangements give way to community bonds, and where the giving of one's time to others takes the place of artificially imposed market relationships based on selling oneself and one's services to others. This sector, once critical to the building of the country, in recent years has slipped to the margins of public life, edged out by the increasing domination of the market and government spheres. Now that the other two realms are diminishing in importance—at least in respect to the hours of available labor time given to either—the possibility of resurrecting and transforming the third sector and making it a vehicle for the creation of a vibrant post-market era should be seriously explored.

The third sector already cuts a wide swath through society. Community activities run the gamut from social services to health care, education and research, the arts, religion, and advocacy. Community-service organizations assist the elderly and handicapped, the mentally ill, disadvantaged youth, the homeless and indigent. Volunteers renovate dilapidated apartments and build new low-income housing. Tens of thousands of Americans volunteer their services in public-supported hospitals and clinics, taking care of patients, including the victims of AIDS. Thousands more serve as foster parents, or as big brothers and sisters for orphaned children. Some provide counseling for runaways and troubled youth. Others are tutors recruited into the campaign to eliminate illiteracy. Americans assist in day-care centers and after-school programs. They prepare and deliver meals to the poor. A growing number of Americans volunteer in crisis centers, helping rape victims and victims of spouse and child abuse. Thousands volunteer their time staffing public shelters and distributing clothes to the needy. Many Americans are involved in self-help programs like Alcoholics Anonymous, and in drug rehabilitation programs. Professionals—lawyers, accountants, doctors, executives—donate their services to voluntary organizations. Millions of Americans volunteer their time to various environmental efforts, including recycling activities, conservation programs, antipollution campaigns, and animal protection work. Others work for advocacy organizations attempting to redress grievances and change public perceptions and laws. Hundreds of thousands of Americans give their time to the arts—participating in local theater groups, choirs, and orchestras. Volunteers often assist municipal governments, serving as volunteer firefighters or donating time to crime prevention work and disaster relief.

While the business sector makes up 80 percent of the economic activity in the United States, and the government sector accounts for an additional 14 percent of the gross national product, the independent sector currently contributes more than 6 percent to the economy and is responsible for 9 percent of the total national employment. More people are employed in third-sector organizations than work in either the construction, electronics, transportation, or textile and apparel industries.[1]

The assets of the third sector now equal nearly half those of the federal government. A study conducted by Yale economist Gabriel Rudney in the early 1980s estimated that the expenditure of America's voluntary organizations exceeded the gross national product of all but seven nations.[2] Although the third sector is half the size of government in total employment and half its size in total earnings, in recent years it has been growing twice as fast as both the government and private sectors.[3]

Despite the fact that the third sector is gaining on the other two sectors in the American economy and boasts economic clout that exceeds the GNP of most nations, it is often ignored by political scientists, who prefer to view America as being made up of just two realms—the private and the public. Yet it is the independent sector that has traditionally played a critical mediating role between the formal economy and the government, taking on tasks and performing services that the other two sectors are unwilling or incapable of handling, and often acting as an advocate on behalf of groups and constituencies whose interests are being ignored by the marketplace or compromised in the councils of government.

According to an extensive 1992 Gallup survey, in 1991 more than 94.2 million adult Americans, or 51 percent of the population, gave their time to various causes and organizations. The average volunteer gave 4.2 hours of his or her time per week. Collectively, the American people gave more than 20.5 billion hours in volunteering. More than 15.7 billion of those hours were in the form of formal volunteering— that is, regular work for a voluntary organization or association. These hours represent the equivalent economic contribution of 9 million full-time employees, and if measured in dollar terms, would be worth $176 billion.[4]

There are more than 1,400,000 nonprofit organizations in the United States: organizations whose primary goal is to provide a service or advance a cause. The Internal Revenue Service defines a nonprofit organization as one in which "no part of the net earnings . . . inures to the benefit of any private shareholder or individual."[5] Most nonprofit organizations are exempt from paying federal taxes, and donations to them are tax deductible.

The growth in the number of tax-exempt organizations in the United States over the past twenty-five years has been extraordinary. In the late 1950s, the IRS processed between 5,000 to 7,000 applications a year for tax-exempt status. By 1985 it was more than 45,000.[6] The total combined assets of the nonprofit sector are now more than $500 billion. This sector is financed in part by private donations and gifts, with the rest coming from fees and government grants. In 1991 the average American household contributed $649, or 1.7 percent of its income, to voluntary organizations. More than 69 million American households reported contributions to the voluntary sector in 1991. Nine percent of all households gave more than 5 percent of their combined income to charity.[7]

Community service is a revolutionary alternative to traditional forms of labor. Unlike slavery, serfdom, and wage labor, it is neither coerced nor reduced to a fiduciary relationship. Community service is a helping action, a reaching out to others. It is an act entered into willingly and often without expectation of material gain. In this sense, it is more akin to the ancient economics of gift giving. Community service stems from a deep understanding of the interconnectedness of all things and is motivated by a personal sense of indebtedness. It is, first and foremost, a social exchange, although often with economic consequences to both the beneficiary and the benefactor. In this regard, community activity is substantially different from market activity, in which the exchange is always material and financial and where the social consequences are less important than the economic gains and losses.

French social scientists introduced the term *social economy* in the 1980s in an attempt to clarify the distinction between the third sector and the market-exchange economy. The French economist Thierry Jeantet says that the social economy is not "measured the way one measures capitalism, in terms of salaries, revenues etc., but its outputs integrate social results with indirect economic gains, for example the number of handicapped persons well cared for at home and not in hospitals; the degree of solidarity between persons of different age groups in a neighborhood." Jeantet makes the point that "the social economy is best understood in terms of results that add considerably to what traditional economics does not know how to or want to measure."[8]

The third sector is the most socially responsible of the three sectors. It is the caring realm that ministers to the needs and aspirations of millions of individuals who, for one reason or another, have been left out, excluded from consideration, or not been adequately taken care of by either the commercial or public spheres.

An Alternate Vision

Alexis de Tocqueville, the French statesman and philosopher, was the first to take notice of America's voluntary spirit. After visiting the United States in 1831, he wrote of his impressions of the young country. Tocqueville was awed by the American propensity to enter into voluntary associations—a phenomenon little in evidence in Europe at the time: "Americans of all ages, all stations in life, and all types of disposition are forever forming associations. There are not only commercial and industrial associations in which all take part, but others of a thousand different types—religious, moral, serious, futile, very general and very limited, immensely large and very minute. Americans combine to give fetes, found seminaries, build churches, distribute books and send missionaries to the antipodes. Hospitals, prisons, and schools take shape that way. Finally, if they want to proclaim a truth or propagate some feeling by the encouragement of a great example, they form an association."[9]

Tocqueville was convinced that the Americans had discovered a revolutionary new form of cultural expression that would prove essential to the flourishing of the democratic spirit:

> Nothing, in my view, more deserves attention than the intellectual and moral associations in America. American political and industrial associations easily catch our eyes, but the others tend not to be noticed. And even if we do notice them, we tend to misunderstand them, hardly ever having seen anything similar before. However, we should recognize that the latter are as necessary as the former to the American people; perhaps more so. In democratic countries, knowledge of how to combine is the mother of all other forms of knowledge; on its progress depends that of all the others.[10]

For more than 200 years, third-sector activity has shaped the American experience, reaching into virtually every corner of American life, helping transform a frontier culture into a highly advanced modern society. While historians are quick to credit the market and government sectors with America's greatness, the third sector has played an equally aggressive role in defining the American way of life. The nation's first schools and colleges, its hospitals, social service organizations, fraternal orders, women's clubs, youth organizations, civil rights groups, social justice organizations, conservation and environmental protection groups, animal welfare organizations, theaters, orchestras, art galleries, libraries, museums, civic associations, community development organizations, neighborhood advisory councils, volunteer fire departments, and civilian security patrols are all creatures of the third sector.

Today, voluntary organizations are serving millions of Americans in every neighborhood and community of the country. Their reach and scope often eclipse both the private and public sectors, touching and affecting the lives of every American, often more profoundly than the forces of the marketplace or the agencies and bureaucracies of government.

Although voluntary organizations exist in most other countries, and are rapidly becoming a major social force, nowhere are they as well developed as in the United States. Americans have often turned to voluntary organizations as a refuge—a place where personal relationships can be nurtured, status can be achieved, and a sense of community can be created. The economist and educator Max Lerner once observed that through their affiliations with volunteer organizations Americans hope to overcome their sense of personal isolation and alienation and become part of a real community. This is a primordial need that cannot be filled by either the forces of the market or the dictates of government. Lerner writes, "It is in them [voluntary associations] . . . that the sense of community comes closest to being achieved."[11]

While much has been said over the years about America's rough and tumble frontier tradition and the fierce competitive ethic that has made the nation an economic superpower, the caring side of the American experience, the one that makes Americans join together in collective service to each other, is given little notice. The independent sector serves as a haven for millions of Americans, a place where they can be themselves, express their views, and exhibit their talents in ways not possible in the more narrow confines of the workplace, where only production and efficiency rule. Walter Lippmann sums up the enormous value of the third sector to the lives of millions of Americans: "It is this social placing of an American—in Church, lodge, service or women's club, eating club, community fund drive, veterans groups, country club, political party—that defines his social personality. Through it he has the sense of effectiveness he does not have as a minor part of the machine process of the corporate organization. Here he can make his way as a person, by his qualities of generosity and friendliness, his ability to talk at a meeting or run it or work in a committee, his organizing capacities, his ardor, his public spirit. Here he stretches himself, as he rarely does on the job, by working with others for common non-profit ends."[12]

The independent sector is the bonding force, the social glue that helps unite the diverse interests of the American people into a cohesive social identity. If there is a single defining characteristic that sums up the unique qualities of being an American, it would be our capacity to join together in voluntary associations to serve one another. The anthropologist Margaret Mead once remarked, "If you look closely you will see that almost anything that really matters to us, anything that embodies our deepest commitment to the way human life should be lived and cared for, depends on some form—often many forms—of volunteerism."[13] Yet strangely enough, this central aspect of the American character and experience is little examined in the history and sociology textbooks used in our nation's high schools and colleges. Instead, our children are taught about the virtues of the marketplace and the checks and balances built into our representative form of government. The third sector, if it is mentioned at all, is usually glossed over as a footnote to the American experience, despite its critical role in forging the American way of life.

Third-sector organizations serve many functions. They are the incubators of new ideas and forums to air social grievances. Community associations integrate streams of immigrants into the American experience. They are places where the poor and the helpless can find a helping hand. Nonprofit organizations like museums, libraries, and historical societies help preserve traditions and open up doors to new kinds of intellectual experiences. The third sector is where many people first learn how to practice the art of democratic participation. It is where companionship is sought and friendships are formed. The independent sector provides a place and time for exploring the spiritual dimension. Religious and therapeutic organizations allow millions of Americans to leave behind the secular concerns of daily life. Finally, the third sector is where people relax and play, and more fully experience the pleasures of life and nature.

The third sector incorporates many of the necessary elements for a compelling alternative vision to the utilitarian ethos of the marketplace. Nonetheless, the spirit of the social economy has yet to gell into a powerful countervailing world view capable of setting the agenda for a nation. This is due, in large part, to the extraordinary hold that the values of the marketplace continue to exert over the affairs of the nation.

The market vision, wedded to a materialistic cornucopia, glorifies production principles and efficiency standards as the chief means of advancing happiness. As long as people's primary identification is with the market economy, the values of expanded production and unlimited consumption will continue to influence personal behavior. People will continue to think of themselves, first and foremost, as "consumers" of goods and services.

The materialist world view has led to a rapacious consumption of the earth, leaving the planet's biosphere compromised by resource depletion on the front end and environmental pollution at the back end. Alan Durning of the Worldwatch Institute observes that "Since mid-century the per capita consumption of copper, energy, meat, steel, and timber has approximately doubled; per capita car ownership and cement consumption have quadrupled; plastic use per person has quintupled; per capita aluminum consumption has grown seven-fold; and air travel per person has multiplied 33 times."[14] The United States alone, with less than 5 percent of the earth's human population, is now consuming more than 30 percent of the world's remaining energy and raw materials.

The rapid conversion of the earth's resources into a cornucopia of goods and services has led to global warming, ozone depletion, mass deforestation, spreading deserts, the wholesale extinction of species, and the destabilization of the biosphere. The overexploitation of the earth's chemical and biological riches has also left developing nations resource-poor and their populations without adequate means to sustain their growing numbers.

The third-sector vision offers a much-needed antidote to the materialism that has so dominated twentieth-century industrial thinking. While work in the private sector is motivated by material gain, and security is viewed in terms of increased consumption, third-sector participation is motivated by service to others and security is viewed in terms of strengthened personal relationships and a sense of grounding in the larger earth community. The very idea of broadening one's loyalties and affiliations beyond the narrow confines of the marketplace and the nation-state to include the human species and the planet is revolutionary and portends vast changes in the structuring of society. The new visionaries view the earth as an indivisible organic whole, a living entity made up of myriad forms of life brought together in a community. Acting on behalf of the interests of the entire human and biological community, rather than on one's own narrow material self-interest, makes the third-sector paradigm a serious threat to the consumption-oriented vision of the still-dominant market economy.

The notion of restructuring a myriad of relationships based on participation, first with those immediately around us, then with the larger human community, and finally with the other creatures that make up the earth's organic community, may seem an unlikely prospect. However, we need only remind ourselves that the vision of the technological utopians—of a world in which machines replace people, creating a cornucopia of material things and the possibility of greater leisure—seemed unlikely and unattainable to many just one hundred years ago.

There is reason to be hopeful that a new vision based on transformation of consciousness and a new commitment to community will take hold. With millions of human beings spending more and more of their waking hours away from work in the formal economy, in the years ahead the importance of formal work to their lives will diminish as well—including its hold over their concept of self-worth. The diminution of work life in the formal economy is going to mean decreased allegiance to the values, world view, and vision that accompany the marketplace. If an alternative vision steeped in the ethos of personal transformation, community restoration, and environmental consciousness were to gain widespread currency, the intellectual foundation could be laid for the post-market era.

In the future, a growing number of people around the world will be spending less time on the job and have more time on their hands. Whether their "free" time will be coerced, involuntary, and the result of forced part-time work, layoffs, and unemployment, or leisure made possible by productivity gains, shorter workweeks, and better income remains to be worked out in the political arena. If massive unemployment of a kind unknown in history were to occur as a result of the sweeping replacement of machines for human labor, then the chances of developing a compassionate and caring society and a world view based on transformation of the human spirit are unlikely. The more likely course would be widespread social upheaval, violence on an unprecedented scale, and open warfare, with the poor lashing out at each other as well as at the rich elites who control the global economy. If, instead, an enlightened course is pursued, allowing workers to benefit from increases in productivity with shorter workweeks and adequate income, more leisure time will exist than in any other period of modern history. That free time could be used to renew the bonds of community and rejuvenate the democratic legacy. A new generation might transcend the narrow limits of nationalism and begin to think and act as common members of the human race, with shared commitments to each other, the community, and the larger biosphere.

· 17 ·

Empowering
the Third Sector

I N THE COMING CENTURY, the market and public sectors are going to play an ever-reduced role in the day-to-day lives of human beings around the world. The power vacuum will likely be taken up either by the growth of an increasing outlaw subculture or by greater participation in the third sector. That is not to suggest that either of the other two sectors is going to wither away or disappear—only that their relationship to the masses of people will probably change in fundamental ways. Even with the technological strides of the Third Industrial Revolution, most people, in the foreseeable future, will still have to work in the formal market economy to make a living although their hours of employment will continue to drop. As for the increasing number for whom there will be no jobs at all in the market sector, governments will be faced with two choices: finance additional police protection and build more jails to incarcerate a growing criminal class or finance alternative forms of work in the third sector. Community-based organizations will increasingly act as arbiters and ombudsmen with the larger forces of the marketplace and government, serving as the primary advocates and agents for social and political reform. Third-sector organizations are also likely to take up the task of providing more and more basic services in the wake of cutbacks in government aid and assistance to persons and neighborhoods in need.

The globalization of the market sector and the diminishing role of the governmental sector will mean that people will be forced to organize into communities of self-interest to secure their own futures. Making a successful transition into a post-market era will depend largely on the ability of an aroused electorate, working through coalitions and movements, to effectively transfer as much of the productivity gains as possible from the market sector to the third sector in order to strengthen and deepen community bonds and local infrastructures. Only by building strong, self-sustaining local communities will people in every country be able to withstand the forces of technological displacement and market globalization that are threatening the livelihoods and survival of much of the human family.

A NEW ROLE FOR GOVERNMENT

The government is likely to play a far different role in the emerging high-tech era, one less tied to the interests of the commercial economy and more aligned with the interests of the social economy. Forging a new partnership between the government and third sector to rebuild the social economy could help restore civic life in every nation. Feeding the poor, providing basic health care services, educating the nation's youth, building affordable housing, and preserving the environment top the list of urgent priorities in the years head. All of these critical areas have been either ignored or inadequately attended to by the forces of the marketplace. Today, with the formal economy receding from the social life of the nation and the government retreating from its traditional role of provider of last resort, only a concerted effort spearheaded by the third sector and adequately supported by the public sector will be able to deliver basic social services and begin the process of revitalizing the social economy in every country.

The downsizing of government's direct role in the formal economy and its shift to activities that enhance the welfare and well-being of the independent sector is likely to change the nature of politics. The Clinton administration has already taken a first tentative step in the direction of creating a new partnership between the public and third sector by announcing on April 12, 1994, the creation of the Non-Profit Liaison Network, to be made up of twenty-five Administration officials who will "work with the nonprofit sector on common goals." The officials will be charged with building cooperative networks between their departments and agencies of government and third-sector organizations. In making the announcement, President Clinton said that he had "long advocated the role of the non-profit sector." He reminded the public that "throughout our history, the nonprofit community has helped our nation adapt to a changing world by strengthening the core values that shape American life." The President said that the Network will create better collaboration between the Administration and advocacy and service groups in a mutual effort to solve the problems of crime, housing, health care, and other pressing national needs. Although the President's action is likely to be viewed more as a symbolic gesture than a change in political paradigms, it suggests both a growing awareness of the potential role of the third sector in American life and the need to create new working relationships between the government and the nonprofit community.[1]

The Clinton administration is not the first to appreciate the importance of the third sector. In the 1980s the Republicans rode into the White House, in large part, on the shirt-tails of the volunteer theme. The Grand Old Party dominated the political landscape for more than a decade with the plea to "return government to the people." The Reagan forces realized, early on, the potential symbolic and emotional power of third-sector images and used them to their advantage, building a Republican mandate in the 1980s. In both the Reagan and Bush White House, third-sector themes were continually manipulated in a cynical effort to mask a free-market agenda. "Returning the government to the people" became a convenient euphemism to push for deregulation of industry, fewer corporate taxes, and cutbacks in social services and entitlement programs for the working poor and those trapped below the poverty line. In the end, the third sector was seriously compromised and undermined by the very political forces that professed to be its champions and advocates. To avoid a similar occurrence in the future, it is necessary to understand both the disarming ways the Reagan people were able to manipulate third-sector images and the responses they evoked from Democrats and progressive forces.

THE THIRD SECTOR AND PARTISAN POLITICS

From his first day in office, President Reagan made volunteerism a key theme of his Administration, suggesting that government had taken over many of the tasks previously performed by the third sector, making Americans far too reliant on the public sector and far less willing to provide for themselves and their neighborhoods. In an attempt to rekindle the spirit of free association that Tocqueville had first seen burning bright in the early years of the new nation, he continually harked back to America's volunteer tradition. Writing in *Reader's Digest* in 1985, the President praised America's volunteer spirit: "This spirit of volunteerism, then, flows like a deep and mighty river through the history of our nation. Americans have always extended their hands in gestures of assistance."

The President went on to criticize what he regarded as the increasing usurpation of the volunteer sector by big government programs in the postwar era: "But after World War II, the levels of that river of volunteerism receded. As government expanded we abdicated to it tasks that used to be done by the community and the neighborhood. 'Why should I get involved?' people asked. 'Let the government handle it.'"[2]

The President lamented the change in public attitudes that had "let government take away many things we once considered were really ours to do voluntarily, out of the goodness of our hearts and a sense of neighborliness." He said, "I believe many of you want to do those things again."[3]

President Reagan's appeal to homespun values and old-fashioned good works touched a responsive chord. Although the "liberal" establishment was quick to ridicule the President, charging him with being naive, even disingenuous, millions of Americans, many of whom were themselves volunteers and committed to the principles of voluntary association, saw in his message a call to renew the American spirit, and they threw their support behind the White House's call to action. In 1983 volunteerism became the theme of the annual Rose Bowl Parade and was made into a national advertising campaign by the Ad Council. A commemorative stamp was issued by the Postal Service.[4]

President Bush later picked up on the volunteerism theme during his inaugural. In his now famous "Points of Light" speech, the new President reminded the country that the volunteer sector was the spiritual backbone of the American democratic spirit:

> It is individuals doing their part to make America a better place in which to live. It is the student who stays after school to tutor a classmate. It's a community leader who raises the money to build a day-care center for underprivileged children. It is the busi-

nessman who adopts a school and pays the college tuition of
every student who has made the grade. It's the volunteer who
delivers meals to the homes of the elderly. And there are a
thousand points of light for everyone who pitches in and builds
up. This is America's greatness. . . . It is the ambition of my
presidency to make these thousand points of light shine brighter
than ever before.[5]

Bush subsequently introduced his Points of Light Initiative—a
$50 million program to be financed jointly by the federal government
and private funds. The program's mission, according to the White
House, was to find innovative and inspiring examples of volunteer
efforts and help publicize them so that other communities could begin
duplicating them. No funds were to be used to extend grants to efforts
in the volunteer sector. The President's Points of Light Initiative was
savaged by the national press and even by many progressive volunteer
groups and associations. John Buchanan, Jr., chairman of the liberal
political group People for the American Way, chided the White House
initiative, saying, "This is little more than a nationwide pep rally."[6]

Criticism of the Reagan-Bush theme of renewed volunteerism was
heard from many quarters. The American left charged that volunteerism was a cynical attempt by Republican administrations to abdicate
government responsibility to aid the poor and working people of the
country. Many liberal critics pointed to the power and influence giant
foundations exert over nonprofit organizations by reason of their
control over the flow of funds to the volunteer sector. Controlling the
purse strings, they contended, ensured that grass-roots organizations
would remain docile and afraid to engage in direct political confronta-
tion or advocacy—traditional roles of the volunteer sector. Others
argued that volunteer efforts by their very nature fragmented attempts
to mount effective political movements for fundamental change. The
notion of "service," they said, prevented people from understanding
the institutional roots of class oppression and kept them mired in futile
attempts at Band-Aid reforms.

In the 1980s the volunteer theme became so associated in the
public mind with Republican politics that it was, like so many important issues in American life, reduced to a partisan cause. The Democrats and most liberal thinkers and constituent groups either openly
opposed the volunteer theme or steadfastly ignored it. The National
Organization for Women (NOW) passed a resolution against volun-

teerism in the 1970s, saying that it was traditionally used as a means to deny women—who make up the majority of the volunteer force—pay for their services. Volunteerism, they contended, was looked down on as less professional, less serious, and of less importance than professional, paid work, and for that reason ought to be discouraged among women. Typical is the response of one woman when asked if she would volunteer her services. She replied, "I think it's terrible. I want to get paid for what I do. I want people to value it. And money is the only way anybody will think it's important."[7]

Public-employee unions have also opposed volunteer efforts in the past, fearing that they would replace paid work performed by public employees. Kathleen Kennedy Townsend, a progressive liberal who worked for the Governor's Office on Human Resources for the state of Massachusetts in the early 1980s, cites several examples of public-employee unions actively opposing volunteer efforts. In North Carolina, teachers unions discouraged efforts to train volunteer tutors, concerned that they might reduce the number of paid teachers. In New York City, she recalls the story of volunteers attempting to scrub a filthy subway station. The Transport Workers Union ordered the group to stop their efforts, saying that if the unions didn't do the work, then it couldn't be done by anyone else.

Townsend says that "the liberals' failure to embrace volunteerism can also be explained by their preference for professionals with academic credentials." The notion of the caring professional has became a popular part of the progressive lexicon in recent years, and many liberal thinkers have come to believe that better, more effective service can be given to those in need by paid professionals than by well-meaning, but uncredentialed amateurs.[8]

Finally, many liberal critics of volunteerism associate the third sector with a patronizing form of elitism. Charity, they contend, disparages the victims, making them objects of pity rather than persons of inherent worth and inalienable rights who deserve a helping hand. Government programs, by contrast, start with the assumption that needy citizens have a right to services, not out of an act of charity but because of the responsibility of government to provide for the general welfare. It is, they remind us, a constitutional guarantee.

The liberal community, to be sure, has not all spoken with a common voice on the matter of volunteerism. Betty Friedan, the founder of NOW, argues for a "new passionate volunteerism." She contends that the "polarization between feminism and volunteerism [is] as false . . . as the [feminists'] seeming repudiation of family." Friedan predicts that in the coming decades "voluntary organizations will be the only way to promise the services essential to further social change and the living of equality, now that it appears we will have to rely less on government agencies and the courts."[9]

Townsend recounts numerous incidents in which liberal criticism of volunteerism failed to reflect the reality of volunteer efforts. For example, on the issue of professionalism and the supposition that "caring professionals" generally provide more effective services, Townsend points out that oftentimes that is not the case. She tells of a personal experience with two boardinghouses, one professionally administered and paid for by the government, the other staffed by volunteers and supported by private donations. In the publicly supported, professionally administered home, "Dozens of men and women crowded together on couches or folding chairs in a dimly lit room that smelled of urine, dirty bodies and ammonia. In one corner a black and white TV flickered; the aides stood off in a corridor, talking among themselves. . . . Though an aide told me they had just completed a summer celebration, there wasn't a trace of gaiety in the place."

The second home, Rosie's Place, is a shelter for homeless women run by volunteers: "The home was bright and cheery, and the walls were fashionably decorated with light blue and white painted flowers. The wooden tables were clean and polished, and there was fresh coffee and just baked chocolate chip cookies. [The volunteers make] all the women who stay there feel welcome."[10]

The nurturing commitment of volunteers often leads to better results in the providing of care services than the more detached care of salaried professionals. More often than not, the combination of small professional staffs and large numbers of volunteers offers the ideal combination of expertise and empathy needed to assist others.

On the more complex issue of volunteers taking the jobs of public employees, the facts suggest that when volunteers become involved in activities that cross over into the public sector—like tutoring, neighborhood clean-up, health-care providing—they begin to see the need to direct more public funds toward these critical social services and often voice their concerns by supporting increased government expenditures.

Today, a growing number of progressive thinkers are taking a second look at the independent sector. They are beginning to realize that it is the only viable alternative people can turn to now that the market economy's role as employer is shrinking, and the government's role as provider of last resort is diminishing as well. The jockeying between conservatives and liberals, Republicans and Democrats, on how best to redirect the nation's energies and commitments to the third sector is going to be one of the most closely watched political issues of the coming decade.

MAKING THE THIRD SECTOR WORK

For all their talk of redirecting the government's mission to assist the third sector, neither President Reagan nor President Bush was willing to carry through on his pledge with concrete programs designed to accomplish such ends. In fact, the Reagan White House actively lobbied to change the Internal Revenue Service Code governing tax-exempt work to further restrict the activities of nonprofit groups and narrow the kind and number of deductions a taxpayer could claim for charitable contributions.

If the third sector is to be transformed into an effective force that can lay the groundwork for a viable post-market era, the government will need to play a supportive role in the transition. At the outset, the needs of two distinct groups will have to be addressed if the country is to effectively redirect millions of hours of available labor time into substantive activity designed to rebuild communities and strengthen the third sector's role in American society. First, the appropriate incentives will need to be put in place to encourage those who still have a job in the market sector, but are working fewer hours, to give a portion of their increasing leisure time over to service in the third sector. Second, legislation will need to be enacted to provide millions of permanently unemployed Americans meaningful work in community service in the third sector to help rebuild their own neighborhoods and local infrastructures.

SHADOW WAGES FOR VOLUNTARY WORK

The government could encourage greater participation in the third sector by providing a tax deduction for every hour of volunteer time given to legally certified tax-exempt organizations. To insure an honest accounting of hours volunteered, every tax exempt organization would be required to report the number of hours donated to it to both the federal government and the individual volunteer at the end of the fiscal year, in the form of a standardized IRS form, similar to a W-2 form. The concept of a "shadow wage," in the form of a deduction on personal income taxes for volunteer hours given, would go a long way toward encouraging millions of Americans to devote a greater share of their leisure time to volunteer efforts in the third sector. While the idea is new, the concept is already firmly established in the laws governing tax-exempt gifts. If giving money to charitable efforts is deemed worthy of tax deductions, why not extend the idea to cover deductions for the donation of hours given to the same efforts and causes?

Providing tax deductions for persons donating their time to volunteer efforts would ensure greater involvement in a range of social issues that need to be addressed. While there would be a loss of taxable revenue at the front side, it would likely be more than compensated for by a diminished need for expensive government programs to cover needs and services best handled by volunteer efforts in the third sector. By extending tax deductions directly to the volunteers donating their services and skills at the point of engagement, the government bypasses much of the expense that goes into financing the layers of bureaucracy that are set up to administer programs in local communities. Then too, improvements in the living conditions and quality of life of millions of disadvantaged Americans inevitably rebounds to the economy itself in the form of greater employment opportunities and increased purchasing power, all increasing the amount of taxable income available to every level of government.

Some might argue that providing a tax deduction for voluntary hours would undermine the spirit of volunteerism. The chances of that occurring are unlikely. After all, making charitable contributions tax deductible seems to have only encouraged the philanthropic spirit, and the likelihood is that creating a shadow wage would only encourage those who are volunteering to give more of their time to the social economy rather than moonlighting at an extra job to make ends meet or sitting in front of the television set every evening.

The advantages in legislating a shadow wage for volunteer activity are obvious and far-reaching. Helping ease the transition of millions of workers from formal employment in the market economy to community service in the social economy is going to be essential if civilization is to effectively cope with the decline of mass work in the twenty-first century.

To ensure that society does not disintegrate into thousands of local initiatives lacking a coherent national purpose and direction, the government might consider leveraging the volunteer sector with the appropriate incentives. Deductions for volunteer work could be prioritized, with larger deductions going to volunteer efforts that the public and their elected officials in Congress and the White House deem more urgent and pressing. In addition, Congress should consider prioritizing deductions for charitable contributions as well, granting larger write-offs for contributions earmarked to activities considered critical to the national interest. By prioritizing deductions for charitable contributions and the donation of volunteer time, the government could play an important role in helping guide the social economy. In the coming years, legislative changes in the tax-exempt provisions of the Internal Revenue Code are likely to be viewed as an important fiscal tool for regulating the social economy, just as other tax policies have been important in regulating the market economy.

A SOCIAL WAGE FOR COMMUNITY SERVICE

While shadow wages would probably encourage greater participation in volunteer efforts by those still gainfully employed, the state and federal governments should also consider providing a social wage as an alternative to welfare payments and benefits for those permanently unemployed Americans willing to be retrained and placed in jobs in the third sector. The government should also award grants to nonprofit organizations to help them recruit and train the poor for jobs in their organizations.

Providing a social wage—as an alternative to welfare—for millions of the nation's poor, in return for working in the nonprofit sector, would help not only the recipients but also the communities in which their labor is put to use. Forging new bonds of trust and a sense of shared commitment to the welfare of others and the interests of the neighborhoods in which they serve is what is so desperately needed if we are to rebuild communities and create the foundation for a caring society. An adequate social wage would allow millions of unemployed

Americans, working through thousands of neighborhood organizations, the opportunity to help themselves.

It is often argued that simply providing income or job training is of little help if not accompanied by concrete programs to help educate the young, restore family life, and build a sense of shared confidence in the future. Extending a social wage to millions of needy Americans and providing funds for neighborhood-based organizations to recruit, train, and place people in critical community-building tasks that advance these broader social goals, would help create the framework for real change. Public-works projects and menial work in the formal economy, even if they were available, would do little in the way of restoring local communities.

In addition to providing a social wage for the nation's poorest citizens, serious consideration should be given to an expanded concept of social income that would include social wages for skilled workers and even management and professional workers whose labor is no longer valued or needed in the marketplace. A viable third sector requires a full range of skills, from minimum entry-level competence to sophisticated managerial experience. By providing a job classification scheme, grading system, and salary scale similar to the ones used in the public sector, third sector organizations could recruit from the broad ranks of the unemployed, staffing their organizations with the proper mix of unskilled, skilled, and professional labor that would insure success in the communities they serve.

The idea of providing a social income first received widespread national attention back in 1963 when the Ad Hoc Committee on the Triple Revolution advocated the scheme as a way to deal with the dual threat of technological unemployment and growing poverty. It should be emphasized that at the time there was no thought of tying a social income to a reciprocal agreement to perform community service. Proponents of the social income theory—also known as the guaranteed annual income—included W. H. Ferry of the Center for the Study of Democratic Institutions, liberal economists Robert Theobald and Robert Heilbroner, and J. Robert Oppenheimer, the director of the Institute for Advanced Study at Princeton. As discussed in chapter 6, they disagreed with the prevailing economic orthodoxy that technical innovation and rising productivity would guarantee a full-employment economy. On the contrary, the computer revolution, they contended, would increase productivity, but at the expense of replacing more and more workers with machines, leaving millions unemployed and underemployed, and without sufficient purchasing power to buy the increased output of goods and services being produced by the new automated production technologies. Stimulating demand through sophisticated advertising and marketing schemes, lower interest rates, increased tax credits and deductions, and more generous consumer credit terms would do little to increase employment, as companies would continue to substitute machines for workers because machines are more efficient and cheaper and guarantee a greater return on investment.

Robert Theobald argued that since automation would continue to boost productivity and replace workers, it was necessary to break the traditional relationship between income and work. With machines doing more and more of the work, human beings would need to be guaranteed an income, independent of employment in the formal economy, if they were to survive and the economy were to generate adequate purchasing power for the public to buy the goods and services being produced. Theobald, among others, perceived the guaranteed annual income as a turning point in the history of economic relationships, and hoped that its eventual acceptance would transform the very idea of economic thinking from the traditional notion of scarcity to the new ideal of abundance. He wrote, "For me, therefore, the guaranteed income represents the possibility of putting into effect the fundamental philosophical belief which has recurred consistently in human history, that each individual has a right to a minimal share in the production of society. The perennial shortage of almost all the necessities of life prevented the application of this belief until recent years: the coming of relative abundance in the rich countries gives man the power to achieve the goal of providing a minimum standard of living for all."[11]

The call for a guaranteed annual income was given an unexpected political boost when America's leading neoconservative economist, Milton Friedman, advocated his own variation on the theme in the form of a negative income tax. He disagreed with the liberal view that automation would steadily eliminate jobs and eventually lead to a decline of mass formal work, forcing a societal decision to separate income from work for the millions of Americans who would be left out of the market economy. Friedman, who served as an adviser to both President Nixon and President Reagan, was more concerned with what he regarded as a failed welfare system. He argued that it would be far better to give the poor a guaranteed annual income than continue to finance the maze of costly bureaucratic welfare programs that were often counterproductive and served only to perpetuate poverty rather than alleviate it.

Under the provisions of a negative income tax, the federal government would guarantee a minimum income level for every American and create a system of incentives that would encourage recipients to supplement the government subsidy by their own labor. While the government allowance would diminish as personal earnings rise, it would decrease at "a less rapid rate so as to preserve the incentive to work."[12] Friedman argued that his approach was not all that radical since the existing "grab-bag of relief and welfare measures" already amounted to "a governmentally guaranteed annual income in substance, though not in name." He pointed out that under current programs, income earned meant loss of benefits, creating a disincentive to get off the dole. "If a person on relief earns a dollar, and obeys the law, his or her relief payment is reduced by a dollar—the effect is to penalize either industry or honesty or both. The program tends to produce poor people, and a permanent class of poor people living on welfare." Friedman said he favored a direct cash payment to the poor so that they could make their own personal consumption decisions in the free market, unencumbered by the dictates of bureaucrats.[13]

Although liberal and conservative economists differed in their reasons for supporting a guaranteed annual income, the growing interest in the idea led President Lyndon Johnson to establish a National Commission on Guaranteed Incomes in 1967. After two years of hearings and studies, the commission, made up of business leaders, representatives of organized labor, and other prominent Americans, issued their report. Commission members were unanimous in their support of a guaranteed annual income. The report stated that "Unemployment or underemployment among the poor is often due to forces that cannot be controlled by the poor themselves. For many of the poor, the desire to work is strong but the opportunities are not. . . . Even if the existing welfare and related programs are improved, they are incapable of assuring that all Americans receive an adequate income. We have therefore recommended the adoption of a new program of income supplementation for all Americans in need."[14]

The report was largely ignored. Many Americans, and most politicians, found it difficult to accept the notion of providing people a guaranteed income. Despite the recommendations that incentives be included to encourage recipients to supplement their subsidy with work, a number of politicians believed that the very idea of guaranteeing an annual income would seriously undermine the work ethic and produce a generation of Americans unwilling to work at all. While the commission's recommendations languished, the federal government did carry out a number of pilot projects to test the viability of providing a guaranteed annual income. To its surprise, the government found that it did not appreciably reduce the incentive to work, as many politicians had feared.[15]

Today, the discussion of a guaranteed annual income is being heard more frequently again, by a growing number of academicians, politicians, and labor and civil rights leaders in search of solutions to the twin problems of long-term technological unemployment and rising poverty levels. But, unlike earlier schemes which would have required little or nothing in return from the recipients, today's reformers are linking the idea of a social income to an agreement by the unemployed to perform community service in the third sector—in effect, advancing the notion of a social wage in return for real work in the social economy.[16]

Many Western European nations have legislated guaranteed minimum income schemes over the past twenty-five years, with varying degrees of success. The French plan is particularly interesting because it includes a contractual arrangement whereby "entitlement to the minimum income is made conditional on acceptance by the beneficiary of work that is socially or culturally useful to the community or on enrollment in courses for retraining or reintegration into active life."[17] With fewer and fewer jobs available in the increasingly automated market economy, the French plan to provide a guaranteed income in return for an agreement to perform community service will likely be taken up by other countries anxious to address the issue of providing both income and worthwhile work in the absence of formal employment.

In the past, the government has often been accused of throwing large sums of money at the social economy with little of it getting to the people and communities in need. Much of the expense involved in government programs has been eaten up in the delivery of social services, with little left over to assist the impacted communities. Still, there have been notable exceptions. Volunteers in Service to America (VISTA), the Student Community Service Program, the National Senior Service Corps, the Peace Corps, the National Health Service

Corps (NHSC), and, more recently, AmeriCorps are federal programs designed to promote individual service and support volunteer efforts in local communities in the United States and abroad.

VISTA, founded in 1964, is made up of volunteers recruited primarily from the communities in which they serve, who give their time and skills to volunteer organizations and community activities to reduce poverty. In return for their services, they receive a token stipend to cover minimum living expenses. The Student Community Service Program helps promote volunteerism among high school and college students. Grants are awarded to community agencies, schools, and civic organizations to promote a range of service activities including day care, tutoring, drug-abuse prevention, and health services. The National Senior Service Corps includes the Retired Senior Volunteer Program (RSVP), the Foster Grandparent Program (FGP), and the Senior Companion Program (SCP). Volunteers in these three federally sponsored programs are sixty or older and work part-time in community-service activities. Grants are awarded to local nonprofit organizations and public-sponsored agencies that recruit, place, and supervise senior-citizen volunteers. The Peace Corps dates back to 1961, and consists of thousands of young Americans who volunteer to work overseas for up to two years, generally assisting poverty-stricken rural and urban communities in third-world countries. The National Health Service Corps, a program of the Public Health Service, recruits and places health-care providers in poor, generally rural communities that lack basic medical care. The NHSC provides tuition fees and monthly stipends to students in return for an agreement to serve a two-year term in a designated community upon completion of studies. AmeriCorps, set up by President Clinton in 1993, provides tuition aid and living expenses to thousands of American students in return for a commitment to serve two years after graduation as a volunteer in the areas of education, environment, human needs, or public safety.[18]

State and local governments are also introducing innovative programs to assist efforts in the third sector. In the 1980s the State of North Carolina established a special office for volunteers to recruit and train people for volunteer service in the community. Over 70 percent of the adults in the state volunteered time under the government program, and the donation of their services was estimated to exceed $300 million. The governor, Jim Hunt, volunteered one day of his workweek tutoring students in math, while his wife volunteered her time to the Meals on Wheels program. The governor became a strong advocate of government assistance to the volunteer sector and argued that "a new kind of thinking among Democrats" was needed in which "volunteerism is the key" to social reform.[19]

Although the costs of these government-sponsored programs in community service are small, the economic returns to the community are enormous and often exceed the expenditures by many times. Dollar for dollar, government investment in programs designed to complement and support the volunteer sector have proven to be among the most cost-effective means of providing social services in local communities. Yet, despite scores of successful experiments and programs in recent years, the money given over to such programs is small compared with other governmental expenditures in the social economy.

Many traditional Democrats, as well as a number of Wall Street analysts and academicians, are looking instead to government-sponsored public-works programs to hire the unemployed and those who have slipped under the social safety net and into the permanent underclass. Felix Rohatyn, the investment analyst who is widely credited with saving New York City from bankruptcy in the 1970s, advocates a massive public-works program to fix the country's bridges and tunnels, mend highways, and create high-speed rail and mass transit. Rohatyn says that the program he envisions would cost at least $250 billion over a ten-year period, but could generate up to a million new jobs annually. The effort could be paid for largely by floating special issues of infrastructure bonds, secured by "modest increases in gasoline taxes." Rohatyn suggests that private and public pension funds also be used to invest in the long-term bonds.[20] While Rohatyn's proposal is laudable, it might not prove politically salable, given the public's clamor for less government, and the new climate of austerity in Washington and in state capitals.

In addition to public-works programs, the Clinton administration is considering offering corporations tax credits for hiring welfare recipients. The Administration and Congress have set aside $2.3 billion in tax credits and $1 billion in new financing to set up Empowerment Zones in a select number of inner-city ghettos. These designated areas would receive special tax credits and other government benefits to help attract new business. Businesses that employ a resident of the Empowerment Zone would save up to $3,000 a year in payroll taxes. Despite the political fanfare surrounding the President's plan to empower poor inner-city communities, few politicians are sanguine that many new businesses are going to relocate in the urban ghettos of America, or that many new private-sector jobs will be generated from the latest urban-development scheme to come out of Washington.[21]

By focusing too much attention on financing public-works projects and providing incentives to the private sector to hire the poor, the government is working against a historical curve that is steadily moving society away from public- and private-sector employment and toward work in the third sector. Talk of massive public-works programs makes little sense right now when the public will is not sufficient to create such programs on the scale required to meet the current crisis. Similarly, continued efforts to find nonexistent jobs in the formal economy, or jobs that will likely be eliminated by re-engineering and automation a few years down the line, seem equally misdirected.

The federal government might do better to redirect its efforts away from costly public-works projects and quixotic attempts to create model economies inside poor inner-city core areas and, instead, greatly expand existing community-service programs in impoverished communities. Recruiting, training, and placing millions of un-employed and poverty-stricken Americans in jobs in nonprofit organizations in their own neighborhoods and communities is likely to have a far greater impact, per dollar spent, than more traditional public-works-oriented programs and market-directed initiatives.

Sara Melendez, the president of the Independent Sector, a national umbrella organization representing third-sector groups, argues that the nonprofit community is often better able to address issues more quickly and effectively at the local level than government agencies. She advocates creative new partnerships between the two sectors and says that at least in some cases the federal government can best accomplish social goals "by funding non-profits, through contracts and grants, tailoring the services to different population groups according to their language, cultural background, and local needs."[22]

The federal government has begun to move tentatively in the direction of guaranteeing income and encouraging some form of community service in current welfare-reform proposals. It already provides a tax credit of up to $3,033 a year per family to supplement the wages of the nation's working poor—essentially guaranteeing a portion of their income. Both Republicans and Democrats have supported the plan, arguing that the additional guaranteed income provides a necessary incentive to keep people working and off the welfare rolls. Moreover, in December 1993, the Administration announced that it would seek an overhaul of the current welfare system and would include among its proposals a plan to encourage work by supplementing earned income when the job performed paid less than the welfare one is entitled to. The White House also said that it would consider imposing a two-year term limit on welfare benefits, after which a recipient would "be forced to find a job or perform community service work."[23]

Under the draft plan currently under review, if after extensive re-education and training, the recipient was still unable to secure a job in the private sector after two years on welfare benefits, he or she would be paid by the government to perform public-work assignments for a minimum of fifteen hours a week at the minimum wage. Or, alternately, the recipient would have to enroll in a "community work experience program" in order to continue to receive benefits.

An even more ambitious welfare-reform program was announced by the Governor of Massachusetts, William F. Weld, in January 1994. The Massachusetts plan would require all able-bodied persons receiving Aid to Families with Dependent Children (AFDC) to go to work in the private sector or enroll in a community-service program called Transitional Employment for Massachusetts Parents (TEMP) within one year. The state government, in turn, would replace their welfare grants with day care, child support and medical care to make sure parents could provide for their families while working. Since those working in community-service programs as part of TEMPS would receive less than the minimum wage, the government would continue to provide a partial AFDC grant to supplement their income. Governor Weld said he was launching the new reforms "to change the welfare paradigm so that we have a public-assistance program based on paychecks, not on cash grants."[24]

Not unexpectedly, the nation's public-employee unions have already weighed in on the new welfare-reform proposals, expressing concern that hundreds of thousands of their members could be displaced by poor people forced off the relief rolls to perform community service. Lee A. Saunders, assistant to the president of the American Federation of State, County and Municipal Employees union

(AFSCME), told the White House Task Force on Welfare Reform that between 1.2 and 2 million workfare jobs would probably have to be created under the President's proposed plan. "There is absolutely no way so many positions can be created without displacing regular public-sector jobs even with strong anti-displacement rules" says Saunders.[25]

The concern of the public employees unions over job displacement could be allayed in large part by the enactment of legislation reducing the workweek from forty to thirty hours for all public employees. The government has long maintained the principle that public employees ought to be compensated in terms comparable to those in the private sector. A reduction in the workweek in the formal market economy would inevitably be matched by a similar reduction of hours worked in the public sector. By reducing the workweek of public employees from forty to thirty hours and increasing the compensation per hour worked to bring salaries in line with gains in national productivity, the local, state, and federal governments could more than assure the job security of existing public employees. At the same time, a 25 percent reduction in the workweek of public employees would create a work vacuum that could be filled, in part, by persons performing community service work.

In the debate over how best to divide up the benefits of productivity advances, every country must ultimately grapple with an elementary question of economic justice. Put simply, does every member of society, even the poorest among us, have a right to participate in and benefit from increases in productivity brought on by the information and communication technology revolutions? If the answer is yes, then some form of compensation will have to be made to the increasing number of unemployed whose labor will no longer be needed in the new high-tech automated world of the twenty-first century. Since the advances in technology are going to mean fewer and fewer jobs in the market economy, the only effective way to ensure those permanently displaced by machinery the benefits of increased productivity is to provide some kind of government-guaranteed income. Tying the income to service in the community would aid the growth and development of the social economy and facilitate the long-term transition into a community-centered, service-oriented culture.

FINANCING THE TRANSITION

Paying for a social income and for re-education and training programs to prepare men and women for a career of community service would require significant government funds. Some of the money could come from savings brought about by gradually replacing many of the current welfare bureaucracies with direct payments to persons performing community-service work. With community organizations and non-profit groups taking greater responsibility for addressing needs traditionally handled by government, more tax money would be freed up to provide community-service incomes and training for the millions who would be working directly in their own neighborhoods to help others.

Government funds could also be freed up by discontinuing costly subsidies to corporations that have outgrown their domestic commitments and now operate in countries around the world. The federal government provided transnational corporations with more than $104 billion in subsidies in 1993 in the form of direct payments and tax breaks. Agribusiness companies alone received $29.2 billion, nearly twice the amount allocated to Aid to Families with Dependent Children (AFDC). The giant food company Sunkist received $17.8 million to promote orange juice overseas. Gallo wines received $5.1 million to promote its wine abroad, while M&M/Mars received more than one million dollars to promote candy bars around the world. Even McDonald's was awarded $465,000—in tax money—to promote its Ch:cken McNuggets in overseas markets. Three global grain companies, Cargill, Continental, and Dreyfus, received more than $1.1 billion of federal funds between 1985 and 1989 as part of the Agriculture Department's Export Enhancement Program. Ranchers, mining companies, timber companies, pharmaceutical companies, and other business concerns are also the beneficiaries of government giveaway programs and handouts. Elimination of these corporate subsidies could free up enough funds to guarantee a social wage for several million Americans.[26]

Additional moneys could be raised by cutting unnecessary defense programs. Despite the fact that the Cold War is over, the federal government continues to maintain a bloated defense budget. While Congress has scaled down defense appropriations in recent years, military expenditures are expected to run at about 89 percent of Cold War spending between 1994 and 1998.[27] In a 1992 report, the Congressional Budget Office (CBO) concluded that defense spending could be cut by a rate of 7 percent a year over a five-year period without compromising the nation's military preparedness or undermining national security. If the CBO recommendations were to be taken up by Congress and the White House, the country could save upwards of $63 billion a year by 1998—enough to make a substantial difference if transferred to the building up of the third sector and the providing of a social wage for millions of displaced workers willing to perform service in the social economy.[28] Even though some jobs would be lost in military-related industries as a result of the cost cutting, far more are likely to be generated if the savings are used directly to finance third-sector employment. The reason is fairly obvious. A great deal of military spending goes to paying for the military hardware itself. If, instead, virtually all of the savings from the military budget were to be used to provide a social wage for third-sector work and for helping rebuild local communities, far more jobs could be generated with far greater potential purchasing power.

Cuts in defense, the elimination of unnecessary subsidies to transnational companies, and the paring down of the welfare bureaucracy, while essential, would still not be sufficient in the long run to raise the money necessary to provide income for millions of displaced workers and rebuild the third sector of American society. Much of the revenue for financing a social wage and community-service program will probably have to come from new taxes.

The most equitable and far-reaching approach to raising the needed funds would be to enact a value-added tax (VAT) on all nonessential goods and services. While the VAT is a new and untried idea in the United States, it has been adopted by more than fifty-nine countries, including virtually every major European nation.[29]

The tax is called value added because it is collected at each stage of the production process—on the "value added" to the product. In other words, a tax is "levied on the difference between the value of each firm's output and the value of its inputs."[30] Advocates of the tax point out the many advantages in taxing consumption rather than income. To begin with, says Murray L. Weidenbaum, formerly chairman of President Reagan's Council of Economic Advisors and now director of the Center for Business at Washington University in St. Louis, shifting the primary base of taxation from income to consumption makes more sense from a societal perspective. "It is fairer to tax people on what they take from society than on what they contribute by working, investing, and saving." Secondly, by taxing consumption instead of income, the VAT encourages saving rather than spending. Comparing the many advantages of the value-added tax over the income tax, Weidenbaum concludes, "A consumption tax encourages savings because every dollar saved and not spent on current consumption is exempt from the consumption tax. The fundamental way for an individual to minimize consumption tax liabilities is to consume less; the incentives to work, save, and invest are unimpaired. By contrast, the basic way one can minimize income tax liabilities is to earn less, which dampens incentives to work, save, and invest."[31]

Champions of the value-added tax believe fervently that "people should be taxed on what they take out of the society's resources, not what they put into them."[32] By taxing what people spend rather than what they earn, the burden is shifted from penalizing work to placing constraints on overconsumption.

There are a number of advantages in implementing a value-added tax over simply raising income taxes in order to finance a guaranteed income, the most important being the overall impact on the economy. The Congressional Budget Office says that a VAT would have a more positive effect on growth, and that national output would be nearly one percent higher if a VAT were used instead of higher income taxes to raise revenue.[33]

The main disadvantage of a value-added tax is its regressive nature. A sales tax falls disproportionately on lower-income groups, especially if it is imposed on basic necessities like food, clothing, housing, and medical care. A VAT also places a greater burden on small businesses, which are less able to absorb and pass on the costs. Many countries have greatly reduced and even eliminated the regressive nature of value-added taxes by exempting basic necessities and small businesses.

By enacting a value-added tax of between 5 and 7 percent on all nonessential goods and services, the federal government would generate billions of dollars of additional revenue—more than what would be required to finance a social wage and community-service program for those willing to work in the third sector.

Alternatively, a more narrow value-added tax could be levied on the expanding goods and services of the new high-technology revolution. For example, serious thought might be given to placing a VAT on all computer, information, and telecommunication products and services. Sales in the computer and information-technology industry have been growing by 8 percent a year for the past ten years and topped $602 billion in 1993. Sales are expected to continue their sharp climb in the years ahead as the economy pushes into the high-tech era.[34] A value-added tax on the products and services of the Third Industrial Revolution, to be used exclusively to help finance the transition of America's neediest citizens into third-sector work, makes sense and ought to be explored. To insure against any potential regressive use of the tax, all nonprofit organizations, including schools and charitable institutions, should be exempt from paying it.

A value-added tax might also be put on the entertainment and recreation industries, which are among the fastest-growing sectors of the economy. In 1991 consumer spending in these two fields jumped by 13 percent, or more than twice the overall rate. In 1993 Americans spent more than $340 billion on amusements, from video rentals to theme parks and casinos. Much of the increase in spending on entertainment and recreation reflects the spending habits of America's new "symbolic analysts" class. A breakdown of the spending on entertainment is revealing. For example, more than $58 billion was spent in 1993 on VCRs, videotapes, cellular phones, and other high-tech communications equipment. Another $8 billion was spent on home computers for personal use. America's wealthiest consumers spent $7 billion on boats and aircraft. Another $14 billion was spent on amusement parks and other commercial participant amusements. Toys and sporting equipment accounted for $65 billion of the total, while movie admissions and video rentals contributed $13 billion. Live entertainment exceeded $6 billion, and gambling took in more than $28 billion.[35]

When the new information superhighway is completed in a few years, entertainment sales are expected to climb even higher. While working and poor people also spend their consumer dollars on entertainment and recreation, they spend a far smaller percentage of their disposable income than do the wealthiest groups in the population. Few of the nation's poor can afford home computers, cellular phones, and expensive trips to theme parks, resorts, and casinos.

Entertainment and recreation are going to account for an even larger share of the nation's growth in the coming information era. Imposing a value-added tax on the consumption of entertainment and recreation appears a fair and equitable way of transferring a small portion of the gains of the new high-tech economy from the purveyors and beneficiaries to those most in need and least likely to benefit from the advances of the third industrial marketplace.

Consideration should also be given to enacting a VAT on advertising. More than $130 billion was spent on advertising in the United States in 1992.[36] In the coming information age, advertising is going to play an even larger role in the economy—especially in the wake of the flood of media advances expected to come with the creation of an information superhighway. A sales tax on advertising could generate additional billions of dollars of revenue for use in government programs to guarantee income and work for millions of the nation's less-well-off citizens.

The state of Florida successfully passed legislation in 1987 imposing a blanket sales tax on all services, including those of lawyers, accountants, and companies that buy advertising, only to have the law repealed six months later because of the strenuous objections of out-of-state advertisers. According to Douglas Lindholm, head of the state tax policy division at Price Waterhouse, "The advertisers have tremendous access to the national media because they essentially pay their bills." In Florida, says Lindholm, "they were able to turn the whole issue against the legislature."[37]

Although powerful vested interests within the business community are likely to resist value-added sales taxes, the alternatives of taxing income or leaving the problem of technological unemployment unattended are even more onerous. By imposing a targeted value-added tax, and then using the revenue exclusively to build up the third sector and ease the transition into the social economy for the millions of workers displaced by the new technologies, a closed loop is created between the market, public, and third sectors. The newly emerging symbolic analyst class—the top 20 percent of the population who are the immediate beneficiaries of the high-tech global economy—are asked to redistribute a small portion of their purchasing power to help those who have been cast aside by the market forces of the Third Industrial Revolution. Providing a social wage to millions of Americans, in return for performing meaningful work in the social economy, will, in turn, benefit both the market and public sectors by increasing purchasing power and taxable income as well as reducing the crime rate and the cost of maintaining law and order.

Along with the enactment of a value-added tax, Congress might also consider passing legislation to increase tax-deductible corporate contributions to the third sector. Under existing laws, corporations are allowed to deduct up to 10 percent of their taxable income in the form of contributions to nonprofit programs and activities. In practice, they pay out far less. In 1992 manufacturing firms contributed a medium of 1.5 percent of U.S. pretax income while nonmanufacturing companies paid out less than 0.8 percent. Although corporate philanthropy has increased steadily from $797 million in 1970 to nearly $5 billion in 1992, it represents less than 5 percent of all giving to the third sector. Health and human services received the lion's share of corporate giving, nearly 34.6 percent in 1992. Education received 30.4 percent of corporate donations in the same year, while culture and art received 9.6 percent, and civic and community programs were given 10.4 percent.[38]

With profits expected to rise sharply in the years ahead from increasing globalization of markets and automation of production and services, transnational companies ought to be encouraged to contribute more of their gains to helping rebuild and sustain the many communities in which they do business around the world. Legislation should be introduced and enacted to provide more favorable deductions for companies willing to expand their corporate giving to the third sector. To assure a fair and equitable sharing of the productivity gains coming out of the Third Industrial Revolution, corporate contributions could include a sliding charitable index geared to increases in productivity by industry and sector. If, for example, productivity for a particular industry were to rise by 2 percent for the year, the government could provide an additional tax deduction for those companies willing to increase their contribution by a like percentage. By sharing their gains with the third sector, businesses enjoy the advantage of being able to participate more directly in the rebuilding of the social economy, rather than simply handing over tax moneys to the government to dispense.

Preparing for the decline of mass formal work in the market economy will require a fundamental restructuring of the nature of human participation in society. By providing shadow wages for millions of working Americans who are devoting more of their time to volunteer activity in the social economy, as well as providing a social wage to millions of the nation's unemployed and poor who are willing to work in the third sector, we can begin to lay the groundwork for a long-term transition out of formal work in the market economy and into service work in the social economy. As the various levels of government begin to shift their focus away from activities and programs designed to benefit the marketplace and toward activities and programs that promote the social economy, proposals of the kind mentioned above are likely to gain support. Forging new working alliances between government bodies and the third sector will help build self-sufficient and sustainable communities across the country.

· 18 ·

Globalizing the
Social Economy

THE INDEPENDENT SECTOR is playing an increasingly important
social role in nations around the world. People are creating new
institutions at both the local and national levels to provide for needs
that are not being met by either the marketplace or public sector. Jim
Joseph, president of The Council on Foundations, notes that in virtually every country "People are reserving for themselves an inter-
mediary space between business and government where private
energy can be . . . deployed for the public good."[1] The third sector has
grown dramatically in recent years and is quickly becoming an effective force in the lives of hundreds of millions of persons in scores of
countries.

England's experience is closest to that of the United States: it has
thousands of volunteer associations, and in recent years has engaged in
a similar political debate over the role of the third sector. There are
currently more than 350,000 voluntary organizations in the United
Kingdom, with a total income in excess of £17 billion, or 4 percent of
the gross national product. As in the United States, the volunteer spirit
is highly developed in England. A 1990 poll found that more than
39 percent of the population participated in voluntary activities in the
third sector.[2]

In France, the third sector is just now beginning to emerge as a
social force. In one recent year, more than 43,000 voluntary associations were created. Employment in the third sector has been growing
lately, while jobs in the formal economy have been declining. The
social economy now accounts for more than 6 percent of total employ-

ment in France, or as many jobs as are provided by the entire consumer-goods industry. As noted earlier, the French government has been at the forefront in providing training and placement of the unemployed in third-sector activities. In an attempt to reduce the number of unemployed youth, it launched the Collective Utility Works. Under the program, more than 350,000 young French men and women are paid a monthly salary by the government in return for performing work in either the nonprofit third sector or in the public sector. Although many of the volunteer groups in France are poorly financed and enjoy only limited memberships, they are growing in number and clout and are likely to play a greater role in French life in the years ahead.[3]

The third sector in Germany is growing at a faster rate than either the private or public sector. Between 1970 and 1987, the nonprofit sector grew by more than 5 percent. In the late 1980s there were more than 300,000 voluntary organizations operating in Germany. While most function without paid staff, the nonprofit sector still accounted for 4.3 percent of the country's total paid employment in 1987. By the end of the decade—just prior to reunification—the nonprofit sector contributed nearly 2 percent of the country's GNP and employed more people than the agricultural sector and nearly half as many jobs as the banking and insurance industries. In recent years, employment in the nonprofit sector has been growing while overall employment has declined. Nearly one third of the nonprofit groups in Germany are tied to churches and religious organizations.[4]

In Italy, the voluntary sector was largely centered around the Catholic Church until the 1970s. In the past two decades however, nonreligious volunteer associations and groups have sprung up and are playing an increasingly important role in local communities. It is estimated that more than 15.4 percent of the adult population in Italy volunteer their time to activities in the third sector.[5]

In Japan, the third sector has grown dramatically in recent years, in part to address the many new social issues facing the country. The rapid restoration and reconstruction of Japan in the postwar period left Japanese society with a new set of problems, ranging from environmental pollution to care for the young and the elderly. The weakening of the traditional family, long regarded as the primary institutional mechanism for guaranteeing personal welfare, created a vacuum at the neighborhood and community level that has come to be filled by third-sector organizations.

Today, thousands of nonprofit organizations functioning through-out Japanese society attend to the cultural, social, and economic needs of millions of people. Some 23,000 charitable organizations, called *koeki hojin*, currently operate in Japan. These are private philan-thropic organizations, incorporated by the government and involved in the fields of science, art, religion, charity, and other public-interest endeavors. In addition to the *koeki hojin*, there are more than 12,000 social-welfare organizations, known as *shakaifukushi hojin*, which ad-minister day-care centers, services for the elderly, maternal and child health services, and women's protective services. Most of these orga-nizations are dependent on public-sector support—between 80 and 90 percent—with the remainder of their expenses raised by fees, sales, charges, and private donations, largely from community chests. The third sector also includes thousands of private schools, religious institutions, and medical facilities as well as charitable trusts and cooperatives. There are also more than one million community and mass organizations, including children's associations, which are formed in most primary school districts and organize outdoor activ-ities, festivals, sporting events, and fund-raising activities. The elderly are likely to belong to one of the 130,000 *Rozin* clubs that exist throughout the country to meet the social and cultural needs of senior citizens.[6]

One of the potentially most powerful third-sector forces in Japan is the community-based mutual-help organization, which includes more than 90 percent of all Japanese households. Neighborhood associa-tions began to proliferate in the 1920s and 30s, in large part to address the issues of rapid industrialization and urbanization. In the late 1930s, the Imperial government incorporated these associations into the state machinery. In 1940 the government ordered every community in Japan to form neighborhood associations and made membership com-pulsory. The groups were used to spread wartime propaganda and control the distribution of food and other goods and services. After the war, neighborhood groups resurfaced as self-governing associations without legal ties to the government. Known as *jichikai*, these organiza-tions now exist in more than 270,000 neighborhoods. A local *jichikai* generally consists of between 180 and 400 households. Its leaders are elected and usually serve two-year terms.[7]

The *jichikai* provide a range of services. They help people who are in need of financial assistance, are homeless, or who have a serious illness. Oftentimes the local *jichikai* will provide free building mate-rials and labor to rebuild a neighbor's house that has burnt down. It also sponsors cultural activities and trips and hosts local festivals and fairs. Many of the associations have become advocates, fighting unwanted development and unfair housing laws. In recent years the *jichikai* have also become increasingly active in environmental issues and often lobby the government to clean up the environment and enforce pollution statutes.

Because they have no formal legal recognition, *jichikai* receive no government funds and have to rely almost exclusively on membership fees. But even without government money, these associations have continued to grow and flourish, in large part because of the high degree of participation by their members. The Confucian tradition, with its emphasis on cooperation and harmonious relations, has helped spur voluntary efforts in every community, making Japan's third sector a formidable force in the life of the country. In the years ahead, third-sector organizations are likely to play an even more critical role as local communities are forced to take on increasing responsibilities in the wake of the government cutbacks in social services.

A New Voice for Democracy

Not surprisingly, the new interest in third-sector associations is also paralleling the worldwide spread of democratic movements. In December 1993, representatives from dozens of countries announced the formation of a new international organization, called Civicus, whose mission is to help "cultivate volunteerism and community service," especially in regions where the third sector is just beginning to flourish. The organization's first executive director, Miklos Marschall, the former deputy mayor of Budapest, said, "We are witnessing a real revolution throughout the world involving tens of thousands of associations, clubs and non-governmental groups." Marschall believes that "the 90s will be the decades of the third sector because throughout the world there has been ... a great deal of disappointment concerning the traditional established institutions such as trade unions, political parties and churches." The power vacuum, argues Marschall, is being filled by the creation of small Non-Governmental Organizations (NGOs) and community groups in dozens of countries.[8] Marschall says that the new organization "will provide a forum for these groups, an opportunity for international advocacy, and serve also as a moral world court."[9]

The growing influence of the third sector has been most noticeable in the former communist nations of the Soviet bloc. NGOs played a decisive role in the collapse of the Soviet Union and the former satellite regimes of Eastern Europe and now figure prominently in the reconstruction of that region. In 1988 more than 40,000 illegal nongovernmental organizations were active in the Soviet Union.[10] Many of the volunteer organizations in Russia and Eastern Europe were nurtured by Church authorities, who provided a safe haven for their activities. Volunteer groups engaged in a wide range of programs, from promoting cultural reforms to waging war on environmental degradation. Many engaged directly in political activity, challenging the power and prerogatives of the state.

These nascent democratic groups proved a far more effective force in toppling the authoritarian regimes in Eastern Europe and the Soviet Union than traditional resistance groups steeped in political ideology and buttressed by paramilitary campaigns. Reflecting on the developments that led to the fall of communism in Central and Eastern Europe, Soviet historian Frederick Starr argues that the rapid growth of third-sector activity placed enormous pressure on the already weakened Party apparatus. "The extraordinary effervescence of NGOs of all types," says Starr, "is the single most distinctive aspect of the revolutions of 1989."[11]

In the wake of the collapse of the Communist Party in Central and Eastern Europe, the third sector has become the wellspring for new ideas and reforms as well as for political leadership. It is estimated that there are upwards of 70,000 NGOs in Central Europe and the former Soviet Union, offering a grass-roots training ground in the exercise of participatory democracy.[12] With the private sector struggling to be born, and the newly reformed public sector still in its infancy, the third sector is playing a unique role in the politics of the region. Its ability to respond quickly and effectively to local concerns and at the same time instill the democratic spirit throughout society should, to a large measure, determine the success of reform efforts in the former communist countries.

As the high-technology revolution and new market forces make their way into Eastern Europe and Russia, questions regarding technological displacement and growing unemployment are likely to come to the fore and become central to the political debate there. The rising tide of xenophobia, nationalism, and fascism, fueled by increasing unemployment, population pressures, and the globalization of the market economy, is going to seriously test the fledgling democratic spirit of the newly emerging third sector as well as the political stability of these newly liberated nations. The political future of Central and Eastern Europe will probably be decided by how well the third sector can fend off the new wave of neo-fascist sentiment and build a strong grass-roots infrastructure for popular democratic participation. If the third sector fails to mount an effective response to the problems of technological displacement and long-term structural unemployment, these countries may well succumb to the emotional appeals of fascism, plunging that part of the world into a new dark age.

While the third sector is playing a pivotal role in the reconstruction of Central and Eastern Europe, its emergent role in the developing nations of Asia and the Southern Hemisphere is no less significant. NGOs in the third world are a relatively new phenomenon. They have accompanied the movement for human rights and democratic reforms in the postcolonial era and are now a major force in the political and cultural life of countries throughout the Southern Hemisphere.

Today there are more than 35,000 voluntary organizations in the developing nations.[13] Third-world NGOs are involved in rural development and land reform, food relief, preventive health care and family planning, early-childhood-education and literacy campaigns, economic development, housing, and political advocacy, and are often the only voice of the people in countries where the governments are weak and corrupt and the market economy small or nonexistent. In many developing nations, the third sector is becoming a more effective force for dealing with local needs than either the private or public sectors. This is especially true where the formal market economy plays little role in the economic life of the community. It is estimated that volunteer organizations already impact the lives of more than 250 million people in developing nations, and their outreach and effectiveness will continue to grow in the coming years.[14]

The third sector has experienced its greatest growth in Asia, where there are more than 20,000 volunteer organizations.[15] In Orangi, a suburb of Karachi, Pakistan, the Orangi Pilot Project has enlisted the voluntary help of 28,000 families to construct 430,000 feet of underground sewers and build more than 28,000 latrines for local residents. In India, the Self-Employed Women's Association (SEWA), a trade union of poor women in Ahmedabad, provides free legal services for women, child-care services, and training courses in carpentry, plumbing, bamboo work, and midwifery.[16] In Nepal, grass-roots NGOs, working with local populations, built sixty-two dams at one fourth the cost of comparable construction done by the government.[17] In Sri Lanka, the Sarvodaya Sharanadana Movement (SSM) claims 7,700 on its staff and works in more than 8,000 villages, helping local populations mobilize resources and create self-sufficient communities. SSM projects include nutrition programs for preschool children, assistance to the deaf and disabled, and income-generating training programs for sewing, mechanical repair, printing, and carpentry.[18] In Malaysia, the Consumers Association of Penang (CAP) works with rural communities, helping them secure government assistance and protecting them from exploitative development schemes.[19] In Senegal, the Committee to Fight for the End of Hunger (COLUFIFA), with its 20,000 members, helps farmers promote food crops rather than exports. The group also provides training assistance for farmers in better cultivation and storage techniques as well as programs to raise literacy standards and improve the health of rural villagers.[20] In the Philippines, PAMALAKAYA, an NGO representing 50,000 fishermen, lobbies the government to preserve communal fish ponds and provides ongoing training and education for its members.[21]

Much of the NGO effort in Asia has centered around ecological concerns. Forest-protection groups, for example, have been set up in South Korea, Bangladesh, Nepal, and other Asian nations to save the remaining forests from the hands of loggers and developers. There are currently more than 500 environmental organizations in India alone, helping save the soil, plant trees, conserve water, and fight agricultural and industrial pollution. One of the most effective environmental efforts of recent years was launched by women villagers determined to protect their forests from logging companies. The Chipco movement gained worldwide attention when peasant women lay down in front of advancing bulldozers and hugged trees to save their forests from being uprooted.[22]

Women's organizations have also proliferated in Asia in the past decade. In Indonesia and Korea, mothers' clubs are helping women develop effective family planning. In Bangladesh, members of a national association of women lawyers have traveled to more than 68,000 villages, informing women of their basic legal rights and providing legal assistance to women who have been victims of mistreatment at the hands of spouses and the government.[23]

Latin America, like Asia, has seen an explosion of volunteer organizations in the past twenty-five years. Much of the impetus for the emerging third sector has come from the Catholic Church. Priests, nuns, and lay people have created a network of local action groups called Christian Base Communities. In Brazil alone, more than 100,000 base communities, with more than 3 million members, have been created. About an equal number of similar communities exists throughout the rest of Latin America. These CBCs combine self-help and advocacy efforts, creating a bottom-up democratic movement among the continent's poorest people.[24] In Lima, some 1,500 community kitchens have been established. More than 100,000 mothers work through these kitchens, distributing powdered milk to the poor. In Chile, hundreds of urban volunteer organizations, called Organizaciónes Económicas Populares, or OEPs, have been set up to address public needs long ignored by the government and market sectors. Some OEPs have established consumer and housing cooperatives. Others have established health and education programs, alternative schools, and community kitchens.[25] In the Dominican Republic, women have joined together to form the Centro de Investigación para la Acción Fémina (CIPAF), an NGO that works on improving the lot of peasant women and poor women of the urban barrios.[26] In Colombia, more than 700 nonprofit community-housing groups are building housing units for the homeless.[27]

Neighborhood-improvement associations—*juntas de vecinos*— exist throughout Latin America. These volunteer groups help build schools and water taps, organize garbage removal, and arrange transportation services. Parent associations have mushroomed throughout Latin America over the past decade, helping parents establish childcare centers, community vegetable gardens, and producer cooperatives. In countries where small landowning elites still own and control much of the countryside, peasant associations and unions have been formed to press for land reforms. The Mexican National Union of Autonomous Regional Peasant Organizations and the Movement of Landless Rural Workers in Brazil are among the best-known and most visible groups.[28]

Africa too is experiencing a rapid growth in third-sector activity. There are more than 4,000 NGOs currently operating on the African continent, and many observers regard them as "the most significant driving force behind development" in that part of the world.[29] In Uganda, 250 local NGOs provide emergency assistance and healthcare programs to the poor. In Burkina Faso, 2,800 community work groups, called *Naams*, with more than 160,000 members, dig ditches, construct raw-water-storage tanks, build small dams, tend community forests, operate literacy programs, build maternity hospitals, phar-macies, schools, and village clinics. The Naams even promote cultural activities and host sporting events in local communities across the country.[30]

In Kenya, the Green Belt Movement, made up of some 80,000 women, has planted more than 10 million trees and taught its mem-bers how to restore and conserve their soil and use natural fertilizer.[31] In Zaire, the Église du Christ, with 12 million followers, works in sixty-two communities establishing health-promotion programs, primary schools, and tree-planting campaigns.[32]

In many Southern Hemisphere countries where the formal market economy is virtually nonexistent, especially in the countryside, NGOs play a somewhat different role than their northern counterparts in the nonprofit sector. In the United States and other industrial countries, third-sector organizations often take over activities that the market cares little about or ignores—for example, rehabilitating low-income housing and building homeless shelters. However, in the third world, says Julie Fisher, of the Program on Non-Profit Organizations at Yale University, NGOs "are getting into precisely the areas that the market does provide for in the developed countries," because the market sector barely exists. "Because people are so desperately poor," says Fisher, "there's literally no opportunity for them in the formal economy—it's essentially irrelevant to most people in the world." Local populations often have little choice, says Fisher, but to develop alternatives to the market. These substitutes often metamorphose into market activities. The setting up of microenterprises, cooperatives, and intervillage trading networks is often a precursor to establishing a rudimentary market in a region or an entire country. Fisher says that "what you have in the third world is the third sector promoting the private sector on a massive scale." The gains made from the market sector are often used, in turn, to finance the continued expansion of third-sector activity.[33]

The third sector is emerging in every region of the world. Its meteoric rise is attributable in part to the increasing need to fill a political vacuum left by the retreat of both the private and public sectors from the affairs of local communities. Global corporations operating in a global marketplace are usually impervious to the needs of individual communities. In many third-world countries, the global market economy is largely absent. Where it does exist, local commu-nities are powerless to negotiate the terms of trade. The rules and regulations are set by faceless men operating from behind closed doors in corporate boardrooms thousands of miles away. Similarly, national governments are less involved in local communities. In most second- and third-world countries, the governments are fragile arrangements, tangled in bureaucratic red tape and rife with corruption.

Plagued by slow growth, stubborn unemployment, and mounting debt, and trapped by a global marketplace that forces each nation to compete on the lowest plane of international commerce and trade, governments are losing their hold over local populations. Unable to deliver basic services and unresponsive to demands from below for greater participation, they are becoming increasingly tangential to the lives of their citizens. This is especially true in the developing world, and is reflected by the subtle change in the way international aid and development funds are channeled. Although most foreign-assistance aid still flows from government to government, an increasing number of public-assistance grants are being funneled from northern governments directly to NGOs in second- and third-world countries. In the United States, the Inter-American Foundation and the African Development Foundation, both created by Congress, provide funds directly to grass-roots organizations in developing countries, generally to support sustainable development projects in local communities. The United States Agency for International Development (AID) also supports local NGO projects and initiatives throughout the third world.[34]

While foreign-assistance grants to second- and third-world NGOs are beginning to inch upwards, most of the money for third-sector initiatives in the developing nations still comes directly from NGOs operating in northern industrial countries. Between 1970 and 1990, northern NGOs increased their grants to southern NGOs from $1 billion to $5 billion. In 1991 the United States accounted for nearly half of all the private funds transferred to third-sector activity in the developing world.[35]

Direct foreign assistance to NGOs in the developing world is likely to increase in the years ahead as the third sector becomes more established and better equipped to deal with human needs at the local level. At the same time, the social economy is going to "play a much more significant role in the labor market in these countries," says Miklos Marschall. Like others, Marschall believes "that one of the most important functions of the NGO sector . . . is offering community based job opportunities to people." He says he is convinced that many of the new jobs that will be created will be in the third sector, and that much of the funding for community-based jobs will come from central governments contracting out to NGOs rather than creating costly public-sector programs.[36]

Martin Khor, Director of the Third World Network, worries about how central governments in the third world are going to finance social incomes for those persons who are willing and able to work in the third sector. While direct foreign assistance to community-based NGOs will help provide some of the necessary funding, inevitably the governments in the third world will have to come up with additional monies through taxation. Khor argues that if a value-added tax is imposed, it should be on the technologies, products, and services purchased by the wealthiest members of society. The third-world activist says that governments can play a key role in "offsetting the gross inequalities" that exist in developing countries by "taxing the rich . . . as a means to employ the poor." Khor cautions that the redistribution of income is the key to advancing the social economy in developing countries. If "you haven't solved the problem of the social distribution of income," warns Khor, "then you can't solve the issue of the development of the third sector, because how else are you going to finance [it]?"[37]

The extraordinary growth in third-sector activity is beginning to foster new international networks. NGOs in northern and southern nations are exchanging information, organizing around common objectives, and banding together to make their voices heard in the international community. If there is a shared aphorism that unites their individual pursuits, it is the oft-heard phrase, "Think globally and act locally." NGOs in most nations share a new vision that transcends both the conventional wisdom of the marketplace and the narrow ideology of geopolitics and nationalism. Theirs is a biospheric perspective. The new activists of the third sector are wedded to democratic participation at the local level, the re-establishment of community, service to their fellow human beings, and stewardship of the larger biotic community that makes up the earth's common biosphere.

Although united in a shared vision of the future, NGOs of the Northern and Southern hemispheres are confronted with a variety of challenges and priorities on the eve of the Third Industrial Revolution. While urban NGOs, in both the north and south, will need to address the issue of rising unemployment brought on by dramatic gains in productivity and technological displacement, southern NGOs are going to be confronted with a second, equally profound problem—the

introduction of agricultural biotechnology and the possible elimination of outdoor farming on the planet. The specter of hundreds of
millions of peasant farmers being made redundant by the genetic-
engineering revolution is mind-boggling. The loss of international
agricultural-commodity markets could plunge the Southern Hemisphere nations into an economic tailspin and force an international
banking crisis of unprecedented proportions. Civilization would likely
descend into a long-term decline that could last for centuries. For that
reason alone, Southern Hemisphere NGOs are going to feel increasing
pressure to resist the biotechnology revolution in agriculture while at
the same time working for land reform and more ecologically sustainable approaches to farming their land.

Dr. Vandana Shiva, Director of the Research Foundation for
Science, Technology and National Resource Policy, in India, worries
that in her own country, upwards of 95 percent of the farm population
could be displaced in the coming century by the biotechnology revolution in agriculture. If that were to happen, warns Shiva, "We will have
Yugoslavia multiplied a thousand times," with separatist movements,
open warfare, and the fragmentation of the Indian subcontinent. The
only viable alternative to mass social upheaval and the potential collapse of the Indian State, argues Shiva, is the building up of "a new
freedom movement" rooted in land reform and the practice of ecologically sound, sustainable agriculture.[38]

NGOs throughout the third world are beginning to band together
to fight the incursion of agricultural biotechnology. In the years ahead,
opposition to both the patenting of native seeds by transnational
companies and the wholesale takeover of agriculture by the global
biotech industry is likely to intensify in virtually every Southern
Hemisphere nation, as millions of farmers fight for their survival
against the new labor-displacing gene-splicing technologies.

THE LAST, BEST HOPE

Northern and Southern hemisphere countries alike face the threats
and opportunities brought on by powerful market forces and new
technological realities. Transnational corporations are blazing a path
across national boundaries, transforming and disrupting the lives of
billions of people in their search for global markets. The casualties of
the Third Industrial Revolution are beginning to mount as millions of

workers are riffed to make room for more efficient and profitable machine surrogates. Unemployment is rising and tempers are flaring in country after country caught up in the corporate crossfire to improve production performance at all costs.

Third-sector service and advocacy groups are lightning rods for rechanneling the growing frustration of large numbers of unemployed people. Their efforts to both kindle the spirit of democratic participation and forge a renewed sense of community will, to a large extent, determine the success of the independent sector as a transformative agent for the post-market era. Whether the third sector can grow and diversify fast enough to keep up with the increasing demands placed on it by a disinherited workforce is an open question. Still, with the shrinking of work in the formal market and the diminution of the role of central governments in the day-to-day affairs of the people, the social economy becomes the last best hope for re-establishing an alternative institutional framework for a civilization in transition.

The high-tech savants remain unconvinced of the crisis at hand. From deep inside the gleaming new global village, surrounded by sophisticated technological hardware capable of performing stupendous feats, the future looks hopeful. Many in the emerging knowledge-class envision a world of near-utopian grandeur, a place of overflowing abundance. In recent years, scores of futurists have written breathless tracts prophesying the end of history and our final deliverance into a techno-paradise mediated by free-market forces and ruled over by detached scientific expertise. Our politicians tell us to begin preparing ourselves for the grand exodus into the postmodern era. They hold out visions of a new world of glass and silicon, global communication networks and information superhighways, cyberspace and virtual realities, soaring productivity and unlimited material riches, automated factories and electronic offices. They tell us that the price of admission to this new and wondrous world is re-education and retraining, acquiring new skills for the many job opportunities opening up along the spanking new commercial corridors of the third industrial marketplace.

Their predictions are not without merit. We are, indeed, experiencing a great historic transformation into a Third Industrial Revolution and heading inexorably toward a nearly workerless world. The hardware and software already exist to speed our passage into a new silicon-based civilization. The yet-unresolved question is how many human beings will be left behind on this final leg of the industrial journey, and what kind of world ultimately awaits the rest of us on the other side.

The apostles and evangelists of the Information Age entertain few if any doubts about the ultimate success of the experiment at hand. They are convinced that the Third Industrial Revolution will succeed in opening up more new job opportunities than it forecloses and that dramatic increases in productivity will be matched by elevated levels of consumer demand and the opening up of new global markets to absorb the flood of new goods and services that will become available. Their faith, and for that matter their entire world view, hinges on the correctness of these two central propositions.

The critics, on the other hand, as well as a growing number of people already left at the wayside of the Third Industrial Revolution, are beginning to question where the new jobs are going to come from. In a world where sophisticated information and communication technologies will be able to replace more and more of the global workforce, it is unlikely that more than a fortunate few will be retrained for the relatively scarce high-tech scientific, professional, and managerial jobs made available in the emerging knowledge sector. The very notion that millions of workers displaced by the re-engineering and automation of the agricultural, manufacturing, and service sectors can be retrained to be scientists, engineers, technicians, executives, consultants, teachers, lawyers and the like, and then somehow find the appropriate number of job openings in the very narrow high-tech sector, seems at best a pipe dream, and at worst a delusion.

Then there is the oft-heard argument that new technologies, products, and services not yet even imaginable will come along, providing new business opportunities and jobs for millions. Critics, however, point out that any new product lines introduced in the future will probably require far fewer workers to assemble, produce, and deliver and thus not add significant numbers to the employment rolls. Even if a product with a universal market potential were to emerge today— one similar to radio or television—its production would likely be highly automated and require few on-line workers.

Similarly, many observers wonder how an increasingly under-employed and unemployed global workforce, displaced by the technologies of the Third Industrial Revolution, is going to be able to afford all of the products and services being turned out by the new highly automated production systems. While the advocates contend that the loosening up of trade barriers and the opening up of new global markets will stimulate pent-up consumer demand, the naysayers argue that soaring productivity will face increasingly ineffective and weak consumer demand throughout the world as growing numbers of workers are displaced by technology and lose their purchasing power.

The skeptics are probably right in their concern over technological displacement, job loss, and reduced purchasing power. However, there is little reason to believe that the technological and market forces already set in motion are going to be effectively slowed or stopped by any kind of organized resistance movement in the years ahead. Short of a long-term global depression, chances are that the Third Industrial Revolution will continue to run its course, elevating productivity and displacing growing numbers of workers, all the while providing some new job opportunities but not nearly enough to absorb the millions made redundant by the new technologies. Global markets are also likely to continue to expand, but not nearly fast enough to absorb the overproduction of goods and services. Rising technological unemployment and declining purchasing power will continue to plague the global economy, undermining the capacity of governments to effectively manage their own domestic affairs.

Already, central governments are straining under the weight of a technological revolution that is leaving millions jobless and destitute. The globalization of the market economy and the automation of the agricultural, manufacturing, and service sectors is fast changing the political landscape in every country. World leaders and governments are at a loss on how to soften the blow of a Third Industrial Revolution that is ripping through whole industries, flattening corporate hierarchies, and substituting machines for workers in hundreds of job categories.

The middle class, long the voice of reason and moderation in the political life of industrialized nations, finds itself buffeted on every side by technological change. Squeezed by reduced wages and rising unemployment, growing numbers of the middle class are beginning to search for quick solutions and dramatic rescue from the market forces and technological changes that are destroying their former way of life. In virtually every industrial nation, fear of an uncertain future is driving more and more people from the mainstream to the margins of society, where they seek refuge in extremist political and religious movements that promise to restore public order and put people back to work.

Rising levels of worldwide unemployment and the increasing polarization between rich and poor are creating the conditions for social upheaval and open class warfare on a scale never before experienced in the modern age. Crime, random violence, and low-intensity warfare are on the rise and show every sign of increasing dramatically in the years immediately ahead. A new form of barbarism waits just outside the walls of the modern world. Beyond the quiet suburbs, exurbs, and urban enclaves of the rich and near-rich lie millions upon millions of destitute and desperate human beings. Anguished, angry, and harboring little hope for an escape from their circumstances, they are the potential levelers, the masses whose cries for justice and inclusion have gone unheard and unaddressed. Their ranks continue to swell as millions of workers find themselves pink-slipped and suddenly and irrevocably locked outside the gates of the new high-tech global village.

Still our leaders talk of jobs and crime, the two great issues of our time, as if they were only marginally related, refusing to acknowledge the growing nexus between technological displacement, job loss, and the rise of an outlaw class for whom crime is the last means to secure a piece of a shrinking economic pie.

This then, is the situation the world finds itself in during the early years of the transition into a Third Industrial Revolution. In industrial countries, concern over the jobs issue has led to growing ideological battles between warring groups. The free-marketers accuse the trade unionists of obstructing the process of globalization of trade and of inciting the public with xenophobic appeals to protectionism. The labor movement counters that the transnationals are pushing wages down by forcing its workers to compete with cheap labor from the third world.

The technological optimists accuse the critics of high technology of trying to hold back progress and of harboring naive neo-Luddite fantasies. The technology critics charge that the technophiles care more about profits than people, and that in their pursuit of quick productivity gains, they are unmindful of the terrible toll that automation takes on the lives of millions of workers.

In the United States, some liberal politicians are calling for a new New Deal and massive expenditures on public-works programs, aid to cities, and welfare reform. Most political observers, however, as well as a majority of the electorate, are reluctant to cast the government back into the role of employer of last resort, for fear of greatly increasing budget deficits and the national debt. The conservative forces are rallying around the theme of laissez-faire, arguing that less government interference with the market will help speed the process of globalization and automation, ultimately providing a larger economic pie for everyone to share. Bogged down by so many conflicting and contradictory ideas of what should be done, our leaders continue to muddle along with few constructive suggestions on how to reduce unemployment, create jobs, cut the crime rate, and ease the transition into the high-tech era.

This much we know for sure: We are entering into a new period in history where machines will increasingly replace human labor in the production of goods and services. Although timetables are difficult to predict, we are set on a firm course to an automated future and will likely approach a near-workerless era, at least in manufacturing, by the early decades of the coming century. The service sector, while slower to automate, will probably approach a nearly automated state by the mid-decades of the next century. The emerging knowledge sector will be able to absorb a small percentage of the displaced labor, but not nearly enough to make a substantial difference in the rising unemployment figures. Hundreds of millions of workers will be permanently idled by the twin forces of globalization and automation. Others, still employed, will work far fewer hours in order to more equitably distribute the remaining work and provide adequate purchasing power to absorb the increases in production. As machines increasingly replace workers in the coming decades, the labor of millions will be freed from the economic process and the pull of the marketplace. Unused human labor is the central overriding reality of the coming era and the issue that will need to be confronted and addressed head-on by every nation if civilization is to survive the impact of the Third Industrial Revolution.

If the talent, energy, and resourcefulness of hundreds of millions of men and women are not redirected to constructive ends, civilization will probably continue to disintegrate into a state of increasing destitution and lawlessness from which there may be no easy return. For this reason, finding an alternative to formal work in the marketplace is the critical task ahead for every nation on earth. Preparing for a post-market era will require far greater attention to the building up of the third sector and the renewal of community life. Unlike the market economy, which is based solely on "productivity" and therefore amenable to the substitution of machines for human input, the social economy is centered on human relationships, on feelings of intimacy, on companionship, fraternal bonds, and stewardship—qualities not easily reducible to or replaceable by machines. Because it is the one realm that machines cannot fully penetrate or subsume, it will be by necessity the refuge where the displaced workers of the Third Industrial Revolution will go to find renewed meaning and purpose in life after the commodity value of their labor in the formal marketplace has become marginal or worthless.

The resurrection and transformation of the third sector into a powerful independent realm capable of absorbing the flood of displaced workers let go by the market sector must be given urgent priority if we are to weather the technological storm clouds on the horizon. Thoughtful ways must be found to transfer a growing portion of the productivity gains of the Third Industrial Revolution from the market to the third sector, to keep pace with the increasing burden that will be placed on the social economy.

Faced with the daunting prospect of absorbing growing numbers of workers cast off by the marketplace, and providing more and more basic social services and cultural amenities, the third sector will need significant infusions of both volunteer labor and operating funds. Providing shadow wages for volunteering time, imposing a value-added tax on the products and services of the high-tech era to be used exclusively to guarantee a social wage for the poor in return for performing community service, and increasing the tax deductions for corporate philanthropy tied to productivity gains are just a few of the steps that can be taken now in the United States to increase the third-sector profile and effectiveness in the years ahead. In other countries, different approaches and incentives will likely be advanced to strengthen and broaden the mandate of the social economy.

Up to now, the world has been so preoccupied with the workings of the market economy that the notion of focusing greater attention on the social economy has been little considered by the public or by those who make public policy. That is likely to change in the coming years as it becomes increasingly clear that a transformed third sector offers the only viable means for constructively channeling the surplus labor cast off by the global market.

We are entering a new age of global markets and automated production. The road to a near-workerless economy is within sight. Whether that road leads to a safe haven or a terrible abyss will depend on how well civilization prepares for the post-market era that will follow on the heels of the Third Industrial Revolution. The end of work could spell a death sentence for civilization as we have come to know it. The end of work could also signal the beginning of a great social transformation, a rebirth of the human spirit. The future lies in our hands.

Postscript

THE OPPORTUNITY NOW EXISTS to create millions of new jobs in the Third Sector—the civil society. Freeing up the labor and talent of men and women no longer needed in the market and government sectors to create social capital in neighborhoods and communities will cost money. Taxing a percentage of the wealth generated by the new Information Age economy and redirecting it into the neighborhoods and communities of the country, and toward the creation of jobs and the rebuilding of the social commons, provides a new agenda and a powerful vision of what life could be like in the twenty-first century.

Re-envisioning work, however, requires that we rethink our notion of the body politic. While politicians traditionally divide the United States into a polar spectrum running from the marketplace on one end, to the government, on the other, it is more accurate to think of society as a three-legged stool made up of the market sector, the government sector, and the civil sector. The first leg creates market capital, the second leg creates public capital, and the third leg creates social capital. Of the three legs, the oldest and most important, but least acknowledged, is the Third Sector.

In the old scheme of things, finding the proper balance between the marketplace and government-dominated political discussion. In the new scheme, finding a balance between the marketplace, government, and civil sector forces becomes paramount. Thinking of society as creating three types of capital—market capital, public capital, and social capital—opens up new possibilities for reconceptualizing both the social contract and the meaning of work in the coming era.

The key to a genuine attempt to recast the political landscape will depend on the political will to increase the clout and elevate the profile of the civil society, making it an equal player with both the marketplace and government. But since the Third Sector relies on the marketplace and government for its survival and well-being, its future will depend, in large part, on the creation of a new social force that can make demands on both the market and government sectors to pump some of the vast financial gains of the new Information Age economy into the creation of social capital and the restoration of the civil life of the country.

The potential for a new third force in American life exists but has not yet been galvanized into a mainstream social movement. It consists of the 89 million Americans—one out of every two adults—who give an average of four or more hours of their time each week serving in more than one million nonprofit organizations that make up the sprawling civil society. These Americans already understand the importance of creating social capital in their own neighborhoods and communities.

Up to now, however, the millions of Americans who volunteer and work in this sector have not seen themselves as part of a potentially powerful constituency—one that could help reshape the national agenda. Third Sector participants come from every race and ethnic background, and from every class and walk of life. They are Republicans, Democrats, and Independents. The one thing they share is a belief in the importance of service to the community and the creation of social capital. If that shared value could be transformed into a sense of common purpose and identity, we could redraw the political map along entirely new lines in this country. Mobilizing these millions of Americans into a broad-based social movement that can make tough demands on both the market and public sectors will be the critical test of the new politics of social capital.

The wild card in the new political dynamic is government. We need to recall that nation-states are a creature of the industrial era. Capitalism required political institutions large enough to oversee and secure broad geographical markets. Now that commerce is moving from the Industrial Age to the Information Age and from the land to the electromagnetic spectrum, geographically bound nation-states suddenly find themselves increasingly irrelevant and without a clearly defined mission.

In the new world that's emerging, government is likely to play a much reduced role in the affairs of commerce and a far greater role in the civil society. Together, these two geographically bound sectors can begin to exert tremendous political pressure on corporations, forcing some of the gains of the new commerce into the communities.

Notes

FOREWORD

1. J.C.L. Simonde de Sismondi, *New Principles of Political Economy,* trans. Richard Hyse, Transactions Publishers, 1991, p. 563.

2. Data from *Historical Statistics of the United States,* Department of Commerce, Washington, D.C., 195, Series D 152–166 (p. 138); also *Economic Indicators,* Government Printing Office, March 1994, pp. 11, 14.

2004 INTRODUCTION

1. "ILO's World Employment Report 2001: Despite Improved Employment Outlook, Digital Divide Looms Large," International Labor Organization, January 24, 2001, *www.ilo.org.*

2. "Labor Force Statistics from the Current Population Survey," U.S. Department of Labor, Bureau of Labor Statistics, October 24, 2003, *data.bls.gov.*

3. Ibid.

4. Harnischfeger, Uta. "International News: It is degrading—I feel like a man going to his urologist," *Financial Times,* May 7, 2003; "German Jobless Rate Climbs in December," *Deutsche Wette,* January 8, 2004, *www.dw-world.de.*

5. "Euro-zone unemployment up to 8.7%," *Eurostat,* February 2003, *europa.eu.int/comm/eurostat/.*

6. Ibid.

7. ."Japan Jobless Rate Jumps to Post War High of 5.5%," *The Wall Street Journal,* February 28, 2003; "Main Economic Indicators: Indonesia Country Report," Organization on Economic Cooperation and Development, September 2003, *www.oecd.com;* "CIA—The World Factbook—India," Central Intelligence Agency, September 17, 2003, *www.cia.gov/cia;* "New ILO Report on Global Employment Trends 2003," International Labor Organization, January 24, 2003, *www.ilo.org/public/english/bureau/inf/pr/2003/1.htm.*

8. Juhn, Chinhui; Kevin Murphy; and Robert Topel. "Current Unemployment, Historically Contemplated." Prepared for the Brookings Panel on Economic Activity, March 2002, p. 25, *www.nber.org/~confer/2002/lss02/juhn.pdf.*

9. Davey, Monica, and David Leonhardt. "Jobless and Hopeless, Many Quit the Labor Force," *The New York Times,* April 27, 2003.

10. Harrison, Paige M., and Allen J. Beck, Ph.D. "Prisoners in 2002," U.S. Department of Justice, Bureau of Justice Statistics, July 2003, *www.ojp.usdoj.gov/bjs;* "Key Facts at a Glance: Correctional Populations," U.S. Department of Justice, Bureau of Justice Statristics, July 27, 2003, *www.jp.usdoj.gov.*

11. "Labor Force Statistics from the Current Population Survey," U.S. Department of Labor, Bureau of Labor Statistics, August 12, 2003, *data.bls.gov;* "Prisoners in 2002," U.S. Department of Justice, Bureau of Justice Statistics, July 2003.

12. "U.S. Personal Savings Rates," Bureau of Economic Analysis, October 3, 2003.

13. Uchitelle, Louis. "U.S. Overcapacity Stalls New Jobs," *The New York Times,* October 19, 2003.

14. "Current Bankruptcy Statistics," American Bankruptcy Institute, September 16, 2003, *www.abiworld.org.*

15. Mishel, Lawrence, Jared Bernstein, and Heather Boushey. *The State of Working America,* Economic Policy Institute, Ithaca, NY: Cornell University Press, 2003.

16. Cowell, Alan. "Personal Debt Surges in Britain," *The New York Times,* September 3, 2003.

17. "Annex Table 24: Household Saving Rates," OECD, October 3, 2003.

18. Leonhardt, David. "'No Help Wanted' Sums Up U.S. Economy," *The New York Times,* October 2, 2003.

19. Uchitelle, Louis. "Defying Forecast, Job Losses Mount for a 22nd Month," *The New York Times,* September 6, 2003.

20. Ibid.

21. Leonhardt, David. "Unemployment Rate Rises to a 9-Year High of 6.1%," *The New York Times,* June 7, 2003.

22. Greenhouse, Steven. "Looks Like a Recovery, Feels Like a Recession," *The New York Times,* September 1, 2003.

23. "Jobs Picture," Economic Policy Institute, June 5, 2003, *www.epinet.org.*

24. Leonhardt, David. "108,000 Jobs Lost in March, U.S. Says," *The New York Times,* April 5, 2003.

25. Dixon, K.A., and Carl E. Van Horn, Ph.D. "The Disposable Worker: Living in a Job-Loss Economy," John J. Heldrich Center for Workforce Development, Rutgers, The State University of New Jersey, *Work Trends,* Vol. 6, No. 2, July 2003.

26. Greenhouse.

27. "Long-Term Unemployed More Likely to Be Educated, Older Professionals," Economic Policy Institute, May 15, 2003, *www.epinet.org.*

28. "College Hiring Falls 36 Percent from 2001 to 2002." National Association of Colleges and Employers (NACE), September 29, 2003, *www.collegerecruiter.com.*

29. Rawe, Julie. "Young and Jobless," *Time,* June 10, 2002.

30. Uchitelle, Louis. "A Recovery for Profits, but Not for Workers." *The New York Times,* December 21, 2003; Meyerson, Harold. "Un-American Recovery." *The Washington Post,* December 24, 2003.

31. Herbert, Bob. "Another Battle for Bush." *The New York Times,* December 15, 2003.

32. Uchitelle, Louis. "A Recovery for Profits, but Not for Workers."

33. "Jobs Picture," Economic Policy Institute, May 2, 2003, *www.epinet.org.*

34. Leonhardt, David. "Jobless Rate Rose to 6% Last Month," *The New York Times,* May 3, 2003.

35. "Gross Domestic Product and Corporate Profits," Bureau of Economic Analysis, September 26, 2003, *www.bea.doc.gov;* "Productivity and Costs, Second Quarter 2003, revised," Bureau of Labor Statistics, September 4, 2003, *www.bls.gov;* Berry, John M., and Mike Allen. "U.S. Economic Growth Surges," *The Washington Post,* October 31, 2003; "Productivity," Bureau of Labor Statistics, December 3, 2003, *www.bls.gov.*

36. Berry and Allen.

37. Fisher, Kenneth L. "Don't Sweat Small Moves," *Forbes,* October 11, 2003, *www.forbes.com.*

38. Gilpin, Kenneth. "Layoffs Rose Sharply Last Month, Report Says," *The New York Times,* September 5, 2003.

39. Ibid.

40. McKinnon, John D. "Projected Budget Deficit Narrows Due to Strengthening Economy," *The Wall Street Journal,* October 9, 2003.

41. Jones, Jeffrey, and Joseph Carroll. "Six in 10 Americans Know Someone Recently Unemployed," The Gallup Organization, May 7, 2003, *www.gallup.com.*

42. "Jobs and the Jobless," *The Washington Post,* May 5, 2003; Herbert, Bob. "Despair of the Jobless," *The New York Times,* August 7, 2003.

43. Leonhardt.

44. "New ILO Study highlights labour trends worldwide: US productivity up, Europe improves ability to create jobs," International Labour Organization, September 1, 2003, *www.ilo.org*; "Productivity and Costs, Second Quarter 2003, revised," Bureau of Labor Statistics, September 4, 2003, *www.bls.gov*; Berry, John M. "Efficiency of U.S. Workers Up Sharply," *The Washington Post,* February 7, 2003.

45. Challenger, John A. "It May Be 2008 Before Next Job Boom," Challenger, Gray & Christmas, Inc., November 11, 2003.

46. Gilpin.

47. Altman, Daniel. "U.S. Jobless Rate Increases to 6.4%, Highest in 9 Years," *The New York Times,* July 4, 2003.

48. Andrews, Edmund. "Rapid Growth Seen for U.S. Economy," *The New York Times,* September 13, 2003.

49. Carson, Joseph G. "U.S. Weekly Economic Update: Manufacturing Payrolls Declining Globally: The Untold Story (Part 2)," *AllianceBernstein,* October 24, 2003.

50. ———. "U.S. Weekly Economic Update: Manufacturing Payrolls Declining Globally: The Untold Story," *AllianceBernstein,* October 10, 2003.

51. Ibid.

52. Ibid.

53. Ibid.

54. Ibid.; ———. "U.S. Weekly Economic Update: Manufacturing Payrolls Declining Globally: The Untold Story (Part 2)."

55. Schwartz, Nelson D. "Will 'Made in the USA' Fade Away?" *Fortune,* November 24, 2003, p. 102.

56. Ibid.

57. Ibid.

58. Ibid.

59. Jones, Del, and Barbara Hansen. "Companies Do More with Less," *USA Today,* August 13, 2003.

60. Arthur, W. Brian. "Why Tech Is Still the Future," *Fortune,* November 24, 2003, p. 121.

61. Jones, Del, and Barbara Hansen. "Companies Do More with Less."

62. Miller, Scott, Bhushan Bahree, and Jeffrey Ball. "Prodi Hopes to Vault EU to Front of Hydrogen Race," *The Wall Street Journal,* October 16, 2002.

63. For further information, please see Rifkin, Jeremy, *The Hydrogen Economy,* New York, NY: Tarcher/Putnam, 2002.

64. Williams, Frances. "Job Creation 'Essential to Halve Poverty,'" *Financial Times,* June 9, 2003.

65. Miller, Steven E. *Civilizing Cyberspace: Policy, Power, and the Information Superhighway* (New York, NY: Addison-Wesley, 1996), p. 206.

66. "Electricity Technology Roadmap: Powering Progress," 1999 Summary and Synthesis, Economic Policy Research Institute, Palo Alto, CA: EPRI, July 1999, pp. 96–97.

67. De Soto, Hernando. *The Mystery of Capital* (New York, NY: Basic Books, 2000), p. 6.

68. Honore, Carl. "A time to work, a time to play: France's 35-hour week: shorter hours result in a social revolution," *National Post,* January 31, 2002.

69. Ibid.; Trumbull, Gunnar. "France's 35 Hour Work Week: Flexibility Through Regulation," The Brookings Institution, January 2001, *www.brook.edu/dybdocroot/fp/cusf/ analysis/workweek.htm.*

70. Honore; Bloom, Jonty. "France's jobless rises again," *BBC News,* June 29, 2001.

71. "How to extract flexibility from rigidity," *Financial Times,* July 29, 1999.

72. "The Law on a negotiated shorter working week in France," French Ministry of Social Affairs, Labour and Solidarity, October 15, 2002, *www.35h.travail.gouv.fr/ index.htm.*

73. Jeffries, Stuart. "The World: C'est magnifique! Le weekend just goes on and on for French workers," *The Guardian,* May 27, 2001.

74. Ibid.

75. McGuckin, Robert H., and Bart van Ark. "Performance 2002: Productivity, Employment, and Income in the World Economies," The Conference Board, 2003, p. 14.

76. Jeffries.

77. "2002 Annual Review for Belgium," European Industrial Relations Observatory, January 2003, *www.eiro.eurofound.eu.int;* "Working Time Developments–2002." European Industrial Relations Observatory, January 2003, *www.eiro.eurofound.ie.*

78. "Working Time Developments–2002," pp. 3–4.

79. "Changeover from career breaks to time credits proves complex," European Industrial Relations Observatory, August 2001, *www.eiro.eurofound.eu.int.*

80. "Inter-community dispute on time credit scheme." European Industrial Relations Observatory, February 2002, *www.eiro.eurofound.ie/2002/02/inbrief/BE0202305N.html.*

81. Ibid. "Changeover from career breaks to time credits proves complex."

82. McGuckin and van Ark.

83. Salamon, Lester M., Helmut Anheier, Regina List, Stefan Toepler, and Wojciech S. Sokolowski. "Global Civil Society: Dimensions of the Nonprofit Sector," Comparative Nonprofit Sector Project, The Johns Hopkins Center for Civil Society Studies, 1999, *www.jhu.edu/~ccss/pubs/books/gcs.*

84. Ibid.

85. Ibid., Chart. "Changes in Nonprofit Sector FTE Employment, by Country, 1990–1995."

86. Ibid., pp. 29–30.

87. Ibid., Table 4: "Civil Society sector FTE revenue, by field, 32 countries."

88. Ibid.

89. Jørgensen, Christian Ege. "Environmental Fiscal Reform: Perspectives for Progress in the European Union," The European Environmental Bureau, June 2003, p. 35.

90. Ibid.

91. Fischlowitz-Roberts, Bernie. "Restructuring Taxes to Protect the Environment." Earth Policy Institute, July 25, 2002, *www.earth-policy.org.*

92. Ibid.

93. "Shifting Tax Burdens to Polluters Could Cut Taxes on Wages and Profit by 15%," WorldWatch Institute, May 10, 1997, *www.worldwatch.org;* Jørgensen, p. 20.

94. Fischlowitz-Roberts.

95. "Shifting Tax Burdens to Polluters Could Cut Taxes on Wages and Profit by 15%."

96. Fischlowitz-Roberts; "Shifting Tax Burdens to Polluters Could Cut Taxes on Wages and Profit by 15%."

97. Jørgensen, p. 15.

98. Ibid., p. 19.

99. "Fatty Foods 'should be taxed,'" *BBC News,* June 9, 2003, *news.bbc.co.uk.*

100. Salamon, Anheier, List, Toepler, and Sokolowski.

101. "What Is a Time Bank?" Time Banks UK, *www.timebanks.co.uk.*

102. "Member to Member," Elderplan, *www.elderplan.org/free/mtm.htm.*

103. "Links Between Neighbors," Grace Hill, October 7, 2003, *www.gracehill.org/ NeighborhoodServices/NS.L.LinksbetwNeighbors.htm.*

104. Cahn, Edgar S. "Time Dollars at Work," *New Democrats Online,* April 1, 1999, *www.ndol.org.*

105. "IRS Question," Hour Dollars Service Exchange Program, *www.hourdollars.org/ irs.html.*

106. "Giving and Volunteering in the United States," Independent Sector, November 2001, *www.independentsector.org.*

INTRODUCTION

1. International Labor Organization, press release (Washington, D.C.: ILO, March 6,1994); International Labor Organization, *The World Employment Situation, Trends and Prospects* (Geneva, Switzerland: ILO, 1994).

2. "Retooling Lives: Technological Gains Are Cutting Costs, and Jobs, in Services," *Wall Street Journal,* February 24, 1994, p. A1.

3. "77,800 Managers at AT&T Getting Job Buyout Offers," *New York Times,* November, 16, 1995, p. A1.

4. "The Case for Corporate Downsizing Goes Global," *Washington Post,* April 9, 1995, p. A22.

CHAPTER 1

1. "When Will the Layoffs End?" *Fortune,* September 20, 1993, p. 40.

2. Ibid., pp. 54–56.

3. "Retooling Lives: Technological Gains Are Cutting Costs, and Jobs, in Services," *Wall Street Journal,* February 24, 1994, p. A1.

4. "Strong Employment Gains Spur Inflation Worries," *Washington Post,* May 7, 1994, pp. A1, A9.

5. "Siemens Plans New Job Cuts as Part of Cost Reductions," *New York Times,* July 6, 1993, p. D4; "On the Continent, a New Era Is Also Dawning," *Business Week,* June 14, 1993, p. 41; "NT T's Cut of 10,000 Jobs Could Pave Way for Others," *Financial Times,* September 1, 1993, p. 5.

6. "Stanching the Loss of Good Jobs," *New York Times,* January 31, 1993, p. C1.

7. Leontief, Wassily, *National Perspective: The Definition of Problems and Opportunities,* paper presented at the National Academy of Engineering Symposium, June 30, 1983, p. 3.

8. "Businesses Prefer Buying Equipment to Hiring New Staff," *Wall Street Journal,* September 3, 1993.

9. "Price of Progress: Re-engineering Gives Firms New Efficiency, Workers the Pink Slip," *Wall Street Journal,* March 16, 1993, p. 1.

10. "Conference Stresses Job Innovation," *Washington Post,* July 21, 1993, p. D5.; "A Rage to Re-engineer," *Washington Post,* July 25, 1993, p. H1.

11. Cited in "Into the Dark: Rough Ride Ahead for American Workers," *Training*, July 1993, p. 23.

12. "Price of Progress."

13. "Germany Fights Back," *Business Week*, May 31, 1993, p. 48.

14. Attali, Jacques, *Millennium: Winners and Losers in the Coming World Order* (New York: Random House, 1991), p. 101.

15. Barlett, Donald L., and Steele, James B., *America: What Went Wrong?* (Kansas City: Andrews and McMeel, 1992), p. xi.

16. "Germany Fights Back," p. 49.

17. Barlett and Steele, p. 18; Drucker, Peter F., *Post-Capitalist Society* (New York: HarperCollins, 1993), p. 68.

18. Krugman, Paul, and Lawrence, Robert, "Trade, Jobs and Wages," *Scientific American*, April 1994, pp. 46, 47.

19. "The Myth of Manufacturing's Decline," *Forbes*, January 18,1993, p. 40; Judis, John, "The jobless Recovery," *The New Republic*, March 15, 1993, p. 22.

20. Winpisinger, William W., *Reclaiming Our Future* (Boulder: Westview Press, 1989), pp. 150–151.

21. Masuda, Yoneji, *The Information Society as Post-Industrial Society* (Washington, D.C.: World Future Society, 1980), p. 60.

22. "Price of Progress."

23. Churbuck, David, and Young, Jeffrey, "The Virtual Workplace," *Forbes*, November 23, 1992, p. 186; "New Hiring Should Follow Productivity Gains," *Business Week*, June 14, 1993.

24. Harrison, Bennett, *Lean and Mean: The Changing Landscape of Corporate Power in the Age of Flexibility* (New York: Basic Books, 1994), pp. 45–47, 51.

25. U.S. Bureau of Census, *1987 Enterprise Statistics, Company Summary* (Washington, D.C.: U.S. Government Printing Office, June 1991), Table 3.

26. U.S. Department of Labor, Bureau of Labor Statistics, *Employment and Earnings*, January 1994, p. 182; Mishel, Lawrence, and Bernstein, Jared, *The Joyless Recovery: Deteriorating Wages and Job Quality in the 1990s* (Washington, D.C.: Economic Policy Institute, Briefing Paper).

27. Peterson, Wallace C., *Silent Depression: The Fate of the American Dream* (New York: W. W. Norton & Co., 1994), p. 33.

28. "The Puzzle of New Jobs: How Many, How Fast?" *New York Times*, May 24, 1994, p. D1.

29. U.S. Bureau of Labor Statistics, *Current Population Survey*, 1993.

30. "Apocalypse—But Not Just Now," *Financial Times*, January 4, 1993, p. D1.

31. Drucker, p. 68.

32. "Life on the Leisure Track," *Newsweek*, June 14, 1993, p. 48.

33. "From Coast to Coast, from Affluent to Poor, Poll Shows Anxiety Over Jobs," *New York Times*, March 11, 1994, p. A1.

CHAPTER 2

1. Bell, John Fred, *A History of Economic Thought*, (New York: Ronald Press Co., 1985), pp. 285–286.

2. Jones, Barry, *Sleepers Wake! Technology and the Future of Work* (Oxford: Oxford University Press, 1982), p. 23; Standing, Guy, "The Notion of Technological Unemployment," *International Labour Review*, March/April 1984, p. 131.

3. McLellan, David, tr., *Marx's Grundrisse der Kritik der Politischen Ökonomie* (New York: Harpers, 1977) pp. 162–163.

4. Clark, John Bates, *Essentials of Economic Theory* (London, 1907) p. 452.

5. Leiserson, William M., "The Problem of Unemployment Today," *Political Science Quarterly* 31, March 1916, p. 12.

6. La Fever, Mortier, W., "Workers, Machinery, and Production in the Automobile Industry," *Monthly Labor Review,* October, 1924, pp. 3–5.

7. Akin, William, *Technocracy and the American Dream: The Technocrat Movement, 1900–1941* (Berkeley: University of California Press, 1977), p. 76; Fano, Ester, "A 'Wastage of Men': Technological Progress and Unemployment in the United States," *Technology and Culture,* April 1991, pp. 274–275.

8. Lubin, Isadore, *The Absorption of the Unemployed by American Industry,* Brookings Institution Pamphlet Series, vol. 1 #3 (Washington, D.C., 1929); "Measuring the Labor-Absorbing Power of American Industry," *Journal of the American Statistical Association,* suppl., March 1929, pp. 27–32.

9. Hunnicutt, Benjamin, *Work Without End: Abandoning Shorter Hours for the Right to Work* (Philadelphia: Temple University Press, 1988), p. 38.

10. Schor, Juliet, *The Overworked American: The Unexpected Decline of Leisure* (New York: Basic Books, 1991), p. 109.

11. Cowdrick, Edward, "The New Economic Gospel of Consumption," *Industrial Management,* October 1927, p. 208.

12. Kettering, Charles F., "Keep the Consumer Dissatisfied," *Nation's Business,* January 1929; Galbraith, John Kenneth, *The Affluent Society,* 4th ed. (Boston: Houghton Mifflin, 1984), p. 127.

13. Dorfman, Joseph, *The Economic Mind in American Civilization* (New York: 1949), vol. 5, pp. 593–94.

14. Allen, Frederick Lewis, *Only Yesterday: An Informal History of the Nineteen-Twenties* (New York, 1964), p. 140.

15. Kyrk, Hazel, *A Theory of Consumption* (Boston, 1923), p. 278.

16. Braverman, Harry, *Labor and Monopoly Capital: The Degradation of Work in the Twentieth Century* (New York: Monthly Review Press, 1974), p. 276.

17. Strasser, Susan, *Satisfaction Guaranteed: The Making of the American Mass Market* (New York: Pantheon Books, 1989), p. 88.

18. "One Dreadful Malady": Collins, James H., "Remarkable Proprietary Beverage," *Printers Ink,* November 4, 1908, pp. 3–4.

19. Strasser, p. 133.

20. Marchand, Roland, *Advertising the American Dream: Making Way for Modernity,* (Berkeley: University of California Press, 1985), pp. 4, 5.

21. Pitkin, Walter, *The Consumer: His Nature and Changing Habits* (New York, 1932), pp. 387–388.

22. Cross, Gary, *Time and Money: The Making of Consumer Culture* (New York: Routledge, 1993), p. 169.

23. Committee on Recent Economic Changes, *Recent Economic Changes* (New York, 1929), p. xv.

24. Harrison, Bennett, and Barry Bluestone, *The Great U-Turn: Corporate Restructuring and the Polarizing of America* (New York: HarperCollins, 1990), p. 38.

25. Akin, p. 77.

26. Mills, Frederick C., *Employment Opportunities in Manufacturing Industries in the United States,* National Bureau of Economic Research, Bulletin #70 (New York, 1938), pp. 10–15.

27. Keynes, John Maynard, *The General Theory of Employment, Interest and Money,* reprinted in *Essays in Persuasion* (New York: Macmillan, 1931).

28. Roediger, David, and Foner, Philip, *Our Own Time: A History of American Labor and the Working Day* (Westport, CT: Greenwood Press, 1989), p. 243.

29. Engels, Frederick, "Socialism, Utopian and Scientific," in *Ten Classics of Marxism* (New York: International Publishers, 1946), pp. 62–63.

30. Kimball, Dexter S., "The Social Effects of Mass Production," *Science 77,* January 6, 1933), p. 1.

31. Hunnicutt, p. 83.

32. Ibid., p. 76.

33. Russell, Bertrand, *In Praise of Idleness and Other Essays* (London, 1935), p. 17.

34. Bergson, Roy, "Work Sharing in Industry: History, Methods and Extent of the Movement in the United States, 1929–33" (unpublished Ph.D. dissertation, University of Pennsylvania, 1933), pp. 7–8.

35. Hunnicut, p. 148.

36. "The Death of Kellogg's Six-Hour Day," Hunnicutt, Benjamin Kline (Iowa City: University of Iowa) p. 9.

37. Ibid., p. 92.

38. Ibid., p. 23.

39. Ibid., p. 24.

40. "5-Day Week Gains Throughout Nation," *New York Times,* August 5, 1932, p. 15.

41. *New York Times,* August 14, 1932, p. 1, cited in Hunnicutt, pp. 148–149.

42. *Labor,* December 22, 1932, and January 10, 1933; *Congressional Record,* 72nd Congress, 2nd Session, vol. 76, part 3, p. 4303, cited in Roedinger and Foner, p. 246.

43. *Thirty-Hour Week Bill,* Hearings on S.5267, 72nd Congress, 2nd Session, pp. 13–14.

44. "Great Victory," *Labor,* April 11, 1933.

45. *Labor,* October 8, 1935, cited in Roedinger and Foner, pp. 252–253.

46. *Congressional Record,* 75th Congress, 2nd Session, vol. 82, part 1, p. 6.

47. Rosenman, S. I., comp., *The Public Papers and Address of Franklin D. Roosevelt,* vol. 2, *The Year of Crisis,* 1933 (New York, 1938), pp. 202, 255.

48. Walker, F. A., *The Civil Works Administration* (New York, 1979), pp. 31, 39.

49. Hopkins, Harry, "They'd Rather Work," *Collier's,* November 16, 1935, p. 8.

50. *Congressional Digest,* July 1938, p. 29, cited in Hunnicutt, p. 201.

51. Hunnicutt, p. 206.

52. Strobel, Frederick R., *Upward Dreams, Downward Mobility: The Economic Decline of the American Middle Class* (Lanham, MD: Rowman and Littlefield Publishers, 1993), p. 23.

53. "Anti-Depression Economics," *The Atlantic Monthly,* April 1993, p. 102.

54. Renner, Michael, "National Security: The Economic and Environmental Dimension," Worldwatch Paper #89 (Washington, D.C.: Worldwatch Institute, 1989), p. 8.

55. "No Business Like War Business," *Defense Monitor* #3, 1987, p. 1; U.S. Office of Management and Budget, *Budget of the U.S. Government, Fiscal Year 1988,* Table 3–2 (Washington, D.C.: OMB, 1989); "Looting the Means of Production," *Ploughshares,* November–December 1982.

56. Alperovitz, Gar, "The Clintonomics Trap," *The Progressive,* June 18, 1993, p. 20.

57. U.S. Department of Labor, Bureau of Labor Statistics, Labstat Series Report, *Current Employment Statistics Survey,* 1975.

58. Biotechnology Industry Organization (BIO), *The U.S. Biotechnology Industry: Facts and Figures* (Washington, D.C.: BIO, 1994), p. 4; Interview, March 16, 1994, with Dennis Chamot, former executive assistant to the president, Department for Professional Employees, the AFL-CIO.

59. Interview, April 5, 1994, with Murray Weidenbaum, former chairman of the Council of Economic Advisors.

60. "Corporate Spending Booms, But Jobs Stagnate," *New York Times,* June 16, 1944, p. D1.

61. Judis, John B., "The Jobless Recovery," *The New Republic,* March 15, 1993, p. 22; Kennedy, Paul, *Preparing for the 21st Century* (New York: Random House, 1993), p. 297.

62. "Middle Class Debt Is Seen as a Hurdle to Economic Gains," *New York Times,* March 28, 1994.

63. "Retrained for What?" *Time,* November 22, 1993, p. 38; "Training for Jobs: O Brave New World," *The Economist,* March 12, 1994, p. 3.

64. "Statement of Robert B. Reich, Secretary of Labor, Before the Subcommittee on Elementary, Secondary and Vocational Education, Committee on Education and Labor, United States House of Representatives," *Hearings on HR1804-Goals 2000: Educate America Act* (Washington, D.C.: Government Printing Office, May 4, 1993), p. 1.

65. "Retrained for What?"

66. Interview, April 12, 1994. Charles Albrecht, Jr., says that as the new technologies have become more sophisticated and displaced an increasing number of workers up the corporate pyramid, even at the level of middle management and above, the issue of inadequate educational background continues to lock more and more workers out of the new high-tech job opportunities opening up.

67. "Literacy of 90 Million Is Deficient," *Washington Post,* September 9, 1993, p. A1.

68. Kozol, Jonathan, *Illiterate America* (New York: Anchor Press/Doubleday, 1985), pp. 4, 10.

69. Cited in Fano, p. 265.

70. Judis, p. 22.

71 Kennedy, Paul, *Preparing for the 21st Century* (New York: Random House, 1993), p. 297; *Historical Tables, Fiscal Year 1995* (Washington, D.C.: Office of Management and Budget, 1994), p. 57.

72. "Can Defense Pain Be Turned to Gain?" *Fortune,* February 8, 1993, p. 84.

73. Ibid., pp. 84–85.

74. U.S. Department of Labor, Bureau of Labor Statistics data cited in *Economic Report of the President,* Washington, D.C., January 1989, pp. 356–37, and *Economic Report of the President,* Washington, D.C., February 1992, pp. 344–345. Computations by Strobel, pp. 68, 70.

75. "Gore vs. Grace: Dueling Reinventions Show How Clinton, Reagan Views of Government Differ," *Wall Street Journal,* September 8, 1993, p. A14.

76. "Free the Economy from Congress," *New York Times,* August 8, 1993, p. E15; quote in Alperovitz, p. 20.

77. Alperovitz, p. 18.

78. Ibid., pp. 18–19.

79. Cyert, Richard M., and Mowery, David C., *Technology and Employment: Innovation and Growth in the U.S. Economy* (Washington, D.C.: National Academy Press, 1987), pp. 1–2.

CHAPTER 3

1. Marvin, Carolyn, "Dazzling the Multitude: Imagining the Electric Light as a Communications Medium," in Corn, Joseph, ed. *Imagining Tomorrow: History, Technology, and the American Future.* (Cambridge, MA: MIT Press, 1986), p. 203.

2. Ibid., pp. 203–204.

3. Macey, Samuel L., *Clocks and the Cosmos: Time in Western Life and Thought* (Hamden, CT: Archon Books, 1980), p. 73.

4. Carlyle, Thomas, "Signs of the Times," *Edinburgh Review 49,* June 1829, pp. 439–459, reprinted in abridged version as "The Mechanical Age" in Clayre, Alasdair, ed., *Nature and Industrialization: An Anthology* (Oxford: Oxford University Press, 1977), pp. 229–231.

5. Segal, Howard, "The Technological Utopians," in Corn, pp. 119–120; Segal, *Technological Utopianism in American Culture* (Chicago: University of Chicago Press, 1985), p. 20.

6. Howard, Albert, *The Milltillionaire* (Boston: 1895), p. 9.

7. Segal, "The Technological Utopians," in Corn, p. 124.

8. Schindler, Solomon, *Young West: A Sequel to Edward Bellamy's Celebrated Novel "Looking Backward"* (Boston: Arena, 1894), p. 45.

9. Howard, p. 17.

10. Clough, Fred M., *The Golden Age, Or the Depth of Time* (Boston: Roxburgh, 1923), p. 34.

11. Kirwan, Thomas, *Reciprocity (Social and Economic) in the 30th Century, the Coming Cooperative Age; A Forecast of the World's Future* (New York: Cochrane, 1909), p. 53.

12. Bellamy, Edward, *Looking Backward 2000–1887,* ed. Thomas, John (Cambridge, MA: Harvard University Press, 1967), p. 211.

13. Gillette, King Camp, *Human Drift* (Boston: New Era, 1894), p. 97; and *World Corporation* (Boston: New England News, 1910), p. 232.

14. Wooldridge, Charles W., *Perfecting the Earth: A Piece of Possible History* (Cleveland: Utopia, 1902), p. 325; Gillette, *World Corporation,* p. 240.

15. Kihlstedt, Folke T., "Utopia Realized: The World's Fairs of the 1930's," in Corn, p. 111.

16. Lippmann, Walter, *A Preface to Morals* (New York: Macmillan, 1929), p. 120.

17. Bell, Daniel, "The Clock Watchers: Americans at Work," *Time,* September 8, 1975, p. 55.

18. Braverman, Harry, *Labor and Monopoly Capital: The Degradation of Work in the 20th Century* (New York: Monthly Labor Press, 1974), p. 88.

19. Cited in Tichi, Cecelia, *Shifting Gears: Technology, Literature, Culture in Modernist America* (Chapel Hill: University of North Carolina Press, 1987), p. 75.

20. Galbraith, John Kenneth, *The New Industrial State* (Boston: Houghton Mifflin, 1979), pp. 101, 94.

21. Segal, *Technological Utopianism in American Culture,* p. 115.

22. Warren, Maude Radford, *Saturday Evening Post*, March 12, 1912, pp. 11–13, 34–35.

23. Callahan, Raymond, *Education and the Cult of Efficiency* (Chicago: University of Chicago Press, 1964), pp. 50–51.

24. National Education Association, *Proceedings*, 1912, p. 492.

25. Frederick, Christine, "The New Housekeeping," *The Ladies' Home Journal*, vol. 29 #9, September 1912.

26. Frederick, Christine, *Housekeeping with Efficiency* (New York, 1913), preface.

27. Tichi, p. 102.

28. Ibid., pp. 98, 102.

29. Ibid., p. 105.

30. Ibid., pp. 116–117.

31. Veblen, Thorstein, *The Engineers and the Price System* (New York: B. W. Huebsch, 1921), pp. 120–121.

32. Akin, William, *Technocracy and the American Dream: The Technocrat Movement, 1900–1941* (Berkeley: University of California Press, 1977), p. 139.

33. Chaplin, Ralph, foreword by Scott, Howard, *Science vs. Chaos* (New York: Technocracy Inc., 1933), reprinted in *Northwest Technocrat*, July 1965, p. 28.

34. "Technocracy—Boom, Blight or Bunk?" *Literary Digest*, December 31, 1932, p. 5.

CHAPTER 4

1. Cited in Kurzweil, Raymond, *The Age of Intelligent Machines* (Cambridge, MA: MIT Press, 1990), p. 189.

2. Ibid., p. 14.

3. "Japan Plans Computer to Mimic Human Brain," *New York Times*, August 8, 1992, p. C1.

4. "The Quest for Machines That Not Only Listen, But Also Understand," *Washington Post*, May 3, 1993.

5. "The Information Technology Revolution," *Technological Forecasting and Social Change*, 1993, p. 69.

6. Cited in Brand, Stewart, *The Media Lab: Inventing the Future at MIT* (New York: Viking Press, 1987), p. 181.

7. Negroponte, Nicholas, *The Architecture Machine* (Cambridge, MA: Massachusetts Institute of Technology, 1970), pp. 11–13.

8. Kurzweil, p. 413.

9. Negroponte, cited in Brand, p. 149.

10. Cited in Fjermedal, Grant, *The Tomorrow Makers: A Brave New World of Living-Brain Machines* (New York: Macmillan Publishers, 1986), p. 94.

11. Simons, Geoff, *Robots: The Quest for Living Machines* (New York: Sterling, 1992), pp. 52–53.

12. Pascal, Blaise, Pensées (New York: E. P. Dutton, 1932), p. 96, no. 340.

13. Babbage, Henry Prevost, *Babbage's Calculating Engines* (1889), Charles Babbage Institute Reprint Series for the History of Computing, vol. 2 (Los Angeles: Tomash Publishers, 1982), pp. 220–222; Bernstein, Jeremy, *The Analytical Engine: Computers—Past, Present, and Future*, revised ed. (New York: William Morrow, 1981), pp. 47–57.

14. Augarten, Stan, *Bit by Bit: An Illustrated History of Computers* (New York: Ticknor and Fields, 1984), p. 77; Austrian, Geoffrey D., *Herman Hollerith: Forgotten Giant of In-*

formation Processing (New York: Columbia University Press, 1982), p. 312; Shurkin, Joel, *Engines of the Mind: A History of the Computer* (New York: W. W. Norton, 1984), p. 92.

15. Kurzweil, pp. 176–177.

16. Zientara, Marguerite, *The History of Computing* (Framingham, MA: CW Communications, 1981), p. 52.

17. Noble, David, *Forces of Production: A Social History of Industrial Automation* (New York: Alfred Knopf, 1984), p. 50; Fjermedal, Grant, *The Tomorrow Makers*, p. 70; Davidow, William, and Malone, Michael, *The Virtual Corporation: Restructuring and Revitalizing the Corporation for the 21st Century* (New York: HarperCollins, 1992), p. 37.

18. Davidow and Malone, p. 37.

19. Masuda, Yoneji, *The Information Society as Post-Industrial Society* (Bethesda, MD: World Future Society, 1981), p. 49.

20. Kurzweil, p. 186.

21. Ceruzzi, Paul, "An Unforeseen Revolution: Computers and Expectations, 1935–1985," in Corn, Joseph J., *Imagining Tomorrow: History, Technology, and the American Future* (Cambridge, MA: Massachusetts Institute of Technology, 1986), p. 190.

22. Ibid., pp. 190–191.

23. Jones, Barry, *Sleepers, Wake: Technology and the Future of Work* (New York: Oxford University Press, 1990), pp. 104–105.

24. "The First Automation," *American Machinist*, December 1990, p. 6; Noble, p. 67.

25. "Automatic Factory," *Fortune*, November 1946, p. 160.

26. "Machines Without Men," *Fortune*, November 1946, p. 204.

27. Noble, p. 25.

28. *Business Week*, January 1946, cited in "The End of Corporate Liberalism: Class Struggle in the Electrical Manufacturing Industry 1933–50," *Radical America*, July-August 1975.

29. Noble, p. 249.

30. Philipson, Morris, *Automation: Implications for the Future* (New York: Vintage Books, 1962), p. 89.

31. Langefors, Boerje, "Automated Design," in Colborn, Robert, *Modern Science and Technology* (Princeton: Princeton University Press, 1965), p. 699.

32. *Management Report on Numerically Controlled Machine Tools* (Chicago: Cox and Cox Consulting, 1958).

33. Alan A. Smith to J. O. McDonough, September 18, 1952, N/C Project Files, MIT Archives.

CHAPTER 5

1. Wilson, William Julius, *The Declining Significance of Race: Blacks and Changing American Institutions* (Chicago: University of Chicago Press, 1980), p. 65.

2. Lemann, Nicholas, *The Promised Land: The Great Black Migration and How It Changed America* (New York: Vintage Books, 1992), pp. 5, 8.

3. Ibid., p. 5.

4. Ibid., pp. 48–49.

5. Ibid., pp. 49–50.

6. Peterson, Willis, and Kislev, Yoav, *The Cotton Harvester in Retrospect: Labor Displacement or Replacement?* (St. Paul: University of Minnesota, September 1991), pp. 1–2.

7. Jones, Marcus, *Black Migration in the United States with Emphasis on Selected Central Cities* (Saratoga, CA: Century 21 Publishing, 1980), p. 46.

8. Lemann, pp. 50, 287.

9. Ibid., p. 6.

10. Jones, Marcus, p. 48.

11. Lemann, p. 17.

12. Ibid., p. 51.

13. Kahn, Tom, "Problems of the Negro Movement," *Dissent*, Winter 1964, p. 115.

14. Ibid., p. 113; Wilson, William Julius, *The Truly Disadvantaged* (Chicago: University of Chicago Press, 1987), p. 30.

15. Kahn, p. 115.

16. Wilson, *Declining Significance of Race*, p. 93; Sugrue, Thomas J., "The Structures of Urban Poverty: The Reorganization of Space and Work in Three Periods of American History," in Katz, Michael, ed., *The Underclass Debate: Views from History* (Princeton: Princeton University Press, 1993), p. 102.

17. Sugrue, in Katz, p. 103.

18. Ibid.

19. Ibid., p. 104.

20. UAW data submitted to *Hearings before the United States Commission on Civil Rights,* held in Detroit, December 14–15, 1960 (Washington, D.C.: Government Printing Office, 1961), pp. 63–65.

21. Judis, John, "The Jobless Recovery," *The New Republic,* March 15, 1993, p. 20.

22. Boggs, James, "The Negro and Cybernation," in Lauda, Donald P., *Advancing Technology: Its Impact on Society* (Dubuque: W. C. Brown Company, 1971) p. 154.

23. Wilson, *Declining Significance of Race,* pp. 111–112.

24. Kasarda, John D., "Urban Change and Minority Opportunities," in Peterson, Paul E., ed., *The New Urban Reality* (Washington, D.C.: The Brookings Institution, 1985), p. 33.

25. Brown, Michael, and Steven Erie, "Blacks and the Legacy of the Great Society," *Public Policy,* vol. 29, #3, Summer 1981, p. 305.

26. U.S. Bureau of the Census, *Census of the Population,* 1960 and 1970, Subject Reports, Occupational Characteristics, in Wilson, William Julius, *Declining Significance of Race,* p. 103.

27. Lemann, p. 201.

28. Brown and Erie, p. 321.

29. Willhelm, Sidney, *Who Needs the Negro?* (Cambridge, MA: Schenkman, 1970), pp. 156–157.

30. Wilson, *The Truly Disadvantaged,* p. 22; Magnet, Myron, *The Dream and the Nightmare* (New York: William Morrow and Co., 1993), pp. 50–51.

31. Moynihan, Daniel Patrick, "Employment, Income, and the Ordeal of the Negro Family," *Daedalus,* Fall 1965, p. 761.

32. "Endangered Family," *Newsweek,* August 30, 1993, p. 18.

33. "Losing Ground: In Latest Recession, Only Blacks Suffered Net Employment Loss," *Wall Street Journal,* September 14, 1993, p. 1.

34. Ibid., p. A12.

35. Interview, May 2, 1994. John Johnson worries that with the downsizing of the armed services and the re-engineering of other government agencies, job opportunities for African-Americans will continue to shrink disproportionately to the rest of the working population of the country. "There is a need to look at how we bridge the gap between

where people have traditionally looked . . . for employment opportunities" and new ways of "providing employment to people at a livable wage," says Johnson.

36. Weiner, Norbert, *The Human Use of Human Beings: Cybernetics and Human Beings* (Boston: Houghton Mifflin, 1950).

37. Willhelm, p. 162.

38. Ibid., p. 163.

39. Quoted by Peter Bart, "Bitterness Rules in Placing Blame," *New York Times*, August 15, 1965.

40. Willhelm, p. 172.

CHAPTER 6

1. "The Ad Hoc Committee on the Triple Revolution Memorandum," March 22, 1964, Appendix 1, in MacBride, Robert, *The Automated State: Computer Systems as a New Force in Society* (Philadelphia: Chilton Book Co., 1967), pp. 192–193.

2. Ibid., p. 193.

3. Ibid., p. 199.

4. Announced in "Special Message to the Congress on the Railroad Rules Dispute," July 22, 1963, *Public Papers of the Presidents, 1963, John F. Kennedy*, January 1–November 22, 1963 (Washington, D.C.: Government Printing Office, 1964), p. 310.

5. "Annual message to the Congress on the State of the Union, January 8, 1964," *Public Papers of the Presidents, 1963–4, Lyndon B. Johnson*, Book 1, November 22, 1963–June 30, 1964 (Washington, D.C.; U.S. Government Printing Office, 1965), p. 114; see also "Letter to the President of the Senate and to the Speaker of the House Proposing a National Commission on Automation and Technological Progress, March 9, 1964," in *Public Papers*, Book 1, p. 357, and "Remarks Upon Signing Bill Creating the National Commission on Technology, Automation and Economic Progress, August 19, 1964," in *Public Papers*, Book 2, July 1, 1964–December 31, 1964, p. 983.

6. "Report of the National Commission on Technology, Automation, and Economic Progress," Appendix 2, in MacBride, Robert, *The Automated State*, p. 213.

7. Ibid., pp. 210–211.

8. Ibid., p. 218.

9. Ibid., p. 212.

10. Ibid., p. 220.

11. "A New Fortune Series: Automation and the Labor Market," cover, *Fortune*, January 1965; Silberman, Charles, "The Real News About Automation," *Fortune*, January 1965, p. 124.

12. See Noble, David, *Forces of Production: A Social History of Industrial Automation* (New York: Alfred A. Knopf, 1984), p. 75.

13. Norbert Weiner to Walter Reuther, August 13, 1949, Weiner Papers, MIT Archives.

14. Reuther, Walter P., "Congressional Testimony," in Philipson, Morris, ed., *Automation: Implications for the Future* (New York: Vintage Books, 1962), pp. 269, 275–276.

15. Noble, p. 250.

16. Ibid., p. 253.

17. CIO Committee on Economic Policy, *Automation* (Washington, D.C.: Congress of Independent Organizations, 1955), pp. 21–22.

18. U.S. Bureau of Labor Statistics, *Major Collective Bargaining Agreements—Train-*

ing and Retraining Provisions, Bulletin no. 1425–7 (Washington, D.C.: Government Printing Office, 1969), p. 4; U.S. Bureau of Labor Statistics, *Characteristics of Major Collective Bargaining Agreements*, January 1, 1980, Bulletin no. 2095, p. 105.

19. Kalleberg, Arne L., et al., "Labor in the Newspaper Industry," in Cornfield, Daniel B., *Workers, Managers and Technological Change: Emerging Patterns of Labor Relations* (New York: Plenum Press, 1987), p. 64.

20. Raskin, A. H., "A Reporter at Large: Part 1, 'Changes in the Balance of Power'; Part II, 'Intrigue at the Summit,'" *The New Yorker,* January 22, 29, 1979.

CHAPTER 7

1. Harrison, Bennett, and Barry Bluestone, *The Great U-Turn: Corporate Restructuring and the Polarizing of America* (New York: HarperCollins, 1990), p. 7.

2. Ibid., pp. 8–10.

3. "The Technology Payoff," *Business Week,* June 14, 1993, p. 58.

4. Roach, Stephen S., *Technological Imperatives* (New York: Morgan Stanley and Co., January 21, 1992), p. 2.

5. Quoted by Gary Loveman, "Why Personal Computers Have Not Improved Productivity," minutes of Stewart Alsop, 1991 Computer Conference, p. 39.

6. "Technology Payoff," p. 58.

7. Brynjolfsson, Erik, and Lorin Hitt, "Is Information Systems Spending Productive?" (abstract) and "New Evidence on the Returns to Information Systems" (Sloan School, MIT, WP#3571–93), June 4, 1993. In an interview, March 17, 1994, Brynjolfsson says that because the new productivity gains are so dramatic, "the amount of output is increasing faster than the number of people working." In the short run, says the MIT economist, the "more routine jobs, like low end office jobs, are tending to be automated away." Brynjolfsson says that "those people are going to have a harder and harder time finding work, unless they get skills that allow them to do something that computers can't do." However, Brynjolfsson cautions that the Third Industrial Revolution has not yet reached the stage when computers will make it impossible for people to find a job. "When that happens," he says, "then we'll have to start thinking about new ways of organizing work or income distribution."

8. "Plug in for Productivity," *New York Times,* June 27, 1993, p. 11. In an interview, March 15, 1994, Stephen Roach points out, "The biggest cost in service companies is people. . . . We found that in some but not all occupations, white collar workers could be replaced by information technologies. And some [occupations] have a surplus in the amount of white collar staff reductions, the likes of which have never happened in modern day experience." Substituting computers and other information and communication technologies for white collar and service workers, says Roach, "is a cost efficient alternative that allows companies to regain their competitive edge."

9. Interview in Davidow, William H., and Michael S. Malone, *The Virtual Corporation: Restructuring and Revitalizing the Corporation for the 21st Century* (New York: HarperCollins, 1992), p. 66.

10. Chandler, Alfred, *The Visible Hand: The Managerial Revolution in America* (Cambridge, MA: Harvard University Press, 1977), p. 97, cited in Beniger, James, *The Control Revolution: Technological and Economic Origins of the Information Society* (Cambridge: Harvard University Press, 1986), p. 224.

11. Reich, Robert, *The Work of Nations: Preparing Ourselves for 21st Century Capitalism* (New York: Random House, 1993), p. 51.

12. Ibid., p. 46.

13. Womack, James, Daniel Jones, and Daniel Roos, *The Machine That Changed the World* (New York: Macmillan Publishing, 1990), pp. 21–22.

14. Ibid., p. 29.

15. Ibid., p. 13.

16. Ibid.

17. Ibid.

18. Machlis, Sharon, "Management Changes Key to Concurrent Engineering," *Design News*, September 17, 1990, pp. 36–37.

19. Harbour, James, "Product Engineering: The 'Buck' Stops Here," *Automotive Industries*, 1985, p. 32.

20. Kagono et al., *Strategic vs. Evolutionary Management: A U.S./Japan Comparison of Strategy and Organization* (New York: North-Holland, 1985), pp. 112–113.

21. Lincoln, James, Mitsuyo Hanada, and Kerry McBride, "Organizational Structures in Japanese and U.S. Manufacturing." *Administrative Science Quarterly*, vol. 31, 1986, pp. 338–364; Kenney, Martin, and Richard Florida, *Beyond Mass Production: The Japanese System and Its Transfer to the U.S.* (New York: Oxford University Press, 1993), pp. 42, 105, 107.

22. Ohno, Taiichi, *Toyota Production System* (Cambridge, MA: Productivity Press, 1988), pp. 25–26.

23. Womack et al., pp. 71–103.

24. Cited in Davidow and Malone, p. 126.

25. Kenney and Florida, p. 54.

26. Womack et al., p. 12; also cited in *Technology and Organizational Innovations, Production and Employment* (Geneva, Switzerland: International Labor Office, July 1992), p. 33.

27. Interview, March 21, 1994. Like others, Loveman's studies indicate "an increasing bifurcation of the labor market" with "highly skilled, highly educated people doing rather well, while those in lower skill occupations [including middle management] are getting trounced." Loveman says that the trend will continue in the future.

28. Hammer, Michael, and James Champy, *Re-engineering the Corporation: A Manifesto for Business Revolution* (New York: HarperCollins, 1993), pp. 36–37.

29. Ibid., pp. 37–38.

30. Ibid., p. 38.

31. Ibid., p. 39.

32. Interview, May 6, 1994. Michael Hammer says that "as organizations become astoundingly more productive, they will either be able to maintain their current size with far fewer employees, or dramatically increase without increasing employment significantly." He worries about "a nightmare scenario" in which "you create a two-tiered world society" made up of "those who have jobs and are creating value for others" and "significant numbers of people . . . who are unemployable."

33. Hammer and Champy, pp. 60–62.

34. Bradley, Stephan, *Globalization, Technology and Competition: The Fusion of Computers and Telecommunications in the 1990's* (Cambridge, MA: Harvard Business School Press, 1993), p. 130.

35. Ibid., p. 129.

36. Davidow and Malone, p. 10.

37. Ibid., p. 168.

38. McBride, Al, and Scott Brown, "The Future of On-line Technology," in Leebart, Derek, ed., *Technology 2001: The Future of Computing and Communications* (Cambridge, MA: MIT Press, 1991), p. 29.

39. "Economy May Be Tokyo Power Broker," *Financial Times*, September 1, 1993, p. 5.

CHAPTER 8

1. *Country Tables: Basic Data on the Agricultural Sector* (Rome: Food and Agriculture Organization, FAO, 1993), p. 332.

2. *Technology on the Farm* (Washington, D.C.: U.S. Department of Agriculture, 1940), p. 63.

3. McWilliams, Carey, *Ill Fares the Land, Migrants and Migrating Labor in the United States* (Boston: 1942), pp. 301–330.

4. "Why Job Growth Is Stalled," *Fortune*, March 8, 1993, p. 52.

5. Goodman, David, et al., *From Farming to Biotechnology: A Theory of Agro-Industrial Development* (New York: Basil Blackwell, 1987), pp. 25, 169; Reimund, Donn A., and Judith Z. Kalbacher, *Characteristics of Large-Scale Farms, 1987* (Washington, D.C.: USDA Economic Research Service, April 1993), Summary, p. iii.

6. Reimund and Kalbacher, p. iii.

7. Tosterud, R., and D. Jahr, *The Changing Economics of Agriculture: Challenge and Preparation for the 1980's* (Washington, D.C.: Subcommittee on Agriculture and Transportation, Joint Economic Committee, Congress of the United States, December 28, 1982), p. 18; Smith, Stewart, "Is There Farming in Agriculture's Future? The Impact of Biotechnology," presentation at the University of Vermont, November 14, 1991, revised October 21, 1992, p. 1.

8. Goodman et al., p. 163.

9. Cochrane, Willard, *Development of American Agriculture: A Historical Analysis*, second edition (Minneapolis: University of Minnesota Press, 1993), pp. 190, 195.

10. Ibid., pp. 195–196.

11. Goodman et al., p. 25; Cochrane, p. 197.

12. Cochrane, p. 126.

13. Ibid., p. 197.

14. Fite, G., "Mechanization of Cotton Production since World War II," *Journal of Agricultural History*, 1980, 54(1).

15. Goodman et al., pp. 35–37.

16. Cochrane, p. 127.

17. *Impacts of Applied Genetics*, Office of Technology Assessment (Washington, D.C.: U.S. Congress, 1981), p. 190.

18. Cochrane, pp. 126–127.

19. "The Mechanization of Agriculture," *Scientific American*, September 1982, p. 77.

20. Cochrane, pp. 137, 158–159.

21. *Poverty in the United States: 1992* (Washington, D.C.: Bureau of the Census, 1993), table 1, p. 1.

22. *A New Technological Era for American Agriculture*, Office of Technology Assessment (Washington, D.C.: U.S. Government Printing Office, August 1992), p. 102.

23. Ibid., pp. 104–105.

24. Ibid., p. 103.

25. Ibid., p. 109.

26. "Israel Moves to Automate Its Agriculture," *Wall Street Journal*, June 9, 1993.

27. "Robot Farming," *The Futurist*, July/August 1993, p. 54.

28. "Israel Moves to Automate."

29. "Robot Farming," p. 54.

30. Goodman et al., p. 122.

31. Engelberger, Joseph, *Robotics in Service* (Cambridge, MA: MIT Press, 1989), p. 157.

32. "Computers Help Feed Cows," *Dairy Report*, 1981–1982, p. 28.

33. "Distributed Intelligence and Control: The New Approach to Dairy Farm Management," in *Computers in Agricultural Extension Programs: Proceedings of the 4th International Conference* (St. Joseph, MI: American Society of Agricultural Engineers, 1992), p. 174.

34. Holt, Donald A., "Computers in Production Agriculture," *Science*, April 26, 1985, pp. 422–424.

35. Fox, Michael, *Superpigs and Wondercorn* (New York: Lyons and Burford Publishers, 1992), p. 114.

36. *New Technological Era*, pp. 4, 45, 86.

37. Ibid., p. 4; Busch, Lawrence, et al., *Plants, Power and Profit* (Cambridge, MA: Basil Blackwell, 1991), p. 8.

38. *New Technological Era*, p. 49; Busch, p. 9.

39. U.S. Office of Management and Budget, *Use of Bovine Somatotropin in the United States: Its Potential Effects*, January 1994, pp. 29–33.

40. "The New Biotech Agriculture: Unforeseen Economic Consequences," *Issues in Science and Technology*, Fall 1985, p. 128.

41. *New Technological Era*, p. 4.

42. *New Scientist*, April 28, 1988, p. 27, cited in Fox, p. 103.

43. *New Technological Era*, p. 87.

44. Cooney, Bob, "Antisense Gene Could Knock Out Broodiness in Turkeys," Science Report, Agricultural and Consumer Press Services, College of Agricultural and Life Sciences, Research Division, University of Wisconsin at Madison; "Building a Badder Mother," *American Scientist*, July 1993, p. 329.

45. "The Blossoming of Biotechnology," *Omni*, vol. 15 #2, November 1992, p. 74.

46. Fox, p. 106.

47. Goodman et al., pp. 123, 184, 189.

48. *Vanilla and Biotechnology—Update* (Pittsboro, NC: Rural Advancement Fund International [RAFI] Communique, July 1991); "Vanilla Beans," *Food Engineering*, November 1987.

49. Mooney, Pat, and Cary Fowler, *Vanilla and Biotechnology* (RAFI Communique, January 1987), p. 1.

50. "Cell Culture System to Produce Less-Costly Natural Vanilla," *Bioprocessing Technology*, January 1991, p. 7

51. *Vanilla and Biotechnology—Update* (RAFI Communiques, July 1991 and June 1989), p. 1; interview, May 13, 1994. Cary Fowler says that the secondary impacts of replacing field-grown vanilla with a laboratory-produced form could "create economic impacts along a whole range of levels" for the vanilla-growing countries. He believes that in the short run, tissue-culture propagation techniques are likely to be used to produce "relatively high value items . . . [like] spices and flavorings."

52. *Vanilla and Biotechnology* (RAFI Communique, June 1989), p. 1. Interview, May 13, 1994.

53. *Biotechnology and Natural Sweeteners* (RAFI Communique, February 1987), p. 1.

54. Ibid., p. 3.

55. "Product Substitution Through Biotechnology: Impact on the Third World," *Trends in Biotechnology,* April 1986, p. 89.

56. Busch, p. 173; see also Rogoff, Martin H., and Stephen L. Rawlins, "Food Security: A Technological Alternative," *BioScience,* December 1987, pp. 800–807.

57. "Tricking Cotton to Think Lab Is Home Sweet Home," *Washington Post,* May 29, 1988, p. A3.

58. Rogoff and Rawlins, "Food Security"; interview, May 11, 1994. Stephen Rawlins says that in the coming era of highly automated laboratory farming, the only part of the process that needs to remain outdoors is capturing the energy of the sun in biomass plants. "You have to capture the energy outdoors because that's where the sun is. But the rest of the processes, once you have the energy, don't have to be outdoors." Rawlins adds that "by bringing [farming] indoors . . . you don't have all of the environmental problems."

59. "Biotechnology and Flavor Development: Plant Tissue Cultures," *Food Technology,* April 1986, p. 122.

60. Busch, p. 183.

CHAPTER 9

1. Gompers, Samuel, *Seventy Years of Life and Labor: An Autobiography* (Cornell, NY: Industrial and Labor Relations Press, 1925), pp. 3–4.

2. Chandler, Alfred D., *The Visible Hand: The Managerial Revolution in American Business* (Cambridge, MA: Harvard University Press, 1977), pp. 249–251.

3. Ibid.

4. Drucker, Peter, *The Concept of the Corporation* (New York: John Day, 1946).

5. Clark, Wilson, *Energy for Survival* (Garden City, NY: Doubleday/Anchor Books, 1975), p. 170.

6. Ford, Henry, *My Life and Work,* 1923, pp. 108–109.

7. Reich, Robert, *The Work of Nations: Preparing Ourselves for 21st Century Capitalism* (New York: Random House, 1992), p. 214.

8. Attali, Jacques, *Millennium: Winners and Losers in the Coming World Order* (New York: Random House, 1990), pp. 95–96.

9. "GM Drive to Step Up Efficiency is Colliding with UAW Job Fears," *Wall Street Journal,* June 23, 1993, p. A1.

10. "Mercedes Aims to Improve German Plants' Efficiency," *Wall Street Journal,* September 2, 1993, p. A7; "German Auto Job Cuts Seen," *New York Times,* August 16, 1993, p. D5.

11. van Liemt, Gijsbert, *Industry on the Move: Causes and Consequences of International Relocation in the Manufacturing Industry* (Geneva: International Labor Office, 1992), p. 76; "Labor-Management Bargaining in 1992," *Monthly Labour Review,* January 1993, p. 20.

12. "Mazda Pushing Toward 30% Automation," *Automotive News,* April 14, 1993, p. 24.

13. Cited in James, Samuel D. K., *The Impact of Cybernation on Black Automotive Workers in the U.S.,* p. 44.

14. Wallace, Michael, "Brave New Workplace," *Work and Occupations,* vol. 16 #4, November 1989, p. 366.

15. Kennedy, Paul, *Preparing for the 21st Century* (New York: Random House, 1993), p. 86; Winpisinger, William, *Reclaiming Our Future: An Agenda for American Labor* (San Francisco: Westview Press, 1989), p. 149.

16. "Boost for Productivity," *Financial Times*, March 23, 1993.

17. Beniger, James, *The Control Revolution: Technological and Economic Origins of the Information Society* (Cambridge, MA: Harvard University Press, 1986), p. 238; Temin, Peter, *Iron and Steel in Nineteenth Century America: An Economic Inquiry* (Cambridge, MA: Massachusetts Institute of Technology Press, 1964), pp. 159, 165.

18. Kenney, Martin, and Richard Florida, *Beyond Mass Production: The Japanese System and Its Transfer to the U.S.* (New York: Oxford University Press, 1993), p. 3.

19. Ibid.

20. Ibid., p. 189.

21. Reich, Robert, *The Work of Nations: Preparing Ourselves for 21st Century Capitalism* (New York: Vintage Books, 1992), pp. 214–215.

22. Drucker, Peter, *Post Capitalist Society* (New York: HarperCollins, 1993), pp. 72–73; "Why Job Growth is Stalled," *Fortune*, March 8, 1993, p. 51

23. Drucker, p. 72.

24. Kenney and Florida, pp. 171, 173.

25. van Liemt, p. 202.

26. Ibid., p. 314.

27. Statistics from the International Association of Machinists, May 1994.

28. Winpisinger, William, *Reclaiming Our Future: An Agenda for American Labor* (San Francisco: Westview Press, 1989), pp. 149–150.

29. *Technological Change and Its Impact on Labor in Four Industries* (U.S. Department of Labor, October 1992, Bulletin 2409), p. 25.

30. Interview, April 29, 1994. William Winpisinger says that he "always told the members [of his union], 'work was made for horses and mules, and even they've got the sense to turn their ass to it.'" The former president of the International Association of Machinists (IAM) argues that "anything we can do to make [work] easier and more satisfying, so much the better." He warns, however, that "if there aren't social mechanisms to tax the illicit profits that are attendant with employing 2 percent of the people to make 100 percent of the goods, then we're going to have a hell of a war."

31. *Technological Change and Its Impact*, p. 25.

32. Kenney and Florida, p. 195.

33. Ibid., pp. 195–197.

34. "Jobs in America," *Fortune*, July 12, 1993, p. 36.

35. Radford, G., "How Sumitomo Transformed Dunlop Tyres," *Long Range Planning*, June 1989, p. 28.

36. "1992: Job Market in Doldrums," *Monthly Labour Review*, February 1993, p. 9.

37. "The Mechanization of Mining," *Scientific American*, September 1982, p. 91.

38. *Technological Change and Its Impact*, p. 1.

39. Ibid.

40. Noble, David, *Forces of Production: A Social History of Industrial Automation* (New York: Alfred Knopf, 1984), pp. 63–65.

41. "Chemical Productivity jumped in Second Quarter," *Chemical and Engineering News*, September 14, 1992, p. 21; Braverman, Harry, *Labor and Monopoly Capital: The Degradation of Work in the Twentieth Century* (New York: Monthly Review Press, 1974), p. 224.

42. "Strong Companies Are Joining Trends to Eliminate Jobs," *New York Times,* July 26, 1993, p. D3; "Jobs in America," *Fortune,* July 12, 1993, p. 40.

43. "Why Japan Loves Robots and We Don't," *Forbes,* April 16, 1990, p. 151.

44. *Technology and Labor in Copper Ore Mining, Household Appliances and Water Transportation Industries* (Washington, D.C.: U.S. Department of Labor, Bureau of Labor Statistics, May 1993, Bulletin 2420), p. 22.

45. Ibid., pp. 22–24.

46. Ibid., p. 24.

47. Bradley, Stephen, *Globalization, Technology and Competition* (Cambridge, MA: Harvard Business School, 1993), p. 190; Davidow and Malone, p. 57.

48. "New Technologies, Employment Shifts, and Gender Divisions Within the Textile Industry," *New Technology, Work and Employment,* Spring 1991, p. 44.

49. "Production Restructuring in the Textile and Clothing Industries," *New Technology, Work and Employment,* March 1993, p. 45.

50. Interview, April 14, 1994. Jack Sheinkman says that technology displacement played a role in the loss of some of the 500,000 jobs in textile in the past decade. While he believes that further automation is inevitable, he argues for a more equitable sharing of productivity gains with the employees, including a shortening of the workweek.

51. "New Technologies, Employment Shifts, and Gender Divisions Within the Textile Industry," p. 47.

CHAPTER 10

1. "Retooling Lives: Technological Gains Are Cutting Costs and Jobs in Services," *Wall Street Journal,* February 24, 1994, p. A1.

2. "AT&T to Replace as Many as One-Third of Its Operators with Computer Systems," *Wall Street Journal,* March 4, 1992, p. A4; "Voice Technology to Replace 6000 Operators," *Washington Post,* March 4, 1992, p. B1.

3. Wallace, Michael, "Brave New Workplace," *Work and Occupations,* November 1989. p. 375.

4. *Outlook for Technology and Labor in Telephone Communications* (Washington, D.C.: U.S. Department of Labor, Bureau of Labor Statistics, July 1990, Bulletin 2357), pp. 1, 11–12.

5. Ibid., p. 12.

6. "Postal Service's Automation to Cut 47,000 Jobs," *Washington Post,* September 28, 1991, p. A10. Interview, April 6,1994: Michael Coughlin, Deputy Postmaster General, predicts that even newer technologies like "remote computer reading" will eliminate still more personnel in the coming years, making the postal service even more automated in its overall delivery system.

7. Interview, March 15, 1994. Stephen Roach says, "In the 1970s, when the debate was held over the state of the post-industrial era, the myth was that the service sector . . . would fill the void left by the downsizing and shrinking of manufacturing." According to Roach, "That seemed to work until we figured out that the service sectors were not very productive in the way they used their workers. And when they faced competitive pressures, they too had to disgorge excess workers." Roach argues that the "key is to find new sources of job creation to employ workers productively," but adds that thus far "we have not yet done that."

8. "Service Jobs Fall as Business Gains," *New York Times,* April 18, 1993, p. 1.

9. *Vision 2000: The Transformation of Banking* (New York: Andersen Consulting, Arthur Andersen and Co., 1991), pp. 2, 6–7.

10. "Computers Start to Lift U.S. Productivity," *Wall Street Journal*, March 1, 1993, p. B3.

11. Leontief, Wassily, and Duchin, Faye, *The Future Impact of Automation on Workers* (New York: Oxford University Press, 1986), p. 84.

12. "Retooling Lives," p. A7; *Vision 2000*, p. 43.

13. *Vision 2000*, p. 43.

14. Ibid., p. 59.

15. "Re-engineering Work: Don't Automate, Obliterate," *Harvard Business Review*, July/August 1990, p. 107.

16. "Re-engineering Aetna," *Forbes ASAP*, June 7, 1993, p. 78; "The Technology Payoff," *Business Week*, June 14, 1993, p. 60.

17. "Re-engineering Aetna," p. 78.

18. Beniger, James, *The Control Revolution: Technological and Economic Origins of the Information Society* (Cambridge, MA: Harvard University Press, 1986), pp. 280–284.

19. "Can You Afford a Paperless Office?" *International Spectrum*, May/June, 1993, pp. 16–17.

20. "Technology Payoff," p. 60.

21. "Advances in Networking and Software Push Firms Closer to Paperless Office," *Wall Street Journal*, August 5, 1993, pp. B1, B6.

22. Interview, March 29, 1994. John Loewenberg says that the company used to have to continuously send out manuals and updated policy statements to keep everyone current on "what the rules were," and still it was "almost impossible" to get everyone reading the same information at the same time. "By being able to electronically update all those instruction manuals, operations manuals, policy manuals, in one point and electronically distribute them, everybody's [now] looking at the same thing."

23. "Reducing the Paper Mountains," *Financial Times*, March 23, 1993, technology section, p. 7.

24. "Software Giant Aiming at the Office," *New York Times*, June 9, 1993, p. D1.

25. Ibid., p. D5.

26. "The Paperless Office Looms on the Horizon Again," *New York Times*, May 30, 1993, sect. 4, p. 2.

27. Green, J. H., "Will More Computers Mean Fewer Jobs?" *Desktop Publishing*, August 1982, pp. 52–54.

28. Leontief and Duchin, p. 82.

29. "Secretaries Down the Chute," *U. S. News and World Report*, March 28, 1994, p. 65.

30. "Receptionist Keeps Track of Mobile People," *Wall Street Journal*, July 19, 1993, p. B1.

31. "Computers Take On a Whale of a Job: Sifting Through Résumés," *Washington Post*, May 30, 1993, p. H2.

32. "Homework for Grownups," *American Demographics*, August 1993, p. 40; "Home Is Where the Office Is," *Financial Times*, August 16, 1993, p. 8.

33. "Home Is Where the Office Is," p. 8.

34. Ibid.

35. "Vanishing Offices," *Wall Street Journal*, June 4, 1993, p. A1.

36. Interview, March 24, 1994, with Steve Patterson, vice president of Gemini Consulting Company.

37. "Vanishing Offices," p. A6.

38. "Being There," *Technology Review,* May/June 1992, p. 44.

39. *Technology and Labor in Three Service Industries* (U.S. Department of Labor: September 1990, Bulletin 2367), p. 19.

40. Harrison, Roy, *Reinventing the Warehouse: World Class Distribution Logistics* (New York: Free Press, 1993), pp. 331–335.

41. "1992: Job Market in Doldrums," *Monthly Labour Review,* February 1993, p. 9.

42. *Technology and Labor in Three Service Industries,* p. 21.

43. Ibid., pp. 21–22.

44. "Job Losses Don't Let Up Even as Hard Times Ease," also titled "Job Extinction Evolving Into a Fact of Life in U.S.," *New York Times,* March 22, 1994, p. D5.

45. "Technology Is Fueling Retail Productivity, But Slowing Job Gains," *Business Week,* May 10, 1993, p. 16.

46. *Technology and Labor in Five Industries,* U.S. Department of Labor, Bureau of Labor Statistics, Bulletin 2033 (Washington, D.C., 1979).

47. "Roboclerk in Tune with Service Industry," *Chicago Tribune,* May 28, 1990, sect. 3, p. 1.

48. "The Retail Revolution," *Wall Street Journal,* July 15, 1993, p. A12.

49. *Technological Change and Its Impact on Labor in Four Industries* (U.S. Department of Labor, October 1992, Bulletin 2409), p. 37.

50. Ibid., p. 42.

51. Ibid., p. 41.

52. Ibid., pp. 38, 42.

53. "Record Store of Near Future," *New York Times,* May 12, 1993, p. A1.

54. Interview, April 2, 1994. Jack McDonald says the digitized distribution system being developed for Blockbuster Video "is truly just-in-time inventory." McDonald points out that with the new made-to-order system, Blockbuster will significantly reduce inventory costs and save on the traditional high costs of returning unsold merchandise.

55. "Retailing Will Never Be the Same," *Business Week,* July 26, 1993, p. 54.

56. Ibid., pp. 54–56.

57. Ibid., p. 57; "Macy to Start Cable TV Channel, Taking Stores into Living Rooms," *New York Times,* June 2, 1993, p. A1.

58. "The Fall of the Mall," *Forbes,* May 24, 1993, p. 106.

59. "Retailing Will Never Be the Same," p. 56; "Fall of the Mall," p. 107.

60. "Fall of the Mall," p. 108.

61. Ibid., p. 112.

62. "Introducing Robodoc," *Newsweek,* November 23, 1992, p. 86.

63. "Good-Bye Dewey Decimals," *Forbes,* February 15, 1993, p. 204.

64. "Potboiler Springs from Computer's Loins," *New York Times,* July 2, 1993, p. D16; "Soft Porn from Software: Computer Churns Out a Salacious Novel," *International Herald Tribune,* July 5, 1993, p. 3.

65. "Pianomorte," *Washington Post,* August 9, 1993, p. A10.

66. "Synthesizers: Sour Sound to Musicians," *Los Angeles Times,* December 6, 1985, p. 24.

67. Ibid., pp. 24–25.

68. Ibid.

69. "Strike Out the Band," *Los Angeles Times,* November 28, 1991, p. F8.

70. "Synthesizers," p. A1.

71. "What's New in Music Technology," *New York Times,* March 1, 1987, p. 19.

72. "Strike Out the Band," p. F8.
73. "Hollywood Goes Digital," *Forbes ASAP*, December 7, 1992, p. 58.
74. "How'd They Do That?" *Industry Week*, June 21, 1993, p. 34.
75. Ibid., p. 35.
76. "Waking Up to the New Economy," *Fortune*, June 27, 1994, p. 37.

CHAPTER 11

1. "The American Dream: Fired Up and Melted Down," *Washington Post*, April 12, 1992, p. A1.
2. Ibid.
3. Reich, Robert, *The Work of Nations: Preparing Ourselves for 21st Century Capitalism* (New York: Random House, 1992), p. 213.
4. Harrison, Bennett, and Barry Bluestone, *The Great U-Turn: Corporate Restructuring and the Polarizing of America* (New York: HarperCollins, 1988), pp. 110–111.
5. Strobel, Frederick, *Upward Dreams, Downward Mobility: The Economic Decline of the American Middle Class* (Lanham, MD: Rowman and Littlefield, 1993), p. 147.
6. Mishel, Lawrence, and Jared Bernstein, *The State of Working America 1992–93* (Washington, D.C.: Economic Policy Institute, 1992), p. 249.
7. "The Perplexing Case of the Plummeting Payroll," *Business Week*, September 20, 1993, p. 27; U.S. Department of Labor, *Re-employment Increases Among Displaced Workers* (Washington, D.C.: Bureau of Labor Statistics, October 14, 1986).
8. "The 6.8% Illusion," *New York Times*, August 8, 1993, p. 15; "Into the Dark: Rough Ride Ahead for American Workers," *Training*, July 1993, p. 22.
9. "Family Struggles to Make Do After Fall from Middle Class," *New York Times*, March 11, 1994, p. A1.
10. "Into the Dark," p. 22; "The 6.8% Illusion," p. 15.
11. "Retrain Who to Do What?" *Training*, January 1993, p. 28; "Jobs in America," *Fortune*, July 12, 1993, p. 35.
12. Mitchell, Daniel J. B., "Shifting Norms in Wage Determination," *Brookings Papers on Economic Activity*, #2 (Washington, D.C.: Brookings Institution, 1985), p. 576.
13. Mishel and Bernstein, p. 191.
14. Harrison and Bluestone, p. 115.
15. Interview, March 25, 1994, with Jared Bernstein, economist at the Economic Policy Institute.
16. "Sharp Increase Along the Borders of Poverty," *New York Times*, March 31, 1994. At the end of 1992, 18 percent of the nation's full-time workers were earning less than $13,091 a year, compared to 12 percent in 1979.
17. Burns, Scott, "Disaffected Workers Seek New Hope," *Dallas News*, August 21, 1988, p. H1.
18. Reich, pp. 56–57; "RIP: The Good Corporation," *Newsweek*, July 5, 1993, p. 41.
19. Mishel and Bernstein, pp. 3–4.
20. "The Next Priority," *Inc.*, May 1989, p. 28.
21. Mishel and Bernstein, p. 155.
22. "RIP," p. 41.
23. Mishel and Bernstein, p. 157.
24. "Not Home Alone: Jobless Male Managers Proliferate in Suburbs, Causing Subtle Malaise," *Wall Street Journal*, September 20, 1993, p. A1.

25. Ibid.

26. Ibid.

27. "Caught in the Middle," *Business Week*, September 12, 1988, p. 80.

28. "Not Home Alone," p. A6.

29. "A Nation in Transition," *Washington Post*, May 28, 1992, p. A19.

30. Mishel and Bernstein, p. 41.

31. Ibid., p. 2.

32. Ibid., p. 14.

33. "College Class of '93 Learns Hard Lesson: Career Prospects Are Worst in Decades," *Wall Street Journal*, May 20, 1993, p. B1.

34. Barlett, Donald, and James Steele, *America: What Went Wrong?* (Kansas City: Andrews and McMeel, 1992), pp. 19–20.

35. "Bring CEO Pay Down to Earth," *Business Week*, May 1, 1989, p. 1.46; "Median Pay of Chief Executives Rose 19% in 1992," *Washington Post*, May 10, 1993; Reich, *Work of Nations*, p. 204; See also "Pay Stubs of the Rich and Corporate, *Business Week*, May 7, 1990, p. 56; "A Great Leap Forward for Executive Pay," *Wall Street Journal*, April 24, 1989, p. B1.

36. Mishel and Bernstein, pp. 6, 249.

37. U.S. Bureau of the Census data, reported in the *New York Times*, September 27, 1990, p. 10, cited in Strobel, p. 165.

38. "The 400 Richest People in America," *Forbes*, October 96, 1987, p. 106; "Economists Suggest More Taxes on Rich," *Christian Science Monitor*, April 23, 1992, p. 15.

39. Mishel and Bernstein, p. 255.

40. Barlett and Steele, p. xi.

41. Reich, pp. 259–260.

42. Ibid., pp. 177–178.

43. Ibid., p. 104.

44. Ibid.

45. Harrison and Bluestone, pp. 69–70.

46. Quoted in "Into the Dark," p. 27.

47. Reich, pp. 302–303.

48. Phillips, Kevin, *The Politics of Rich and Poor: Wealth and the American Electorate in the Reagan Aftermath* (New York: Harper Perennial, 1991), p. 201.

49. Interview, March 23, 1994. Paul Saffo notes that the increasing polarization of rich and poor is happening all over the world, and especially in former communist countries, where market forces have spawned a new entrepreneurial class overnight. "In Moscow," says Saffo, "you've got some serious millionaires emerging and they're living in buildings where babushka grandmas are sitting outside selling their last possessions." Saffo warns that "when change like that clusters at the extremes it's a virtual sure bet that more fundamental change lies ahead."

50. "Number of Americans in Poverty up for Third Year, Health Care Drops, Census Bureau Announces," *Commerce News*, October 4, 1993, pp. 1, 4, 9, 12, 13; "Number of Poor Americans Rises for 3rd Year," *Washington Post*, October 5, 1993, p. A6.

51. "Number of Poor Americans Rises for 3rd Year."

52. "Food Stamps Now a Fact of Life for 25 Millions in U.S.," *Washington Post*, May 24,1992, p. A1; "Growing Hunger," *Utne Reader*, November/December 1993, p. 63.

53. "Growing Hunger," pp. 63, 65.

54. Ibid., p. 63.

55. Interview, March 29, 1994, with Don Reeves, an economic policy analyst at Bread for the World.

56. "Number of Americans," p. 20.

57. Merva, Mary, and Richard Fowles, *Effects of Diminished Economic Opportunities on Social Stress: Heart Attacks, Strokes, and Crime* (Washington, D.C.: Economic Policy Institute, October 16, 1992, pp. 1–2.; In an interview, March 14, 1994, Fowles worries that the nation's preoccupation with government deficits is keeping the White House and Congress from appropriating the necessary funds to deal with the related problems of rising unemployment and the rising incidences of disease and crime. "I think one of the real tragedies in the discussion of large deficits is that it now seems politically impossible for a person in Congress to propose higher government spending to reinstitute the social safety net." Fowles agrees with economists like Gar Alperovitz that the nation could afford to increase its deficits in the short run to stimulate the economy, but, like Alperovitz, believes that for political reasons it is not likely to happen anytime soon.

58. "Number of Americans," pp. 2, 20.

59. Mishel and Bernstein, p. 9.

60. "Even with Good Pay, Many Americans Are Unable to Buy a Home," *Wall Street Journal*, February 5, 1988.

61. Mishel and Bernstein, p. 389.

62. Phillips, p. 184.

63. "The Economic Crisis of Urban America," *Business Week*, May 18, 1992, p. 38.

64. Ibid., p. 40.

65. Reich, p. 303.

CHAPTER 12

1. Irvine, Lieutenant General C. S., "Keynote Address," Proceedings of the Electronics Industries Association Symposium, 1957.

2. Olesten, Nils O., "Stepping Stones to N/C," *Automation*, June 1961.

3. Kuusinen, Larry, Boeing machinist, interview, June 5, 1979, with David Noble, in *Forces of Production. A Society History of Industrial Automation* (New York: Alfred Knopf, 1984), p. 242.

4. Dohse, Knuth, Ulrich Jurgerns, and Thomas Malsch, "From Fordism to Toyotism? The Social Organization of the Labor Process in the Japanese Automobile Industry," *Politics and Society* 14 #2, 1985, pp. 115–146.

5. Sakuma, Shinju, and Hideaki Ohnomori, "The Auto Industry," ch. 2 in *Karoshi: When the Corporate Warrior Dies*, National Defense Council for Victims of Karoshi (Tokyo: Mado-sha Publishers, 1990).

6. Kenney, Martin, and Richard Florida, *Beyond Mass Production: The Japanese System and Its Transfer to the U. S.* (New York: Oxford University Press, 1993), p. 271.

7. Ibid., p. 278.

8. "Management by Stress," *Technology Review*, October 1988, p. 37. Also see Parker, Mike, and Jane Slaughter, *Choosing Sides: Unions and the Team Concept* (Detroit: Labor Notes, 1988).

9. "Management by Stress," p. 39.

10. Ibid., p. 42.

322   *Notes*

11. See "Workers at Risk," *Detroit Free Press,* July 7, 1990, pp. 1A, 6A–7A; "Injury, Training Woes Hit New Mazda Plant," *Automotive News,* February 13, 1989, pp. 1, 52.

12. Kenney and Florida, p. 265. See also *Karoshi: When the Corporate Warrior Dies.*

13. Simons, Geoff, *Silicon Shock: The Menace of the Computer Invasion* (New York: Basil Blackwell, 1985), p. 165.

14. Brod, Craig, *Techno-Stress: The Human Cost of the Computer Revolution* (Reading, MA: Addison-Wesley Publications, 1984), p. 43.

15. Ibid., pp. 43, 45.

16. Ibid.

17. OTA report cited in "Big Brother Is Counting Your Key Strokes," *Science,* October 2, 1987, p. 17.

18. Rawlence, Christopher, ed., *About Time* (London: Jonathan Cape, 1985), p. 39.

19. Brod, p. 43.

20. NIOSH study cited in Brod, p. 26.

21. "Employers Recognizing What Stress Costs Them, UN Report Suggests," *Washington Post,* March 28, 1993, p. H2.

22. *World Labour Report 1993* (Geneva: International Labor Office, 1993), pp. 65, 70.

23. Ibid., pp. 66, 68.

24. Ibid., p. 66.

25. Ibid., p. 67.

26. "Age of Angst: Workplace Revolution Boosts Productivity at Cost of Job Security," *Wall Street Journal,* March 10, 1993, p. A8.

27. "Temporary Workers Are on Increase in Nation's Factories," *New York Times,* June 6, 1993, pp. A1–D2.

28. "Into the Dark: Rough Ride Ahead for American Workers," *Training,* July 1993, pp. 24–25.

29. "Cutbacks Fuel Contingent Workforce," *USA Today,* March 3, 1993, p. 1B.

30. "Hired Out: Workers Are Forced to Take More Jobs with Few Benefits," *Wall Street Journal,* March 11, 1993, p. A1.

31. "Cutbacks Fuel Contingent Workforce."

32. "Into the Dark," p. 26.

33. Interview, March 28, 1994. Belous acknowledges that corporate restructuring and the growing reliance on contingent workers is going to lead to turbulence in the years ahead. "What we're going through," he says, "is as radical and revolutionary as the first and second industrial revolutions." While he cautions that the future is not "going to be a bed of roses," especially for skilled blue collar workers, he says that in the long run he is "fairly optimistic" that at least the knowledge workers will be able to keep their skills current enough to accommodate the rapid changes in hiring policies and practices that are likely to continue in the fast-paced global economy.

34. "Temporary Work: The New Career," *New York Times,* September 12, 1993, p. F15. Interview, March 16, 1994: Nancy Hutchins says that with greater reliance on just-in-time employment, "the fundamental question is what happens to the class structure of the United States if we don't have a middle class with very large numbers of people with predictable employment. . . . What are the implications for people who literally don't know where they are going to work, if they are going to work, or how much money they're going to make?"

35. "Cutbacks Fuel Contingent Workforce."

36. U.S. Department of Labor, *Employment and Earnings,* January 1988, cited in duRivage, Virginia L., *New Policies for the Part-Time and Contingent Workforce* (Washington, D.C.: Economic Policy Institute), November 18, 1992, pp. 3, 7, 12.

37. "Outsource Tales," *Forbes ASAP,* June 7, 1993, p. 37.

38. Cited in "The Disposable Employee Is Becoming a Fact of Life," *Business Week,* December 15, 1986, p. 52.

39. Harrison, Bennett, and Barry Bluestone, *The Great U-Turn: Corporate Restructuring and the Polarizing of America* (New York: HarperCollins, 1988), p. 48.

40. "Temporary Workers Are on Increase."

41. "Jobs in America," *Fortune,* July 12, 1993, p. 47; "Temporary Work: The New Career."

42. "Jobs in America," p. 48.

43. "Cutbacks Fuel Contingent Workforce."

44. "Experimenting with Test-Tube Temps," *USA Today,* October 11, 1993.

45. "Abuse of Temporary Workers Compared to a 'Sweatshop,'" *Washington Post,* June 23, 1993.

46. Tilly, Chris, *Short Hours, Short Shrift: Causes and Consequences of Part-Time Work* (Washington, D.C.: Economic Policy Institute, 1990), cited in duRivage, p. 4.

47. "UAW Faces Test at Mazda Plant," *New York Times,* March 27, 1990, p. D8.

48. "Job Seeking, Reemployment, and Mental Health: A Randomized Field Experiment in Coping with Job Loss," *Journal of Applied Psychology,* October 1989, p. 759.

49. Cottle, Thomas T., "When You Stop You Die," *Commonweal,* June 19, 1992, p. 16.

50. "Violence in the Workplace," *Training and Development,* January 1994, p. 27.

51. Ibid., pp. 28, 30.

52. Ibid., p. 32.

53. Cottle, p. 17.

CHAPTER 13

1. *The OECD Jobs Study: Facts, Analysis, Strategies* (Paris: Organization for Economic Cooperation and Development, 1994), p. 7.

2. *Human Development Report 1993,* U.N. Development Program (New York: Oxford University Press, 1993), p. 35.

3. "Clues to Rising Unemployment," *Financial Times,* July 22, 1993, p. 18.

4. "Japan Begins to Confront Job Insecurity," *Wall Street Journal,* September 16, 1993, p. A10.

5. "Japan Inc. Slams Its Entrance Doors in the Faces of New College Graduates," *Wall Street Journal,* October 5, 1993, p. B1.

6. Ibid.

7. "The American Economy," *New York Times,* February 27, 1994, p. F6.

8. "EC Expects Economy to Contract 0.5% This Year, Led By 2% Decline in Germany," *Wall Street Journal,* July 1, 1993.

9. "Pull Me Up, Weigh Me Down," *The Economist,* July 24, 1993, p. 57; "Ireland's Jobless Rate," *Wall Street Journal,* November 10, 1992; "Italian Jobless Rate Increases," *Wall Street Journal,* February 1, 1993, p. A7A; "Belgian Jobless Rate Unchanged," *Wall Street Journal,* November 5, 1992, p. A9; "Denmark's Jobless Rate Rose," *Wall Street Journal,* October 8, 1992, p. C26; "Spain's Jobless Rate Climbs," *Wall Street Journal,* February 16, 1993, p. A3.

10. Crash Landing for West German Economy," *Financial Times*, March 1, 1993; "Rips in the Employment Featherbed," *Financial Times*, March 30, 1993.

11. "How Germany Is Attacking Recession," *Fortune*, June 14, 1993, p. 132.

12. Ibid.

13. "Massive Layoffs Foreseen in Western Europe," *Washington Post*, September 21, 1993, p. C3.

14. *Employment/Unemployment Study: Interim Report by the Secretary General* (Paris: Organization for Economic Co-operation and Development, 1993), p. 6.

15. "Threat to 400,000 Jobs in Europe's Auto Parts Sector," *Financial Times*, October 18, 1993.

16. *World Labour Report 1993*, pp. 19–20.

17. *Employment/Unemployment Study*, p. 6; "Europeans Fear Unemployment Will Only Rise," *New York Times*, June 13, 1993, p. A1.

18. "Europeans Fear Unemployment."

19. *Employment Outlook July 1993* (Organization for Economic Co-operation and Development, July 1993), p. 20; *Human Development Report 1993*, p. 37.

20. *Employment Outlook July 1993*, p. 18.

21. "Europe's Safety Nets Begin to Tear," *Wall Street Journal*, July 1, 1993; "Europe's Recession Prompts New Look at Welfare Costs," *New York Times*, August 9, 1993, p. A8.

22. "Europe's Safety Nets."

23. Ibid.

24. "Europeans Fear Unemployment."

25. "A labour market 'gripped by Euro-sclerosis,'" *Financial Times*, June 21, 1993.

26. "Is Europe's Social-Welfare State Headed for the Deathbed?" *Newsweek*, August 23, 1993, p. 37.

27. "Europe's Recession Prompts Look," p. A8.

28. Interview, May 9, 1994. EU commissioner Padraig Flynn says that Europe is "going to have to have another look at the way we finance our social welfare system." While he argues that the social net "has to remain," he advocates a rethinking of current social welfare programs with particular emphasis on "which of our social welfare policies actively encourage the reintegration of people into the working life" of society.

29. "Wage Cuts Anger French Students (cf. May 1968)," *New York Times*, March 24, 1994, p. A3; "Passions Ignited, French March for Wages Again," *New York Times*, March 26, 1994, international section, p. 3.

30. "An Unemployment Boom," *World Press Review*, February 1993, p. 40.

31. "Homeless in Europe," *Parade*, August 15, 1993, p. 8.

32. Interview, May 5, 1994, with Harley Shaiken, Professor of Labor and Technology at the University of California, Berkeley.

33. *Human Development Report 1993*, p. 35.

34. van Liemt, Gijsbert, *Industry on the Move: Causes and Consequences of International Relocation in the Manufacturing Industry* (Geneva: International Labor Office, 1992) p. 313; "Your New Global Workforce," *Fortune*, December 14, 1992, p. 52.

35. "Those High-Tech Jobs Can Cross the Border Too," *New York Times*, March 28, 1993, sect. 4, p. 4.

36. "Northern Mexico Becomes Big Draw for High-Tech Plants," *New York Times*, March 21, 1993, p. F1.

37. "Global Workforce," pp. 52–53.

38. Interview, May 5, 1994. Harley Shaiken says that in developing nations like Mexico, transnational companies are determined to hold down wages by building high-tech, state-of-the-art, automated plants. Even the highly skilled labor that is fortunate to have a job is woefully underpaid by U.S. standards. While the companies save money on the front end, at the production stage, they lose at the consumption end because the new markets aren't able to generate enough purchasing power to absorb the products being produced. Says Shaiken, "If you depress wages, you depress purchasing power. So the very factors that make production cheap ensure that you will not have a robust consumer market."

39. "Rendered Surplus," *Far Eastern Economic Review,* July 22, 1993, p. 18.

40. "China's Much-Needed Effort to Improve Productivity Will Take Economic Toll," *Wall Street Journal,* February 16, 1944, p. A13.

41. "Indians, Foreigners Build Silicon Valley," *Washington Post,* August 1, 1993, p. A21.

42. Kennedy, Paul, *Preparing for the 21st Century* (New York: Random House, 1993), pp. 182–183, 189.

43. *Population Pressures Abroad and Immigration Pressures at Home* (Washington, D.C.: Population Crisis Committee, 1989), pp. 18–20.

44. *Human Development Report 1993,* p. 37.

45. *Population Pressures,* p. 20.

CHAPTER 14

1. Merva, Mary, and Fowles, Richard, *Effects of Diminished Economic Opportunities on Social Stress* (Washington, D.C.: Economic Policy Institute), October 16, 1992, pp. 1–2.

2. Ibid., p. 11; "Nation's Prison Population Rises 7.2%," *Washington Post,* May 10, 1993.

3. "Life on the Shelf," *Newsweek,* May 9, 1994, p. 14.

4. "Youth Joblessness Is at Record High in New York City," *New York Times,* June 4, 1993, Metro section.

5. "Shootout in the Schools," *Time,* November 20, 1989, p. 116; "Reading, Writing and Intervention," *Security Management,* August 1992, p. 32.

6. "Wild in the Streets," *Newsweek,* August 2, 1993, p. 43.

7. "Getting Ready to Die Young," *Washington Post,* November 1, 1993, p. A1.

8. "Unhealed Wounds," *Time,* April 19, 1993, p. 30.

9. Ibid., p. 28.

10. Wacquant, Loic, "When Cities Run Riot," *UNESCO Courier,* February 1993, p. 10.

11. "Gang Membership Grows in Middle-Class Suburbs," *New York Times,* July 24, 1993, p. 25, Metro section.

12. "Danger in the Safety Zone," *Time,* August 23, 1993, p. 29.

13. Ibid., p. 32.

14. "A City Behind Walls," *Newsweek,* October 5, 1992, p. 69.

15. Louv, Richard, *America II* (Boston: Houghton Mifflin, 1983), p. 233.

16. "Enclosed Communities: Havens, or Worse?" *Washington Post,* April 9, 1994, p. E1.

17. "Reengineering Security's Role," Security Management, November 1993, p. 38.

18. "Security Industry Trends: 1993 and Beyond," *Security Management,* December 1999, p. 29.

19. Ibid.

20. "When Cities Run Riot," p. 8.

21. Ibid.

22. Ibid., p. 11.

23. "Germany's Furies," *Newsweek*, December 7, 1992, p. 31.

24. "Italy's Neo-Fascists Gain Dramatically," *Washington Post*, March 31, 1994, p. A25.

25. "Every Man a Tsar," *The New Yorker*, December 27, 1993.

26. Gardels, Nathan, "Capitalism's New Order," *Washington Post*, April 11, 1993, p. C4.

27. Van Creveld, Martin, *The Transformation of War* (New York: Free Press, 1991). Business leaders are also beginning to worry about the prospects of low-intensity conflict breaking out. In an interview, March 24, 1994, Lincoln Electric's assistant to the CEO, Richard Sobow, warns that the biggest problem facing the United States is the growing polarization of the country into two nations—one a wealthy first-world society and the other a pauperized third-world culture. He says that improving the education of the growing underclass without providing jobs might as easily lead to rebellion as reform, arguing that with education comes leadership and with leadership comes the potential for an organized resistance. Sobow says that "eventually we will see a revolution," and he adds, "I think it will be a bloody one."

CHAPTER 15

1. Marcuse, Herbert, *Eros and Civilization* (Frankfurt, Germany: Suhrkamp, 1979), preface.

2. Roediger, David, and Foner, Philip, *Our Own Time: A History of American Labor and the Working Day* (Westport, CT: Greenwood Press, 1989), p. vii.

3. Masuda, Yoneji, *The Information Society as Post-Industrial Society* (Washington, D.C.: World Future Society, 1981), p. 74.

4. *Society for the Reduction of Human Labor Newsletter*, Hunnicutt, Benjamin Kline, and William McGaughey, eds., Winter 1992–1993, vol. 3 #1, p. 14.

5. Schor, Juliet, *The Overworked American: The Unexpected Decline of Leisure* (New York: Basic Books, 1991) pp. 1, 2, 5, 29, 32.

6. Jones, Barry, *Sleepers Wake! Technology and the Future of Work* (New York: Oxford University Press, 1982), ch. 9.

7. Interview, March 18, 1994. Former Senator Eugene McCarthy argues that in the emerging high-tech era, the need to redistribute work becomes the essential battle cry of the forces fighting for economic justice. "What you have to look to," says McCarthy, "is a redistribution of work, through which you establish a claim to what is being produced."

8. Interview, April 8, 1994: Lynn Williams says that the loss of manufacturing jobs to high-technology automation is going to continue to accelerate in coming years. The outspoken labor leader says, "We ought to be able to handle this technological revolution more rationally" by finding creative ways for workers to share in the dramatic gains in productivity.

9. "VW Opts for Four Day Week in Move to Cut Wage Costs," *Financial Times*, October 25, 1993, p. 1.

10. Interview, May 3, 1994. Peter Schlilein says that Volkswagen had no choice but to either eliminate thousands of workers or shorten the workweek to 28.8 hours because of declining worldwide demand for automobiles and "more important, the very big progress in our productivity." Rising productivity and falling purchasing power are likely going to force similar decisions to shorten the workweek and share the available work in other industries in the years ahead.

11. "Europeans Ponder Working Less So More of Them Can Have Jobs," *New York Times*, November 22, 1993, p. A1, 6.

12. Ibid.

13. Ibid., p. A6.

14. Ibid.

15. *Memorandum on the Reduction and Reorganization of Working Time* (Brussels: Commission of the European Communities, 1982), p. 60.

16. *Report on the Memorandum from the Commission of the European Communities on the Reduction and Reorganisation of Working Time*, D. Ceravolo (European Parliament, Committee on Social Affairs and Employment, 1983), p. 9.

17. *The Five-Year Economic Plan: Sharing a Better Quality of Life Around the Globe*, Economic Planning Agency, Government of Japan, June 1992; "Labor Letter: Japan's Diet Slims the National Work Week by Four Hours," *Wall Street Journal*, July 13, 1993, p. 1.

18. "Japan Finds Ways to Save Tradition of Lifetime Jobs," *New York Times*, November 28, 1993, p. A1.

19. Cited in William McCaughey, "The International Dimensions of Reduced Hours," *Society for the Reduction of Human Labor Newsletter*, vol. 1, no. 1, p. 6.

20. Barber, Randy, and Teresa Ghilarducci, *Pension Funds, Capital Markets and the Economic Future* (Washington, D.C.: Center for Economic Organizing, January 24, 1993), p. 1.

21. Leontief, Wassily, "The Distribution of Work and Income," *Scientific American*, September 1982, pp. 194–195. In an interview, March 14, 1994, Leontief argues that free time should be considered a "part of your income" and says that "ways must be found to encourage leisure." He is concerned, however, that "if we work less," we might "simply spend more time in front of the television set." The constructive use of leisure, argues Leontief, can come about only with an "improvement in education."

22. Zalusky, John, *The United States: The Sweatshop Economy* (Washington, D.C.: AFL-CIO, Economic Research Department, 1993), p. 1.

23. Zalusky, p. 6.

24. "U.S. Unions Back Shorter Week, But Employers Seem Reluctant," *New York Times*, November 22, 1993, p. A6; Zalusky, p. 5.

25. Ibid., p. 1.

26. Interview, March 21, 1994. John Zalusky admits that the unions, acting alone, lack the political muscle to push through changes in the Fair Labor Standards Act. He is particularly concerned about the growing roadblocks put in the way of organizing activity in the United States and cites the fact that the United States was one of only a handful of countries found in violation of the human rights clause of the International Labor Organization of the United Nations in 1993, which guarantees workers the right to freedom of association and the right to bargain. Such antiunion practices, says Zalusky, create a chilling effect and hamper organized labor's attempts to reform labor standards and practices, including the provisions on overtime compensation.

27. "Labor Wants Shorter Hours to Make Up for Job Losses," *New York Times*, October 11, 1993, p. A10.

28. Interview, March 18, 1994. Dennis Chamot argues that the new wave of technology displacement is not a new phenomenon. "We've gone through these kinds of massive changes before," he says, and each time "we have adjusted to the increased levels of productivity by reducing work time." While Chamot is not hopeful that the thirty-hour week will be passed anytime soon, he says we need to begin preparing the political groundwork for its eventual adoption if we are to effectively address the ever-widening gap between

productivity gains and over-production, on the one hand, and rising unemployment and loss of consumer purchasing power on the other.

29. U.S. Congress, House Committee on Education and Labor, Subcommittee on Labor Standards, *Hearings on H.R. 1784: To Revise the Overtime Compensation Requirement of the Fair Labor Standards Act of 1938*, 96th Congress, 1st Session, October 23–25, 1979. See also Conyers, John, "Have a Four-day Workweek? Yes." *American Legion*, April 1980, p. 26. Quote from a personal letter by Conyers to Members of the House of Representatives, photocopy with the author, dated February 15, 1979, in Hunnicutt, p. 311.

30. Congressman Lucien Blackwell, U.S. Congress, House of Representatives, *H.R. 3267, The Full Employment Act of 1994*, March 23, 1994.

31. McCarthy, Eugene, and William McGaughey, *Non-Financial Economics: The Case for Shorter Hours of Work* (New York: Praeger, 1989), p. 143.

32. Interview, May 6, 1994. Michael Hammer argues that "if you're going to reduce work hours and reduce compensation along with it, that's basically asking people to have a more communitarian approach to their incomes, which you may or may not be able to do." Hammer also says that he's "not sure we can depress work . . . because, in this society, at least, a lot of people aren't sure what to do with their existing leisure and it's not clear to me people will be quite sure what to do with more."

33. McCarthy and McGaughey, p. 156.

34. "Survey Says Employees Less Willing to Sacrifice," *Washington Post*, September 3, 1993, p. A2.

35. Robert Haft International Poll, "Family Time Is More Important Than Rapid Career Advancement: Survey Shows Both Men and Women Support Parent Tracking," *San Francisco*, June 28, 1989, pp. 4–5, cited in Schor, p. 148.

36. Labor Department study cited in Roediger and Foner, p. 275.

37. Schor, pp. 12–13.

38. Roediger and Foner, p. 276.

39. See James, Selma, *Women, Unions and Work* (London, 1976), p. 15.

CHAPTER 16

1. Van Til, Jon, *Mapping the Third Sector: Voluntarism in a Changing Social Economy* (Washington, D.C.: Foundation Center, 1988), p. 3; O'Neill, Michael, *The Third America: The Emergence of the Nonprofit Sector in the United States* (San Francisco: Jossey-Bass Publishers, 1989), p. 6.; *Nonprofit Almanac 1992–1993* (Washington, D.C.: Independent Sector), p. 29.

2. Van Til, p. 113; Rudney, Gabriel, *A Quantitative Profile of the Independent Sector*, Working Paper no. 40 (Program on Non-Profit Organizations, Institution for Social and Policy Studies, Yale University, 1981), p. 3.

3. O'Neill, p. 6.

4. Hodgkinson, Virginia A., and Murray S. Weitzman, *Giving and Volunteering in the United States: Findings from a National Survey*, 1992 Edition (Washington, D.C.: Independent Sector, 1992), p. 2.

5. *The Non-profit Almanac 1992–1993*, p. 6; quote in O'Neill, p. 2.

6. Weisbrod, B. A., *The Voluntary Non-profit Sector* (Lexington, MA: Heath, 1977), p. 170.

7. Hodgkinson and Weitzman, p. 1; O'Neill, p. 8.

8. Jeantet, Thierry, *La Modernisation de la France par l'Economie Sociale* (Paris: Economica, 1986), p. 78, translated in van Til, pp. 101–102.

9. Eisenberg, Pablo, "The Voluntary Sector: Problems and Challenges," in O'Connell, Brian, ed., *America's Voluntary Spirit* (Washington, D.C.: Foundation Center, 1983), p. 306.

10. O'Neill, p. 13.

11. Lerner, Max, "The Joiners," in O'Connell, p. 86.

12. Ibid., p. 82.

13. Krikorian, Robert, "Have You Noticed? An American Resurgence Is Underway," *Vital Speeches of the Day*, March 1, 1985, p. 301.

14. Alan Durning, *How Much Is Enough?* (New York: W. W. Norton, 1992), p. 29.

CHAPTER 17

1. White House press release, April 12, 1994.

2. "Now It's Our Turn," *Reader's Digest*, May 1985, p. 109.

3. Ronald Reagan, as quoted from televised budget message, in "A Vision of Voluntarism," *Time*, October 19, 1981, p. 47.

4. Ellis, Susan, and Noyes, Katherine, *By the People: A History of Americans as Volunteers* (San Francisco: Jossey-Bass Publishers, 1990), pp. 290–291.

5. "2 Million Points of Light," *Across the Board*, March 1989, p. 12.

6. "The Elusive 1000 Points," *Newsweek*, December 1, 1989, p. 49.

7. Townsend, Kathleen Kennedy, "Americans and the Cause of Voluntarism: The Forgotten Virtue of Voluntarism," *Current*, February 1984, p. 11.

8. Ibid.

9. Ibid., p. 15.

10. Ibid., pp. 16, 17.

11. Theobald, Robert, *The Guaranteed Income* (New York: Anchor Books, 1967), p. 19.

12. "A Minimum Guaranteed Income: Experiments and Proposals," *International Labour Review*, May–June 1987, p. 263.

13. Friedman, Milton, "The Case for the Negative Income Tax," *National Review*, March 7, 1967, p. 239; "PRO and CON Discussion: Should the Federal Government Guarantee a Minimum Annual Income for All U.S. Citizens?" *Congressional Digest*, October 1967, p. 242.

14. "Guaranteed Annual Income: A Hope and Question Mark," *America*, December 11, 1971, p. 503.

15. Hum, Derek, and Wayne Simpson, "Economic Response to a Guaranteed Annual Income: Experience from Canada and the United States," *Journal of Labor Economics*, January 1993, part 2, pp. S280, S287.

16. Interview, March 23, 1994. Don Kennedy worries that the "supply-siders" are ignoring the question of aggregate demand. He asks, "What do you do when you build the finest products in the world, at the lowest cost and the highest quality, and no one can afford to buy them?" Since "demand is a function of income," says Kennedy, "we've got to be thinking of income distribution, not just the cost of cutting jobs." The problem is how "to get income to people who cannot find gainful employment. . . . If workerless technology produces society's wealth, then we need to figure out a whole different way of sharing that wealth, rather than through the wage system."

17. "Minimum Guaranteed Income," p. 271.

18. "Federal Volunteer Programs," *Congressional Digest,* May 1990, p. 132; *Seasons of Service* (Washington, D.C.: Corporation for National Service, 1994).

19. Interview, April 13, 1994: North Carolina Governor's Office of Citizens' Affairs.

20. "The American Economy and the Rest of the World: Two Sides of the Same Coin," address by Felix G. Rohatyn at the John F. Kennedy School of Government, Harvard University, 1993, Albert H. Gordon Lecture on Finance and Public Policy, November 30, 1993.

21. "Too Few Good Enterprise Zones," *Nation's Business,* October 1993, p. 30.

22. Interview, March 18, 1994, with Sara Melendez, president of the Independent Sector.

23. "U.S. Is Paying More Low-Earners for Working, I.R.S. Survey Finds," *New York Times,* April 17, 1994, p. 23; "Hill to Get Welfare Bill, Clinton Officials Predict," *Washington Post,* December 27, 1993, p. A8.

24. "Weld, Cellucci File Plan to Replace Welfare with Work Benefits," press release from the Commonwealth of Massachusetts, Executive Department, State House, Boston, January 14, 1994; "Massachusetts Welfare Reform Would Drop Cash Benefits, Require Work," *Washington Post,* January 15, 1994, p. A6.

25. "Unions Fear Job Losses in Welfare Reform," *Washington Post,* January 6, 1994.

26. Center for Study on Responsive Law, *Aid for Dependent Corporations (AFDC)* (Washington, D.C.: Essential Information Inc., January 1994). Survey based on spending data obtained from the *Catalogue of Federal Domestic Assistance* (U.S. Office of Management and Budget, 1993) and *Estimates of Federal Tax Expenditures for Fiscal Years 1994–1998* (Joint Committee on Taxation, 1993); "The Fat Cat Freeloaders," *Washington Post,* March 6, 1994, p. C1.

27. Peterson, Wallace, *Silent Depression* (New York: W. W. Norton, 1994), p. 202.

28. Ibid., p. 203.

29. "A New Kind of Tax: Adopting a Consumption Tax," *Current,* May 1993, p. 17.

30. "The VATman Cometh," *The Economist,* April 24, 1993, p. 17.

31. "New Kind of Tax."

32. Ibid.

33. "VATman Cometh."

34. *Information Technology Industry Data Book 1960–2004,* (Washington, D.C.: Computers and Business Equipment Manufacturers Association, CBEMA, 1993), p. 4.

35. "The Entertainment Economy," *Business Week,* March 14, 1994, p. 60.

36. "Ad Gains Could Exceed 6% This Year," *Advertising Age,* May 3, 1993, p. 4.

37. "A Federal Value-Added Tax Could Compete with Mainstay of the States: The Sales Tax," *The Bond Buyer,* July 6, 1993, p. 1.

38. *Corporate Contributions, 1992* (New York: The Conference Board, 1994), pp. 6, 9–11; *Non-profit Almanac, 1992–3,* (Washington, D.C.: Independent Sector), p. 60.

CHAPTER 18

1. Interview, March 18, 1994. Jim Joseph says that, increasingly, "people are turning to non-governmental alternatives to meet human needs and to serve public purposes." He says that if government subsidies were available to supplement community resources in the third sector, many people "could find meaningful and productive jobs that contribute to the public good."

2. "Policy Issues for the UK Voluntary Sector in the 1990s," in Ben-Ner, Avner, and Benedetto Gui, eds., *The Non-Profit Sector in the Mixed Economy* (Ann Arbor: University of Michigan Press, 1993), pp. 224, 230.

3. "Public Authorities and the Non-Profit Sector in France," in Anheier, Helmut, and Wolfgang Seibel, eds., *The Third Sector: Comparative Studies of Non-profit Organizations* (New York: Walter de Gruyter, 1990), pp. 298–299.

4. "Employment and Earnings in the West German Nonprofit Sector: Structure and Trends 1970–1987," in Ben-Ner and Gui, pp. 184, 188; "A Profile of the Third Sector in Western Germany," in Anheier and Seibel (New York: Walter de Gruyter, 1990), p. 323.

5. "The Italian Nonprofit Sector: An Overview of an Undervalued Reality," in Ben-Ner and Gui, pp. 206, 211.

6. Amenomori, Takayoshi, *Defining the Non-Profit Sector: Japan* (Baltimore: The Johns Hopkins University Institute for Policy Studies, July 1993).

7. "Traditional Neighborhood Associations in Industrial Society: The Case of Japan," in Anheier and Seibel, pp. 347–358.

8. Interview, May 4, 1994. Miklos Marschall says that in his own country of Hungary as well as in other Eastern European nations "NCOs were the driving force of the changes" that helped topple the old communist regimes. Because political parties were banned, "opposition activity was confined to the only legal organizations available—the voluntary organizations."

9. "World Volunteerism Group Forms," *New York Times*, December 21, 1993, p. A12.

10. Starr, S. Frederick, "The Third Sector in the Second World," *World Development*, Vol. 19 #1, p. 69.

11. Ibid., p. 65.

12. Ibid., p. 70.

13. Fisher, Julie, *The Road from Rio: Sustainable Development and the Non-Governmental Movements in the Third World* (Westport, CT: Praeger, 1993), p. 91.

14. *Human Development Report 1993*, United Nations Development Project Program (New York: Oxford University Press, 1993), p. 93.

15. Fisher, pp. 89–91.

16. *Human Development Report 1993*, pp. 86–87.

17. Fisher, p. 167.

18. Durning, Alan, *Action at the Grass Roots: Fighting Poverty and Environmental Decline* (Washington, D.C.: Worldwatch Institute, 1989), p. 11; *Human Development Report 1993*, p. 95.

19. Cordoba-Novion, Cesar, and Sachs, Céline, *Urban Self-Reliance Directory* (Nyon, Switzerland: International Foundation for Development Alternatives, January 1987), p. 33.

20. "Colufifa: 20,000 Individuals Fighting Hunger," *African Farmer*, #4, July, p. 81.

21. "Philippenes: Pamalakaya, Small Fishermen's Movement," *IFDA Dossier* (Nyon, Switzerland: International Foundation for Development Alternatives, 1987), #61, pp. 68–69.

22. Fisher, p. 124; Rush, James, *The Last Tree* (New York: The Asia Society, distributed by Westview Press, 1991), p. 55.

23. Fisher, pp. 40, 104.

24. Durning, p. 11.

25. "Alternative Resources for Grass Roots Development: A View from Latin America," *Development Dialogue*, vol. 1, 1987, pp. 114–134; "Another Development Under Repressive Rule," *Development Dialogue*, vol. 1, 1985.

26. *Human Development Report 1993*, p. 87.

27. Fisher, p. 23.

28. Lopezlera-Mendez, Luis, *Sociedad Civil y Pueblos Emergentes: Las Organizaciónes Autonómas de Promoción Social y Desarrollo en Mexico* (Mexico City: Promoción del Desarrollo Popular, 1988), p. 60.

29. Fisher, p. 89; "In Search of Development: Some Direction for Further Investigation," *The Journal of Modern African Studies*, vol. 24 #2, 1986, quote on p. 323.

30. *Human Development Report 1993*, pp. 93–94.

31. "Kenya's Green Belt Movement," *The UNESCO Courier*, March 1992, pp. 23–25; "Reforestation with a Human Touch," *Grassroots Development*, vol. 12 #3, 1988, pp. 38–40.

32. Fisher, p. 108.

33. Interview, March 22, 1994. Fisher says that "most governments in the third world are very comfortable with the growth of the non-profit or voluntary sector because it represents alternative sources of power in the country." Nonetheless, according to Fisher, the third sector continues to grow into a potent and viable institutional force in many developing nations and is likely to play a critical role in helping to shape national agendas in the years ahead.

34. Durning, p. 47.

35. *Human Development Report 1993*, p. 88.

36. Interview, May 4, 1994. Miklos Marschall says that while he doesn't believe that "NGOs can ever substitute for the government's responsibility," he argues that "small NGOs are much more efficient in handling unemployment than big government bureaucracies. Because they are based in the community and are much more familiar with the real needs, they have a much clearer picture about the labor situation in a given region as opposed to huge government programs putting people simply on welfare." Marschall says that the key to broadening the roles and responsibilities of NGOs and advancing the interest of the social economy is "to encourage partnership schemes between the government and the third sector."

37. Interview, May 18, 1994. Martin Khor says that while the third sector is going to play an increasingly important role in terms of both advocacy and reform and providing social services, the governments in third-world countries are still going to be looked to in the foreseeable future as the primary institutions for ensuring the well-being and security of the masses of people.

38. Interview, April 27, 1994. Vandana Shiva says that in countries like India, the Third Industrial Revolution is likely to further widen the gap between rich and poor as the new information technologies create a new elite class of symbolic analysts on the one hand, while the new biotechnologies eliminate, en masse, small family farmers on the other. Shiva warns that "India cannot survive with enclaves of prosperity while the rest of the people have absolutely no right to a livelihood and to work for their own survival."

Bibliography

Akin, William, *Technocracy and the American Dream: The Technocrat Movement, 1900–1941.* Berkeley: University of California Press, 1977.

Andersen Consulting, *Vision 2000: The Transformation of Banking.* Chicago, 1991.

Anheier, Helmut, and Seibel, Wolfgang, eds., *The Third Sector: Comparative Studies of Nonprofit Organizations.* New York: Walter de Gruyter, 1990.

Attali, Jacques, *Millennium: Winners and Losers in the Coming World Order.* New York: Random House, 1991.

Barlett, Donald, and Steele, James, *America: What Went Wrong?* Kansas City, MO: Andrews and McMeel, 1992.

Beniger, James, *The Control Revolution: Technological and Economic Origins of the Information Society.* Cambridge, MA: Harvard University Press, 1986.

Ben-Ner, Auner, and Gui, Benedetto, eds., *The Non-Profit Sector in the Mixed Economy.* Ann Arbor: University of Michigan Press, 1993.

Berardi, Gigi, and Geisler, Charles, eds. *The Social Consequences and Challenges of New Agricultural Technologies.* Boulder, CO: Westview Press, 1984.

Bradley, Stephen, et al., eds., *Globalization, Technology, and Competition: The Fusion of Computers and Telecommunications in the 1990s.* Cambridge, MA: Harvard Business School Press, 1993.

Brand, Stewart, *The Media Lab: Inventing the Future at MIT.* New York: Viking Press, 1987.

Braverman, Harry, *Labor and Monopoly Capital: The Degradation of Work in the 20th Century.* New York: Monthly Labor Press, 1974.

Brod, Craig, *Techno Stress: The Human Cost of the Computer Revolution.* Reading, MA: Addison-Wesley, 1984.

Brynjolfsson, Erik, and Hitt, Lorin, *Is Information Systems Spending Productive? New Evidence and New Results.* Cambridge, MA: Massachusetts Institute of Technology, Working Paper #3571–93, June 4, 1993.

Busch, Lawrence, Lacy, William, and Burckhardt, Jeffrey, *Plants, Power, and Profit: Social, Economic, and Ethical Consequences of the New Biotechnologies.* Cambridge, MA: Basil Blackwell, 1991.

Callahan, Raymond, *Education and the Cult of Efficiency.* Chicago: University of Chicago Press, 1964.

Carnevale, Anthony Patrick, *America and the New Economy.* Washington, D.C.: U.S. Department of Labor, 1991.

Chandler, Alfred Jr., *The Visible Hand: The Managerial Revolution in American Business.* Cambridge, MA: Harvard University Press, 1977.

Clinton/Gore National Campaign, *Technology: The Engine of Economic Growth,* 1992.

Cochrane, Willard, *The Development of American Agriculture: A Historical Analysis.* Minneapolis: University of Minnesota Press, 1993.

Corn, Joseph, ed., *Imagining Tomorrow: History, Technology, and the American Future.* Cambridge, MA: MIT Press, 1986.

Cornfield, Daniel, *Workers, Managers and Technological Change: Emerging Patterns of Labor Relations*. New York: Plenum Press, 1987.

Council on Competitiveness, *Gaining New Ground: Technology Priorities for America's Future*. Washington, D.C.: March 1991.

Cross, Gary, *Time and Money: The Making of Consumer Culture*. New York: Routledge, 1993.

Cyert, Richard, and Mowery, David, eds. *Technology and Employment: Innovation and Growth in the U.S. Economy*. Washington, D.C.: National Academy Press, 1987.

Davidow, William, and Malone, Michael, *The Virtual Corporation: Restructuring and Revitalizing the Corporation for the 21st Century*. New York: HarperCollins, 1992.

Derek, Leebart, ed., *Technology 2001: The Future of Computing and Communications*. Cambridge, MA: MIT Press, 1991.

Drucker, Peter, *Post-Capitalist Society*. New York: HarperCollins, 1993.

duRivage, Virginia, *New Policies for the Part-Time and Contingent Workforce*. Washington, D.C.: Economic Policy Institute, November 18, 1992.

Durning, Alan B., *Action at the Grassroots: Fighting Poverty and Environmental Decline*. Washington, D.C.: Worldwatch Institute, 1989.

———, *How Much Is Enough?* New York: W. W. Norton, 1992.

Edquist, Charles, *Technological and Organisational Innovations, Productivity and Employment*. Geneva: International Labor Organization, 1992.

Ellis, Susan, and Noyes, Katherine H., *By the People: A History of Americans as Volunteers*. San Francisco: Jossey-Bass, 1990.

Ellul, Jacques, *The Technological Society*. New York: Random House, 1964.

Engelberger, Joseph, *Robotics in Service*. Cambridge, MA: MIT Press, 1989.

Ferman, Louis, Kornbluh, Joyce, and Miller, J. A., eds., *Negroes and Jobs*. Ann Arbor: University of Michigan Press, 1968.

Fisher, Julie, *The Road from Rio: Sustainable Development and the Nongovernmental Movement in the Third World*. Westport, CT: Praeger, 1993.

Fjermedal, Grant, *The Tomorrow Makers: A Brave New World of Living Brain Machines*. New York: Macmillan, 1986.

Fox, Michael, *Superpigs and Wondercorn: The Brave New World of Biotechnology and Where It May Lead*. New York: Lyons and Burford, 1992.

Gideon, Siegfried, *Mechanization Takes Command*. New York: W. W. Norton, 1948.

Gimpel, Jean, *The Medieval Machine: The Industrial Revolution of the Middle Ages*. New York: Holt, Rinehart and Winston, 1976.

Goodman, David, Sorj, Bernardo, and Wilkinson, John, *From Farming to Biotechnology: A Theory of Agro-Industrial Development*. New York: Basil Blackwell, 1987.

Gorz, Andre, *Critique of Economic Reason*. New York: Verso, 1988.

Grant, George, *Technology and Empire*. Toronto: House of Anansi Press, 1969.

Green, Mark, ed., *Changing America: Blueprints for the New Administration*. New York: New Market Press, 1992.

Gumpert, Gary, *Talking Tombstones & Other Tales of the Media Age*. New York: Oxford University Press, 1987.

Hammer, Michael, and Champy, James, *Re-engineering the Corporation: A Manifesto for Business Revolution*. New York: HarperCollins, 1993.

Harmon, Roy, et al., *Re-Inventing the Factory: Productivity Breakthroughs in Manufacturing Today*. New York: Free Press, 1989.

———, *Re-Inventing the Factory II: Managing the World Class Factory*. New York: Free Press, 1992.

———, *Re-Inventing the Warehouse: World Class Distribution Logistics*. New York: Free Press, 1993.

Harrison, Bennett, and Bluestone, Barry, *The Great U Turn: Corporate Restructuring and the Polarizing of America*. New York: HarperCollins, 1990.

Harrison, Bennett, *Lean and Mean: The Changing Landscape of Corporate Power in the Age of Flexibility*. New York: HarperCollins, 1994.

Heilbroner, Robert, *The Making of Economic Society*. Englewood Cliffs, NJ: Prentice-Hall, 1980.

Hodgkinson, Virginia, and Weitzman, Murray, *Giving and Volunteering in the United States: Findings from a National Survey*, 1992 Edition. Washington, D.C.: Independent Sector, 1992.

Humphrey, John, *New Technologies, Flexible Automation, Work Organisation and Employment in Manufacturing*. Geneva: International Labor Organization, 1992.

Hunnicutt, Benjamin Kline, *Work Without End: Abandoning Shorter Hours for the Right to Work*. Philadelphia: Temple University Press, 1988.

Innis, Harold, *Empire and Communications*. Buffalo, NY: University of Toronto Press, 1972.

International Labor Organization, *The World Employment Situation, Trends and Prospects*. Geneva: ILO, 1994.

———, *World Labour Report 1993*. Geneva: ILO, 1993.

James, Samuel, D. K., *The Impact of Cybernation Technology on Black Automotive Workers in the U.S.* Ann Arbor: UMI Research Press, 1985.

Jarratt, Jennifer, and Mahaffie, John, *Future Work: Seven Critical Forces Reshaping Work and the Work Force in North America*. San Francisco: Jossey-Bass, 1990.

Jenkins, Clive, and Sherman, Barrie, *The Collapse of Work*. London: Eyre Methuen, 1979.

Jones, Barry, *Sleepers, Wake! Technology and the Future of Work*. New York: Oxford University Press, 1990.

Jones, Marcus, *Black Migration in the United States with Emphasis on Selected Central Cities*. Saratoga, CA: Century 21 Publishing, 1980.

Juenger, Frederich Georg, *The Failure of Technology*. Chicago: Gateway Editions, 1956.

Katz, Michael, ed., *The Underclass Debate: Views from History*. Princeton, NJ: Princeton University Press, 1993.

Kennedy, Paul, *Preparing for the Twenty-first Century*. New York: Random House, 1993.

Kenney, Martin, and Florida, Richard, *Beyond Mass Production: The Japanese System and Its Transfer to the United States*. New York: Oxford University Press, 1993.

Kern, Stephen, *The Culture of Time and Space*. Cambridge, MA: Harvard University Press, 1983.

Korten, David, *Getting to the 21st Century: Voluntary Action and the Global Agenda*. Hartford: Kumarian Press, 1990.

Kozol, Jonathan, *Illiterate America*. New York: Anchor Press/Doubleday, 1985.

Kraut, Robert, ed., *Technology and the Transformation of White Collar Work*. Hillsdale, NJ: Lawrence Erlbaum Associates, 1987.

Kurzweil, Raymond, *The Age of Intelligent Machines*. Cambridge, MA: MIT Press, 1990.

Le Goff, Jacques, *Time, Work and Culture in the Middle Ages*. Chicago: University of Chicago Press, 1980.

Lemann, Nicholas, *The Promised Land: The Great Black Migration and How it Changed America*. New York: Vintage Books, 1992.

Leontief, Wassily, and Duchin, Faye, *The Future Impact of Automation on Workers*. New York: Oxford University Press, 1986.

Louv, Richard, *America II*. Boston: Houghton Mifflin, 1983.

MacBride, Robert, *The Automated State: Computer Systems as a New Force in Society*. Philadelphia: Chilton Book Co., 1967.

Magnet, Myron, *The Dream and the Nightmare: The Sixties' Legacy to the Underclass*. New York: William Morrow, 1993.

Masuda, Yoneji, *The Information Society as Post-Industrial Society*. Bethesda, MD: World Future Society, 1980.

McCarthy, Eugene, and McGaughey, William, *Non-Financial Economics: The Case for Shorter Hours of Work*. New York: Praeger, 1989.

McCarthy, Kathleen, Hodgkinson, Virginia, and Sumariwalla, Russy, *The Nonprofit Sector in the Global Community: Voices from Many Nations*. San Francisco: Jossey-Bass Publishers, 1992.

McLuhan, Marshall, *Understanding Media: The Extensions of Man*. New York: McGraw-Hill, 1964.

Merva, Mary, and Fowles, Richard, *Effects of Diminished Economic Opportunities on Social Stress: Heart Attacks, Strokes, and Crime*. Washington, D.C.: Economic Policy Institute, October 16, 1992.

Meyrowitz, Joshua, *No Sense of Place: The Impact of Electronic Media on Sociable Behavior*. New York: Oxford University Press, 1985.

Mishel, Lawrence, and Bernstein, Jared, *The State of Working America 1992–1993*. Washington, D.C.: Economic Policy Institute, 1992.

Mumford, Lewis, *Technics and Human Development*. New York: Harcourt Brace Jovanovich, 1966.

Nelson, Robert, *Reaching for Heaven on Earth*. Savage, MD: Rowman & Littlefield, 1991.

Noble, David, *Forces of Production: A Social History of Industrial Automation*. New York: Alfred A. Knopf, 1984.

O'Connell, Brian, ed., *America's Voluntary Spirit*. Washington, D.C.: Foundation Center, 1983.

Offe, Claus, and Heinze, Rolf, *Beyond Employment*. Philadelphia: Temple University Press, 1992.

Office of Management and Budget, *A Vision of Change for America*. Washington, D.C.: U.S. Government Printing Office, February 1993.

O'Neill, Michael, *The Third America: The Emergence of the Nonprofit Sector in the United States*. San Francisco: Jossey-Bass, 1989.

Organisation for Economic Co-operation and Development, *Employment Outlook July 1993*. Paris: OECD, 1993.

———, *Employment/Unemployment Study Interim Report by the Secretary General*. Paris: OECD, 1993.

———, *The OECD Jobs Study: Facts, Analysis, Strategies*. Paris: OECD, 1994.

Parker, Mike, and Slaughter, Jane, *Choosing Sides: Unions and the Team Concept*. Detroit: Labor Notes, 1988.

Peterson, Wallace, *Silent Depression: The Fate of the American Dream*. New York: W. W. Norton, 1994.

Peterson, Willis, and Kislev, Yoav, *The Cotton Harvester in Retrospect: Labor Displacement or Replacement?* St. Paul: University of Minnesota Press, 1991.

Philipson, Morris, *Automation: Implications for the Future*. New York: Vintage Books, 1962.

Phillips, Kevin, *The Politics of Rich and Poor: Wealth and the American Electorate in the Reagan Aftermath*. New York: HarperCollins, 1990.

Reich, Robert, *The Work of Nations: Preparing Ourselves for 21st Century Capitalism*. New York: Random House, 1992.

Renner, Michael, *Jobs in a Sustainable Economy*. Washington, D.C.: Worldwatch Institute, 1991.

Rifkin, Jeremy, *Algeny*. New York: Viking, 1983.

———, *Biosphere Politics*. New York: Crown, 1991.

———, *Declaration of a Heretic*. Boston: Routledge and Kegan, Paul, 1985.

———, *Entropy*. New York: Bantam Books, 1980.

———, *The North Will Rise Again*. Boston: Beacon Press, 1978.

———, *Time Wars*. New York: Simon & Schuster, 1987.

Rivkin, Steven, et al., *Shortcut to the Information Superhighway*. Washington, D.C.: Progressive Policy Institute, 1992.

Roach, Stephen, *Making Technology Work*. New York: Morgan Stanley, April 1993.

———, *Technology Imperatives*. New York: Morgan Stanley, January 1992.

Roediger, David, and Foner, Philip, *Our Own Time: A History of American Labor and the Working Day*. Westport, CT: Greenwood Press, 1989.

Salamon, Lester M., and Anheier, Helmut, *Toward an Understanding of the International Nonprofit Sector*. Baltimore: Working Papers of the Johns Hopkins Institute for Policy Studies, 1992.

Schor, Juliet, *The Overworked American: The Unexpected Decline of Leisure*. New York: Basic Books, 1991.

Segal, Howard, *Technological Utopianism in American Culture*. Chicago: University of Chicago Press, 1985.

Simons, Geoff, *Robots: The Quest for Living Machines*. New York: Sterling, 1992.

———, *Silicon Shock: The Menace of the Computer Invasion*. New York: Basil Blackwell, 1985.

Strasser, Susan, *Satisfaction Guaranteed: The Making of the American Mass Market*. New York: Pantheon, 1989.

Strobel, Frederick, *Upward Dreams, Downward Mobility: The Economic Decline of the American Middle Class*. Lanham, MD: Rowman and Littlefield, 1993.

Theobald, Robert, *The Guaranteed Income*. New York: Anchor Books, 1967.

Tichi, Cecilia, *Shifting Gears: Technology, Literature, Culture in Modernist America*. Chapel Hill: University of North Carolina Press, 1987.

Tilly, Chris, *Short Hours, Short Shift: Causes and Consequences of Part-Time Work*. Washington, D.C.: Economic Policy Institute, 1990.

Turkle, Sherry, *The Second Self: Computers and the Human Spirit*. New York: Simon & Schuster, 1984.

United Nations Development Programme (UNDP), *Human Development Report 1993*. New York: Oxford University Press, 1993.

U.S. Congress Office of Technology Assessment, *A New Technological Era for American Agriculture*. Washington, D.C.: U.S. Government Printing Office, March 1985.

U.S. Department of Labor, Bureau of Labor Statistics, *Outlook for Technology and Labor in Telephone Communications*. July 1990, Bulletin 2357.

———, *Technological Change and Its Impact on Labor in Four Industries: Coal Mining, Pharmaceutical Preparations, Metalworking Machinery, Eating and Drinking Places*. October 1992, Bulletin 2409.

———, *Technology and Labor in Copper Ore Mining, Household Appliances, and Water*. May 1993, Bulletin 2420.

———, *Technology and Labor in Three Service Industries: Utilities, Retail Trade, and Lodging*. September 1990, Bulletin 2367.

van Creveld, Martin, *The Transformation of War*. New York: The Free Press, 1991.

van Liemt, Gijsbert, ed., *Industry on the Move: Causes and Consequences of International Relocation in the Manufacturing Industry*. Geneva: International Labor Office, 1992.

Van Til, Jon, *Mapping the Third Sector: Volunteerism in a Changing Social Economy*. Washington, D.C.: The Foundation Center, 1988.

Watson, Dennis, Zazueta, Fedro, and Bottcher, A., eds., *Computers in Agricultural Extension Programs: Proceedings of the 4th International Conference*. St. Joseph, MO: American Society of Agricultural Engineers, 1992.

Weiner, Norbert, *The Human Use of Human Beings: Cybernetics and Human Beings*. Boston: Houghton Mifflin, 1950.

Willhelm, Sidney, *Who Needs the Negro?* Cambridge, MA. Schenkman, 1970.

Wilson, William Julius. *The Declining Significance of Race: Blacks and Changing American Institutions*. Chicago: University of Chicago Press, 1980.

———, *The Truly Disadvantaged*. Chicago: University of Chicago Press, 1987.

Winpisinger, William, *Reclaiming Our Future: An Agenda for American Labor*. Boulder, CO: Westview Press, 1989.

Womack, James, Jones, Daniel, and Roos, Daniel., *The Machine That Changed the World*. New York: Macmillan, 1990.

Wooley, Benjamin, *Virtual Worlds: A Journey in Hype and Hyperreality*. Cambridge, MA: Blackwell, 1992.

Zalusky, John, *The United States: The Sweatshop Economy* (AFL-CIO). Presentation at the Industrial Relations Research Association Meeting, Anaheim, CA, January 6, 1993. Washington, D.C.: AFL-CIO Economic Research Department, 1993.

Index